A LIBERAL THEOLOGY FOR THE TWENTY-FIRST CENTURY

Liberal theology, in its typical form, represents the attempt to approach religion from a rational perspective without denying or belittling the importance of religious experience and religious commitment. Versions of liberal theology can be found in all the great religions.

This book is primarily concerned with a Christian tradition that goes back to the second century and reached a high point in the seventeenth. This tradition includes a method of inquiry which, when re-evaluated in the light of recent discussions on the nature of rationality and applied to contemporary issues, reveals that there are versions of materialism, monism and theism that can accord with rationality. While liberal theology cannot demonstrate the truth of theism, it can present it not only as one of the rational options, but as an option that has uniquely attractive characteristics, and when the liberal tradition is taken at its best, it can support a version of Christianity which continues to refer to God as a transcendent 'reality', and which can continue to support recognizable doctrines of incarnation, redemption and Trinity.

The liberal theology introduced and advanced in this book can be contrasted with many recent 'radical theologies', and could be called 'liberal orthodoxy'. Students of philosophy, theology and religious studies, as well as clergy and interested lay readers, will find this an accessible insight into liberal theology and to current debates on materialism, atheism and inter-faith dialogue.

D1352581

A Liberal Theology for the
Twenty-First Century
A passion for reason

MICHAEL J. LANGFORD
University of Cambridge, UK

Ashgate

Aldershot • Burlington USA • Singapore • Sydney

Published by
Ashgate Publishing Limited
Gower House
Croft Road
Aldershot
Hants GU11 3HR
England

Ashgate Publishing Company
131 Main Street
Burlington VT 05401-5600 USA

Ashgate website: http://www.ashgate.com

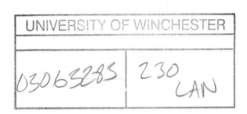

Michael J. Langford has asserted his right under the Copyright, Designs and Patents Act 1988 to be identified as the author of this work.

British Library Cataloguing in Publication Data
Langford, Michael, 1931-
    A liberal theology for the twenty-first century : a passion
    for reason
    1. Theology
    I. Title
    230

Library of Congress Cataloging-in-Publication Data
Langford, Michael J., 1931-
        A liberal theology for the twenty-first century: a passion for reason/Michael J. Langford.
        p.   cm.
    Includes index.
    ISBN 0-7546-0503-5 — ISBN 0-7546-0504-3 (softcover)
    1. Liberalism (Religion)   2. Anglican Communion—Doctrines.   I. Title

    BR1615.L36 2001
    230'.046—dc21

                                                        2001022638

ISBN 0 7546 0503 5 (Hardback)
      0 7546 0504 3 (Paperback)

Typeset by Manton Typesetters, Louth, Lincolnshire, UK.
Printed in Great Britain by MPG Books Ltd, Bodmin, Cornwall.

Contents

Acknowledgements

In the preparation for this book acknowledgement is due to many people from whose ideas and encouragement I have profited. I shall limit my thanks to three. First, to my wife (the Sinologist, Dr Sally K. Church) who has opened my eyes to many Eastern parallels to the issues I am concerned with. Second, to Professor J.D. (Peter) Dawson, who opened my eyes to the centrality of the question 'Where to begin?'. Third, to an anonymous reader for Ashgate Publishing Limited, who helped to enlarge the scope of the inquiry.

MJL

Chapter 1

Introduction

A Castle Story

A certain man was desperately concerned with security, so he surrounded his house with a high perimeter fence and installed an expensive burglar alarm. He still was not satisfied, so he made the walls thicker, the windows smaller, and where the roof overhung the front entrance he put battlements from which he could look down on any visitors. When he had finished the alterations his house looked like a miniature medieval castle. Then he read in a history book that many old castles which were too strong to be taken by assault had been captured by treachery and, fearful of this, he resolved never to let any other person into his home, even though it meant he had to do all the cleaning and internal maintenance. Then he heard on the radio of someone who lived in a similarly fortified house being mugged when they went to the local store, so he decided never to go out but to have all his goods delivered through the letter box, which he enlarged for the purpose.

One can think of several instructive ends for this story. According to one of them the man dies through an unforeseen event, such as a virus in the water supply, thereby stressing the impossibility of finding absolute security. The one I prefer allows the man to find a security that succeeds in protecting him from all his fears, but concludes with the neighbours' comments. They look sadly at their old friend's home, and they do not call it a castle, but a prison, for indeed that is what it has become.

It often spoils a parable to explain it, but in this case I propose to do so because although the first level of meaning is fairly obvious, there is a second which is less so, and this is the level which relates to the main theme of this book. The first level is found in the moral meaning, centred in the insight that a human life that is happy or good cannot escape some vulnerability. Having friends, let alone family, involves being able to be hurt, either physically or, more often, emotionally. Paradoxically, the capacity to be happy – which depends so much on our relationships with others – is intimately linked with the capacity to be hurt. The higher our defensive walls the more we distance ourselves from other people. In addition to this, being truly happy is intimately concerned with the moral life, for that too is rooted in our relations with other people. The more we avoid every kind of risk the less we are able to leave the world a better place than we find it. In the Christian tradition, the vulnerability that is integral to both happiness and goodness is symbolized in the life of Jesus – in the one who chose to 'empty himself' so that he could share human sufferings, even to the point of crying 'My God, My God, why hast Thou forsaken me' as he faced death. This level of meaning may well be accepted as helpful by many people who would not consider themselves religious, for the insight that being a loving person involves being vulnerable is not an exclusively Christian insight. It is rather an insight that is specially stressed in the Christian tradition.

The second and less easily discernible level of meaning concerns the invulnerability of some world-views, or philosophical positions. The Logical Positivists, despite all the objections that can be brought against their theory, followed a profound insight when they rejected positions, including religious ones, against which no possible evidence could be offered. The totally impregnable position may be immune to assault, but it pays the price of becoming an intellectual prison in which the castellan is not open to any challenging idea and is imprisoned in a system, not of reality, but of their own creation. The castle walls are a metaphor for a series of assumptions in which everything is interpreted to fit the chosen position. The paradox is that Logical Positivism itself tended to become just such a prison, for it demanded acceptance of a particular theory of meaning, with the result that the prophetic words of others could not be heard.

One contemporary example of this castle is found among many people who have accepted not science – which is a liberating search for truth – but what is sometimes called 'scientism', that is, the belief (and belief it is) that the empirical sciences, spearheaded by Darwinian theory, are the key to all understanding.[1] The possibility that there might be other levels of reality, and that behind and beyond the world of sense there could be a spiritual world, is not open to serious investigation. The words of the prophets are like arrows that cannot penetrate the shutters that cover the arrow slits. If the walls were really made of stone, then God – if there be a God – could tear them down in an instant; but the hearts and minds of these prisoners cannot be reached by force, only by a response that opens up the chance of being wounded, in the sense that the very foundations of the position one has come to rely on may be shaken. So the soldiers of scientism are condemned to live in the darkened confines of their keep, secure in a methodology that guarantees no dangerous outside light can enter in. No one must open a shutter, let alone put their head out of a window, or they risk a serious wound. Clever people often build intellectual prisons that are like scientific theories, or rather pseudo-theories, which are adjusted to fit any new fact or any new exierence. Up to a point the adjustment of a theory in order to take account of new data can be legitimate, but when the theory is made to fit *whatever* is experienced, then it is a case of fitting the facts to fit the theory, rather than a case of constructing a theory to explain the facts. On many occasions in the history of science this is what has happened.[2]

Many religious people have built, and still do build, equivalent prisons, but there is a theological tradition which has always involved a breaking away from any such prison. This tradition stresses the nature of belief rather than knowledge; it admits the role of doubt and stresses the importance of an open dialogue in which all views can be challenged. Within this tradition, there is a legitimate assurance that the religious person may claim, but it is found in the rewarding experience of personal commitment to a way of life, not in a conviction that one particular philosophy can be known to be true with absolute certainty. This tradition is generally known as that of rational or liberal theology, and it is the purpose of this book, first, to explore what it has stood for in the past and, second, to expound a version of it that is suitable for the twenty-first century.

The Need for a Rational and Liberal Theology

The present intellectual climate is full of paradoxes. In many contemporary cultures there is much evidence for a spiritual hunger combined with very little awareness or knowledge of the spiritual traditions that have enriched these cultures in the past. Instead, the traditions are frequently rejected, even though the ideas rejected are likely to be caricatures. In the Western world there is an understandable and commendable interest in Eastern religions, but this is often combined with minimal knowledge of the spiritual traditions of the West. Meanwhile in China, the Communist elite tend to combine a fascination with one Western tradition (namely Marxism) with a woeful ignorance of their own, extremely rich spiritual traditions. Another, and related, paradox has been illustrated by the parable of the castle. A general acceptance of scientific claims is often combined with very little understanding of what contemporary science is really like and little openness to explore, first hand, the relatively modest claims actually made by most of those in the forefront of scientific work. As a result, many people are imprisoned within a world-view that is pseudo-scientific. More generally, there is a widespread belief that in order to follow reason we should discard religion, while at the same time, not only is there no clear understanding of what 'reason' means, but many things are believed on authority rather than on any reasoning process. In other words, the irrationalism that used to infect many (but not all) religious people has been replaced by an irrational rejection of religions that have never been examined and, quite often, an irrational acceptance of other beliefs. In the context of the widespread spiritual hunger, which many of the great religions – when experienced at their best – could respond to, the situation is not only paradoxical, but tragic.

Unfortunately, when we turn to those who teach theology, or who preach in the churches, we often find that a rational approach to religion, which has been one hugely important tradition within Christianity, is often sidelined, with the result that the sceptic's suspicion that religion reflects the approach of a bygone age is confirmed. Many of the churches either preach a version of fundamentalism that cannot stand up to rational analysis, or a Barthian gospel that is only alleged to make sense once one is within the circle of faith.[3] In consequence, there is an urgent need for a reappraisal of the tradition of 'liberal theology', a tradition which no one who is truly rational can afford to ignore, even if they end up rejecting it. It can be thought of as part of the 'human enterprise'. Let me explain why this is so.

In human beings, we find a strange mixture of passion and reason. It is in the blending of these two elements that we find the essence of humanity in contrast with animals on the one hand – who often have something akin to passion but, at best, only the rudiments of reason[4] – and computers on the other – which have no passion, but a certain kind of rationality. Exactly what we mean by reason is a complex question that I shall address more directly in the next section; however, whatever our account of it may be, it is something that all of us approve. We may have doubts as to how far reason can answer some questions, or how far it is appropriate for guiding some aspects of our lives but, in principle, we always condemn the 'irrational' and seek what is 'reasonable'. Moreover, although passion is often in tension with reason, many people, perhaps paradoxically, have a positive passion to be rational. They wish to extend the boundaries of the rational to as many spheres of life as they can.

As I have indicated, within the history of theological reflection, in Christian and other forms of religious thought, there has been a tradition in which reason has been a central concern. In its typical form, this tradition has not claimed that there is no place for revelation, meaning religious experience that is believed to indicate knowledge or awareness of a spiritual reality, for without reference to such experience we could not appreciate the history of any of the great religions. However, within this tradition, the content or alleged content of any revelation is reflected upon, sifted, compared with other examples and, as far as possible, described within the context of a general philosophy of life. If we have only a spark of the 'passion for reason', and if we acknowledge that some religious questions are of fundamental importance with respect to what we should believe and how we should live, then this tradition should be of vital interest.

The claim that liberal theology is of importance can be strengthened when we observe the way in which fundamental positions in religion are often caricatured, so that what is attacked or rejected, is not, say, Christianity as many Christians would recognize it, but some strange distortion of it. In the context of partisan debates in which the participants are more concerned with winning than with discerning truth, alternative positions are often painted in grotesque colours. Religious people are often guilty of this irrationalism, for example, in the way they describe the religious views of others, or in claims that only religious people can be morally good. Equally, those who are anti-religion tend to select bad examples of religion (of which, of course, there are many), and then make general conclusions that are quite unjustified. Even normally intelligent and fair-minded people often rely on caricatures. An example is provided by a chapter in Jeremy Paxton's *Friends in High Places* in which a gloomy picture of the Church of England is presented.[5] Here there is an amusing, if one-sided, account of what is said to go on in the upper echelons of the church, but absolutely no reference to the dynamic life of many ordinary parishes. It is as if one were to evaluate an army by going to dinner parties at the officers' mess, while never seeing the regular troops in training or action!

Similar to the problem of caricature is the problem of grave misunderstanding, often within the thought of highly intelligent people. For example, when the scientist and Nobel Prize winner Francis Crick describes his boyhood movement towards becoming 'an agnostic with a strong inclination toward atheism', he describes how he increasingly found certain religious claims untenable, such as fundamentalist statements about the age of the world. He adds: 'if some of the Bible is manifestly wrong, why should any of the rest be accepted automatically?'[6] This attitude is of a piece within a commonly received picture of religious people retreating, stage by stage, as one claim after another must be abandoned in the face of new scientific discoveries, and the God of the Gaps is seen to be less and less relevant.[7]

There are two important misunderstandings here. The first is the failure to distinguish central religious assertions – in the Bible or elsewhere – from factual claims, that in many cases have no essential importance for religion. With regard to the factual claims Crick is quite right. It is unfortunate that again and again many religious people and many churches, especially from the time of Copernicus and Galileo, have made factual assertions that cannot be defended in the light of later discoveries in modern science. (There are *some* factual claims, such as the historical existence of Jesus of Nazareth which *are* central for the historical religions, and some of these will be discussed in Chapter 7.) Within the liberal tradition, once Darwin's theory became generally understood, it was soon realized that the question of whether or not animals and humans evolved over a long period of time was irrelevant to the question of whether or not there was a loving creator behind the creative process. No Christian thought that the gradual development of the baby in the womb entailed that God was not the creator of the individual person it became, so why should the gradual development of a whole species entail that God was not the creator of the species? The distinction between the scientific examination of a process and the religious significance of a process indicates how the essential *religious* assertions of the great religions are not factual claims of the kind that science can investigate. In the case of the Bible, the essential assertions include the claim that behind the whole physical creation there is a loving intelligence that is its ultimate source, and that individual humans are known and loved by this intelligence. In later chapters we shall examine the reasons why religious people make these claims, and how rational people may agree or disagree with the validity of these reasons, but the point is that the essential religious claims should not be lumped together with factual assertions that are logically completely independent. It is only with respect to the latter that a systematic retreat can be seen.[8]

The second misunderstanding is implicit in Crick's objection to beliefs being 'accepted automatically'. Within the liberal religious tradition that is explored here, nothing is accepted 'automatically'. As with many other beliefs, a young child may accept many things purely on trust, but growing to adulthood must include what the Bible calls being ready to give 'a reason' for the hope that is in you.[9]

An illustration may help to illuminate further the difference between the kind of empirical statements that it is the proper business of science to investigate, and what I have called 'essential' religious claims. Let us suppose (what I believe to be extraordinarily unlikely) that new scientific evidence showed not only that the famous shroud of Turin dated from the first century of the Christian era, but that the imprint was made in a totally inexplicable manner – though one that had to be in the context of an extraordinary discharge of energy. These scientific findings would be consistent with Christian claims, and psychologically would boost them for many people, but there would be no logical proof of any metaphysical claim about the nature of Jesus. The same point would emerge *if* we were to have physical proof of Jesus being the product of a virgin birth. This would be extraordinary, perhaps unexplainable, but there would be no logical need for an atheist to say: 'Jesus is the unique son of God.' The logical point is that no amount of physical evidence can by itself be a scientific proof for a metaphysical claim of this kind – by its very nature, with the exception of cosmology, empirical scientific evidence is about parts or aspects of the physical universe. Further, even in the case of cosmology, although the nature of the physical universe as a whole is the object of study, scientists, as scientists, do not concern themselves with alleged purposes or metaphysical realities behind it.

Aquinas shows acute awareness of this point.[10] He defines the word 'miracle' as an event 'in nature' that 'cannot be explained' by natural means, and is done by

God. (Not everyone is happy with this definition, but it certainly captures what many people have meant, and for the sake of the present argument we can use it.) He then goes on to say that some things, notably creation and redemption, are not *in the strict sense* 'miracles', because they are not, and could not be, events 'within nature'. They belong to a still more marvellous category of event. Claims about Jesus being the unique son of God, or of his being eternally present with his people are of this kind, although Aquinas does not discuss them in the same passage. They are metaphysical claims that go beyond any possible purely physical evidence. They are not, in Aquinas' language, events 'within nature'. No physical evidence could prove that Jesus is the unique son of God – including evidence about a virgin birth; nor could it prove Jesus' presence with his followers – including evidence about an empty tomb or a disappearing body. The last point indicates an essential truth behind the controversial claims made by the former Bishop of Durham, Dr David Jenkins. Whether or not we agree with him about the importance of an empty tomb, the essential message of what Christians have meant by the resurrection needs to be separated from a series of traditional claims concerning the details of what happened. At its heart, the resurrection is a belief about Jesus' presence with his disciples that cannot be proved or disproved by purely physical observations. If we saw the tomb emptied in a flash of light, this would not prove the claim of the disciples that they experienced the living presence of Jesus, or the claim that he is present with us now. If we saw his body being stolen away this would raise problems for traditional Christian belief but, strictly speaking, it would not disprove the claim that later on he was seen by the disciples and is now with us. There is no doubt that Aquinas believed in miraculous events – in his sense of the term (such as the emptying of the tomb) – that were associated with the resurrection, but I am claiming that, strictly speaking, these miraculous happenings were ancillary events surrounding the central claim, namely that Jesus was alive and present with his disciples. This central claim, I have argued, if we use the language of Aquinas, was not an event 'within nature'. Similarly, proof of a virgin birth would indicate a surprising, perhaps inexplicable event, but would not show that Jesus was 'the image of the invisible God',[11] and proof that he was the natural son of Joseph, or of someone else, would not disprove that he was.

Lest I be misunderstood, let me add that I personally believe that the tomb of Jesus was found to be empty. In addition to the whole resurrection story being a beautiful parable, it is also, as I see it, 'congruent' with the way that God works in this world. Also, there are rational grounds for holding that something extraordinary did happen on Easter morning. Not only do the gospels and the Acts of the Apostles describe an early Christian tradition: St Paul, probably writing in the mid 50s CE (only some twenty years after the events), makes explicit the nature of the eyewitnesses' claims.[12] Moreover, it is very hard to explain the behaviour of the first disciples if they knew that they had stolen the body, and it is strange that the body was not produced if it were stolen by enemies. However, my point is most important for the logical understanding of what the resurrection means with regard to the central claim about the living presence of Jesus. This is an example of a non-scientific (but not an 'unscientific') belief, and in the light of this I hold that it is a mistake to demand that all Christians must accept the traditional Easter story in all its details. A similar point can be made about the incarnation. The story of the virgin birth was certainly a powerful teaching parable for the first Christians, and it is also, considered as an alleged physical happening, congruous with the teaching, but logically it is not essential to it. (Also, the evidence is a whole generation older than that for the events of the life of Jesus, which was almost certainly written down by eyewitnesses or their associates.) In consequence, a number of Christians prefer to remain agnostic with respect to the physical events surrounding both the birth and resurrection of Jesus.

The importance of avoiding caricatures and misunderstandings, including those that concern the relation of science to religion, should help to explain the approach to secular thought – both atheistic and agnostic – throughout this book. Some religious readers may be surprised, or even annoyed, to find that in the context of the analysis of what it is to be 'rational' and in the account of what 'materialism' means, I shall defend the claim that it is possible to have either an agnostic or an atheistic philosophy that *is* rational. For example, some of those people who call themselves 'secular humanists' have developed a tradition that can properly be called both rational and liberal that parallels in many ways the religious tradition with which I am concerned. This secular tradition, at its best, has the same kind of openness as the tradition of liberal theology, and should certainly command respect. However I shall argue not only that a theistic philosophy can also be rational, but that such a philosophy has some inherent attractions that a rational, secular philosophy does not have. Moreover, most individual atheists and agnostics do not have rational positions, since the pictures they have of theism include a series of caricatures or misunderstandings. In other words, they have never seriously considered a theistic philosophy represented at its best. It is also true that many individual theists hold irrational positions but, in their typical form, contemporary religious positions tend to have one rational advantage over secular ones, especially atheistic ones. Typically, believers in God claim not to know that their religion is true, but to believe it (not blindly, but for a series of reasons that they may try to explain). Some, like Leslie Weatherhead, have put this point particularly strongly, insisting that in the strict sense of the term they are agnostics, since the word 'agnostic' literally means 'not knowing'.[13] They have then objected to popular usage which takes 'agnostic' to mean 'not knowing *and* not believing'. In contrast, many (but not all) atheists have a dogmatic certainty about their secular philosophy, and about what they hold to be the demands of scientific rationality, that reminds one more of the dangerous certainties that often infected older generations of believers rather than the kind of openness that scientific rationality actually supports. In serious debates between religious people and atheists, it is amazing to see how often highly intelligent and educated people attack caricatures. We shall see this, for example, when we come to consider what the liberal tradition says about the nature of divine omnipotence and the manner in which providence is claimed to work, both of which tend to be consistently misunderstood or misrepresented. It is not likely that this book will convert large numbers of atheists, but if it moves some atheists to a rethinking and then to a more rational version of atheism, it will have achieved much.

Given the realization that reason itself can see that there must be limits to reason's power, especially in regard to fundamental questions about the universe as a whole, or about a spiritual dimension that cannot be directly observed with our senses, it is understandable that many thinkers have been suspicious of the liberal tradition. We find, for example, that in the *New Catholic Encyclopedia*, both 'rationalism' and the allied word 'liberalism' are defined in pejorative terms.[14] When we recall the programme of some members of the Enlightenment movement, who believed that scientific reasoning was itself sufficient to cure all human ills, we can have sympathy with these negative definitions. Also, if one reads the doctrines that the Roman Catholic Church associated with theological liberalism, for example, those condemned in the official lists of errors in papal encyclicals of 1864 and 1907, liberals like myself will almost certainly find that they too disagree with many of the offending propositions. Thus the liberalism that this book supports is not primarily committed to lists of traditional liberal claims (only some of which would be supported), but to a *method* of inquiry. To put this in another way, we can adopt part of the Enlightenment's trust in reason without being committed to the overly optimistic view that often accompanied this trust. Hence, while I do not deny that there are many examples of putting too much faith in human reasoning, I am using the terms 'rationalism' and 'liberalism' with a positive rather than a negative force. Later in this chapter I shall give a fuller account of how I recommend using these terms, and I think it will become evident, given this usage, that there are many liberal, Roman Catholic thinkers who would not find major disagreement.

The attempt to find a rational philosophy or theology, within the limits of what reason can hope to achieve, will be recognized by many readers as part of a long tradition within human reflection, a tradition in which philosophy and theology overlap. The Christian version of this tradition is rooted in those apologists of the early church, such as Justin Martyr, who first sought to find some common ground with the Greek philosophers, in the face of others who wanted to distance the new religion from everything pagan. Later, Justin's attempt to find common ground between Christianity and the searching, intellectual spirit of all human beings found strong support in a series of theologians writing in ancient Alexandria. Later still, the situation becomes complicated by the fact that many of the great thinkers of the Middle Ages who could not happily be classed as liberals (among other reasons, because they believed in the persecution of heretics) gave reason a prominent place within their theology. Foremost among these is Thomas Aquinas, writing in the thirteenth century, whose views will frequently be found helpful throughout this book. Moreover, the Scholastic support for the role of reason faced significant opposition from many quarters, including the Nominalist movement. The situation was not immediately changed at the Reformation, since many of the Reformers were extremely hostile to what they considered to be the dangerous pride involved in any rational assessment of Revelation and, very often, a particular view of Revelation as interpreted by them. But even in the sixteenth century, a genuinely liberal tradition (in a sense to be given more precision later in this chapter) began to develop with writers such as Castellio and Hooker, the latter having to fight a rigid Puritanism as well as conservative Catholicism. Most of all, however, the rational tradition that I seek to be part of can be found in a number of seventeenth-century thinkers, mostly Anglican, including what is known as the Great Tew circle, centred from 1632 to 1639 on Lucius Cary,[15] and the group known as the Cambridge Platonists, many of whom got their chief inspiration from Benjamin Whichcote.

This tradition was kept alive by thinkers such as Joseph Butler in the eighteenth century. Reading these writers in the context of the narrow-mindedness of much of the philosophical and theological debate of the time is like taking a breath of fresh air.[16] They were also at the forefront of an ethical tradition that found no genuine Christianity outside a life that was lived for the good of all, and that led, in the eighteenth century, to the first serious movement to abolish institutional slavery.[17] (However, for that movement, the greatest credit must go to the Quakers, whose thinking preceded that of both Anglicanism and Methodism on this matter.)

The reason why Aquinas, and most other scholastic writers of the high Middle Ages, were what I would call 'allies' of the liberal tradition, rather than 'exponents' of it, needs to be explained further. Reason, in a theological context, can refer to at least three kinds of activity. First, there is the capacity that can be found in all people of good will as they reflect on the ordinary data of experience. The religious person may believe (like Justin) that even this kind of reason is due to the illumination of God, but the important point is that there is no appeal to a kind of reason that is only accessible to the few. Second, there is the rational exploration of the data of religious experience, either of a personal kind, or as recorded in the writings of others. This always involves an *interpretation* of experience, even though many theologians have written as if Revelation is some sort of unmediated 'given'. It is a kind of rational activity that I shall be discussing directly in Chapters 4 and 5, when the data of religious experience must be considered. Third, and much more controversially, there is the special sense of reason as informed or guided by faith. On the positive side, this third sense of reason is rooted in the kind of *insight* that comes from reflection within a particular tradition or a particular community. However, the obvious danger that attaches to any doctrine of intuitive or inspired reason is that people can appeal to what (it is alleged) reason *really* shows you if only you are enlightened, in a way that parallels those who offer people 'real' freedom, if only they will give up their false ideologies.

In contrast with this third sense of reason, the first sense is sometimes referred to in theological writings as 'unaided' reason. However, this term is highly misleading, since although there is no appeal to special insight, a religious person may well believe that *all* human reasoning is inspired in some way, either because of divine illumination working within us all the time, or because our reasoning faculty is in itself a kind of participation in the divine, and part of what it means to be made in the image of God. Thus, according to many theists, even the thinking of an atheist is not properly described as unaided. As a result, a better characterization of the first kind of reason is simply to say that it is the kind of reasoning found in all typical members of the human species. When I come to describe this more adequately in the next section, I shall argue that this 'ordinary' kind of reasoning is more than logic, as that term is normally used.

Returning to the third, or inspired form of reason, we should note that this has a long history. It was present in the Stoic conception of 'right reason' (*recta ratio*), and in Christianity one of the founts is Augustine's search for an understanding that is illuminated by faith, encapsulated in the saying 'I believe in order that I may understand' (*credo ut intelligam*). Later, we find a similar idea expressed in Anselm's quest for 'faith seeking understanding' (*fides quaerens intellectum*). In Aquinas the theme returns with the idea that faith must take reason by the hand and lead it aright.[18] One way of describing what the liberal Christian tradition stands for is to indicate its nervousness about this context for the use of reason. This need not imply a denial that there is a form of inspired insight that is found among the faithful (and it must be admitted that several of the seventeenth-century liberals to whom I refer did make reference to 'right reason'), but it does involve a reluctance to rely on any such appeal when there is a genuine debate, either with non-believers concerning the Christian faith, or with fellow believers when there is controversy concerning the interpretation of what is believed to be a revelatory event or experience. To put this in another way: a modest assessment of liberal theology is to see it as a tradition of primal importance in the context of open debate or dialogue between people of good will. This arises in at least two contexts: first, discussions in which Christians or other theists explain their beliefs to non-believers, and second, when Christians or other theists, seek to understand their own faith, prior to or apart from any special insights that they believe have been given to them.

Thus an acceptance of liberal theology, as a vital tradition, does not entail that there could not be other traditions, like that of 'mystical theology', that might be important and legitimate for some theists. In the different context of a believing and worshipping community, it may be the case that shared insights and shared convictions arise that only begin to make sense in the light of the experience. In Chapter 7, when we consider the grounds for Christian teaching about the Trinity, this issue will re-emerge when it may appear that it is not always easy to draw a sharp line between reflection on the religious experience of others, and reflection on one's own experience (for example, among those who speak of being 'in Christ'). However, for the most part, within this book, I am only concerned with the nature and scope of liberal theology, and therefore, as far as possible, I avoid references to appeals regarding intuitive insight.

Given the *range* of attributes that characterize liberalism (as summarized later in this chapter), many writers do not fit neatly into the classifications of liberal or non-liberal, but Abelard, writing in the first half of the twelfth century, is an example of one who can be placed within the liberal tradition, and who was subsequently attacked, by St Bernard among others, for what was held to be a dangerous over-reliance on reason.

It is worth stressing several ways in which Abelard championed what later came to be called liberal theology, without putting him on a pedestal. (There is no doubt that Abelard's brilliance was marred, especially in his early days, by a certain intellectual arrogance, and that – because of the nature of his background and opportunites – he did not produce the kind of comprehensive theology that we find, for example, in Aquinas.) First, like all typical liberals, Abelard does not make a major distinction between natural and revealed theology, precisely because he sees a continuity of rational activity in both. However he was not a rationalist in the twentieth-century sense, although he and his followers were called the equivalent of 'modernists' (*hodierni*, or 'today people').[19] He believed that humans should seek to understand (*intelligere*) Christian doctrine, if they are to believe it in any significant sense, but that they cannot be expected to comprehend it (*comprehendere*). Not only did he accept the way in which God helps to inform all our understandings, when we do begin to understand we have at best only a partial understanding that falls short of 'comprehension'.[20] For this reason, it is misleading to claim that he completely reversed the Augustinian *credo ut intelligam*, as is sometimes alleged, with a *intelligo ut credam* ('I understand so that I may believe'),[21] and on this matter there is evidence that he was consistently misunderstood by Bernard and other opponents.[22] Second, on a related matter, he introduces a legitimate role for *doubt*, for example, in his book *Sic et Non*, in which he places alternative doctrines side by side, with the implication that in many cases there is no one obvious truth. Third, Justin's positive approach to Plato and other gentile philosophers is frequently to be found in Abelard's writings.[23] Fourth, while not going as far in the matter of original sin as some seventeenth-century liberals, he supports an intermediate position in which we cannot, strictly speaking, inherit guilt, although we can inherit the penalties of Adam's guilt.[24] Fifth, in a similar way, while not taking the step of denying the literal truth of any part of the Scriptures, Abelard held what can be called a mid-way position. If a passage of Scripture strikes us as absurd, although we should never think that the author was wrong, we should suspect that the text or translation is faulty, or that we have not grasped the true meaning.[25] (Among Christian theologians, explicit rejection of the doctrine of *verbal inspiration* had to wait until Sebastion Castellio in the sixteenth century and John Smith in the seventeenth.[26] Even in the eighteenth century explicit rejection from Christian writers was rare, Thomas Morgan and the Quaker preacher Hannah Barnard providing important examples.[27]) Sixth, unlike most of his contemporaries, Abelard claims that heretics should be presented with reasoning instead of force.[28] Finally, as we shall see in Chapter 7, he produces an account of the atonement that is free of the rational and moral objections that apply to most other theories.

Liberal theology received a special impetus from within groups of Anglican and Quaker theologians during the seventeenth century, and it is to some of these writers that special attention will be paid throughout this book. Among these liberal thinkers is a member of the Great Tew circle called William Chillingworth. Probably the most brilliant student at Oxford of his generation, in 1628 he shocked his contemporaries by converting to Roman Catholicism and studying in one or more seminaries. He then returned to the Anglican church and began his literary output. In recent years his writings have been much neglected, in part because of their style,[29] but they are of the highest interest. One indication of this is the way in which Chillingworth can be seen to be moving away from an account of reason that is centred in intuitive insight – as found not only in Aquinas, but to a degree, within the thinking of his mentor, Richard Hooker – towards an understanding of reason as an essentially critical faculty that is close to some twentieth-century views.[30] Another is the moving account of how on his death-bed Chillingworth was urged by the Puritan divine, Francis Cheynell, to reject the suggestion that Turks (that is, Muslims), Papists (Roman Catholics), and Socinians (heretics who denied the orthodox doctrine of the Trinity) might be saved. Chillingworth refused.[31] Today such suggestions about how those with very different beliefs can merit God's grace and forgiveness are common, but in the seventeenth century they were exceedingly rare, and help to indicate what the liberal Christian tradition has stood for. Moreover, Chillingworth's position on this matter was a logical consequence of his argument about how an honest search for the truth, together with the implications of this for how we should live, were the *essential* demands of the divine upon us.[32] He insists that 'it cannot consist with the revealed goodness of God to damn him for error that desires and endeavours to find the truth.'[33] Later we shall see how this can be related to what it means to respond to the *logos*, which Christians believe was made flesh in the person of Jesus.[34] In the light of this, it will be apparent that it is perfectly possible to combine Chillingworth's positive approach to honest non-believers with a belief in the actual truth of central Christian doctrines such as those redemption, incarnation and the Trinity, all of which he upheld.

With the benefit of hindsight, two major weaknesses can be detected in the thinking of Chillingworth and his contemporaries (although I do not agree with a recent commentator who blames these writers for the deism and scepticism of the eighteenth century).[35] The first concerns a problem common to many Protestant writers, namely reliance on the 'plain' reading of Scripture; the second problem (one shared with many Catholic writers) was a naive reliance on the miracle stories as providing rational proof for the special authority of the Bible. Among liberals of the seventeenth century, this second line of argument was boosted by its use in Grotius' *De veritate religionis Christianae* (1627). (Grotius was a representative of a liberal version of Protestantism that flourished in seventeenth-century Holland, and was known as Arminianism, after its founder, Arminius.) In 1632 the first of many English editions of this work appeared, along with its claim that miracles provide the 'verification' of Christ's doctrine.[36]

In this book I am not primarily concerned with a scholarly exposition of the history of liberal theology, but with the application of the liberal tradition to theological issues as these are seen in the twenty-first century. Given this aim, in Chapter 7, I shall attempt to reconstruct a case for the fundamentals of Christian doctrine in a way that avoids the two fundamental weaknesses I have just described, while remaining within the ancient liberal tradition that is introduced in this chapter. This aim of the book also explains why I have not included an examination of a host of nineteenth- and twentieth-century theologians, from the time of Schleiermacher, who are commonly regarded as liberals. Any adequate survey of this history would require several volumes. Moreover, although such a survey would illuminate the quest for a twenty-first-century liberal theology in many ways, the most important of the issues that emerges in this history will be taken up directly in the next chapter. This issue concerns the way in which any contemporary quest for objectivity must be described, given the realization that the idea of a 'totally detached observer' is no longer sustainable, whether we are thinking of truth claims in science or history or theology. This matter will be addressed in the context of the debate among postmodernists and others who are centrally concerned with the cultural context of rationality. I shall argue that the quest for objectivity should not be abandoned, but described with more care.

One further comment is appropriate with respect to the complex history of liberal theology in the nineteenth and twentieth centuries. In this period, the theologians commonly called liberal are even more diverse than their predecessors, and many of them propose 'radical' or 'postliberal' theologies that differ dramatically from the kind of liberal theology proposed in this book, especially when they celebrate the death of any God who can be described as an objective reality. In contrast, I shall support what is, in the modern context, sometimes regarded as the conservative view that God should be thought of as reality. Also, although it is typical of liberal theologians to tread somewhat lightly in respect to the traditional *language* of the creeds, the liberal tradition of the seventeenth century generally upheld the central doctrines that the creeds referred to. It is with respect to these two matters that I distinguish between some kinds of radical theology – which depart from the older tradition on one or both counts – and liberal theologies, which I see as a continuation of the tradition found in writers such as Chillingworth. I recognize that here I am not simply describing the liberal tradition as this term is often used, but selecting and recommending a particular usage, based on the distinctions I have just made. However, I think that a distinction along these lines is helpful. It is therefore defensible, since the role of a philosopher is not only to describe how words are used, but also to recommend how they can be used more effectively in the light of distinctions that need to be made. Therefore, I am using the term 'liberal' to refer to a tradition that is found, *par excellence* in writers such as Chillingworth, who apply a rational methodology that does not deny the role of Revelation, and that ends up by supporting a series of traditional Christian claims, even though these are expressed in ways that take into account contemporary thought. Although the line may sometimes be fuzzy, in principle these writers differ from 'radicals' who either reject references to 'reality', or who reject any recognizable doctrines of incarnation, redemption and Trinity.

The stress on the reality of God explains another reason why I concentrate on a group of seventeenth-century rationalist theologians, rather than later ones. In a recent article on liberal theology, Maurice Wiles suggests that its 'eclipse' at the end of the twentieth century is due to the view that it 'has come to be perceived as an intellectual rather than as a religious undertaking'.[37] Even though this perception is largely unfair (as Wiles sees), this is the perception that has been given by many of the writings that have passed for liberal theology since the seventeenth century. In contrast, no one can read the Cambridge Platonists or the Great Tew circle without being conscious of their *religious* as well as their intellectual agenda.

A final introductory comment concerns the nature of the audience for whom this book is intended. It is not primarily aimed at teachers or students of philosophy, except in so far as all thinking people are 'students' of philosophy. In fact, some of my colleagues in the profession of philosophy will probably be irritated by certain passages where I am aware that the issues have been oversimplified. However, many philosophical questions are of the profoundest interest to the ordinary, intelligent person. Also, these same people are quite capable of thinking about the issues with a considerable degree of subtlety, especially if technical terms are avoided as much as possible. Further, there is evidence that what I have called a passion for reason is shared by a large number of people. It is for these serious-minded people who share at least some passion for reason that this book is intended. Technical language is therefore kept to a minimum.

The Meaning of 'Reason'

Many important words do not refer to any single characteristic, but to clusters of typical characteristics. 'Intelligence' is a good example. It is a mistake to rank people on a linear scale of intelligence, since one person may have more of one characteristic, such as speed of thinking, and less of another, such as depth of thinking. The measurement of IQ is only legitimate when we remember that it does not measure 'intelligence' as that word is normally used, which is multi-faceted, but some aspects of intelligence. 'Reason', and the allied words 'rationality' and 'rationalism', are also such 'cluster' words, and it is this which makes it impossible to give a precise definition. According to many postmodernists, rationality does not refer to a faculty that has any universal characteristics, but, as Richard Rorty claims, is only 'a property of what society lets us say'.[38] In the next chapter I shall argue that there are serious flaws in the argument which Rorty uses to support this claim. Here, I shall argue that despite the different ways in which the word 'reason' is used, it is possible to outline a basic, universal sense to the term.[39] This involves the identification of several typical characteristics, which is why, as in the case of intelligence, there can be no simple definition. I also suggest that the meaning of 'reason' and its derivatives is illustrated by their use within this book, which claims to be a rational exploration of some fundamental questions. If I have partially succeeded in this quest, then the book provides a special case of 'narrative' in which these terms are portrayed, as it were, in action. What follows is a series of suggestions concerning the chief characteristics of reason.

If we look at reason in terms of its evolutionary value, then it can be seen as a faculty by which the human species was able to consider the possible as well as the actual. For a species that increasingly depended for its survival on the cunning of its group activity – rather than in strength or speed – in matters such as hunting, and later in agriculture and other communal activities, this ability was of huge importance. Up to a point, therefore, we can give a sort of Darwinian explanation for the emergence of rationality.[40] Central to this ability was the ability to notice similarities – for example, in the behaviour of animals – and then to make predictions about what might occur and what was likely to occur. This preparation for the possible was essentially different from the complex group activities of bees or wolves, to take two examples. Bees certainly communicate with each other, as do wolves, and certainly have group activities which prepare them for the seasons that are likely to lie ahead, but there is no evidence that they have individual reflection on what is possible, along with the language skills to share this reflection with others. Jonathan Bennett has shown that there is a significant difference between 'regular' behaviour, and behaviour that is 'rule-guided', and it is only the latter which would lead us to say that a behaviour is 'rational'. In the light of this we do not have to conclude that even the complex behaviour of bees indicates rationality.[41] On the other hand, when a chimpanzee faces the problem of how to retrieve a fruit that is out of reach, and then uses a piece of wood to move it within range, there really is present something akin to human rationality – in one of its aspects – since an inner reflection on what is possible has taken place. In other words, even if the first glimmerings of rationality are intimations of something *new*, there is no need to insist that only humans can enter into the antechambers of this realm.

As these abilities of imaginative reflection and language developed, possibly by very gradual processes, then there emerged the basis for what would later be called induction, along with the rules of inference that successful induction requires. There does not have to be a moment at which this aspect of rationality suddenly occurs, but by the time the process has advanced to the extent that people can discuss probabilities with respect to the possible future (say, of the weather, or the enemies' likely actions), then one element of rationality is present.

Among the rules that allow for successful induction is a demand for consistency – for example, in the way that we use words. I think it is better to see the relationship of reason to consistency in this way (that is, as a feature of the inductive – and later, of the other rational processes) rather than as a 'free-standing' criterion. Another ground for this approach to consistency is that whereas computers can be consistent, there is a personal element in human reason which involves things other than consistency, and which prevents there being a single criterion that captures what human reason means. This can be seen from the following consideration: the inductive element of rationality involves an exercise of thinking in which different possibilities are balanced or weighed in a process that can be called 'judgement'. Clearly, there is some analogy here to the mechanical process of weighing two material things and seeing which is the heavier, but because the inductive process is an inner one, it involves a personal evaluation of the options in a way that links human reason, right from the start, with the passions or inclinations. This is one of the things that distances all human thinking from the processes that govern computers, at least as these presently exist. It also explains why an individual's reason has an essentially personal aspect, although in so far as the grounds for giving weight to certain options are rooted in shared values and interests a communal reason develops. I suspect that Rorty's denial of the universality of reason is based, in part, on a misreading of this feature of all human thinking. One result of the inner nature of the act of weighing and balancing that accompanies induction (as well as other aspects of rationality) is that no single result of this thinking process can be predicted with absolute certainty. There is no universal truth to the effect that all people will reach a particular conclusion. However, at least two things are genuinely 'universal' (among those who have developed the appropriate abilities). First, there is the univeral nature of the process that is taking place when this process can be characterized as successful thinking of the kind[42] that is required for our species to survive and to flourish, through communal activity. Second, there is the possibility of reaching conclusions, for example in scientific thinking, that have a measure of universality, or objectivity, and that do not depend solely on the hopes and wishes of the individual. This matter will be taken up in the next chapter.

When the human imagination is aware, not only of what is likely to occur, but also of what is *always* going to occur, and therefore of the notion of certainty, in contrast with contingency, then a second element of rationality can be distinguished. In due course this will be called 'deduction', and will be characterized by drawing particular conclusions from more general premises. However this process is dependent on a prior notion of 'necessity', which distinguishes the deductive process from the inductive. When primitive builders used a wooden triangle with sides in the ratio of three, four and five, they could be certain that they could set up an upright pillar (although it would not be until Pythagoras that it would be understood *why* this must be so). They had made what we would call a 'right angle'.

When these elements of reason are present, then already something of the transcending power of thought begins to emerge. Reflection and imagination concerning what is possible begin to take leaps, which in due course include reflection on the processes one is actually using and an awareness of the pressures that bear upon one. Here, if not before, crude deterministic accounts of human behaviour and thought become manifestly inadequate, for increasingly the very things that are claimed to necessitate us are themselves subjected to reflection and criticism. During the early stages of this transcendence, a third characteristic, or ingredient, of reason is manifest (the first being induction, and the second deduction), namely a reflection that is not satisfied with authority as the source of what is held to be true. Indeed, a search for an adequate explanation that was not simply based on ancient authorities formed an essential element in the development of modern science. This does not mean that there can be no place for certain kinds of authority, but that all authorities need to be justified. This, in turn, leads to the need to admit the positive role that doubt should play. It is unfortunate that there has not been more positive and explicit commentary on the valuable role that doubt plays in the rational process, other than in its exaggerated role in Cartesianism. The Scholastic method of stating and answering objections often looks as if there were a systematic use of doubt, but most of the time this was simply part of an exposition in which contrary views were dismissed, without there being any serious misgivings. A questioning doubt is implicit in Plato's dialectical method, but explicit in comparatively few writings prior to the Enlightenment. Abelard, we have seen, is one exception, as is the sixteenth-century Christian humanist Sebastian Castellio;[43] in the East, there is the claim of Zhu Xi (Chu Hsi), 1130–1200 CE, that one should doubt both the views of others and of oneself.[44] However, when great thinkers such as these have stressed the need for critical reflection, and therefore, at least by implication, of doubt, there has been a tendency for their writings to become a new orthodoxy that – paradoxically – repressed the role of doubt. We see this classically in the followers of Plato, who often accepted his theories as a new kind of orthodoxy, and in China when the works of Zhu Xi themselves became part of the orthodox canon that was required for examinations. Another example of a critical approach paradoxically becoming a new kind of orthodoxy is provided by the tradition of scepticism, both in its Greek form, and in that of recent scientific thought, which is rooted in Hume's sceptical philosophy. Sceptical empiricism can be commended for stressing critical inquiry, but in practice, as the parable of the castle illustrates, it easily leads to a new kind of dogmatism, in which whatever does not measure up to the methodology of a scientific naturalism is ruled impossible or 'empty', without sufficient realization of the assumptions that lie behind the methodology. For example, although the psychologist James Leuba made a serious effort to examine mystical experience, he did it from the standpoint of a scientific naturalism in which one cannot detect any serious doubt that might lead him to think: 'Perhaps I've got this wrong, and some of these people were in contact with a transcendent intelligence.' His consistent assumption is: 'For the psychologist who remains within the province of science, religious mysticism is a revelation not of God but of man.'[45] The assumptions involved in his investigations of religion, as in the case of Freud, made it almost impossible to transcend the limitations imposed by the methodology. We know that many theists are infected with a parallel dogmatism, but as already suggested, theism, in its typical forms, is concerned with belief, in contrast with the kind of certainty associated with 'knowledge'. Moreover, when religious writers of the last hundred years have examined religious experience, we sometimes find them agonizing over the issue of whether the experiences represent contact with the divine or whether they should be given a naturalistic interpretation (such as low oxygen levels in the brain).[46] Such writers are far more open and genuinely rational than many of the sceptical writers. This is one reason why, within the liberal tradition of theism, belief can be held to be rational.

With respect to what I have called the third ingredient of reason, namely the rejection of authority as an adequate source of truth, it is interesting to note an additional Eastern equivalent to the Western discovery. When the Mohists, probably around the same time as the emergence of Greek rational disputation, introduced what is often referred to as the first rationalist disputation in ancient China, this was based on three tests that had to be applied to every candidate for truth. The claim was made – which at the time must have been startling – that the soundness of a thought has nothing to do with who thinks it.[47]

For more subtle thinkers, the third ingredient of reason (the questioning of authority) inevitably leads to a fourth, namely the search for rational grounds for an *overall* position. Certainly by 500 BCE, in several parts of the world, some people reflected on moral customs, religious beliefs and philosophical ideas, in a way which attempted to see why one system was to be preferred to another. When we decide to adopt some general position, like a philosophy that covers a range of more particular positions, or a scientific theory that brings together a multiplicity of observations, how does a rational person choose this particular philosophy or theory? It is sometimes suggested that this adoption of a general stance can only be 'non-rational'. I strongly disagree, and take as the basis of my view a suggestion made by D.D. Raphael in his *Moral Philosophy*. The rationality of both philosophy and science, he argues, 'lies in two things, the requirements of consistency and the pursuit of truth'.[48]

Another way of describing this twin requirement would be to say that a rational person, in considering some general position, looks for both internal and external consistency. The internal consistency is a matter of stating the general position in a way that does not involve contradictions; the external consistency is a matter of being faithful to the complexity of our actual experience. (Later, when we examine the notion of paradox, these claims will need some qualification.) One element of truth behind the commonly made claim that the choice of an overall philosophy is non-rational lies in the fact that this approach may not always so much show that a single position is true, as show that many other positions should be rejected. Moreover, it may emerge that there are several positions that, at least for the moment, pass the test of internal and external consistency, or are on a par, in that they all get similarly close to passing it. In this limited context it may well be true that the final choice depends on personal, non-rational factors as one examines the 'living options'. What emerges, however, is that in its later stages what we call reason is typically concerned with a search for a truth that is disinterested. This, Santayana called the 'second degree' of reason, and is characterized by him as a reflective concern with 'the truth about things'.[49]

An illuminating discussion of the use of reason in respect to fundamental questions can be found in Keith Ward's *Rational Theology and the Creativity of God*. After rejecting the view that reason, in this context, can adequately be described as either deductive or inductive he writes: 'The highest use of philosophical reason lies in the conceiving and application of a new organizing idea, or a new interpretation of an existing one, which enables one to build up a new, and more comprehensive scheme for understanding this world.'[50] This suggests that reason, used in this approach to an 'organizing idea', is not limited to the negative one of showing the inadequacy of some views, but may positively support an idea because of its ability to bring together and explain a number of insights. This, in turn, suggests a similarity between the imaginative use of reason in theology and in the frontiers of science, where a similar rationality is used to select which hypothesis is likely to be most fruitful.

A fifth ingredient of reason can be suggested, one which overlaps the fourth. It emerges as the genius of finer minds enables leaps of imagination and reflection in order to see systems and hypotheses of new and seemingly strange kinds. Here, as in the weighing or balancing of different possibilities, the so-called cognitive aspects of our minds are interwoven with some of the so-called non-cognitive. Not only philosophers, mathematicians and empirical scientists, but also poets and musicians, find within themselves a dialogue between imagination, feeling and logical thought forms, to name but three of the participants. The context in which all human acts of judgement take place is exceedingly complex. If Augustine is right, another participant within the very activity of our thinking, especially if we are open and receptive to it, is the illuminating Spirit of the creative source of the universe. (Hence, strictly speaking, for Augustine there is no 'unaided' human reason.)

If I am right in claiming that these mental activities typify human reasoning, then it can be seen why a description in terms of logic is insufficient. Frequently, the term 'logic' is taken to refer to the recognition and use of rules of inference in both induction and deduction. Even if we are thinking of the first two ingredients that I have separated out, although human reasoning could plausibly be called a matter of logic, even here there is something misleading, since 'logic' tends to suggest some quasi-mechanical or inevitable sequence of thoughts, while I have pointed out that the *human* context for any act of weighing or balancing, which is central to induction, involves an internal aspect in which choices are involved that reflect drives or appetites. (Even in the case of deduction, the choice of a more 'elegant' way of doing a calculation indicates an essentially *human* aspect of the process.) More generally, if our starting point is the human capacity for envisioning the possible, in contrast with the actual, a capacity that is essential for survival, then this capacity – which makes possible what can be called 'successful thinking' – includes *imaginative* gifts, which cannot adequately be subsumed under the notion of logic. In order to flourish, and therefore to survive in any adequate sense of the term, we need to respond to claims to authority, and we need to work out general strategies that go beyond the needs of the moment. As a result, at least the beginnings of what I have called the third and fourth ingredients of reason are present, or potentially present, in all typical members of the human species. Moreover, when it comes to any rational evaluation of religion, it is what I have called the fourth ingredient of reason that is most likely to be most involved.

A fuller description of reason might well suggest additional characteristics. I shall mention only one more interesting candidate, namely intuition, or the rather similar 'right reason' of the Stoics, already referred to. As suggested before, here we find ourselves in difficult waters for many people certainly seem to grasp important truths in some immediate way, but the question arises as to whether this is the result of a fast-thinking process that applies known rules of inference, or of some 'direct' way of knowing. Although some cases of what is called insight may turn out to be fast internal processes, there is a case for holding that there is also a faculty that needs a different analysis and part of the perennial difficulty of giving an adequate account of what we mean by reason is that we need to do justice to two different areas of the faculty we refer to by that word. There are what can be called the 'discursive' and the 'insightful' areas of reason. The discursive is exemplified whenever we are conscious of a process of active reflection, leading to some reasoned conclusion or act of judgement, and the first four ingredients of reason I have just described fall under this category; the insightful is exemplified in those moments when a pattern is suddenly seen, or a number of things suddenly 'fall into place'. What I have called the fifth aspect of reason is, at least in part, of this nature.[51] It is not an aspect of reason that I propose to make significant use of, since in the context of a debate with non-believers, it tends too easily to be seen as a case of special pleading.

This account of some basic aspects of reason or rationality does not claim to be exhaustive, but it provides good grounds for the claim that there are some universal aspects of rationality, and for dismissing Rorty's claim that rationality is only 'a property of what society lets us say'.

The Scope or 'Range' of Reason

Any adequate account of reason must not only discuss the nature of reasoning processes, as attempted in the last section, but also consider the limits or range of what reason can hope to achieve. This is an ancient issue, but it has looked different ever since Kant wrote his famous critiques of reason (under the three subheadings of 'pure' or scientific reason, 'practical' or ethical reason, and 'judgement' or aesthetic reason). Prior to Kant, there was a commonly found acceptance, at least in the Western world, that human beings were endowed with a mental instrument that was competent to search out and discover universally *true* answers to many of life's fundamental questions and, in particular, that questions about the reality and nature of God could sensibly be asked and perhaps answered. Not all Westerners approached such questions in the same way, for despite the optimistic view of what reason may achieve, in a tradition that runs from Plato to Whitehead, many thinkers thought that our answers to questions about ultimate reality had to be in a negative form, such as 'God is not x', while others, especially in the Protestant tradition, felt that the Fall had so vitiated all human minds that our reasoning powers were too limited to handle such questions. However, after Kant, all educated writers who have thought about reason have been forced to face up to the challenge he introduced. It is not essential that Kant's position be accepted, but it is essential that it be taken into account.

Kant distinguishes reality as it really is, which he calls 'noumena', from reality as it appears to us, which he calls 'phenomena'. The idea that we, in some degree, distort reality as a result of the way we view it, initially (at least in the case of physical reality) through our senses, had always been obvious and commonplace. For example, we know that a stick can look straight until it is seen half in the water, when it looks bent. However Kant's position is far more radical than a suggestion that we often get things wrong. A precondition of our being able to perceive anything, he argues, is that we perceive things in ways that are modelled so as to fit both our physical senses and the structure of our minds. In particular, the way we see objects as being in *space* and in *time*, and as *causally connected*, is a kind of necessity forced upon us by the human instruments we are compelled to use. However we can see, by reason, that this is and must be the case, and therefore *we know that we cannot know* the noumena as it really is.

This initially sceptical position is mollified by two other ingredients in Kant's philosophy. The first is that although we cannot *know* what reality is like through our senses, we do know that there *is* a reality that, as it were, underlies the phenomena. Second, although speculative or scientific reason cannot find out what noumenal reality is like, we do have certain clues through 'practical reason'.

This is not the place to rehearse the many and often subtle arguments that Kant uses to justify these conclusions, but a general awareness of his position enables us to appreciate the misgivings of all reflective people who are sensitive to Western thought concerning our ability adequately to describe what Kant calls 'noumenal' reality. While the ideas that there is no ultimate reality, or that it is foolish to speculate about it at all, are not views that were commonly accepted in the Western world until the twentieth century, they have long been familiar in the East. The earliest forms of Buddhism appear to disapprove of any speculations about what we might call noumena, since they can distract from our proper spiritual path. (It is misleading, I think, to call this 'atheism', since even the denial that there is a 'divine', on this view, is an inappropriate speculation.) Similarly, early Confucianism appears to disapprove of speculation about what we might call noumena, but for the different reason that this can distract us from concentrating on our social duties. Today, however, many Western philosophers go further, claiming that any reference to ultimate reality is 'empty'. This contrasts with 'old-fashioned' sceptics, like Hume, who, while denying our ability to know, for example, the 'real' causes of things, writes about the 'ultimate springs and principles' that are 'totally shut up from human curiosity and enquiry'.[52] In other words, there is acceptance of the *existence* of some ultimate reality or 'ultimate springs'.

In the chapers that follow I hope to be sensitive to the problems raised by Kant. For example, following the discussion of postmodernism in the next chapter, I shall reconsider what kind of objectivity we may hope to achieve. However for reasons that will be clearer when I discuss the 'transcending power' of reason in Chapter 3, I do not propose to assume the radical distinction between 'phenomena' and 'noumena' that Kant makes. One of the grounds for doubt about Kant's distinction can be indicated here.

According to Kant, an example of a truth that can be known *a priori*, because of the way in which we are bound to see the world, is that 'in all changes of the material world the quantity of matter remains unchanged.'[53] Superficially, given the atomic discoveries of twentieth-century physics, this is not only not *a priori*, but manifestly false. However, Kant's essential claim can easily reappear in a new form, namely through the principle of the conservation of energy. But now the question arises as to whether this principle should be described as something that can be known, absolutely, prior to all experience, based on Kant's claims about a phenomenal world that we are bound to see in certain ways. I suggest that the principle of the conservation of energy is better described as a discovery about the physical universe we inhabit. We cannot know for certain that it applies to other universes that might have been created or come to be in some spontaneous fashion. Moreover, even though a case can be made for the claim that it reflects a 'natural necessity' for any universe in which beings like us could evolve, we cannot *know* absolutely that the principle always applies in this world, for example, in extreme conditions. It is rather a convenient and fruitful assumption to make when we carry out experiments and observations. More generally, when we consider the speculations of scientists about the nature of the physical universe, it seems both hazardous and unnecessary to lay down in advance of these speculations what the limits of our understanding may be. If we suspect that the universe is not only stranger than we imagine, but stranger than we can imagine (recalling a famous remark by J.B.S. Haldane to this effect), we have already begun to stretch our imaginations in ways that were previously not considered.

Notoriously, Kant had little time for the classical arguments of what he considered to be old-fashioned metaphysics, or for arguments based on religious experience, along with any claims to Revelation. He preferred to expound a 'Religion Within the Limits of Reason Alone'. However, I propose not to prejudge the possibility of either an old-fashioned metaphysics, or of revelatory experiences. Instead, I shall discuss both possibilities in later chapters. Therefore I shall leave open the question of whether we can have insights into what he calls a noumenal world (beyond those that he allows), either through rational speculation or through revelatory experiences.

A discussion of the range of reason must also consider the issue of whether speculative or theoretical reason is essentially similar to practical reason. In ancient times, any radical separation between the two would have seemed odd. For example, when Plato or Aristotle described the universe, their descriptions were at the same time an account of what *is*, and an account of what *should be*, since one's proper function or role in life was determined by one's position in 'the great chain of being'. Nowadays, the link between a description of what is and an account of what should be is often taken to be problematic – a kind of illicit move from an 'is' statement to an 'ought' statement. The link – so it is often held – can only be made by bringing in an extra premise such as 'we ought to do what will promote happiness' (J.S. Mill), or an implicit and shared sentiment of sympathy for others (Hume), or a special 'reverence' for moral laws (Kant), any of which could explain how we are *moved* to act in accordance with some theoretical judgement. However, my suggestions about the basic nature of reason may show why such moves are unnecessary. If we are thinking of the strict *logic* of the move from descriptive observations to actions, then it may be necessary to introduce one of these factors as a kind of 'middle term'. However, if we are trying to explain what *moves* a person, then we should see that the *human* context for any act of judgement, even in applying the basic rules of inductive inference, is always one in which a person weighs possibilities in a way that takes into account our drives and passions. Unlike the 'thinking' of the present range of computers, human thinking is always in the context of an organic body. As a result, any absolute divide between theoretical reason, which seeks to see what 'is', and practical reason, which seeks to decide what to 'do', is artificial. There is, of course, a difference of emphasis, and in this book I am primarily concerned with questions of truth, or justified belief, and therefore with the realm of 'is', but it is artificial to separate this radically from all questions of action.

On this matter it can be argued that Kant was essentially right. The categorical imperative (to the effect that we should always act on a maxim – or personal principle – that we could consistently will all other persons to act on) is normally thought of as a guide to moral thinking, but I think that Onora O'Neill has successfully shown that for Kant it is a principle that applies to *all* reasoning. For example, Kant's metaphors of the tribunal and the political debate, used to illustrate the functioning of reason, include the idea that 'any principle of thinking and acting that can have authority cannot enjoin principles on which some members of a plurality cannot (not "would not") act.'[54] Something like this is implicit in what I have described as a third ingredient of reason, for if external authorities are to be questioned and replaced with some kind of internal authority, then the very idea of an 'authority' carries with it the notion of what is proper or appropriate, in other words, something that is not just an 'is'. If even theoretical reason cannot avoid this notion, then there cannot be a chasm between reason acting in the theoretical sphere and reason acting in the practical sphere: it is rather a matter of different emphases.

The Meaning of 'Liberal'

The word 'liberal' is used in many different contexts – for example, in the area of political thought. Although there are some characteristics of the word that apply across the different contexts, I am here only concerned with the use of the word within liberal theology. In this tradition, the word 'liberal' is closely linked with the word 'rational' and, once again, the difficulty of giving a precise definition lies in the fact that there are several, overlapping characteristics. The principal ones can be described as follows.

a)   The desire to use rational methods, including those of the empirical sciences, as far as they can be taken. Moreover (as we have seen), these rational methods are those that can be appreciated by the ordinary, honest and intelligent person, whether or not they are within the 'circle of faith'.

b)   Within the tradition of liberal theology, there is a particular act of *faith* that is typically present. John Habgood makes illuminating comments on this matter. After stressing the slipperiness and many-sidedness of the concept of liberalism, he sees as a constant feature 'the wish to take seriously the intellectual climate in which faith has to be lived', and then, not unexpectedly given his own background in science, he goes on to discuss the relevance of science for any thinking, religious person. The pursuit of *truth*, both here and in other intellectual disciples, is to be welcomed by religious liberals, precisely because they really believe in a God who is active in the world, and who is the source of all that is:

The search for truth, in other words, through rational critical understanding (which needs of course to be self-critical as well) has theological roots no less significant that the theological basis of revelation. Both are from God ... It is this kind of faith, I believe, which undergirds the best liberal approaches to theology. I want to emphasize that this is a theological undergirding, not an absence of faith in God, but a conviction that he is to be found wherever the human mind can reach.[55]

Thus while the first characteristic of liberalism stresses rationality, the second stresses faith – a faith that encourages one to pursue an open dialogue with contemporary thought, precisely because it is believed that all truth, in the end, will point to God.

This reliance of liberal theology on faith puts an interesting twist to the previous discussion of the relationship of faith to reason. In the tradition that stems from Augustine, faith opens the door to an intuitive reason that tends to distance Christian from non-Christian thought. In the liberal tradition, faith in a creative God who is to be found throughout the cosmos leads the Christian to explore the insights of scientists and all other reflective people, since God, it is believed, can be found in all aspects of his creation.

The other typical characteristics are really an articulation of what is implicit in the first two, namely:

c) The refusal to be overawed by tradition or authority when strong objections to a belief or a practice are raised.
d) A dislike of any formal links between church and state.
e) A general scepticism of claims that are not backed up by appeals to reason or experience.
f) A tolerant attitude to those who disagree, including an appeal to reason rather than coercion.
g) A stress on the importance of the individual that rejects the relevance of distinctions based on nationality, race, religion, social standing and gender, except when these things can be shown to be relevant for the issue being considered. Respect for the individual includes encouraging each person to develop their own rationality and their own conscience, rather than being reliant on authority. (The last two characteristics indicate how the use of the word 'liberal' in this book overlaps the usage within the context of political thought.)

Taken together, the seven characteristics also indicate how what I call the liberal tradition in theology is allied to the Christian humanism of the Renaissance. Of special interest in this respect is Marsilius Ficinus, who died in 1499. His concern to unite Christian philosophy with a revitalized Platonism was derived, in part, from his desire to open a dialogue between Christian and secular thinkers, and his belief that this dialogue could lead atheists back to Christianity. He constitutes both a source and an examplar for the liberal tradition of the seventeenth century.

It might be objected that these criteria resemble a description of motherhood, in that just about everyone approves of liberalism when it is described in these terms. However, when it comes to practice, or to the attitudes that actually govern people's

thinking and actions, actual endorsement is not as common as might be thought. Moreover, in the past, even lip-service was less common. In looking at the history of this tradition I shall be concentrating on Anglican and Quaker examples, but it is not the reserve of any single denomination. Until this century, the liberal, Christian tradition faced huge opposition in all the major churches – witness, for example, the debate over evolution. In the context of this opposition, despite the vagueness of the term, it is helpful to contrast those who have generally stood within this tradition from those generally outside it. Within the Christian liberal tradition, as thus described, can be found many individual Roman Catholics (including Erasmus and E(s)tienne Pasquier[56]), Anglicans and Lutherans, along with members of all the other major denominations. All of these denominations also include within their ranks members who could not be called liberal, and many who are liberal in some respects and not others. Outside the Christian tradition, there are many who hold liberal theologies of an analogous kind in all the major religions of the world.

A further comment is needed on the liberal approach to Scripture, and in particular, within Christian liberalism, to the New Testament. The early days of Protestantism were typified by the call *Sola Scriptura* ('by Scripture alone'), indicating the only final source of authority in all spiritual matters, in contrast with the blending of Scripture with tradition and reason in the Catholic tradition. In the final chapter I shall criticize some aspects of the Catholic position in the sense of the official Vatican teaching, but equal criticism is merited for this primitive form of Protestantism. For example, I have already indicated that much as I admire Chillingworth, his claim that there is in all essential points a 'plain' reading of Scripture is hard to sustain. The most obvious problem with *Sola Scriptura* is evidenced in the bitter disputes between the Reformers themselves on the interpretation of Scripture – for example, in the exchanges between Luther and Zwingli on the nature of the Eucharist. Apart from a basic testimony to certain historical events, an understanding of Scripture always involves a complex process of interpretation. In terms of what is actually used by almost all Christians in their interpretative processes, there is much to be said for the 'Wesleyan quadrilateral' of Scripture, Tradition, Reason and (contemporary) Experience. The way in which these elements interact in the judgement of what is true or right is a highly complex matter on which I wish to make only one comment here, and that concerns the sense, if any, in which Scripture should be regarded as the primary authority for Christians.

Contemporary Protestant authors often ground their faith in the primacy of Scripture in a way that liberals may wish to qualify. For example, within the context of a generally perceptive book, Richard Hays claims: 'the hermeneutical [that is, "the interpretative"] primacy of the New Testament is an axiom for the life of the Christian community: tradition, reason and experience must find their places within the world narrated by the New Testament witnesses.'[57] Behind this claim is an argument concerning the way in which the New Testament must be read as a whole, along with an understanding of how within the redeeming work of Christ a particular community arises, and only in the context of this community can the Christian vision of life, including its ethical domain, be appreciated. I have sympathy with this approach until it leads to the conclusion that dialogue between the Christian and an intelligent secular humanist, or follower of another 'way', becomes impossible or, at best, of severely limited value. As I have stressed before, this dialogue becomes virtually impossible as soon as it is claimed that someone cannot appreciate a certain truth or certain value until they stand within the circle of believers. I have argued elsewhere that there is truth in the claim that things look different from within the standpoint of faith and of life in the Spirit;[58] however, this does not mean that things look *totally* different, or that there cannot be much common ground with all people of good will. The Thomistic view (meaning a view that is integral to the philosophy of Thomas Aquinas) of a Christian source of grace that is built upon, and fulfils, nature not only has an equal claim to be based in Scripture, it can be developed to allow for a genuine dialogue in which the Christian can challenge the views of a non-Christian, in matters of truth or of values, in terms that both can understand. Equally, the non-Christian can challenge the Christian tradition in terms that can be understood by both. Challenges to Christian tradition, sometimes coming from within Christendom, sometimes from without, have helped to promote new thinking on issues such as slavery, verbal inspiration and patriarchy.

Nevertheless, it is right for the Christian to accord a certain kind of primacy to the Bible. The Old Testament provides an essential context for understanding the New Testament and the New Testament provides the only written witness we have to the central historical events out of which Christianity arose. These are the events which underlie the doctrines of redemption, incarnation, the coming of the Spirit, and new life 'in Christ', as experienced by the first generation of Christians. This is sufficient to give the New Testament a unique status and importance for the Christian, even before we examine the extraordinary power of some of the writing, which includes an ability to draw the sensitive reader into the very fabric of the narrative. But this kind of primacy should not be confused with an interpretative rule that when there appears to be a tension between contemporary experience and certain passages of Scripture, then experience must give way to Scripture. This view leads Hays, and many others, to positions on many issues (such as pacifism) that do not take seriously enough the kind of reasoning that lies behind, for example, the Thomistic doctrine of the just war. Also, when someone argues for the primacy of a New Testament position, this may often be because a human experience, as described in the New Testament, is actually interpreted in the light of contemporary experience. For example, the Pentecostal experience is sometimes read in the context of those who have contemporary, dramatic experiences of 'speaking with tongues', experiences that may or may not actually resemble the original. Here the claim that the New Testament is given priority may *mask* the fact that it is contemporary experience that is actually given priority. In the light of all the interpretative difficulties, I question the assumption that any single rule of interpretation must be primary. The human situation is typically one in which there is no single rule that will iron out either intellectual or practical difficulties, but rather we are offered *several* rules or principles, among which we must seek a balance.[59] This is quite different from a universal scepticism in which there are no objective rules, or a radical relativism in which no position is ultimately better than another, since the rules or principles frequently show that certain interpretations are *wrong*. However, the rules or principles, initially at least, may only succeed in indicating a range of positions that can be sustained by honest and rational people. In this, all too frequent, human situation, trumping other positions with a primary card only succeeds in isolating oneself from the ongoing dialogue. We should be able to agree on procedural rules that allow for a creative dialogue, but we may not always be able to lay down a substantive truth that all must accept, even within the circle of faith.

The Order of Inquiry

This book is an attempt, not only to explore the method of the liberal Christian tradition, but also to explore what this tradition has to say about certain fundamental questions, particularly questions concerning the nature and reality of God, and the implications for human life of any answers that we give. These two themes are intimately linked, because in the course of exploring the fundamental questions, using the methods and principles of the liberal tradition, the method of this liberal tradition will be exemplified and clarified.

If we are to explore fundamental questions about the nature and reality of God, there is a certain logical order for the inquiry, an order that involves a series of steps. However before I indicate the sequence of steps I propose to follow, it must be stressed that the logic of presentation is often quite different from the process of discovery, which varies enormously from person to person. In the case of science, there is what can be called a 'logic' of discovery,[60] and those who pursue it carefully are more likely to make discoveries than those who do not, but this does not alter the fact that for the individual scientist accident and luck also enter into the discovery process. Various personal experiences may have led someone to what they consider to be a discovery, either in the realm of science or of faith, and it may be only much later that the discoveries can be presented in a systematic way that makes them comprehensible to another. Thus, the suggestions about the logic of presentation should not be taken to imply that this order represents the steps by which any individual should have come to faith.

Let us review the steps in response to a fundamental question put in the form 'Is God a reality?'.

Step One: for any inquirer who is sensitive to the intellectual climate of the past hundred years, the first step in any response is to face the challenge 'Is this question meaningful, or coherent?'. Here, some response to the challenge of the Logical Positivists, namely that the concept of God is empty, or meaningless, must be attempted. To proceed without this response, whether the answer is yes or no, is to assume precisely what many contemporary thinkers will not allow.

Step Two: if we accept the argument against Positivism, if only to the extent of admitting that the case against the meaningfulness of the concept of God has not been proved, there is one more preliminary step to take before any significant answer is examined. The contemporary movement known as postmodernism, in its typical form, denies that there is any universal concept of reason and, largely for this reason, any attempt to respond to the question 'Is God a reality?' cannot proceed on the assumption that one answer may be closer to the truth than another. I have already given a partial response to the postmodernist challenge during the discussion of the nature of reason. This response needs to be amplified, first by a defence of the search for objectivity, of the kind that postmodernists consider to be empty, and then through an examination of how a rational theology that claims some objectivity uses the ideas of analogy and of paradox, both of which are essential for any adequate understanding of religious language.

Steps one and two will be the subject of Chapter 2, under the general heading 'Where to begin?'. The remaining steps will each require one or more whole chapters.

Step Three (which comprises Chapter 3): the materialist response will be examined. This involves a negative answer to the question of God, and implies either atheism or some form of agnosticism (in the popular sense of the term).

Step Four: the monist answer will be examined. This response gives a qualified yes to the question 'Is God a reality?', since belief in a spiritual reality is affirmed, but not a spiritual reality that corresponds to the God of the great monotheistic religions. The word 'God', when it is used by monists, is a way of referring to the 'All', of which our minds are part. Our relationship to the All is like that of a drop of water to the ocean from which it came and to which it will return, or, to use an analogy common to both Stoic and ancient Indian thought,[61] like that of a spark to the great universal Fire.

Step Five: we examine the case for theism – the belief in the God of the great monotheistic religions, a God who in some sense is personal, and the creator of the physical universe. Here, a whole chapter will be devoted to the meaning of the concept of such a God, and another to a re-evaluation of the ancient arguments for the existence of God. I shall argue that, properly stated, these arguments do provide grounds for the rationality of theism.

In Step Six, we shall examine the different forms that theism may take, and in particular the case for describing God, as most Christians do, in Trinitarian language.

Step Seven, with which I shall conclude this quest for rational answers, will ask whether belief in a Trinitarian conception of God has any implications for the acceptance of any particular denomination of Christianity. Here, I shall not be claiming that liberal Anglicanism is the only rational form of Christian belief, but I shall claim that it represents one challenging and attractive form of it.

Reviewing these seven steps, it must be stressed again that this represents an order of presentation. For the individual believer the order may often be the very reverse of these steps. I may begin by being attracted to a particular religious community because of the quality of its life, or because of the way I feel valued as an individual within it. Only later may I begin to reflect on the philosophy which lies behind this community. Alternatively, I may simply be attracted to the person of the Buddha or Jesus Christ or Muhammad, and seek to be a follower of a way of life. Again, it may only be later that the philosophy that lies behind this way of life is explored. As in science, we must not confuse the logic of discovery with the logic of presentation.

Another matter to be stressed is that the relationship of these steps is not only a linear one, in which a person considers step one and then, if prepared to take this step, moves on to step two, and so on, all the way to step seven. Particularly as we come to consider the relationships of materialism, monism and theism (which are analysed separately in steps three, four and five), an adequate assessment of every position cannot be made only in terms of the analysis offered of each one by itself.

This is because a rational decision does not only ask whether a position is rationally possible, in that it can pass the twin test of internal and external consistency already described, but whether, all things considered, it is more rational or more adequate than any other possibility considered. If, in Chapter 3, it were successfully proved that materialism is false, and then, in Chapter 4 that monism is false, and then, in Chapters 5 and 6 that theism is true, we could indeed proceed in a purely linear fashion, moving, as it were, from one clear discovery to the next. However, it will be clear in what follows that this would be an exceedingly naive, and indeed irrational approach. I have already indicated that despite my own preference for theism, some forms of atheistic materialism are 'rational', and I shall make the same positive case for monism. When we bear in mind how the great thinkers of the past and present have espoused different forms of all three positions, there would be an evident absurdity in suggesting that one book could simply dispose of two-thirds of these thinkers as manifestly irrational. The linear approach involves an orderly progression, in which each position is understood in the context of others. As already suggested, many individual positions will turn out to be irrational (as forms of materialism, monism or theism), but more subtle variations on each of these more general approaches can certainly be defended. Our personal decision on where to stand will not only ask what is a possible rational position, but which position, all things considered, is most rational, or – among rational options – most attractive to us. Therefore in addition to the linear process there will also be, within our own reflections, a lateral one.

There is another reason why the rational quest which this book comprises is not simply a linear progression. Each of the options, although generally distinguishable when they are described in an initial and crude way, can be seen to have 'fuzzy edges' as soon as the descriptions take account of the complexity of the issues raised. (We shall find that some religions, such as Confucianism, do not fit comfortably into the classifications I use, even allowing for the fuzzy edges.) This is most clearly the case with the different Christian denominations, but it is also the case across the boundaries of the world's great religions. Members of a liberal Jewish synagogue may find they have more in common with some liberal Christians than with some fellow Jews; monotheistic Hindus might find that they have more in common with many Christians than with other Hindus who still defend a rigid caste system through a particular interpretation of karma, and so on. Individual Muslims, like members of the other great religious traditions, hold a range of views that once again overlap with the views of members of other faiths. This is not only true across religious boundaries. Among those who consider themselves secular are some people who want to stress a spiritual dimension to human life, and these may have as much in common with certain religious people as the latter do with fundamentalists who profess the same religion. The rejection of God is sometimes better described as the rejection of a caricature than as a rejection of the divine as understood by others.

A final comment concerns the order in which the chapters may be read. In most cases, I am assuming that the interested reader will follow the natural order of the chapters, taking the steps in the order of presentation. However, some people may prefer to skip to the step which is of particular interest to them. For example, someone who is already a committed Christian, but who has doubts about what the doctrine of the Trinity is really about, may prefer to skip to Chapter 7. Similarly, an atheist who has no serious misgivings about the meaning of religious terms or about the nature of reason, may wish to skip to the discussion of materialism in Chapter 3, followed by the defence of theism in Chapters 5 and 6. However, in both cases, I hope they will later go back to the earlier chapters, which in several ways prepare the ground for what follows.

Notes and References

1 See Hutton, E.H. (1956), *The Language of Modern Physics*, London: Allen and Unwin, p. 273: 'This belief in the omnipotence of science is, in fact, making a mockery of science: for this *scientism* represents the same, superstitious attitude, which, in previous times, ascribed such power to a spiritual agency' (original emphasis).

2 A good example is provided by phrenologist theory in the nineteenth century. According to the most popular version of the theory, human characteristics, including intelligence, were systematically related to the shape of the skull. When Mark Twain (Samuel Clemens) went incognito to have a character reading from a famous London phrenologist, he received a completely different evaluation of his capacity for humour than when he went in his own name. See Gribben, A. (1972), 'Mark Twain, Phrenology and the "Temperaments"', *American Quarterly*, Philadelphia, **24** (1), 62.

3 I shall expand on this point in the final chapter.

4 Although computers, as they exist today, have a certain reasoning power, this does not mean that we should say they 'think'. See Searle, J. (1989), *Mind, Brains and Science*, London: Penguin, ch. 2.

5 Paxton, J. (1990), *Friends in High Places*, London: Penguin, ch. 8.

6 Crick, F. (1988), *What Mad Pursuit*, London: Penguin, pp. 11–12.

7 This term, used for belief in a God whose hand can only be detected in the places where there is no scientific explanation, has been common since the rejection of a 'God of the Gaps' in Coulson, C.A. (1955), *Science and Christian Belief*, London: Oxford University Press, for example, p. 30.

8 This argument does not entail that science, philosophy and theology exist in totally different compartments. For example, it would be a caricature of science to see it as *only* concerned with 'matters of fact' that can be verified by the senses. What we think of as science and as philosophy originate in a common concern to find *knowledge*, in the sense of the Greek concept of *episteme*, later translated by the Latin *scientia*. From early on there has been an *empirical* aspect to scientific methodology, in the modern sense of the term. (For example, Aristotle was interested in the classification and description of biological phenomena, long before the rise of the more strictly empirical method in the sixteenth century.) This empirical aspect, which gradually developed into the contemporary experimental method, has tended to drive a wedge between science and philosophy in the minds of many people – but it is easy to overlook the common concerns and methods that both still have. Even abstract philosophy makes use of empirical data, and, for example, in the phenomenological tradition, tends to generate what it claims to be a special kind of data. Also, it is increasingly evident that good science has speculative and organizing aspects in which 'rationality' is not very different from what goes on in philosophical argument.

9 1 Peter 3:15.

10 Aquinas, *Summa Theologiae*, 1a Q. 114, 4 and Q. 105, 7.

11 Col. 1:15. The King James translation of the Bible is used except when otherwise indicated.

12   1 Cor. 15:3–8.
13   Weatherhead, L.D. (1965), *The Christian Agnostic*, Abingdon: Hodder and Stoughton.
14   *New Catholic Encyclopedia* (1967), New York: McGraw-Hill. Rationalism is defined
     as 'A theory or system that *exaggerates* reason's independence from the senses in
     philosophy or from supernatural revelation in religion' (emphasis added), while reli-
     gious liberalism is defined as 'an effort at emancipation from supernatural demands'
     (which is pejorative in the context of the *Encyclopedia* as a whole).
15   After 1639, Lucius Cary, later Lord Falkland, was drawn into the political events that
     led to his tragic death in 1643.
16   For an old but excellent introduction to these thinkers, see Tulloch, J. (1872), *Rational
     Theology and Christian Philosophy in England in the Seventeenth Century*, Edinburgh:
     Blackwood.
17   Some individual Christians, Catholic and Protestant had been against slavery long
     before the movement for emancipation, and there had been many authoritative attacks
     on the *manner* in which slaves were treated, but what was lacking before the Quaker
     activist, John Woolman, was any serious effort to rid the world of the institution of
     slavery. One reason for this was the acceptance by the majority of Christian theolo-
     gians that since the Fall slavery was not in itself contrary to natural law. It was contrary
     to an 'original' natural law, but not to the 'relative' natural law that followed the Fall.
     Similarly, in Roman law, slavery was not contrary to *ius gentium*, although it was
     considered to be contrary to *ius naturale*.
18   Aquinas, *De Veritate*, Q. XIV, A. 10. Here Aquinas refers to certain articles of faith *per
     quae manuducatur ad perveniendum in perfectam cognitionem* (by means of which he
     is led by the hand until he reaches perfect knowledge). In many editions the Latin text
     here is corrupt, for example, in putting *manducator* for (the correct) *manuducatur*.
19   See Clanchey, M.T. (1997), *Abelard. A Medieval Life*, Oxford: Blackwell, p. 33.
20   Abelard, *Intr. Ad theologiam*, II, III, 1051D, in *Patrologia Latina*, ed. Migne, (hence-
     forth *P.L.*) vol. 178, Paris 1855. In this passage the distinction is between *intelligere*
     and *congnoscere*.
21   See Sikes, J.G. (1932), *Peter Abailard*, Cambridge: Cambridge University Press, p. 31.
     Cf. Clanchy, *Abelard*, p. 36, where Abelard is interpreted as implying this reversal.
22   See Sikes, *Peter Abailard*, pp. 220 ff. Anselm, despite his general insistence on *fides
     quaerens intellectum*, himself suggests the occasional use of a purely rational ap-
     proach, for example, in his preface to the *Monologium*.
23   Abelard, *Intr. Ad Theologiam*, II, III in *PL* vol. 178, 1012–3.
24   See Abelard, *Expositio in Epistolam ad Romanos*, *PL* vol. 178, 866. On this matter
     Abelard is not always consistent. See Clanchy, M.T. *op. cit.* pp. 272–4. Abelard's
     contemporaries, Pierre de Bruys and Henry of Lausanne (or Le Mans), appear to have
     denied that any guilt could be attributed to infants. For this and other reasons both were
     declared to be heretics.
25   Abelard, Prologue to *Sic et Non*, *P.L.* vol. 178, 1347.
26   Castellio, S. (1563), *De arte dubitandi*, I, chs 12–17. In ch. 14 Castellio stresses the
     different kinds of Scriptural writing, each of which demands an appropriate response;
     in ch. 15 he describes how ambassadors (and hence the Apostles) sometimes had to put
     messages into their own words; in ch. 16 he insists that the authority of Scripture lies in
     the totality or body of doctrine rather than in particular passages. The implication is
     that the New Testament authors did not write everything from direct inspiration. On
     John Smith, see ch. 4.
27   Morgan, T. (1737), *The Moral Philosopher*, 2nd edn (1738), London, pp. 133, 251,
     442. According to Hannah Barnard, what we find in many Old Testament passages
     (such as those in which God appears to command the slaughter of defeated peoples)

was what people believed God commanded, not what he actually commanded. In a similar way she argued that 'Abraham may have believed that the will of God required him to sacrifice his only son ...', but he had misinterpreted God's message. Barnard, H. in *Considerations on the Matter of the Difference between the Friends of London and Hannah Barnard*, Hudson: 1802 (Early American Imprints, 2nd series, 1802, no: 1839. American Antiquarian Society, Worcester, Mass.: 1966) p. 13 (the controversy related to Barnard's preaching in London during the 1790s).

28 *Ratione potius quam potestate eos coerceri* , Abelard, *Intr. Ad Theologiam*, II, III in *PL* vol. 178, 1048.

29 His most important work, *The Religion of Protestants*, dated 1638, but published in the autumn of 1637, consists of a series of long extracts from the writings of his principal Catholic opponent (a Jesuit called Matthew Wilson who wrote under the name of Edward Knott), which were themselves responses to a Protestant writer (Dr Christopher Potter of The Queen's College, Oxford), followed by Chillingworth's systematic refutations.

30 See the study by Orr, R.R. (1967), *Reason and Authority*, Oxford: Clarendon Press, especially ch. VI. Chillingworth's position is not without its difficulties (see, for example, p. 163).

31 *Ibid.*, p. 197. See also Cheynell, F. (1644), *Chillingworthi Novissima*, London: 1725, p. 44.

32 Orr, *Reason and Authority*, pp. 62, 71, 163. Chillingworth maintained the Protestant position that the Bible contains all that is necessary for salvation, but he added important qualifications. It is one thing to say that the Bible contains all that is necessary for salvation, another to say that only those who believe what it contains (leaving aside the question of how this is interpreted) can be saved. He also supported the doctrine of justification by faith, if 'rightly understood' (*The Religion of Protestants*, vii, 33). The doctrine was only understood when it was seen that there is no real faith without obedience (vii, 32), for 'nothing avails with him [God], but faith which worketh by love' (i, 9).

33 Chillingworth, W., *The Religion of Protestants*, iii, 14. cf. ii, 104 where he says of a tyrannical God who damned servants who made honest mistakes: 'I for my part fear I should not love God, if I should think so strangely of him.' See also iii, 52.

34 Among the criticisms made of Chillingworth is the objection that he fudged the issue of what doctrines, if any, were essential or 'fundamental'. But at least part of his response to this issue makes perfectly good sense. It is that the question of what is fundamental has to be asked in context. For example, it is one thing to say what is fundamental for a person of very limited intellect to believe if they are to receive divine grace, another thing to say what should be the fundamentals of church teaching. Although the *Religion of Protestants* is more a polemical work than a systematic treatise, it is clear that Chillingworth regarded the traditional doctrines of incarnation and redemption as fundamental in the latter sense. See, for example, *The Religion of Protestants*, iii, 13. More questionable is the insistence that there is always a clear distinction between the plain teachings of Scripture, open to every honest reader, and the more 'obscure', which should not be the basis of anything deemed 'fundamental', for example, ii, 170. He thought that the whole Apostle's Creed could be defended by appeal to the plain teachings. During the discussion of the Trinity I shall be defending a similar claim, but this issue cannot be dealt with as easily as Chillingworth envisaged.

35 See Beiser, F.C. (1966), *The Sovereignty of Reason*, Princeton, NJ: Princeton University Press, pp. 123–33. More likely causes are the attack on all metaphysical ideas heralded by the Enlightenment, along with a naive acceptance of the omnicompetence of science.

36   Grotius, H., *True Religion*, London trans. of 1632, II, vi.
37   Wiles, M. (2000) in 'Theology in the Twenty-first Century', *Theology*, **103** (816), Nov./ Dec., 406.
38   Rorty, R. (1979), *Philosophy and the Mirror of Nature*, Princeton, NJ: Princeton University Press, p. 181.
39   The issue is complicated by the ambiguity of the term 'universal'. The important questions concern not what is universal in the sense of being found wherever we look within human cultures, but what is universal in the sense of comprising an appropriate ideal towards which cultures could move. The situation is parallel to that of the idea of a *universal* justice. When Aristotle says that natural justice has a universal application (*Ethics*, 1134b), he does not mean that this justice is everywhere to be found, but rather that it is the ideal which must everywhere be sought if human nature is to be fulfilled so that we can truly flourish. Similarly, the kind of universality that applies to rationality concerns the necessary requirements of *successful* thinking whenever conscious minds begin to develop understanding. Initially, the criteria for success concern the ability to survive through communal activities, like hunting, in which an awareness of the possible was essential. Later, the criteria for success depend on how well conscious processes can handle a whole range of problems, some of which have no obvious survival value.
40   Part of this explanation could be biological (and strictly Darwinian), in so far as those humans who had a greater capacity for rationality would be more likely to survive. Part could be sociological (and quasi-Darwinian), in that those groups that encouraged rationality and developed customary means of promoting an inherent capacity would be more likely to survive.
41   Bennett, J. (1964), *Rationality*, London: Routledge and Kegan Paul, p. 15. I do not conclude, with Bennett, that rationality is totally absent from all non-human species, still less do I agree that one should begin by *defining* rationality in terms of something that is exclusive to our species (*Ibid.*, p. 5).
42   This is important in order to distinguish the universal aspects of rationality from particular judgements that *happen*, by chance, to be successful.
43   Castellio, S., *De arte dubitandi et confidendi ignorandi et sciendi*, ed. E.F. Hirsch, Brill, Leiden, 1981 (in French under Castellion, S. *De l'art douter et de croire, d'ignorer et de savoir*, trans. C. Baudouin, (1953), Geneva: Jeheber). This work was written in 1563. Part of it was published in 1613, and the rest only in the twentieth century. Castellio is best known for his book *De haereticis, an sint persequendi* ('Concerning Heretics, and whether they should be persecuted') published in 1654, largely in reaction to the burning to death of Servetus in Geneva the year before. (For a modern edition see *Concerning Heretics*, ed. and trans. R.H. Bainton, Columbia University Press, 1935.) This book, written in conjunction with Caelius Curio, was the first defence of toleration (written after the churches gained power under Constantine) that became a classic. There had been many individuals who advocated toleration, such as Wazo, Bishop Lieges, *ob.* 1048, but little in the way of a systematic defence of toleration from within a Christian perspective. The only earlier example I am aware of appears in the writings of the anabaptist Bathasar Hübmaier, in the 1520s.
44   Chu Hsi, *Learning to be a Sage*, trans. and commentary by D.K. Gardner, (1990), Berkeley: University of California Press, pp. 46–7, 151.
45   Leuba, J.H. (1925), *The Psychology of Religious Mysticism*, London (1972): Routledge and Kegan Paul, p. 318. On the positive side, not only does Leuba make a serious study of mystical writings, his rejection of a direct 'divine causation' account of events in this world has something in common with the view of Providence that I shall be presenting. We should also note how Leuba distances himself from Freud (for example, p. 321).

46 See, for example, Zaehner, R.C. (1961), *Mysticism Sacred and Profane*, Oxford: Oxford University Press, and Katz, S.T. ed. (1978), *Mysticism and Philosophical Analysis*, London: Sheldon Press, for example, p. 255, and (writing with no evident bias for or against a religious interpretation), Norrman, C. (1987), *Mystical Experiences and Scientific Method*, Stockholm: Almqvist and Wiksell International, pp. 93–4, 167–9.

47 The first test is the 'root' of the claim – which allows some use of authority by the back door. The second is the 'evidence' for the claim – which involves an appeal to experience. The third is the 'use' of the claim – which allows a kind of utilitarian criterion to influence what should be believed, and a generally 'pragmatic' approach to truth. See Graham, A.C. (1989), *Disputers of the Tao*, La Salle, Illinois: Open Court, pp. 36–41.

48 Raphael, D.D. (1981), *Moral Philosophy*, Oxford: Oxford University Press, p. 6.

49 Santayana, G. (1968), *The Birth of Reason and Other Essays*, ed. D. Cory, New York: Columbia University Press, p. 54. Another example of a similar viewpoint can be found in Whitehead, who distinguished two aspects of the 'function of reason'. The first is 'practical', and is a matter of rendering our purposes effective (which fits well with my account of the origins of induction); the second comes from a disinterested curiosity 'driven forward by the ultimate faith that all particular fact is understandable', Whitehead, A.N. (1929), *The Function of Reason*, Princeton, NJ: Princeton University Press, p. 29.

50 Ward, K. (1982), *Rational Theology and the Creativity of God*, Oxford: Blackwell, p. 110.

51 These areas of rationality parallel, in some degree, two aspects of what we mean by justice – namely the 'procedural' and the 'substantive'. Procedural justice is relatively easy to describe – in terms of a series of rules, and similarly discursive (or critical) reason is relatively easy to describe – sometimes at least, in terms of rules of inference. On the other hand, just as questions of substantive justice are notoriously difficult, so are questions of insightful reason. However both may be essential. Without substantive justice the procedural rules of justice become an empty shell. Similarly, without a notion of insight, rooted in some basic, self-evident truths, it is hard to see where reason can find all the premises on which discursive reason can work. Bernard Lonergan is one of the thinkers who has illuminated how much rationality has to include an understanding of insight. See Lonergan, B.J.F. (1957), *Insight*, London: Longmans, Green.

52 Hume, D., *An Enquiry Concerning Human Understanding*, Sect. IV, part 1.

53 Kant, *Critique of Pure Reason*, trans. N.K. Smith (1950), London: Macmillan, p. 54. (section V of Kant's 2nd ed.)

54 O'Neill, O. (1989), *Constructions of Reason*, Cambridge: Cambridge University Press, Cambridge, p. 20, cf. pp. 8, 24.

55 Habgood, J. (1991), 'Reflections on the Liberal Position', in D.W. Hardy and P.H. Sedgwick (eds), *The Weight of Glory*, Edinburgh: T. and T. Clark, p. 12.

56 One of Castellio's important works on toleration, the *Conseil à la France desolée* (1562) was inspired by Pasquier's pamphlet, *L'Exhortation au Roi et à son Conseil Privé* (1561).

57 Hays, R.B. (1997), *The Moral Vision of the New Testament*, Edinburgh: T. and T. Clark, p. 296.

58 See Langford, M.J. (1994), 'Fideist responses to atheism and positivism: The rationality of belief revisited', *Studies in Religion*, Canada, **23** (2), 179–92; reprinted (1999) in *Walking the Tightrope of Faith*, H. Hart, R.A. Kuipers and Kai Nielson, eds, Amsterdam: Rodopi.

59 In ethics there is much to be said for a 'pluralistic' position in which there are a number of moral principles (such as respect for life and respect for truth), no one of which is

primary. This approach is fundamentally opposed, from the start, to efforts such as that of Bentham to find a single, supreme principle of morality, and allows for the existence of genuine moral dilemmas when the different principles are in tension. In such situations, the religious person will pray for strength to eschew the manifestly wrong answers (which distances this suggestion from most forms of relativism), and for courage to make the *creative* decisions that have to be made, wisely. Aquinas has a single overarching principle of practical reason, namely 'Good must be sought and done, and evil eschewed' (*ST* 1a2ae, Q. 94, 2), but this is more a statement about the nature of ethical conduct than a guide to the specific content of ethics. The overarching moral commands to love God and our neighbours as ourselves and to treat others as we would have them treat us, do have important, general, implications for conduct, but they do not give any specific guidance when love pulls us in different directions, as is the case in typical moral dilemmas. My position questions the helpfulness of any absolute moral principle that has specific content.

60   See, for example, Popper, K.R. (1958), *The Logic of Scientific Discovery*, London: Hutchinson; and Hempel, C.G. (1966), *Philosophy of Natural Science*, Englewood Cliffs, NJ: Prentice-Hall, pp. 5 and 15–16. For the claim that both writers exaggerate the role of chance and accident in the process of scientific discovery, see Achinstein, P. (1978), 'Discovery and Rule-books' in T. Nickles ed., *Scientific Discovery, Logic, and Rationality*, London: Reidel, p. 117.

61   See, for example, the *Katha Upaniṣad*, II, 2, 9 and *Mundaka Upaniṣad*, II, 1, 1.

Chapter 2

Where to Begin?

The Search for an Absolute Starting-point

One approach to the search for an answer to a fundamental question is to seek a *certain* or indubitable starting-point. Any such starting-point must be certain, not in the sense of a merely psychological certainty, in which we *feel* certain, but in the sense of a justified, rational certainty. Here we can recall how Descartes proposed a way of systematic doubt so that he could end up with just this. He claimed to have found it in his famous *cogito ergo sum*, that is, 'I think, therefore I am.' But unfortunately, as many have seen, Descartes' starting-point is fatally flawed. It is true that we can doubt the evidence of our senses. It is also true that we can, at a pinch, doubt our most primitive mathematical intuitions, for if we find that we are sometimes mistaken when we multiply, say, eleven and twelve, how can we be absolutely certain that we are not having a mental aberration when we multiply two and two, or that our memory about the meaning of mathematical terms is not playing us tricks? But when Descartes insists that even when we doubt these things it is certain that there is an 'I' that doubts, he assumes that the 'I' is, as he calls it, a thinking *thing* – that is, an entity that endures, unchanged, through time. But this can certainly be doubted, and indeed is rejected by many thinkers.

There is an important kind of philosophizing that is common in Continental Europe, centred in the work of Husserl, which claims that without the assumption of an enduring self, the bare experience of thinking is enough to establish an absolutely certain base for philosophy. However, there are equally strong objections to this candidate for certainty.[1] Other people have tried to base absolute certainty in the evidence of our senses, but Descartes' reflections, despite the flaw I have described, succeed in showing the inadequacy of this.

Can religion give us this kind of certainty? Here, even more than in the earlier searches for certainty, we must distinguish rational certainty from psychological certainty. Richard Hooker was one of those theologians who saw this clearly. He distinguishes 'Certainty of Evidence', which we do *not* have in matters of faith (unlike the angels who have 'the light of glory'), and 'Certainty of Adherence', which, by grace, we may have in spiritual matters. The latter relates to conviction, rather than to intellectual certainty, and it is with respect to this kind of certainty that Hooker describes how 'the heart doth cleave and stick unto that which it doth believe'.[2] This distinction can be developed in a way that makes possible an appropriate sense of assurance which the religious person may come to have, and at the same time, a denial that religious conviction can give one a justified, philosophically certain starting-point. This distinction can also be used to argue that religious assurance cannot be a legitimate ground for forcing a belief on others.

At this point an analogy may help to clarify the nature of the conclusion I am leading up to. Let us suppose that sculptor A begins work on a rough piece of marble by fashioning a perfectly formed foot, and then works upwards, bit by bit creating a perfectly formed ankle, then a leg, and so on. Meanwhile sculptor B begins by roughing out the complete statue as it is envisaged, and then, step by step begins to shape the piece more accurately, leaving the final contours of the face until late in the process. In the case of sculptors these are genuine options, although the latter method is how Michelangelo and the vast majority of other sculptors have proceeded. I am arguing that in the case of philosophers we can imagine two, analogous approaches, but in practice only the latter option is a real, or 'living option' (to use a term coined by William James). The reason for this is that it is impossible to find a truly indubitable starting-point that has sufficient significance to be usable as a foundation for any system of rational certainty. Instead, we must assume that when we ask a serious question about what we can know for certain, we *already* have some rough understanding of many things, and what we need to do is continually to test first one and then another of our convictions. We cannot make an absolutely fresh start with some absolutely secure foundation. What is sometimes called 'foundationalism' is not a possible starting-point for any intellectual discipline. We must start where we are, and then go in a series of circles, or – using another metaphor – a series of zigzags. In the words of John Donne:

> On a huge hill,
> Cragged and steep, Truth stands, and hee that will
> Reach her, about must, and about must goe;
> And what the hills suddennes resists, winne soe ...[3]

At first sight this conclusion might seem to introduce a radical form of scepticism that would run counter to any search for answers to fundamental questions. However, if we are satisfied with something less than absolute certainty, we can still have grounds for claiming that it is appropriate to use the word 'know' for some of our most established scientific or other discoveries, and a term such as 'rational belief' for other claims. In no way does acceptance of the second approach to the problem of where to begin deny the legitimacy of searching for answers that are better than others. Nor does this conclusion rule out the possibility that there are methods of reflection that are intrinsically more suited than others to the consideration of fundamental questions.

What does this conclusion about a process of 'roughing out' mean with respect to this chapter's basic concern with 'Where to begin'? The answer is somewhat banal: since there is no guaranteed starting-point it may not matter very much exactly where we begin, provided that, having begun, we immediately start on a process of doubt about the details of our view (unlike Descartes' systematic doubt about everything *at the same time*), and seek, in a process that may go on for ever, to question and then to refine all our conclusions.

By way of illustration let us imagine a history student who suddenly decides to reject everything that cannot be fully demonstrated. It soon becomes evident that even within the field of history (let alone practical matters of living), *complete* scepticism renders the entire discipline impossible. The student can doubt whether the battle of Hastings has been accurately described, but although it *can* be doubted that there was any such battle, if this doubt is extended, simultaneously, to all the (alleged) major historical events, this so undermines the use of established historical records that all history, as an intellectual exercise, becomes impossible. Hence a compromise has to be reached. One can doubt particular events and particular sources, and then go round in a series of circles, doubting this and then that, but one cannot usefully doubt everything at the same time without rendering the inquiry futile. A similar point can be made about historical methodology. One can question each suggested methodology, but one cannot avoid the use – if only in a provisional way – of some methodology, if one is to do any history at all.

In this book I am not primarily concerned with ethical issues, but it is worth pointing to an interesting parallel with 'where to begin' in ethics. Many writers have tried to find a 'supreme principle' or 'absolute value' on which to base a whole series of arguments. But perhaps this is a mistake that parallels Descartes' mistake in the theory of knowledge. Stanley Hauerwas, for example, has suggested that any serious moral thinking must begin with the recognition that we are already *within* a personal story or narrative: 'Ethics begins with the recognition that we are *already* in the moral adventure.'[4] My own position differs from that of Hauerwas in several ways, but on this point we are in accord.[5] However, as with the case of the fundamental questions, the fact that there is no essential starting-point, or indubitable beginning, does not mean that a *presentation* of ethics cannot proceed in a systematic way.

The claim that all questions must be posed within the context of a story or narrative in which we are already engaged is also important in relation to a kind of invasive scepticism that is sometimes presented, one that is rooted in the alleged inadequacy of all human words. Let us suppose that an extreme sceptic dismisses all our truth claims on the grounds that our words are *totally* inadequate. This dismissal, and the questions that are posed in order to suggest it, are themselves making use of words that the sceptic employs in the belief that a claim, in this case a totally sceptical claim, is being made. In other words, the sceptical assertions or questions are themselves part of a 'narrative' from which the sceptic *cannot* escape – even in order to issue a challenge. The challenge itself arises only in the context of this narrative, and uses words that are integral to it. In consequence, this *total* scepticism cannot be rationally stated, or even rationally thought, if thinking involves words of any kind. What is possible, and I hold rational, is a modified scepticism which seeks continually to correct the inadequacies that we suspect are present within our world-views. The analogy of the sculptor can be used to express this point.

Step One: The Response to Positivism – Are the Fundamental Questions 'Meaningful'?

The kind of positivism that insists on the emptiness of all 'metaphysical' questions, including those about an alleged 'God', has lost many of its followers, even among the purely sceptical. The positivist A.J. Ayer refused to call himself an atheist, because – as he saw it – to say that there is no God is to deny that some entity exists, and this denial itself assumes that there is some coherent meaning to the word 'God'. Today, unlike Ayer, sceptics are more likely to call themselves atheists, basing their rejection of theism in a materialistic philosophy that does not begin with a denial of the *meaning* of the concept of God, but with a denial of his existence. However the fact that positivism has lost much of its popularity does not prove it is false. Here I shall indicate two of the reasons that have led many to find positivism inadequate, and then suggest that despite this inadequacy there are important lessons to learn from positivism, lessons that can assist the later discussion. (An indication of some other objections to positivism is placed in the notes.[6])

The first reason for disenchantment with positivism (or more strictly, 'Logical Positivism', which is one form of positivism) concerns its commitment to a *theory* of meaning that is itself subject to dispute. It is fair to say that positivists *believe* in their theory of meaning, or are *committed* to it, in a way that has some analogy with religious belief, especially since a whole range of attitudes to life may depend on this initial belief. Positivists often claim that their theory of meaning is *the* theory, demanded by a rational or scientific approach, but in view of the massive disagreement in this area, even among atheistic philosophers, this is an assertion rather than an argument. The second reason for the decline of positivist thinking lies in the ambiguities that have emerged within the central positivist claim that all meaningful statements about 'matters of fact' must, in principle, be verifiable.[7] When, under the heat of criticism, this gave way to the lesser claim that all meaningful statements about 'matters of fact' must, in principle, be verifiable *or* falsifiable, the central claim became exceedingly cloudy. For example, some religious people said that 'God loves me' is falsifiable in principle, and pointed out that many people have abandoned religion precisely because they have concluded, after much unexplained suffering, that God did not love them. In other words, their belief had been falsified. This did not impress the positivists, who said that only *some* people give up faith on this ground, and those who did not often proposed to stick to their faith *whatever* happened, and so for them there could be no falsification.[8] But others said that if suffering were held by these religious people 'to count as a reason for considering giving up on faith', even if they did not give it up, then there was the possibility of falsification 'in principle', akin to the falsification 'in principle' of scientific theories that many scientists continue to accept even though some evidence is acknowledged 'to count against them'. The debate has continued, but what is clear is that behind claims about what is truly meaningful, there lie *theories* of meaning that are themselves disputable. Here we return to the first objection.

However, despite this criticism of positivism, there are at least three useful ideas that emerge from an understanding of the movement, concepts that will be of value in the quest for answers followed in this book.

First, there is the need to be careful about the meaning we attribute to words, and the danger of the assumption that all of those who, for example, use the word 'God', have the same concept in mind. The positivists were justified in asking for an account of the meaning of 'God'; the problem lay in their hidden (or sometimes not so hidden) agenda, which was designed to reject any suggested answer on what were, in effect, doctrinal grounds.

Second, the positivist concern with meaning can challenge us to seek alternative and more satisfactory theories of meaning. One theory which is stressed in many contemporary authors places the emergence of meaning in the context of *narrative*.[9] In Chapter 5 we shall note how, in the context of the Old Testament, the concept of God undergoes an interesting development, as the idea of the 'holy', which is held to be one of the attributes of God, changes from being a kind of dangerous and unpredictable force (propitiated by ritual purity) to being described in terms of justice (propitiated by our just actions), and later, of love. Thus the *meaning* of the concept of God can be seen to shift as we work through the long and complex narrative that the Bible comprises. To ask for a clear account of the meaning of 'God' outside the context of narratives such as this is to demand something that is necessarily going to be extremely vague and general. However, within the context of a narrative, the way in which a concept is used, and the ways in which the concept changes, and the many ways in which the concept is related to other concepts can be observed. This is a much more fruitful way of searching for the meaning of many interesting concepts than the provision of a definition. For example, the meaning of 'virtue' and the way its meaning has changed (while retaining some common elements) from its context in ancient Greece to, let us say, Victorian England, can only be fully appreciated by comparing the literature of ancient Greece and Victorian England. Positivist accounts of meaning are exceedingly narrow in their neglect of this context for the understanding of concepts.

Third, although we may reject the claim that all meaningful statements must be verifiable or falsifiable, positivism may well be right to insist that significant statements *assert* something that makes a difference. I agree with Renford Bambrough in his insistence that theology must involve making assertions about the world and its nature, assertions that can be objectively true or false.[10] This is one of the grounds on which, later in this chapter, I shall argue that a *via negativa*,[11] in which we only say what God is *not*, should be supplemented with an 'analogy of attribution' (or a *via positiva*) in which something positive is said about the nature of God which *does make a difference*. However the 'difference' is the kind of difference that is appropriate for a religious assertion. Consider, for example, the religious statement 'God is love'. Although there is no empirical way of verifying or falsifying this claim, it does, in my view, 'make a difference' to both understanding and practice, and therefore it can be seen as an *assertion* of a truth. In terms of understanding it means that our concept of God really is illuminated by our vision of human love, at its best. In terms of practice, it means (for the believer) that our love must be continually enlightened and enlarged by the examples of divine love that we are given.

Step Two: The Response to Postmodernism – Universal Aspects of 'Reason' and 'Objectivity'

The postmodernist movement comprises a huge variety of positions, but typical of them is a scepticism about both reason and objectivity. Although there are links with positivism, postmodernism is different because within positivism there is a general acceptance of the competence of reason to 'discover' genuine 'matters of fact' in *some* spheres, for example, in science. Indeed, in the positivist movement of the nineteenth century from which the positivism I have been writing about springs, science was held to be the true exemplar of knowledge, and its rational method was the one which all other forms of knowledge should try to copy. In contrast, many postmodernist writers claim that 'reason' itself refers not to any universal faculty, but to a particular mode of thinking that typifies a certain culture. Therefore *any* claim to *universal* truth, or justified belief, in *any* field, including science, is rejected. It is not held that 'truth claims' should not be made, but that they should be understood as pragmatic or political statements of one kind or another. 'Truth' is always relative to a culture and never universal. Any serious attempt to defend a liberal theology in which true or relatively true positions are sought, must take account of this view, even if it seems initially implausible to many readers.

A proper treatment of postmodernism should consider more than a hundred individual thinkers and an interconnecting web of complex issues and terms. Later in this chapter I shall indicate how many of these thinkers illuminate the human condition in a variety of ways. The negative views of rationality and of objectivity are my targets, and therefore I have concentrated on the question of the nature of 'reason' in the first chapter, and shall concentrate on the related question of 'objectivity' in this.[12] The representative of the movement I shall consider in this section is Richard Rorty, although he himself dislikes the label 'postmodernist',[13] since he defends positions on objectivity and rationality which are central to much postmodernist thought. Also, to his credit, he writes in a much clearer way than many others who hold similar views. He writes 'It is no truer that "atoms are what they are because we use 'atom' as we do" than that "we use 'atom' as we do because atoms are as they are." *Both* of these claims, the anti-representationalist [like Rorty] says, are entirely empty.' In another passage he writes: 'For pragmatists [like Rorty himself], the desire for objectivity is not the desire to escape the limitations of one's community, but simply the desire for as much intersubjective agreement as possible, the desire to extend the reference of "us" as far as we can.'[14] In the light of this, Rorty totally rejects the traditional search for the kind of objectivity he had previously described. In the discussion of the moral argument in Chapter 6 we shall find another objection to postmodernist philosophy, but here I shall indicate one major objection to this rejection of objectivity, as the term has usually been understood.

Prior to a discussion of this major objection it will be helpful to consider the 'short way' that is often alleged to refute the whole postmodernist theory, a way which I do not think is adequate.

The 'short way' goes like this. Postmodernists claim: 'There are no objectively true statements.' What is the status of such a claim? Any response to this challenge (so the 'short way' alleges) exposes an Achilles' heel, since if the utterance is itself a significant truth claim there seems to be a manifest contradiction, while if it is not, nothing significant seems to have been asserted. (Here we may recall Aristotle's discussion of theories that destroy themselves because they involve inherent contradictions.[15]) Despite my disavowal of postmodernism I do not think this difficulty provides the knock-out blow it is often alleged to be, for two reasons. First, not all those who adopt Rorty's position *make assertions* to the effect that their position is true; rather they adopt the Rortian position as a kind of programme to live by. They are not so much asserting a rival truth, as living a different set of values. In such cases it is not fair to charge them with making inconsistent *state-*

ments. An indication that some postmodernists are aware of the apparent circularity of their position is their frequent use of the concept of *irony* by which any 'truth' in their position is only signified indirectly. A variation on this defence is to describe postmodernism as the *negative* truth of modernity which (as Terry Eagleton puts it) 'allows one to reject modernity without claiming that you do so from some loftier vantage-point'.[16] Second, if assertions are made, we shall see, when we come to issues relating to Russell's paradox, that it may be a mistake to demand of statements that refer to a whole system the same kind of criteria that we apply to any statement within the system. Nevertheless, prior to a consideration of the more substantial objection that follows, even the 'short' way raises significant difficulties for postmodernism. For example, it is hard to see what sense can be made of the irony defence without *assuming* some intrinsic superiority in the postmodernist position. Moreover, with respect to a 'Russellian defence', it is reasonable for a sceptic about postmodernism, like myself, to suggest that any 'overall' statement is seen as a *claim* that needs justification, and then it is deeply puzzling to be told that there are no 'objective' criteria for justification.

Let us consider the more serious criticism. Rorty defends his position on the *emptiness* of truth claims through one recurring argument, although it appears in different formulations. It is impossible, he claims, to have a truly '*independent*' test of the accuracy of any alleged representation of reality, or to have a 'God's eye standpoint' or a 'skyhook' on which to hang our representations.[17]

Even if we grant that there is no totally independent standpoint available to us, at least in this life, it does not follow that talking about 'reality' or about a 'truth' that we are hoping to move towards, is *empty*. It only follows that we could never have absolute certainty. Here, there seems to be a systematic confusion between the question of the *meaning* of a term, like 'truth', and the question of *establishing* that something is true. (The claim that these two matters cannot be separated, even conceptually, was one of the dogmas of Logical Positivism.) I may, and in fact do, share Rorty's suspicion of claims to have certain knowledge, but I deny his inference that this makes the search for greater objectivity empty.[18]

Two examples can illustrate this point. First, consider the following scenario. During the reign of Stalin the secret police frame a political opponent for murder. The fact is that he was asleep while another person killed the victim, but the police rewrite the files, bribe the witnesses, and the false allegation is 'proved' in court. Twenty years later all the witnesses, including the police who were involved in this rewriting of history, are dead, and *nothing* remains in the way of testimony except the falsified documents. It would not be 'empty' for a relative of the victim to claim 'this is not what *really* happened'. Rorty might be able to agree, but on grounds that, in my view, would not be the right ones. He might say, for example, that there was intersubjective agreement about a systematic abuse of documents in Stalin's time. He might also say that it is pragmatic systematically to reject Stalinist accounts of the past. But even if no possible evidence *could* come forward, the claim is not 'empty'. On Rorty's view, when I described this scenario, I should not be allowed to say 'the fact is that he was asleep ...', for this use of the word 'fact' presupposes an acceptance of the kind of objectivity that Rorty rejects. But the systematic rejection of this and similar words, in law, history, science, and so on, would do extraordinary violence to ordinary language. With the systematic use of his recommendations we would simply not be allowed to say many of the things we wish to say.[19] In ordinary language, when we claim that a certain event 'really happened', this should not be confused with claims about how we could know that it happened.[20]

The following observation on the question 'What is the meaning of "truth"?' may be helpful here. The question can easily lead to misunderstanding because quite different things may be being asked. The question may indicate a request to show what the *word* 'truth' means, while another request, framed in the same language, may be for an indication of *what* (if anything) can be said to be true, or ultimately true. (The question can also have other implications.[21]) At present, I am only concerned with the first of these requests, although this book as a whole is clearly concerned with the second. (A similar distinction needs to be made when someone asks 'What is 'good'?', and in several other instances.[22]) With respect to the former, verbal question: 'truth', I suggest, is a concept that is embedded within the use of human language, especially indicative language,[23] and for this very reason there cannot be a straightforward definition of the term that is not circular (because it uses words like 'objectivity' with which truth is interlinked). Many fundamental concepts, including that of 'God', cannot have simple definitions, but in the case of 'truth' the problems associated with definition have an extra layer of difficulty, since the use of all human language relies implicitly on the concept. However, once again, the significance of the term can emerge by seeing how it is used in narrative or discourse – in this case when we discover the need to make a contrast, in many contexts, between 'the way it is' and 'the way it appears'. If I am asked what it means to refer to 'the way it is', I am back with my original problem, for any response is likely to be circular. When we recognize that the concept of truth is a kind of 'category' that we need for communication, then we can see how Rorty's position cannot do justice to the concept of 'objectivity', or the related concept of 'truth'. For example, in the foregoing scenario, Stalin's police tried to cover up a 'truth' in a way that we can understand perfectly well. However, asking for a definition of this 'truth' (in the verbal sense) itself involves a misunderstanding of what the concept is, while to *demand* a definition is to *assume* a dubious philosophical position that includes a questionable theory of language. Similarly, when a typical scientist, investigating let us say the DNA of a primate, says that they are seeking to discover 'the way it is', we know that the *meaning* of the claim refers to the belief that there is a 'real' difference between the answer they are seeking, and 'false' answers, based on misinformation or fraud.

The second example concerns the different kinds of divisions we make when we classify things in nature. It is certainly the case that many human classifications are either primarily or purely a matter of human convenience, and in such cases to regard the division we make as corresponding to 'reality' may often be unjustified. The traditional way in which we divide plants and animals into species since the time of Linnaeus may be an example of this, although there is room for disagreement about this example because of cases where interbreeding cannot take place. It is quite another thing to say that *all* our divisions are of this kind. Water, for example, is made by combining the *elements* of hydrogen and oxygen, and the grounds for referring to 'elements' relate to basic structures that we have *discovered* to be in nature. Of course, the models of the elements that we draw, in which we picture a nucleus surrounded by a series of circles of electrons, are *models*, but there are strong reasons for claiming that some of these enable us to get *closer* to an objective truth than earlier speculations about matter. It is implausible to argue that the division of the elements based on the work of Dalton and Mendeleyev is purely for human convenience.[24] It is much more plausible to see the 'periodic table' of the elements as what Plato called 'dividing nature at the joints'.[25] (The Chinese philosopher, Zhuang Zi (or Chuang Tzu), writing at about the same time, uses the almost identical image of a good butcher who goes 'along with the natural makeup' and strikes 'in the big hollows'.[26]) In contrast, postmodernist language makes it impossible to think of these 'joints' except in purely pragmatic terms, and such language cannot allow any talk of 'scientific discoveries' in the usual sense of the term.

However, as in the case of positivism, there are lessons to learn from postmodernism that will be useful for the rational quest that follows. In view of the large number of intelligent people who have fallen under the spell of the movement, this is not surprising. Even if we reject some central claims that typify postmodernism (in particular, the denial of any universal notion of reason, and the alleged emptiness of any search for objective truth), certain important insights can be accepted, insights which partially explain the strong following the movement has enjoyed. The insights are rooted in the understanding that there is a simple form of objectivity theory, along with a simple-minded correspondence theory of truth, which cannot be sustained in the context of contemporary science. Scientific and other objective statements, like those of the historian, do not simply describe a world that is 'out there', waiting for us to depict in a way that is completely independent of our activity of exploration. We *select* bits of information that are of particular interest to us; we *interpret* the data that comes to us both by the ways that our physical faculties channel information, and by the way we try to make sense of the data. We *interact* with our environment, most crucially when we try to measure subatomic activity, but to a lesser extent whenever we observe anything.[27] Postmodernist writers can do us a service by making us more aware of the greater sensitivity we need to have about all three of these aspects of understanding. A fourth, though related insight into the way in which human reason does not operate in a totally detached manner comes from the findings of psychoanalysis. Although I criticize some of the assumptions that lie behind Freudian viewpoints, some understanding of how the unconsious helps to shape our thinking is a discovery for which great credit must be given to Freud. As Emilia Steuerman puts it, we need 'an understanding of rationality which fully acknowledges that which is not conscious and explains the ways in which thinking is shaped by emotional life'.[28] However in response to all four of these factors which bear upon the observer, it must be stressed that the search for objectivity and truth does not have to be abandoned; rather, it should be made with a greater care. For example, when psychoanalyists reflect on the implications of their own psychoanalysis, it is unlikely they will think that this reflection is simply a response to some still deeper level of the unconscious that has not been explored, even though the existence of such a deeper level may be acknowledged; they are almost certain to think – and rightly – that the analysis has permitted a greater level of objectivity. Further, an awareness of all four of these factors is itself an example of gaining some measure of objectivity!

The way in which contemporary science is beginning to move away from the type of objectivity that typified nineteenth-century thought can be seen with reference to Goethe's view of science. There has been a revival of interest in Goethe, in part because of the way in which he is said to have anticipated Darwin, in part because of a new sympathy with his understanding of the historicity of science, and in part because of his claim that we need to see particular phenomena in the context of a whole 'which is present in the part'.[29] But in this appreciation of a holistic approach to nature there is a temptation to let the pendulum swing too far and to deny the legitimate role of an analytical aspect in science through which genuine discoveries have often been made, and which allows one to assert that certain claims are true and certain claims are false. Thus we can properly say that Goethe's account of the glacial transportation of boulders was both original and *true*, but by the same token we must say that his rejection of Newton's composite theory of white light was *mistaken*.[30] He may well have been right to ask that we explore the phenomenon of light and colour in a broader, more human context, but this should not lead us to overlook his mistakes as well as his discoveries. Also, although Goethe did stress the relationship of humans to other animals (for example, in denying that the human jaw was totally different from that of primates – a claim that was widely used at the time to defend the view that man was a special creation), there is no evidence that he held a Darwinian principle of natural selection. This appraisal of Goethe's views only makes sense if we are prepared to say that in some ways he was right, and in some ways he was wrong, and the significant use of these notions of right and wrong simply do not make sense within the kind of postmodernist philosophy to which I have been referring. We continue to need a sense of 'objectivity' which allows us to say that some statements are true and some false, even though, much of the time, we do not know which are which.

This reaction to the rejection of all objectivity is especially important in the light of a tendency, in much contemporary theological thinking, to stress the *metaphorical* nature of religious language and imagery. In many contexts I am fully supportive of this approach. For example, in meditating on a passage of Scripture (from any of the great religious traditions), it is usually much more helpful to ask 'How does this passage illuminate the way I see life and how I should pray?' than to ask 'Is it true?'. However, to take the extreme position, namely that no theological statements can express objective truth, is another matter and, in my view, is based on a serious misunderstanding of the many *different* uses that religious language can have. The good side of the contemporary emphasis on metaphor is the realization that learning to live within a religious tradition is not simply a matter of accepting a series of true propositions – it is, to a large degree, learning to see the rich, metaphorical power of language, and to see the implications of this for life and for prayer. But if *all* claims to objectivity are removed from religious language, the metaphors themselves lose much of their power, and the crucial difference between fantasies of the mind, and belief in the reality of God, is undermined. The kind of liberal Christianity that I am supporting in this book is 'traditional' in certain crucial ways, and one of them is manifest in the assertion that when we say 'God is love' we are not only advocating a way of life, we are making a truth claim about the creative source of the universe.

Reason and Paradox

When we ponder a fundamental question like 'Is God a reality?', I have suggested that the attempt to find an answer is worth making, even if only a partial and incomplete answer may be found. In supporting the case for this rational quest, I have described a certain tradition of thinking, commonly called 'liberal theology'. So far the quest has had to face two rational objections, the first from those who think the quest is futile because the question is essentially meaningless; the second, because it is denied that there is a universal sense of reason which could render any answer significant. A third attack often comes from *within* certain religious circles. Although many thinkers have made a serious effort to build bridges between faith and reason, in others there is a special pleasure in pointing out the (alleged) *irrationality* of religion. A 1998 *Times* review of a book refers to the claim that 'faith's departure from logic and reason is its glory',[31] a viewpoint that goes back to the later writings of Tertullian in the first decades of the third century. Without going so far, many religious people speak of the 'paradoxes' that accompany their faith, and this has led many to doubt whether faith and reason can properly be combined. Such positions provide much ammunition for the sceptic.

Before responding to this issue we need to look carefully at the notion of 'paradox'. The word 'paradox' comes from two Greek words, and means, literally, contrary to opinion (*doxa*). In this original meaning, that I shall call sense (a), there does not need to be any implication of an inherent, logical contradiction. For example, in the Christian tradition, the claim that the true Messiah died as a criminal on a cross was supremely paradoxical for the orthodox Jew, because it was contrary to expectation. However, Christians tried to show that if one understood the loving purposes of God one could see that although this looked like foolishness *to humans*, it was in fact congruent with the purposes of God.[32] Thus (we might say) there was nothing *inherently* contradictory or *illogical* in the Messiah dying on a cross. Similarly, many, perhaps all other type (a) paradoxes pose no challenge to rationality as such.

Closely linked with type (a) paradoxes are what I shall call type (b). Again, there is no need here for a suggestion that something is intrinsically irrational – the stress is rather on what is a *surprising* discovery, or alleged discovery. A good example is the claim, for example, in J.S. Mill, that you cannot achieve happiness by seeking primarily to be happy; instead happiness is discovered to be a kind of by-product of something else. According to Aristotle, who held a similar view, it is a by-product of ethical and rational living. If, in the light of human experience, one finds this claim sound there is no need to introduce the idea of the 'irrational' into the suggestion, but the claim is surprising and 'paradoxical' to some, especially when it is first heard. Many religious paradoxes fall into this category, such as 'Blessed [happy] be ye poor: for yours is the kingdom of God'.[33]

The word 'paradox' is often used to refer to stronger claims, namely either (c) that two or more 'truths' *appear* to be in logical contradiction, or (d) that two or more 'truths' really *are* in logical contradiction. One must note the important difference between (c) and (d). Take the example of two people looking at an object in a box where one sees a circle and the other a rectangle. If both are correct in their judgement we *appear* to have a contradiction, but as soon as we realize that one is looking through a hole that shows a cylinder end on, while the other is looking from a hole that shows the same cylinder lengthwise, from the side, then the contradiction disappears. The apparent contradiction disappears when we see both observers from above by moving, as it were, to another dimension. The important question that now arises is whether what are claimed to be examples of type (d) paradox are really always examples of type (c). If they are not, then the idea of a truly rational approach to reality is dealt a severe blow, for whatever rationality means exactly, it surely includes the notion that *in principle* there is no radical inconsistency in nature, and that (as Anaxagoras held)[34] reality is ultimately intelligible.

Consider the famous case of the 'paradoxical' nature of light. It appears as a wave when investigated in certain contexts, and as a stream of particles in other contexts. The two views certainly seem to be at odds, so do we have a logical contradiction within nature? It seems to me that the answer is 'No'. The situation is rather that the phenomenon we know as light is only partially understood, and we are continually forced to describe what we have found through inadequate models. The situation is really a sophisticated version of the cylinder example, the difference being that we are still searching for the viewpoint from which the apparent contradiction will disappear. It isn't that nature is inherently contradictory, only that we have, either temporarily (because of the current state of science) or permanently (because of a Kantian-type problem with human capacities) to live with models that appear to be contradictory. Although this view is certainly controversial, I cannot see why, *in principle*, it cannot be applied to all the other paradoxes that arise in science. Moreover (and this is my essential claim), if we are to pursue the discipline of science we have to work on this assumption that nature is 'intelligible'. Congruously, when scientists investigate light, the foregoing paradox is a *challenge* to them, precisely because they feel forced to look for a deeper understanding in which the apparent contradiction will be overcome.

The foregoing claim, if correct, does not mean that we cannot find logical contradictions, only that these contradictions are not 'in nature' or 'in reality'. Take, for example, the process of proving something by *reductio ad absurdum*. In mathematics and elsewhere this is a useful process that, far from proving that there is something basically irrational in nature, depends on the assumption that there is not. One tries a suggested hypothesis, and if the conclusions that one draws from it lead to a logical contradiction (as in Plato's dialectical method), then one rejects the original hypothesis because it has led to absurdity. Here the logical contradiction 'exists' in an abstract sense, namely as a kind of idea, but only so that one can deny that a certain alleged aspect of nature, or a certain allegedly consistent piece of reasoning, is what it was first claimed to be.

There is a special kind of paradox that is important for us to examine, first because of what it does *not* prove – so that a common misunderstanding can be avoided – and second for what it *does* prove – which has implications for the relationship of faith to reason. Consider the old problem of the librarian who wishes to make a general catalogue of all the catalogues within a library, like that of the rare books, that do not refer to themselves. When the new catalogue is nearly finished the question arises: 'Should this new catalogue of catalogues refer to itself?' If the catalogue does not refer to itself, then it ought to be included (since it is, after all, another catalogue that does not refer to itself). However, if it does include itself, then by this very fact, it becomes a catalogue that ought not to be included! But the inability to make the proposed catalogue seems paradoxical.

Similar problems arise with a series of suggestions about statements that refer to themselves, like the claim: 'Everything I say, including this sentence, is false.' More important versions of the self-referential problem occur in 'Russell's paradox' and in 'Gödel's theorem',[35] which raise huge problems for any system that attempts to explain itself. One of the things that emerges is that the trust and expectation of mathematicians that their systems are consistent, in the face of an inability to prove them so, parallels a 'trust' or 'faith' that the world is intelligible in a way that the whole scientific enterprise is forced to assume.

Let us consider an example of the self-referential paradox which has important implications for the limits of both human and divine prediction. Suppose I am constructing a computer that will assist me in foretelling the movements on the stock exchange. My hope, eventually, is to feed in *all* the factors that influence the market so that I can make certain predictions, and then become very rich. Let us ignore the practical difficulty that I could never include all the human and physical factors that are relevant, and suppose, *per impossibile*, that I succeeded. Then I have to face the question: 'Do I include the influence of the forecasts that this super computer will make?' But here is harsh example of the self-referential problem, for if it is known that the computer says that x will do y, as soon as x knows this he may well say: 'No I won't, I'll do z.' In other words, the forecast actually affects what will happen. Suppose, in an attempt to avoid this problem, I keep the forecast secret. If I keep it secret from *everyone*, then the computer is a very odd forecaster, for it has as a precondition of its being able to forecast that it *tells* no one. (Moreover, even for this strange, totally secret forecast to be possible, we must assume that Jung and others are wrong when they suggest that all things influence each other in some way. In other words, the mere fact that something is 'known and recorded', be it only in a computer, may influence the outcome.) Suppose I keep the secret of the forecast from all but myself. Now the computer tells me not simply what it would be wise to do, but what I shall do. But, again, it is perfectly obvious, given the fact of human perversity, that when I am told that I shall do p I may decide to do q. So the computer cannot infallibly tell anyone what they will do.

What this, and similar paradoxes do *not* show is that there are any contradictions 'in nature'. They show instead that certain things cannot *exist* in nature, and that someone who sets out to produce a complete catalogue (that didn't refer to itself), or a computer of the kind described, is wasting their time. In some cases, like square circles, this is obvious, in others, it takes some time to realize – by using arguments like that of the cataloguer – that the things cannot exist. Therefore arguments that seek to prove that nature is inherently irrational, based on a series of famous paradoxes, prove nothing of the kind. They only prove that some problems have no solutions – and this knowledge can be used to make computers whir round and round, trying to solve problems that we know have no answers.

What then of claims like that referred to at the beginning of this section – that a living faith is typically full of irrational paradoxes, and that without these we take away the very soul of religion? Very often a truth is being expressed, but in a misleading way. There is a simple-minded but valuable distinction often made at the level of a children's confirmation class. It is one thing to be 'beyond' reason, quite another thing to be 'contrary' to reason. Chillingworth makes an equivalent distinction, claiming to believe 'many mysteries, but no impossibilites; many things above reason, but nothing against it'.[36] Long before, Aquinas had written 'The Apostles and prophets under divine inspiration have never said anything contrary to the dictate of natural reason. Nevertheless, they have said things which go beyond the comprehension of reason, and so to this extent seem to contradict reason, although they do not really oppose it.'[37] Many things in life, not only in religion, are clearly 'beyond' reason, in so far as we can understand things *now*. However nothing should be accepted that is 'contrary' to reason. Further, in order to take seriously anything classed as the former (that is, 'beyond' reason), we need, first, to have experiential grounds for affirming the two or more things that appear to be in tension and, second, at least a suggestion as to how the tension might be resolved. Otherwise, we may be invited to believe nonsense.

A similar distinction should be made between the 'irrational' and the 'non-rational', allowing for the fact that in ordinary English the two words may be used interchangeably. If we are thinking philosophically, emotions like love are not 'irrational' (although they may lead to irrational behaviour or thinking), but 'non-rational'. When distinctions like these are appreciated there is no need for a liberal like myself to deny both the reality and importance of the *mysterious* element in religion. Indeed, when we come to discuss the significance of mystical experience, later in this book, we shall see how certain 'non-rational' experiences form part of the life-blood of all the great religions.

This section will conclude with an examination of an important example of a religious paradox that occurs in most monotheistic systems. God is said to allow human freedom, and yet to 'foreknow', providentially, *everything* that will happen. When sceptics say that here is a contradiction their objection is often brushed off with the remark: 'This is a divine mystery.' This is not a satisfactory response unless it is combined with an *attempt* to unravel the mystery, for otherwise the sceptic is being asked to accept something quite fundamental on a faith which they don't have. The believer needs to show, first, *why* monotheists have been led to make both claims (that is, the claims concerning human freedom and divine fore-knowledge), and second, to indicate a route to an explanation. All other paradoxes demand this minimum, twofold response, if we are to have any justification for not joining the sceptical ranks. With regard to the first half of the response we may note that if a physicist is asked about the paradoxical nature of light, the immediate response would be to describe the observations that have led to the different descriptions. In other words, the problem is not just made up in order to justify a strange claim – it arises out of an honest attempt to face the complexity of experi-ence. Similarly, religious paradoxes can only be taken seriously when they arise out of the complexity of experience. With regard to the second half of the response, the physicist is involved in a discipline whose whole purpose is to try and unravel the 'mysteries' of nature. In the same way, the theologian ought to be seeking a theology that at least begins to explain the religious experiences that seem to be in tension with each other. This is another way of describing what I have called the search for internal and external consistency, which is part of the rational explora-tion of a general position.

Returning to the issue of divine foreknowledge, in addition to the fact that the paradox is rooted in the attempt to be faithful to two different kinds of religious experience, there have been serious attempts to indicate a route to understanding or explanation. I shall refer to two of them. The first, and most well known, is expounded by Aquinas, but he took it over from Boethius and the Neoplatonists.[38] A model is suggested in which we see *human* foretelling as something on the same time-line as the events to be foretold. The result is that human foretelling, as such, is at best good guesswork, because we cannot actually see what is ahead on the line. However God, as the being who transcends space and time, should be seen as the apex of a triangle that has the former time-line as its base. So God 'looks down' on all human history, rather as someone who has read a book right through and then goes back to one of the pages can see the whole story as told. Hence from *within* the system of space and time there can be no absolute foreknowledge (given human freedom, and given the indeterminacy of subatomic particles), but God transcends this system.

This solution, or route to a solution, has satisfied many, but it does not satisfy all. The initial reason for dissatisfaction is that the Thomistic solution runs into difficulties as soon as the God who is beyond space and time is *actively* involved in the temporal order, like my example of the super-computer that actually told people what they were about to do. But such involvement – for example, through responses to individual prayer – is certainly maintained within the Thomistic form of monotheism. But if God is helping to change things within the time-line he is no longer simply to be seen as living 'in another dimension'. Much very subtle thought, in both Christian and Muslim circles, has gone into attempts to reconcile this paradox – for example, in the extensive literature reflecting on predestination. Common to the suggestions is the idea that the active involvements within the time-line are all anticipated in the great timeless order of things. To prove whether any of these suggestions resolve the apparent contradiction would require a lengthy and controversial analysis, but now enters a second reason for disquiet in the form of a question, namely: 'Is it necessary to maintain this *total* omniscience of God?' In Thomistic thought the idea that there have to be some restrictions on the idea of God's power if one is not to talk nonsense is accepted. In particular Aquinas denies, first, that one should think of God 'breaking the law of non-contradiction', or, as we might put it, denying basic logic; and, second, that God can be thought of as doing evil.[39] In both cases Aquinas insists that these should not be thought of as 'limitations' but as ways of preventing nonsense being spoken. My suggestion is that an additional consequence of the Thomistic commitment to logic is that we should not say that God *both* knows the details of all future events, and grants genuine freedom to humans (or angels, if they exist). This is the claim not only of theologians in the movement known as 'process theology', from the time of Whitehead, but also of a number of theologians who support a generally 'classical' form of theism, but who are also referred to as supporters of 'openview' theism.[40] One way of putting this objection to the Thomistic view is to claim that omnipotence and omniscience, when used correctly, apply to what it is logically possible to do or to know. If it is not possible to know the details of the future *and* have freedom, then the denial that God knows these details is not a denial of any coherent doctrine of omniscience. This, essentially, constitutes the second suggestion.

One reason for my preference for this second option is that it adds much light to another familiar paradox, namely that of a good and omniscient God allowing terrible suffering among the innocent. On the view I am promoting, given an essential element of solidarity or mutual interdependence among humans, and given genuine free will, there really are limitations on what an 'omnipotent' God *can* do because he *cannot* know all outcomes. He *cannot* 'make' people good, or they would not be 'people', and similarly, he *cannot* contrive to bring about a situation where no undeserved suffering will ever arise. To seek for such a state of affairs would be like asking a computer to solve an unsolvable problem in logistics. What God *can* do is use the influence of love to bring about huge, though gradual changes, and this is exactly what Whitehead has in mind when he writes of the *persuasive* nature of God.[41]

The foregoing suggestion can be combined with a belief that God can indeed foreknow the *sweep* of history, even if he cannot know the details, except for such details as he directly controls. (We may recall Kant's claim that we can know roughly how many people will be married next year, but not who those individuals will be.[42]) There is therefore nothing to prevent a monotheist calling God 'The Lord of Time', provided this is properly understood as being Lord of all that it is logically possible to know or control.

The situation has some parallel to quantum mechanics, where the individual cannot be predicted, but the greater the quantity of particles involved, the greater the certainty of a prediction relating to the immediate future. The difference is that with humans the impossibility of individual prediction is based on 'freedom' which is not the same as 'randomness'. Given human nature it was *inevitable*, according to Christian belief, that sooner or later God would have to send his son, and sooner or later, during his life, someone would betray him. But, say, in the time of David, it was not inevitable that this would be in the reign of Tiberius nor that Judas would be the betrayer. However by the time of the last supper, Jesus 'knew' who had it in mind to betray him. In all of this, the 'process' view allows for all the prediction that is necessary to make sense of the gospels, without leading one into unnecessary claims concerning logical paradoxes.

Here we have a case where, although I have indicated a preference for the second option, I am not branding the former as 'irrational'. The first option does begin with two aspects of religious experience, both of which it tries to take seriously, despite the tension between them, namely the sense of the 'all-knowing power of the divine', and a sense of genuine human freedom. It then attempts some kind of resolution. Therefore both aspects of 'rationality' (as applicable to apparent paradoxes) are to some extent addressed. My reservations hinge on the claim that the experience of the divine does not actually require the account of omniscience that has traditionally been given.

Reason and Analogy

Let us assume that a primitive hunter who recognizes the footprints of an antelope has a word for this animal. Each individual antelope varies somewhat, but there is sufficient similarity to use the word for different members of the species. This is where a general noun like 'antelope' differs from a name, which refers to a single individual. Even with an individual there are gradual changes which do not prevent the attribution of the same proper name, although we sometimes acknowledge the changes by expressions such as: 'John has not been himself recently.' With nouns a much larger range of differences is acceptable while we continue to use the same word, although puzzling situations arise sometimes, that is, when the differences from the norm are so great that we are not sure whether to use the word. I remember Isaiah Berlin, in the context of a philosophy tutorial, asking me 'When you shorten the legs of a table, when does it become a tray?'.

The foregoing forms the background to our understanding of 'analogy', for we see that ordinary language cannot function without the capacity of words to be 'stretched'. Analogy refers to the practice of 'stretching' some words in *special ways*, and great controversy surrounds the legitimacy of some of these. The central meaning of 'analogy' is given in a classical account given by Aquinas, especially when he reflects on Aristotle's teachings on the subject.[43] According to this there are three, general ways in which a word may be reused: in the first, there is 'univocal' usage, when the word is used in exactly the same sense on both occasions (literally, 'with the same voice'). In the second, there is 'equivocal' usage, when the word is used in completely different senses (literally, 'with equal, different voices'); in the third, there is 'analogical' usage (literally, 'in equal proportion'), when the word, in its secondary usage, is 'stretched'. As I have indicated, this 'stretching' is something different from the ordinary stretching that allows a noun to cover different members of the same species or type. A central question for this section will be to try to elucidate what these 'special ways' are, and an initial clue can be suggested by pointing out that in the ordinary stretching of words there tends to be more or less of the same *measurable* characteristic. For example, different antelopes differ in length, weight, colour, etc. However, when we say that a *place* is 'healthy' (which is one of Aquinas' exemplars of analogy), in a way that is analogous to a *person* being 'healthy', the difference between the terms is not one of degree. The analogy, in this case, depends on a place being conducive to the health of persons. Thus at least a negative account can be given of how analogical description differs from the ordinary stretching of words.

In ordinary language, exploiting the possibilities of simile and metaphor depend upon analogy. When Louis XIV's courtiers used the simile, 'our king is like the sun', we know that this was not meant to be taken literally, and we also know more or less what was meant. The king (allegedly) was the brightest, most noble thing in the kingdom and the source of France's glorious light. If the same courtiers spoke of the radiant beams that flowed from the monarch's decrees, we know that they were speaking metaphorically, with the implication of the same simile in the background. In both cases, there is something in common between the normal referent of 'sun', technically called 'the prime analogue' and the 'derivative analogue', be it the majesty of the king, or the splendour of his decrees, just as there is between a 'healthy' person (the person's health being the prime analogue) and the 'healthy' place.

Literature, poetry and humour all depend upon analogy to a huge extent. What is common here is the need to say new things, or old things in new ways, and yet not always to be inventing new words to do this, lest our language become excessively cumbersome. Also, if we kept using new words, instead of stretching old ones, we would miss a whole series of similarities and interconnections that the analogical use of language uncovers. Science too finds the need to use analogical language, as when electricity is said to 'flow' through a medium. This has become such a common expression that we can forget how it must first have sounded, with the metaphorical reference to water in a river. If an electron is said to 'skip' from one circular path to another, we know that it isn't really like a lamb jumping over a tussock, but we have some idea of what is meant.

If analogy is so much used in activities like literature and science, why is its use in religion the subject of so much controversy? Once again, Aquinas put his finger on the essential problem. In most analogies, what is sometimes called the 'prime analogue', which reflects the word in its *strict* or primary sense, is the object at its most familiar, and then we use 'extensions' of the term to describe the less familiar. The brightness of the sun is familiar, and then we apply this, by extension, to Louis XIV. However if we say that God is wise, then, Aquinas argued, properly speaking it is God who is most truly wise, and humans can only be wise in a secondary sense. In other words, the analogy is the opposite way round and we are trying to grasp the meaning of divine wisdom from the reflection, instead of trying to understand the reflection from the original. This is particularly true, according to Aquinas, in the most important of all analogies, the 'analogy of being' (*analogia entis*). It is God alone who has true 'reality' or 'existence', and all created things exist 'derivatively'. As the seventeenth-century poet John Mason put it:

> How great a being, Lord, is thine,
> which doth all beings keep!
> Thy knowledge is the only line
> to sound so vast a deep.
> Thou art a sea without a shore,
> a sun without a sphere;
> thy time is now and evermore,
> thy place is everywhere.[44]

Hence if (like Plato) we liken God to the sun, the likeness of the sun to God cannot be explained in the same way as the (alleged) likeness of Louis to the sun.

There is an important practical consequence to this understanding. When we say that God is a Father, it follows that 'true Fatherhood' is what we see in God, not what we see in the average human father. This should challenge all fathers to re-examine what kind of character they should have, and in this context many of the 'patriarchal' models might more clearly be seen to be inadequate. Recalling the argument of Chapter 1 – this is one of the places where a religious assertion can 'make a difference'. The same should be said for 'true Motherhood' and, further, the rarity in Christian literature of a linkage between motherhood and the nature of God until late in the twentieth century is also the result of an inadequate, patriarchal view of God. There is, however, strong evidence for a tradition that did teach the feminine aspects of divinity in the early church, a tradition that tended to languish after the fifth century until revived by some of the medieval mystics.[45] A powerful example of this theme in the medieval tradition is referred to in an anthem by William Mathias in which the fourteenth-century English of Julian of Norwich is paraphrased: 'As truly as God is our Father, so just as truly is he our Mother. In our Father, God almighty, we have our beginning; in our merciful Mother we are remade and restored. Our fragmented lives are knit together. And by giving and yielding ourselves, through grace, to the Holy Spirit we are made whole.'[46] This is one of many passages in which Julian links salvation with the 'ever lovyng Moder Jesus',[47] referring not to the mother of Jesus, but to the way in which Jesus represents the motherhood of God.

To sum up the situation (and to make a concession to the sceptic), because of the special way in which some key religious analogies 'stretch' words, it cannot just be assumed that the doctrine of analogy 'explains' religious language or renders it coherent. Fortunately, however, there are at least two additional aspects of religious analogies which help to forge a link between the familiar and the unfamiliar.

The first concerns the notion of 'proportionality'. If we say 'God is wise', this, technically, can be called an analogy of 'attribution' or of 'proportion'. However if we say that God is a 'Father', although this looks like an analogy of attribution, it can be argued that it is really an analogy of 'proportionality', because it is a way of claiming that one relationship has something in common with another. Thus there are really four terms, not two, since it is a case of 'As A is to B, so C is to D', or (in the words of the Psalmist): 'Like as a father pitieth his own children: even so is the Lord merciful unto them that fear him.'[48] An important point, for the purposes of this discussion, is that when the *relationship* of God to us (rather than *God* himself) is the prime analogue, this is not something utterly beyond our knowledge and experience. On the one hand, we have the experience of the relationship of human parents to their children; on the other, we have a Biblical narrative which claims to describe the divine–human relationship that is its analogue.

An adequate account of the relationships between the different kinds of analogy would introduce many complications, including a discussion of Cajetan's controversial claim that proportionality is the key to theological language because it alone can begin to express the truth of things.[49] Without entering the complexities of this debate (unlike Cajetan), I shall use the term 'analogy of attribution' to refer to any allegedly true statement of the form 'God is x', leaving open the issue of whether behind this two-term expression there is always implict a four-term proportionality.[50] My essential claim is that without some place for an analogy of 'attribution' (dependent on either a two- or a four-term model), we are in danger of robbing theological language of significant meaning. Moreover, the defence of a genuine role for an analogy of attribution is intimately linked with the second additional aspect of analogy that links the familiar with the unfamiliar. This concerns the crucial role of the Jewish and Christian doctrine of the *Imago Dei*, based on the passage in Genesis: 'So God created man in his own image.'[51] What this means, or at least how this has often been interpreted, is to say that when we see humans at their best, and especially when we see their capacities as people with (i) intelligence, and (ii) creative freedom and (iii) love (arguably, archetypes of the Trinitarian conception of God), we see, dimly reflected, something of the reality of God himself. This implies that even if we use what looks like an analogy of attribution in a statement like 'God is our Father', the God who is the prime analogue is not *totally* unknown or unknowable. The resulting claim to the effect that, at its best, the human intellect begins to participate in the divine mind, and therefore, that creative human reflection can reach a measure of real objectivity, acts as a kind of *motif* throughout the rest of this book.

This last point must be stated with caution, and bearing in mind the ancient controversy about whether anything can properly be said about God other than in a pure *via negativa* – that is, through saying what God is not – if God is to be respected for what he is. Also, when it came to positive assertions, using analogies of attribution, Aquinas himself was extremely careful, and limited their use to what he regarded as aspects of the divine perfection, such as wisdom, goodness and power.[52] I am taking a somewhat bolder approach, because the logic of belief in the *Imago Dei* seems to me to allow for a whole series of words, including creativity, freedom, love and conscious awareness, to be predicated of God with *some* positive force. However, I too would claim that all of these words relate to the divine perfection in one way or another. It is only when we see humanity at its best that any of these words can provide some indication of the nature of God.

In popular religious language, one often hears talk of how God is *utterly* transcendent, or *infinitely* different from us. In the light of the foregoing, it is important to qualify such language. We often use words like 'utterly' and 'infinitely' in a loose way, simply to mean 'extremely' or 'immeasurably more', and I have no objection to this. However, if the words are used more strictly, then a further distinction is important. If 'infinite' refers to a matter of *degree*, so that when it is said that God has, for example, infinitely more wisdom than we do, because there is no finite measure of the difference between the wisdom of God and of humans, then the use of the word is appropriate. Indeed, any recognizable form of traditional theism must insist that God's wisdom is 'infinite' in this sense. But when the word refers to a difference of *kind*, we have to tread more carefully. The whole point of the doctrine of the image of God lies in the claim that humans can and do reflect *something* of the divine nature. The minds with which we are endowed really have similarities to the mind of God. They are not *utterly* distinct. Our experience of knowing and feeling and understanding are reflections and clues to the nature of the divine.[53] Most important of all, our experience of loving is rooted in a genuine reflection of the divine love. As a result, when we say 'God is love', this is not only a way of affirming our commitment to love, it is also a statement about the nature of God that has meaning because it is rooted in an insight into human love that – at its best – 'really' reflects the divine love. As we shall see, in monistic thought our minds can properly be described as part of the Mind of God, while in more orthodox Jewish, Islamic and Christian ('theistic') thought, they are better described as reflections of God's mind that can enter in communion with Mind. In both monism and theism there is kinship of mind to Mind. This is one of the reasons why an 'analogy of attribution' can be defended. (An alternative approach, within a Christian philosophy that allows one to make some meaningful statements about the divine nature, is to insist, with Duns Scotus, that words such as 'being' and 'wisdom' are predicated of humans and of God in a *univocal* manner. However a discussion of this option would require a technical analysis that goes beyond the scope of this book.[54])

In reflecting on this matter it is helpful to remember the distinction Christianity makes between the 'image' of God and the 'likeness' of God. According to the traditional teaching we are all born in the 'image' of God, because, whether we like it or not, if we are typical members of the human species and do not suffer some terrible abnormality like anencephaly, we are all *able* to have some understanding, creative activity and love. Leaving aside until Chapter 7 some special questions that relate to the nature of Jesus, none of us is born *like* God, meaning having *his* understanding, creativity or love. However something of this *likeness*, by grace, can be *achieved* during the course of a good life. Thus the saints share both the image and (something of) the likeness.

The Cultural Context of Rationality

Although postmodernism presents the most extreme rejection of universal rationality, a number of people who have no commitment to a programme that could be called postmodernist feel uneasy about any claims regarding universal norms – in respect to reason or any other fundamental concept. For example, increased sensitivity to the work of anthropologists may very properly make us cautious about applying the criteria we are familiar with to other cultures. Without being committed to an extreme relativism, in which we assume that there can be no universal criteria, we may well be attracted to a more moderate relativism, in which – as much as possible – we try to appreciate a tradition from within, rather than judging it from outside. In this section I shall consider a number of individuals and movements that are important for an appreciation of the cultural context for rationality. I shall begin with Alasdair MacIntyre, who does not fit comfortably into any group; I shall follow this with some reflections on the Frankfurt School, with special reference to Jürgen Habermas. This will be followed by a discussion of some feminist writers, then of Georg Lukács – as a representative of a Marxist standpoint, and I shall conclude this section with some comments on 'Radical Orthodoxy'.

Alasdair MacIntyre

Alasdair MacIntyre's *Whose Justice? Which Rationality?* is an important book which tries to appreciate what both justice and rationality mean in the context of different traditions.[55] It should be noted that MacIntyre, in this book, is primarily concerned with 'practical reasoning' or 'practical rationality'[56] while in this chapter I have primarily been concerned with more general rules of theoretical reasoning. Moreover, MacIntyre himself uses many rules of theoretical reasoning, sometimes explicitly, for example in claims about what is 'incoherent', and in seeing the mind as engaged in the logical activities of 'collecting, separating, classifying, naming', and so on.[57] When it comes to rational claims about fundamental ethical principles, then, in my discussion of 'insight', I have already indicated that the claims of a universal rationality are much more problematic. MacIntyre's account of how such claims should be understood within the context of a particular tradition is one I am sympathetic to. But this study is not primarily about ethical principles, but about the foundations of religious thought, and what kind of rational conclusions can be drawn in the sphere of religion – although there is inevitably some overlap with ethical issues. I shall be claiming that in addition to general reflection on the human condition there are some significant religious experiences, and that inquisitive

people are bound to attempt a rational evaluation of these experiences. Thus I am not in the position of having to use as a starting-point a series of ethical 'intuitions' whose status as universal principles can easily be challenged. Instead, my initial starting-point is a general reflection on the human condition, and when it comes to a consideration of monism and theism, an additional starting-point is provided by reflection on certain kinds of religious experience. The reality of this experience (if granted) in no way demonstrates the reality or 'truth' of the claims made by religious people – but it provides additional material which critical, universal reason can explore. As a result, an attempt can properly be made to answer questions about whether the experience justifies religious beliefs of any kind.

Further, even within the field of ethical foundations, MacIntyre allows for the exercise of a certain kind of universal rationality, for towards the end of his book he discusses how one tradition can be found to have a '*richer* conceptual and theoretical framework' than another (my emphasis) in terms of its capacity to pass through an 'epistemological crisis' so that adherents to the tradition can write its history in a more 'insightful' way. Meanwhile, another tradition, faced with a similar crisis, may find itself unable to find a cogent explanation for why it cannot solve its problems or restore its coherence, and decide that an alien tradition is 'superior in rationality'.[58] Thus although there is, according to MacIntyre, no 'neutral standing ground' outside all traditions,[59] this does not mean that there is no rational ground for preferring one position to another. Here, the contrast with Rorty is illuminating. From the claim that there is no 'skyhook', Rorty concludes that there is no universal truth or rationality. From the claim that there is no 'neutral standing ground' – which is clearly a parallel claim – MacIntyre draws very different conclusions. These conclusions, I think, are consistent with my own – namely that we can never be in a position to have justified, absolute certainty with respect to our fundamental questions, but that reflection on human experience, using certain universal criteria for rationality, which make sense of terms such as 'incoherence', shows that some positions are to be preferred to others, not only on pragmatic grounds, but on rational grounds too.

The Frankfurt School

More radical than MacIntyre are some of the writers concerned with the sociology or psychology of knowledge, many of whom are part of what is termed the 'Frankfurt School'. Whatever our ultimate view of these may be, there is no doubt, first, that they illuminate the human condition in a whole variety of ways and, second, that they succeed in expressing a scepticism about traditional claims concerning universal truth, or values, or reason that captures the sentiments of many people. Here, I shall refer to some leading writers in the sociology of knowledge, but the conclusions can also be applied to parallel writers in psychology.

Early in the development of thinking in this field, it was not uncommon to distinguish sharply between philosophical issues in the nature of knowledge or reason, and sociological or psychological issues.[60] If this distinction were rigidly enforced, one might say, for example, that Michel Foucault helped us to understand the ways in which what counted as knowledge was both acquired and used within social contexts, without seeing this as any challenge to traditional philosophical ideas about the actual nature of knowledge. However, this attitude would miss the challenge that the sociology of knowledge has actually posed to the philosophy of knowledge since the latter decades of the twentieth century. In the 1970s, when Foucault declared to an audience of startled students that 'truth' was a human invention,[61] this was not simply a comment on how some societies used the term 'truth', but a rejection of a long tradition of seeing truth as some kind of universal category. Even if people did not think they had the truth, it was still an ideal they hoped to get closer to. Moreover, the movement within the sociology of knowledge towards claims that challenged traditional *philosophical* views of knowledge and of rationality was virtually inevitable, given the programme of Karl Mannheim (one of the seminal writers in the early days of the movement). For Mannheim, no human thought, except for mathematics and parts of natural science, could be immune from the ideologizing influences of the social context.[62] It could not be long before even mathematics and the whole enterprise of natural science would also be 'gathered in'.

When this move is fully developed, as (in different ways) within Rorty and Foucault, a critic of postmodernism may still find much of value in the writings. Foucault's exploration of how knowledge is integrated within patterns of power – for example, in his studies of madness and of punishment – can have much to inform all readers, liberal-minded Christians included. However, acceptance of his full-blown theory would make nonsense of the kind of liberal theology I am exploring.

Of particular interest within this field of inquiry is the contemporary German philosopher Jürgen Habermas who is sometimes held to be more a champion of modernism than of postmodernism. His philosophical development has passed through a number of stages, but in the more recent writings there is an increasing criticism of Heidegger, Adorno, Foucault and Lyotard among others, and an attempt to support the viability of a significant form of rationality. With respect to Foucault, his argument includes a variation on what I have called the 'short way' in the discussion of Rorty (although the issue is drawn out at length), in that in order for Foucault to sustain his position, he must, implicitly, rely on the very kind of rationality that he is rejecting: 'His investigations are caught exactly in the self-referentiality that was supposed to be excluded by a naturalistic treatment of the problematic of validity.'[63] But I have already indicated that suggestive as this 'short way' is, it needs to be supplemented with other arguments. In what might be called the 'long way', one does not only reject the extreme postmodernist positions on truth, objectivity and rationality on the grounds of circularity, one tries to counter them with a more adequate account of what these three concepts stand for. This Habermas certainly seeks to do, for while there is a rejection of a 'radicalized critique of reason' (which he sees as self-defeating), there is also support for what is described as 'communicative reason', in contrast with 'subject-centred reason'.[64]

Habermas' concern with reason 'incarnated in contexts of communicative action and structures of the lifeworld'[65] has interesting parallels with Rorty's concern with 'intersubjective agreement', but in my view the supporting argument is more subtle. It is not rooted so much in a denial of a divine viewpoint (as in Rorty), as in the need to justify the ethical dimension, and provide grounds for emancipation that reflect a Marxist quest for true freedom (even though Marxist claims to scientific rationality are rejected). While Rorty, by his own admission, can give no reason why Hitler's programme was wrong, Habermas believes that he can, even though he is fully aware of the cultural context for all knowledge claims. Communicative reason 'integrates the moral-practical as well as the 'aesthetic-expressive domains'.[66] Habermas' moral agenda also provides one of the reasons for his dislike of Heidegger's position, for he sees Heidegger's active support for Adolf Hitler as being intimately connected with fundamental flaws in his philosophy.[67]

My own support for certain universal aspects of rationality goes beyond that of Habermas, although I too think that certain universals emerge in the context of communication. Also, like him, I do not seek to base a universal claim on 'foundationalism', meaning belief in some sure intellectual starting-point upon which one could build a certain system of knowledge. Indeed, my analogy of the sculptor was designed to distance my view from this approach to knowledge. On the other hand, there is more to be said for a measure of 'subject-centred' reason than Habermas allows. Our capacity, as typical human beings, to reflect in a quiet and solitary way on the eternal and fundamental questions of life may only arise in the context of a material and cultural context but, having arisen, it presents an amazing and puzzling power to *transcend* the conditions in which it arises. This is true even when we add to the strictly material conditions the human and social contexts, including that of the language, in which rationality arises. To assume that these material and social contexts fully 'explain' what reason is, once it has developed, is to commit the old 'fallacy of origins'.[68] The questions concern how adequately to understand and describe the nature of the rationality that has emerged through the biological and social processes.

In his discussion of communication, Habermas holds that in certain contexts a speaker raises validity claims concerning the truth of what is said. It is not that we always speak the truth, or always intend to, but, as Emilia Steuerman puts it: 'What he is saying is that when we engage in communication, we mutually expect each other to speak the truth, truthfully and rightfully, and, moreover, we expect reasons to be given in the case of where these claims would be thought unfounded.'[69] My suggestion is that this insight carries with it the implication that even though we may never be able to *grasp* truth, we can form a concept of a truth that has the possibility of transcending intersubjective agreement. Even if we see the force of the famous simile (exploited by Otto Neurath) that likens scientific thought to the efforts of sailors trying to rebuild a boat while it is still at sea, we can envision the project of *seeking* a universal truth, taking account of our limited abilities as we rebuild our ship bit by bit, or (like the sculptor) remodel our pattern piece by piece.

In the next chapter, when we consider materialism, I shall suggest that the necessity of a material context for the development of human thought implies a certain truth in materialist philosophies, even if they turn out to be inadequate. Here I want to point out that the claim to a measure of transcendence does not only arise out of a religious philosophy, although it is consistent with it, and may – so I would argue – give additional grounds for it. The claim arises, initially at least, from two interrelated factors that are not in any obvious way religious.

First, there is the actual, quasi-empirical *observation* of how human thinking continually breaks the bounds of traditional thought, past and present. It is helpful to recall what I have called the essential 'ingredients' of reason. Some of these ingredients are certainly essential for communication, but they also raise the possibility of a kind of independent reflection that is not adequately captured by the notion of 'communicative rationality'. We are able to mark resemblances or similarities that are of importance for us; we are able to see where there is an inconsistency or contradiction; we are able to reject a familiar source of authority and decide to judge for ourselves; we are able to ponder the potential value of some projected scheme, be it practical or philosophical, in terms of internal and external coherence. In other words, what can later be called induction, deduction, autonomy and judgement characterize developed human thinking. Taken together, along with the other ingredients of human reason that I attempted to describe in Chapter 1, we have the basis for the 'transcending' nature of human reason. Extreme examples arise in the production of the uncertainty principle and in quantum mechanics, but significant examples abound of a much more ancient kind. When past cultures became aware of the manifold moral customs of people in different parts of the world, Socrates was one of many who asked, in all kinds of ways, 'Is there some universal or intrinsic good by which these (positive) "goods" can be truly measured?'. The very posing of such a question (even if we think that the answer is negative) indicates a power that begins to 'break the shackles' of its origins – and this, essentially, is what I mean by 'transcendence' (at least described according to a *via negativa*). A question such as 'Is my understanding of reality adequate, given the way in which it has been culturally conditioned?' is itself a perfectly meaningful question, and itself begins to transcend the cultural conditions. Similarly, when, in their ground-breaking book *Dialectic of Enlightenment*, Adorno and Horkheimer force the Enlightenment to examine itself, their whole attack on 'instrumental rationality' is itself made on both rational and moral assumptions without which their whole critique would make no sense. For example, they rely on the notion of 'conceptual clarity', and they talk of 'a new kind of barbarism', in ways which indicate their own belief in the ability of their analysis to 'break the shackles' of both past thinking and present morality.[70]

Second, there is the intriguing question raised by Anaxagoras (and perhaps by many others whose thought is not recorded), concerning how our intellects are related to the cosmos, out of which, in some sense, they emerge. Perhaps the cosmos is ultimately 'intelligible' because we are products of the same powers or laws that order the rest of the cosmos. In any event, unless we work on the assumption that the universe is intelligible, we cannot embark on the whole enterprise of science – meaning the pursuit of 'knowledge', not necessarily of a *certain* kind, but of a kind that comprises at least justifiable, or 'reasonable', belief. But if the cosmos is 'intelligible', then we have, after all, grounds for holding that a 'subject-centred' reason may have some limited, but real power.

The second line of argument, it might be said, is *already* to introduce a religious, or at least metaphysical dimension into the argument, since any suggestion about a 'natural kinship' between our mental capacities and the actual nature of the universe is already to go beyond a strict empiricism. I think, rather, that this point indicates the unclear and unsatisfactory line that is often drawn between religious and secular positions. In the past, many people who considered themselves to be atheists, because they had no time for a God with any personal qualities, certainly believed that the human intellect, because of its innate capacities, could begin to unravel some of the ways in which 'reality' is constituted. The postmodernist rejection of any such discovery is not just secularism – it is a particular form of secularism, that can be attacked without any resource to (what would normally be considered) religious considerations.

At the same time, a theistic philosophy does, in my view, add a new dimension to the second of the foregoing lines of argument. In this book I deal frequently with the belief that we are made 'in the image of God', on the grounds that it is only in terms of this idea (along with a certain view of the role of analogy) that the liberal tradition in theology can reasonably proceed. In the language of religious poetry, humans are a 'Distinguished link in being's endless chain. Midway from nothing to the Deity.'[71]

Even if, for a secular thinker presented with this suggestion, what we have is only a *possibility*, it presents an exciting and challenging reason for holding that our minds may have a limited transcendence – a transcendence already intimated in the first two lines of argument. 'Reaching for the stars' may not be a fruitless enterprise, and, contrary to Rorty, Foucault and company, we cannot rule out the possibility that at times, quite apart from any suggestions of special revelation, we begin to rise out of our material and cultural heritage, and glimpse a horizon from something like a divine standpoint! In a strange way, when Rorty and Foucault raise fundamental questions about the limits of human knowledge, awareness of these questions is itself an example of such transcendence, so that their very philosophizing undermines a crucial element in their positions. More generally, the denial that such transcendence is even a possibility looks like a particular form of secular dogmatism, rooted in a *commitment* to disputable theories that contrasts sharply with the openness of the kind of liberal theology I am promoting.

Feminist Writers

Initially, it is possible to divide feminist writers in the field of epistemology (that is, theories of knowledge) into holders of 'moderate' or 'reformist' theories of reason on the one hand, and holders of 'extreme' or 'radical' views on the other, the latter frequently overlapping with postmodernist claims. It will soon appear that this distinction is far too simple, but I propose to use it as a starting-point.

According to reformists, the idea of reason that has pervaded past cultures has been distorted by male dominance. An obvious illustration of this has been the way in which most males have systematically excluded women from the opportunity to exercise reason. However, even in the reformist version of the issues, there is more to it than this, because it is reasonable to suppose that the features that are thought to characterize what reason *is* have been partly determined by male agendas. For example, Rae Langton discusses how a traditionally male concern for *objectivity*, which can look innocuous, may reflect the way in which the observers' beliefs effect (rather than affect) what seems to be 'normal'. In many cases the world arranges itself in order to fit what the powerful believe: 'Believing women to be subordinate can make women subordinate ... .'[72] Nevertheless, despite the distortions that have been put into the very idea of reason, the reformist does not want to abandon reason, or what Miranda Fricker calls, 'the aspiration to represent the world truly',[73] but to remove the distortions and achieve a more adequate understanding of rationality. In contrast, the radical view claims that '*reason* is an inherently gendered concept', so that in the thought of writers such as Rosi Braidotti, there is no inherently rational position and all that we can hope to achieve is pictured in the 'nomadic' image of 'constantly evolving creative drifting'.[74]

Seen in this way, the issues relating to the theme of this book would seem to be fairly straightforward. Reformist feminist epistemology is a valuable tool in seeking a better account of reason, while the more radical stance faces all the objections that were mounted against Rorty. However, this is too easy a solution, and ignores the profound insights of many writers who, while not adopting the 'extreme' position as just described, have major reservations about what reason is normally taken to be. An important illustration of this is the hesitation to say that the woman's approach to reason represents a 'distinctive style' or is 'complementary' to that of males, terms which could easily be fitted into a reformist agenda. For example, Genevieve Lloyd points out how references to a 'distinctive style' tend to be an oblique way of downgrading feminine traits, and references to 'complementarity' tend to be a prelude to suppression.[75] A typical male reaction to the suggestion that women have different and complementary insights to their own is to agree, and then simply to ignore these insights. This is particularly insidious when the nature of the alleged male characteristics of reason are those that lead to positions of power, while those alleged to represent the feminine invite some subservient role.

I suggest that the account of reason given in Chapter 1 opens up a possible way of describing the insights that come from the feminist critique of rationality. While remaining agnostic about the degree to which, if at all, there are genetic differences between the male and female that impact on the nature of rationality (a matter which is subject to controversy within the area of feminist writing), the *human* aspects of the rational process allow for significant differences between individuals, and also – potentially – between classes of humans, even though there are, so I claim, 'universal' characteristics. Even in the case of induction and deduction, although the rules of inference that can be known and used are the same for all, the way in which the possible is envisioned or imagined, and the way in which there is a 'balancing' of alternatives, in the actual use of the rules of inference, involves a human activity which is visceral as well as intellectual. More significantly, when we get to what may be 'higher' aspects of rationality, as in the fourth ingredient, in which we assess the merits of alternative strategies or (in more developed cultures) alternative world-views, then the imaginative nature of the enterprise can allow for all kinds of difference.

An additional comment concerns the *practical* emphasis in much of the feminist writing on epistemology, an emphasis which explains why so many are hesitant to move too far into the postmodernist camp. Indeed, here is a concern that is common to many members of the Frankfurt School and more orthodox Marxists as well as feminist writers, since within a Rortian style of postmodernism, all moral language that uses terms such as 'oppression' or 'tyranny' or 'abuse' becomes problematic. It is not (to be fair to Rorty) that these terms become literally meaningless, but that outside some explanation of what it is to be 'better' or 'more free' that goes beyond what Rorty can offer, they lose much of their force. Hence, in typical feminist writers, we find a moral agenda in which a fuller Reason is something to be achieved, different perspectives are to be valued, and there is a commitment to 'political action'.[76]

Marxist Writers

Among other thinkers who stress the importance of the cultural context for rationality are a number of hard-line Marxists. Whereas Habermas and other members of
the Frankfurt School are strongly influenced by Marxism, those that I refer to as
'hard-line' Marxists take a more negative view of all non-Marxist philosophies
(which are alleged to be the irrational results of 'false-consciousness', engendered
by the underlying economic conditions) and a more optimistic belief in the eventual triumph of communism. Unlike many postmodernists and some members of
the Frankfurt School, the total relativism of *all* systems of knowledge is not asserted, since Marxist philosophy is claimed to achieve a kind of 'true-conscious-
ness'. Marx and Engels, for example, both asserted the essentially *scientific* nature
of their own thinking on history and economics.

   Of special interest here is Georg Lukács, perhaps the most perceptive of twentieth-century Marxist writers. Whereas most Marxists have little time for non-Marxist thinkers (other than accepting the importance of Hegel in the development of
dialectic) Lukács shows a profound knowledge of a whole range of writers, including religious ones such as Pascal and Kierkegaard (although, in my view, his
analysis of religious writers is flawed by a consistent failure to distinguish between
the 'irrational' and the 'non-rational',[77] and this leads, inevitably, to a negative
evaluation of all religious experience.)

   In his influential book, *History of Class Consciousness* (1923), Lukács argues
that the different elements of social life must be understood within an integrated
whole, and here there is common ground with the claim I shall be making in
Chapter 3, namely that one of the troubles with older forms of materialism is the
failure to take into account the kinds of relationship that bind the universe together.[78] Further, Lukács powerfully expresses a Marxist doctrine of rationality that
has an interesting resemblance to what I call the 'transcending' power of human
reason. When workers become aware of themselves as 'commodities' within the
capitalist system, understanding how this has happened and how true freedom can
be found (through revolution), then they achieve an objective and 'scientific' viewpoint. Thus, in the fashion of classical Marxism, Lukács identifies 'reason' with
'materialist dialectics'.[79] On this view, the 'proletarian standpoint' achieves precisely that 'Archimedean point' which Rorty claims to be impossible. Whether this
claim is compatible with the Marxist form of materialism in which, in the long
term, all human thought is to be explained by the material, economic base is
subject to debate (and within this debate it must be remembered that in Marxism
the only 'real' philosophical problems are those that can have practical solutions).
Whatever our view of this matter, there is *some* common ground here with Christianity, namely in the denial of the postmodernist's rejection of *any* universal viewpoint. (Also, it may be that the way in which Lukács defends his objective viewpoint,
in terms of the integration of subject and object within the self-conscious prole-
tariat, has parallels with a Christian philosophy in which the immanent and the
transcendent are held in balance.) Nevertheless, one must not exaggerate the similarities. In the first place, although conservative Christians, both Catholic and
Protestant, have sometimes held to the *certainty* of their positions, the grounding of
this certainty is either in religious experience, or a kind of intuitive reason, both of

which are subject to doubt within the liberal tradition. In this tradition there is belief in the existence of an objective truth, along with rational grounds for this belief, but unlike both Marxists and conservative Christians, this is a truth one is striving to attain, rather than something one already grasps, whether guaranteed by some kind of authority or some process of reasoning. Paradoxically, in the context of what science is taken to be in the twenty-first century, this acceptance of doubt makes liberal Christianity closer to the spirit of scientific thinking than classical Marxism.

My own view is that more genuine similarities between Christianity and Marxism are to be found within the moral agenda both have with respect to the overcoming of alienation, and the liberation of the oppressed, themes that will arise within Chapter 7. For both viewpoints, these themes are intimately connected with the need to rise beyond the treatment of people as 'things', or objects of commodity.

Radical Othodoxy

Not all of those who stress the cultural context of rationality reject the religious dimension. I shall close this section with a brief comment on a contemporary religious movement that responds in a creative fashion to the sociological thinking of the last hundred years, a movement sometimes known as 'Radical Orthodoxy'. In John Milbank, one of the writers within this movement, one finds a powerful analysis of the underlying assumptions and shortcomings of materialistic social theory, and, in this context, a powerful reaffirmation of fundamental Christian doctrines.[80] The principal difference between the approach outlined in this book and radical orthodoxy lies in my greater emphasis on the possibility of creative dialogue with members of other faiths, or of no faith, based on universal aspects of rationality. As I have stressed, in no way do I belittle the insights that come from understanding Christianity from *within* the circle of faith, but I am concerned with a broader context, one that is the modern equivalent for what Christians of the Alexandrine tradition called the *praeparatio evangelica*. We need a forum where this debate can take place. On this view, the rejection by Radical Orthodoxy of what is termed a 'supposedly objective reason'[81] is over-stressed. What is supported here is not absolute confidence in a narrowly defined autonomous reason (as, allegedly, in Suarez,[82] and at a later date, in the Enlightenment), but a multi-faceted view of reason that includes (as one 'ingredient') reflection on general positions, and reflection on the data of religious experience, and allows for the possibilities of intuitive insight. As a result, we have in common both the rejection of secular postmodernism and the affirmation of central Christian teachings; we differ in the assessment of the creative possibilites of open dialogue with others who share a common rationality.

Some Religious Options

It is one thing to criticize the adequacy of an alleged Christian philosophy, but another thing to claim that people who hold such philosophies are not 'Christians'.

The kind of liberal Christian tradition explored here encourages one to claim that God is a 'reality', and for this reason it will be regarded by some Christians who consider themselves to be 'liberals' as too conservative. While I strongly disagree with the rejection of 'reality' claims by religious people, I can understand why they take the positions they do. More importantly, in the light of what I shall claim to be the *essential* core of Christian belief (in Chapter 7), rooted in a commitment to the way of life and way of prayer exemplified in Jesus, I think it is wrong to assert that these 'non-realists' cannot be Christian. There are at least three forms of Christian non-realism adopted by people who wish to remain within the Christian fold, even though they accept either the positivist or the postmodernist positions I have argued against.

The first is sometimes called 'fideism', and (in the usage I have in mind) it refers to a decision to have 'faith', without a commitment to give reasons of any kind for this faith, except in terms of references to personal fulfilment or happiness. Sometimes this position takes as its foundation portions of Wittgenstein's later philosophy, for although Wittgenstein himself cannot be described as a typically religious person,[83] his theory allows for the use of religious language as a sort of self-contained frame of reference that does not need to be justified by anything outside itself. Wittgenstein himself wrote: 'religious belief could only be something like a passionate commitment to a system of reference. Hence, although it is *belief* it's really *a way of living*, or a way of assessing life. It's passionately seizing hold of this interpretation.'[84]

The second has been closely associated with a group of Christian thinkers called the 'epiphany philosophers', best known among whom was R.B. Braithwaite. While accepting much of the positivist account of meaning as being tied to verification, he claims that both moral and religious language can have a significant meaning which positivists have overlooked, and which depend on a special *use* of language to indicate proposed types of action. Braithwaite goes on to give an interesting account of how Christian stories (or the stories of other religions), while often being in a sense untrue, play a critical role in the kind of life it is proposed to live.[85]

The third is found within the contemporary movement known as the 'sea of faith', strongly influenced by the writings of Don Cupitt. Here, among typical members, is a rejection of any 'realistic' account of God, coupled with a strong desire to affirm many things within the Christian tradition that are regarded as good, and without which the world would be immeasurably poorer. Let us suppose that, notwithstanding the arguments I present in this book, one really cannot accept *even the possibility* that there may be a God, in the sense of an ultimate 'reality'. At the same time, however, one feels deeply attracted to many aspects of the Christian tradition, including the symbolism of the cross, along with all that this implies for how we should live; and also, one feels deeply unhappy about the secular tone of much modern life. Suppose too that among the things one wishes to identify with is a desire for corporate, symbolic activity, especially that found in the Christian Eucharist. Thus in addition to much of the ethical content of Christianity, there is a desire to see maintained much of the sense of corporate ritual and rhythm that the faith has preserved. Given all of this, I can empathize with someone who seeks to 'rework' the Christian message in this radical way, including the adoption of a very different use for the word 'God'.[86]

Notes and References

1   Using an argument similar to that of Descartes, Husserl sought to establish a starting-point of alleged absolute certainty, rooted in the experience of cognition. 'Without doubt', he says, 'there is a *cogitatio*, there is, namely, the mental process during [the subject's] undergoing it and in a simple reflection upon it.' From this starting-point, which in some places he calls 'Archimedean', he claims to establish a radically new *method* of philosophizing, 'the specifically *philosophical method*'(Husserl, E. (1964), *The Idea of Phenomenology*, trans. W.P. Alston and G. Nakhnikian, The Hague: Nijhoff, pp. 2 and 19.) I have sympathy with this approach, and for the 'phenomenological' tradition to which it has led, since when thinkers have tried to explore the implications of actual, conscious experience, many insights have emerged. However, doubts about whether this method can provide an indubitable starting-point are multiplied when one sees the successive stages of Husserl's own attempts to use his method, and the way in which he gradually developed a claim to the certain existence of what he called a 'transcendental ego', and then modified this claim.

2   Hooker, R. *Works*, ed. J. Keble (3rd edn 1845), Oxford: Oxford University Press, vol. III, pp. 470–71 (from a sermon dating from around 1585). Cf. Chillingworth, W. (1638), *The Religion of Protestants*, i, 9, where the same terminology is used.

3   Cf. John Donne (*c.* 1597), *Satyre: Of Religion*. (Note too Donne's admonition, just before these lines: 'doubt wisely'.)

4   Hauerwas, S. (1984), *The Peaceable Kingdom*, Notre Dame: University of Notre Dame Press, p. 18, original emphasis.

5   I do not think that Hauerwas allows for enough common ground between the ethics of the good person in general, and the Christian.

6   One objection concerns the status of the claim: 'all meaningful statements about the world must be verifiable or falsifiable in principle.' Is this a meaningful truth claim, or a dogmatic ('stipulative') definition, or what? The problem here merges with the first problem discussed in the main text, since it soon becomes apparent that the alleged falsification criterion is itself part of a more general theory which is not open to verification or falsification, at least in any straightforward way. Another problem area arises out of references made by positivists to truth claims about the 'world', or 'matters of fact'. Clearly, if what are sometimes called 'metaphysical' claims (about God, or the soul, for example) are meaningful, they are not – at least directly – about the 'world' in the sense of the physical universe that can be explored by the five senses. To assert, therefore, that metaphysical claims are meaningless because they cannot be explored, at least in a direct way, by the five senses, seems circular or to be another piece of dogmatism – one, yet again, that follows from the acceptance of a *theory* that *rules out* certain truth claims. The dogmatism is particularly odd in view of the fact that many truth claims in modern physics, that most positivists do not want to call meaningless, are also not open to any direct verification. It is true that they form part of an 'explanatory web' that is at its roots open to observation by the five senses, but in a corresponding way, statements about God are part of an 'explanatory web' that is part of a way of life, and part of a way of *seeing* and experiencing everything in the world. There are significant differences between what I have called the 'web' of scientific discourse and the 'web' of religious discourse, but they are precisely the differences one would expect from an understanding of the nature of science and the nature of religion.

7   In contrast with 'relations of ideas', which could be meaningful and true, simply because of the analysis of the terms. This distinction is rooted in Hume's 'fork', in which it is claimed that whatever volumes contain neither 'abstract reasoning concern-

ing quantity or number' (such as mathematical argument) nor 'experimental reasoning concerning matter of fact and existence' (such as inductive argument) should be commited to the flames. Hume, D. *An Enquiry Concerning Human Understanding*, XII, III.

8   See Hab. 3: 17–18 for an example of an expression of faith, *regardless* of what may happen.

9   I do not wish to support the extreme thesis that narrative provides the only source of meaning. This would entail that the 'truthfulness' of a narrative, in terms of how it fits with our own experience of living, completely replaced a concern with the 'truth' of certain claims – for example, with respect to important historical events that non-fictional narratives often depend upon. On this matter, see the three-cornered debate between Julian Hartt, Stephen Crites and Stanley Hauerwas, in *Why Narrative?*, eds S. Hauerwas and L.G. Jones, Grand Rapids, Michigan: Eerdmans.

10   Bambrough, R. (1969), *Reason, Truth and God*, London: Methuen, p. 74.

11   In the Greek Orthodox tradition this is called the 'apophatic' way.

12   For an overview of the important contemporary debate concerning realism between Richard Rorty, Donald Davidson, Hilary Putnam, Michael Dummett and others, along with an interesting defence of a 'modest realism', see Farrell, F.B. (1994), *Subjectivity, Realism, and Postmodernism – The Recovery of the World*, Cambridge: Cambridge University Press. See also Thiselton, A.C. (1992), *New Horizons in Hermeneutics*, London: Harper Collins.

13   Rorty, R. (1991), *Essays on Heidegger and Others*, Cambridge: Cambridge University Press, p. 1.

14   Rorty, R. (1991), *Objectivity, Relativism, and Truth*, Cambridge: Cambridge University Press, pp. 5 and 23, original emphasis.

15   Aristotle, *Metaphysics*, 1012b.

16   Eagleton, T. (1996), *The Illusions of Postmodernism*, Oxford: Blackwell, p. 31. Eagleton goes on to dismiss this defence as spurious.

17   Rorty, R., *Objectivity, Relativism, and Truth*, pp. 6 and 38.

18   Rorty accurately describes a search (which he rejects) for a 'truth', at least from the time of the Greeks, that is to be pursued 'for its own sake' and that is based on a 'realist' or 'objective' search for a correspondence of true statements with reality. Then comes the following claim: 'For pragmatists [like Rorty himself], the desire for objectivity is not the desire to escape the limitations of one's community, but simply the desire for as much intersubjective agreement as possible, the desire to extend the reference of "us" as far as we can.' (ibid., p. 23). In the light of this, Rorty totally rejects the traditional search for the kind of objectivity he had previously described.

19   I acknowledge that there are major problems with a correspondence theory of truth when this is described in simple terms, as if a true statement simply mirrors what is there in reality. However, more subtle versions of the theory can certainly be defended. See Prior, A.N. (1967), 'Correspondence Theory of Truth' in P. Edwards, ed., *The Encyclopedia of Philosophy*, New York: Macmillan, vol. 2, pp. 223 ff.

20   There is an interesting complication to this case. From some religious perspectives the situation in the scenario *could* not arise, since there would always be a witness to the truth, namely God (and perhaps a countless number of other spiritual beings). In this context one can consider a little-known argument for the reality of God that is hinted at in Augustine ('they are, because Thou seest them', *Confessions* 13, 53). If we are convinced that it *is* meaningful to speak of what really happened when we can have no possible evidence, perhaps because the event is alleged to have occurred in a previous state of the universe, before the big bang that started the present cycle of events; and *if* the only way this meaning can be possible is for there to be an 'eternal observer'; then

a prerequisite for holding to the meaning we uphold is that there is such an eternal observer.

21 For example, posing the question may be a rhetorical way of suggesting that nothing is 'really true', or (quite differently) that nothing can certainly be known to be true.

22 In so far as one can give a meaning to the *word* 'good', one can point to how it signifies the most general word of commendation. However, a quite different kind of answer is required if the question is asking *what* is good, or the ultimate good, to which, of course, the answer is controversial. Whether or not there is a 'good', in an 'objective' sense, is part of the controversy.

23 Even in interrogative language the concept is embedded, since for a question to be asked meaningfully, it must be assumed that the words used to ask the question truly represent some standard usage.

24 It is true that the elements are only stable within certain physical conditions, but this does not justify the claim that the division of elements is not a reflection of how nature actually is, unless we introduce assumptions about nothing being truly 'real' that is subject to change (in which case, postmodernism begins to move towards the philosophy of Heraclitus.)

25 Plato, *Phaedrus*, 265e.

26 *The Complete Works of Chuang Tzu*, trans. Burton Watson (1968), New York: Columbia University Press, p. 51.

27 An anthropologist investigating a culture, while living within that culture, provides another clear case of some interaction. In other cases the nature of the interaction is much less obvious and less intrusive. For example, if we measure the speed of sound or light, we use instruments that we have made and calibrated.

28 Steuerman, E. (2000), *The Bounds of Reason*, London: Routledge, p. 21.

29 See Bortoft, H. (1966), *The Wholeness of Nature: Goethe's Way of Science*, Edinburgh: Floris, p. 22. cf. pp. xi and 63.

30 See the article on Goethe by Wells, G.A. (1972) in C.C. Gillispie, ed., *Dictionary of Scientific Biography*, New York: Scribner, vol. V, p. 445.

31 The *Times*, 28/9/98, p. 16, in a preview of Libby Purves' *Holy Smoke*.

32 See 1. Cor. 1.

33 Luke 6: 20; cf. Matt. 5: 3 where there may be an early attempt to soften the paradox.

34 When Anaxagoras said 'everything is mind (*nous*)' he was not simply putting forward another candidate for the universal stuff that binds all things together (like the water of Thales). There must be some speculation about the exact meaning of his claim, since the point is not so much what he actually meant (about which we cannot be certain), but how his suggestion can be, and has been interpreted. The key to the significance of the claim is that since mind is in all things, including us, there is a 'natural congruence' between our minds, and the 'all', or the universe, of which we are part. Hence it is not a case of a totally mysterious, subjective mind, somehow housed in our brains, trying to make sense of an alien universe 'out there', about which all our ideas are inevitably mere speculations. The principle which sustains and invigorates the universe we perceive is the *same* principle which sustains and invigorates our thinking. Thought is not alien to matter, it underlies it, and is capable of understanding it. As a result nature is 'intelligible' and 'science' (*episteme*) is possible.

35 For an introductory account of both, see Singh, S. (1997), *Fermat's Last Theorem*, London: Fourth Estate (pp. 154–5 recount another version of the catalogue problem). Gödel showed that mathematical systems cannot be proved to be consistent.

36 Chillingworth, W., *The Religion of Protestants*, vi, 62.

37 Aquinas, *De veritate*, Q. 14, 10, ad. 7, trans. J.V. McGlynn (1953) as *The Disputed Questions of Truth*, Chicago: Regnery. Here, as suggested in Chapter 1, Aquinas is an

'ally' rather than an exponent of liberal theology, since his view of inspired reason has allowed traditional Christians to accept far more on faith than might be warranted.

38   Boethius, *The Consolation of Philosophy*, 5, 6.

39   Aquinas, *ST* 1a Q. 25, 3–4; 1a 2ae Q. 93, 4.

40   See Michael Robinson, 'Why divine foreknowledge?', *Religious Studies*, **36** (3), Sept. 2000, 251–75. This article usefully distinguishes different kinds of foreknowledge. My principal disagreement is with the claim that on an 'openview' account God could not know 'theogically necessary future events' (p. 262). In my view, he might not know *when* they would happen, but he could know *that* they would happen.

41   On this view of omniscience see Cobb, J.B. Jr and Griffin, D.R. (1977), *Process Theology: An Introductory Exposition*, Belfast: Christian Journals Ltd, pp. 47–8 and 119–20.

42   Kant, I., *Idea for a Universal History from a Cosmopolitan Point of View*, in *On History*, ed. L.W. Beck, (1963), New York: Bobbs-Merrill, p. 11.

43   Aquinas, *ST* 1a, Q. 13. Aquinas also discusses the issue in other works, sometimes with slightly different terminology. See also Aristotle, *Posterior Analytics*, 98a and 99a; *Topics*, 106a–108b and *Metaphysics*, 1003a–b. For a more detailed account of Aquinas' teaching see Anderson, J.F. (1949), *The Bond of Being*, St Louis: Herder.

44   Mason, J. (1683), *Spiritual Songs*, 5th edn (1696), London, p. 2.

45   See, for example, Heimmel, Jennifer P. (1982), *'God is Our Mother': Julian of Norwich and the Medieval Image of Christian Feminine Divinity*, Austria: Universität Salzburg.

46   Mathias, W. (1987), *As Truly as God is our Father*, Oxford: Oxford University Press. Cf. Julian of Norwich, *Shewings*, chapter 59.

47   Ibid., intr. to ch. 60.

48   Psalm 103: 13. Prayer Book (Coverdale translation).

49   See Cajetan, *The Analogy of Names*, trans. E.A. Bushinski, 2nd edn (1959), Pittsburgh: Duquesne Studies, p. 28.

50   Ibid., p. 68 for Cajetan's claim concerning God's wisdom. It should also be noted that many analogies can be called 'three term'. For example, a climate and a complexion are both said to be 'healthy' because they have an implicit reference to a prime analogue, or third term, namely an animal constitution.

51   Genesis 1: 27.

52   Aquinas argues that in the case of words that refer to perfection, from the point of view of what each word means it is used primarily of God, while from the point of view of our use of the word we apply it first to creatures. In contrast, when words are used metaphorically to refer to God, as when we liken God to a lion, then the words refer primarily to creatures. Aquinas, *ST* 1a Q. 13, 6.

53   Thus Nathaniel Culverwell wrote 'though there be still an infinite disproportion between God and the creature *in esse naturali*, yet there is a fit and just proportion between them *in esse intelligibilis*': *An Elegant and Learned Discourse of the Light of Nature* (1652), Toronto: University of Toronto Press, (1971), p. 169.

54   Both Aquinas and Duns Scotus reject the position that all words are predicated *equivocally* of God and humans. Duns Scotus, perhaps unfairly, attributed this view to Henry of Ghent (who wrote shortly after the death of Aquinas). Since Duns Scotus accepts Aquinas' claim that God's being is different from ours (for example, he stresses the way in which God is a *necessary* being more than Aquinas does), the crucial Thomistic point that God has an eternal existence while we have 'derivative' existence, is not denied by the different terminology that he used. However, he held that his account of the univocal use of some words was essential (among other reasons) because it alone made some metaphysical *knowledge* of God possible.

55 MacIntyre, Alasdair (1988), *Whose Justice? Which Rationality?*, London: Duckworth.
56 Ibid., pp. 339 and 346.
57 Ibid., pp. 362 and 356.
58 Ibid., pp. 363–5.
59 Ibid., p. 367.
60 For example, in Berger P.L. and Luckman, T. (1966), *The Social Construction of Reality*, (1984) London: Penguin pp. 13–14, 33.
61 See Steuerman, E. (2000), *The Bounds of Reason*, London: Routledge, p. xi.
62 Berger and Luckman, *The Social Construction of Reality*, p. 21.
63 Habermas, J. (1987), *The Philosophical Discourse of Modernity*, trans. F. Lawrence, Boston, MA: MIT Press, p. 279; cf. pp. xv, 247–8, 269.
64 Ibid., pp. 302, 314.
65 Ibid., p. 322.
66 Ibid., pp. 314–15.
67 Ibid., pp. 155–60.
68 This is the fallacy (pointed out by William James among others), in the argument that in giving an account of the historical origins of an idea one removes the obligation to consider its validity.
69 Steuerman, *The Bounds of Reason*, p. 28.
70 Adorno T.W. and Horkheimer, M. (1947, rev. edn 1969), *Dialectic of Enlightenment*, 1969, trans. J. Cumming (1997), London: Verso, pp. xi, xiv.
71 From Edward Young's poem, *Man*.
72 Langton, R. (2000), 'Feminism in Epistemology: Exclusiveness and Objectification' in Fricker, M. and Hornsby, J., eds, *The Cambridge Companion to Feminism in Philosophy*, Cambridge: Cambridge University Press, p. 139.
73 Fricker, M. (2000), 'Feminism in Epistemology' in ibid., p. 148.
74 These expressions are both explained and criticized in Sabina Lovibond's 'Feminism and the "Crisis of Rationality"', *New Left Review*, **207**, 1994, pp. 72 and 78.
75 Lloyd, G. (1984), *The Man of Reason*, London: Methuen, pp. 104–105.
76 Fricker, M. and Hornsby, J. eds (2000), *The Cambridge Companion to Feminism in Philosophy*, Cambridge: Cambridge University Press. Lloyd, G., *The Man of Reason*, p. 107; Fricker, M., 'Feminism in Epistemology', pp. 149, 160.
77 Lukács, G. (1980), *The Destruction of Reason*, trans. P. Palmer, London: Merlin Press, pp. 114–16; 250–96.
78 Lukács, G. (1923), *Geschichte und Klassenbewusstein*, Berlin: Malik-Verlay, pp. 26–7.
79 Ibid., p. 852.
80 Milbank, J., *Theology and Social Theory*, Oxford: Blackwell, 1990.
81 Milbank, J., Pickstock, C. and Ward, G., eds (1999), *Radical Orthodoxy*, London: Routledge, p. 1.
82 Montag, J. (1999), 'The False Legacy of Suarez' in ibid., pp. 53–4. I use the word 'allegedly' since it is misleading to see Suarez as a consistent supporter of an objective, secular reason. Montag correctly points to Suarez' intention to ground theology in a more general metaphysic (and congruously, we could point to Suarez' account of the social contract, which is surprisingly secular), but in his account of natural law it is clear that human reason depends on divine illumination, and he stresses the notion of a 'right reason' that this illumination bestows upon man. Hence what can be called 'theological reason' is the source of many important themes, for example, the obligatory nature of natural law *because of* its grounding in God, and the legitimate *coercive* power of the papacy in regard to heretical monarchs and infidels who will not allow the preaching of Catholicism in their domains and the punishment of apostates. In these important matters of coercion (in which Suarez follows Bellarmine and other Catholic

writers), there is too much dependence on a 'theological reason', not too little. See Suarez, F., *De legibus* (1612), II; V, 14 and VI, 24 (misnumbered 14); *Defensio Fidei Catholicae* (1613), III, 23; *De Fide* (1621), XVIII, 2 and 3.

83 On Wittgenstein's personal position, which was quite complex, see Cupitt, D. (1994), *The Sea of Faith*, 2nd edn, London: SCM Press, pp. 243–7.

84 Wittgenstein, L. (1980), *Culture and Value*, ed. G.H. von Wright, trans. P. Winch, Oxford: Blackwell, p. 64e.

85 Braithwaite, R.B. (1955), *An Empiricist's View of the Nature of Religious Belief* (Eddington Memorial Lecture), Cambridge: Cambridge University Press, pp. 15 and 23 ff.

86 For a 'non-realist' definition of 'God', see Cupitt, D. *The Sea of Faith*, p. 275.

Chapter 3

Materialism

The Meaning of Materialism

Materialism might also be called 'naturalism' or 'physicalism', but these and the other possible terms all have similar ambiguities. The essential position of materialism is that nature, in the sense of the physical universe, is all that can properly be said to exist. Most importantly, mind and consciousness, in so far as they can be said to exist at all, are seen as essentially *reducible* to, or totally explainable by physical processes. For this reason, 'reductionism' might be considered another candidate for the name of this option, but not all those who consider themselves to be materialists are committed to the systematic reduction of all aspects of human life.[1] However, materialism is always reductionist to the extent that for the materialist, thoughts either simply *are* the neurological activities that take place in the brain, or are 'epiphenomena' that are totally explainable by these activities. In general, therefore, materialism has no place for the God of theism. Nevertheless, a number of materialists in the past have wanted to use the word 'God', sometimes as a way of referring to the *whole* of nature, and sometimes – for example, in the case of a number of Greek thinkers – for a powerful entity that had a special kind of body. More often materialists prefer to call themselves atheists in order to dissociate themselves from both theism and agnosticism. I have heard a number of sermons lambasting such atheists for arrogance. 'How can you *know* that there is no God?' has been the rhetorical question that features in these harangues. However, this challenge, in the case of some atheists, is quite unfair. There are many dogmatic atheists, just as there are many dogmatic theists, but atheism does not have to be dogmatic. Materialism, at least in its more subtle formulations, is a rational option that can be expressed in a way that conforms to the demands for internal and external consistency. If this is the option taken, then there is no more need to demand that it be 'proved', in some absolute way, than in the case of theism. If someone feels, after much reflection, that it is the most plausible option, they cannot be faulted for calling themselves atheists. However reason demands the possibility be considered that one of the other options might be either *as* defendable, by rational criteria, or *more* defendable, which, in the case of theism, is my own conviction.

There is one other ambiguity to refer to in this initial statement of the materialist position. In modern English the word 'materialism' refers to two different positions that may be quite unrelated. The first, with which this chapter is concerned, reflects a view of what constitutes what 'is', or 'reality'. The second concerns an ethical standpoint to the effect that 'material things', as opposed to 'spiritual things', whatever these may be, are the appropriate objects of human pursuit. It is perfectly possible to hold either of these views while rejecting the other. Marx, for example, was a materialist of the first kind, but his philosophy includes a systematic attack on materialism of the second kind. In particular, he describes the materialistic values of bourgeois society as a rapacious egoism, which, he alleges, has replaced the proper human search for justice, consonant with our true nature as 'species beings'.[2]

If matter is the only thing that exists, this suggests to the ordinary person that everything is made out of one or more kinds of 'stuff'. Some early forms of materialism did indeed assert something to this effect. Democritus, probably building on earlier ideas in Leucippus and Empedocles, maintained that there was an infinite number of indivisible particles – the atoms – moving around in the 'void', which is a rough equivalent for our concept of space. The atoms collide and form groups, and from thence arises *everything* that exists. Moreover, and very importantly in the view of Democritus and his followers, there is no need to ask questions about how or why the whole system arose – or, to put this more technically – to invoke a 'teleology'.[3] Later, Epicurus adapted this system, and he did so, in part, to further his purpose of removing 'superstition', in which he included fear of the gods and any belief in human immortality. Like many early atomists he did believe in 'gods', but these, like everything else, were made of atoms and were simply higher beings that took no interest in human affairs. He also believed in the human 'soul', but, again, as made of (special kinds of) atoms which come apart at death. Everything has a 'mechanical' explanation, and, once again, there is no need to introduce a teleology, or any kind of divine intervention.

Non-materialists can properly be amazed at the ingenuity of the primitive speculation about atoms, and the brave attempt to *explain* movement and difference in a way that anticipates so much recent thought. In Democritus there even seems to be the realization that in the void there is no real top or bottom, and hence an extraordinary anticipation of one aspect of relativity. We should also note that although the ethical systems that these philosophers built often emphasized the sensual they were in nearly all cases far from being amoral or immoral or purely egoistic. Once again we see that materialism, in the sense of egoism, is not necessarily connected with philosophical materialism, and we note too that theists have too easily argued that you must have a God in order to have an ethic.[4] Another misconception is that recent advances in physics, in which the idea of 'stuff' or 'material' tends to give way to fields and flows of energy, somehow destroys the viability of a materialist philosophy. Modern science does demand that the essential picture be described in different ways, but not necessarily by the reintroduction of teleology.

A good example of a materialist who moves away from an emphasis on matter to a more modern form of materialism is Hobbes, who wrote in the middle of the seventeenth century. The essence of Hobbes' materialism is the claim that everything is reducible to laws of motion. Thus the discovery that atoms or, later, subatomic particles, are not the solid entities they were once thought to be does not destroy the essential features of the materialist position, especially its denial that there are existing spirits that have no 'body'. In Hobbes' system, without any reliance on a solid account of matter, we have explicit claims to the machine-like nature of animals and humans: 'For what is the heart but a spring; and the nerves, so many strings ... .'[5] The claim that humans are special examples of machines is one of the themes that runs through materialism, from its beginnings to modern comparisons of humans with computers. The very title of La Mettrie's most famous book, *L'Homme machine* (1747), provides a classical case of this view. Returning to Hobbes, sense, imagination and reason are all claimed to be different forms of interior motion: 'All fancies are motions within us, reliques of those made in the sense ... .'[6] Hobbes has his own doctrine of God and, unlike most materialists, of immortality, but nothing can exist without 'body', and this applies both to God and to our future estate: 'Though men may put together words of contradictory signification, as *Spirit, and Incorporeall*; yet they can never have the imagination of any thing answering to them ... .'[7]

Among the thousands of other materialists one could name, including important examples in Chinese and Indian thought, I shall mention here only Richard Dawkins, because of the popularity of his ideas, and because of the clarity of his writings. Also, here again we see that materialism in the primary sense need have no link with egoistic materialism, and this is important in view of the title of Dawkins' well-known book *The Selfish Gene*. In fact, Dawkins stresses his desire *not* to advocate an ethic based on selfishness.[8] What he succeeds in doing is building up an appealing case for a complete Darwinian explanation of all things, and thence of a universe in which there is 'no design, no purpose, no evil and no good ...'.[9] We, and all other animals, are machines created by our genes. There is no room and no need in this universe for God, the idea of which has had remarkable survival power, he asserts, 'for its great psychological appeal. It provides a superficially plausible answer to deep and troubling questions about existence.'[10]

As with the early atomists and with Hobbes, one can admire and approve the bold attempt to seek a total explanation in terms of a scientific theory without accepting some of the conclusions that are reached, especially when these conclusions are not, strictly speaking, part of the scientific enterprise but stray into more general areas of philosophy. I shall describe two ways in which materialism, when espoused as an overall philosophy, is vulnerable to attack. These relate, first, to materialistic claims concerning the universe *as a whole*, and second, to materialistic accounts of thought and consciousness. Later, I shall argue that when materialist philosophies become more subtle, they may cease to be 'materialistic' in a way that necessarily conflicts with all forms of theism.

The Physical Universe as a 'Whole'

By way of an introduction to the critique of materialism I want to consider what Dawkins says about 'why' questions. He refers disparagingly to those who, after hearing about 'how' evolution works, then ask 'why' questions, and points out that 'the mere fact that it is possible to frame a question does not make it legitimate or sensible to do so'.[11] This is true, but overlooks a fundamental distinction. *Within* the context of explaining individual parts of the universe, it is certainly not clear that a 'why' question is legitimate, except in a special sense. For example, one might ask 'why' a bird has colour vision, and an answer could be given in terms of survival value. In such cases there is no *extrinsic* purpose being referred to, and the 'why' is really a special case of the 'how'. So far I am on Dawkins' side, fully accepting, for example, Darwinian evolutionary theory as by far the best attempt to say how (and in a sense why) things are as they are within the universe. I do not see any need to introduce an external teleological principle into the workings of *individual* things within the universe (in contrast with the process as a whole), and I think that science is right to avoid any temptation to do so.[12]

Despite what Dawkins claims, when reflective people ask 'why' in reference to the universe as a whole, or to the workings of evolution as a whole, it may well be that they are not asking *scientific* questions, but metaphysical questions. If a religious person *assumes* that the questions are meaningful, then an assumption has been made that – at least in the context of those who disagree – requires justification. But if Dawkins says that such questions are meaningless, then he, likewise, is making an assumption that needs justification – again, at least in the context of those who disagree with him. To put this in another way: the status of metaphysical questions about the 'whole' is controversial, and the greatest minds continue to disagree about them, so no side in the debate should use their alleged meaningfulness or meaninglessness as a *premise*. Such claims should be the *conclusions* of argument. Hence some of the 'why' questions might be fair questions, and to tackle them Dawkins must step outside his area of special expertise, and enter into the more general realm of philosophy.

Let us turn to a typical question that concerns the whole process of evolution rather than any particular aspect of the process. Suppose someone asks: 'How is it that evolution is able to bring forth consciousness and love?' We can predict two things a follower of Dawkins is almost certain to say. First, up to a point a scientific answer can be given, for a gradual process is increasingly understandable in which the survival of certain genes leads to all kinds of new, complex organisms. With this a theist should have no problem. Second, when the process as a *whole* is surveyed, while a feeling of wonder at the beauty and majesty of some of the products of the process is perfectly natural, the assumption that the question could have any kind of meaningful answer is mistaken and naive. Very often this refusal to consider questions about the whole universe is supported by the following argument. The universe just *is*, and no reason for why it is can be given, or should be sought. Moreover, if you suggest a reason, such as 'the universe is the product of a creative Mind, and all the potentialities of evolution are built into nature by this creative Mind', the question is not answered, but merely postponed. Just as you mistakenly ask 'why' there is a universe, or an evolutionary process that leads to conscious life, so I could ask 'why' there is a Mind behind this process. The questioning has to stop somewhere, and why not stop with the universe, and just accept that no 'reason' can be given for it? Perhaps (the materialist might concede) it is difficult to accept that the universe just *is*, given our natural propensity to look for reasons, but a theistic response, like the one suggested, simply replaces one puzzle with another.

One natural response to this materialist language is to point out that some questions about the 'whole' are in fact asked within the context of scientific cosmology. It is interesting to note that such questions – for example, about what explanation, if any, can be given for the 'big bang' – are rejected as improper by some scientists, and eagerly sought after by others. In this controversial area I would make the following suggestion. When questions are asked about the whole universe to which scientific methods of observation and prediction apply, because empirical *evidence* for or against a theory might be forthcoming, then these questions should be treated as scientific. For example, new evidence about the distribution of 'dark matter' is relevant to the issue of whether or not there will be a 'big crunch', and rival theories involve different predictions about this distribution. However the 'why' questions which some intelligent listeners to one of Dawkins' lectures on evolution may ask could be non-scientific, but nevertheless perfectly genuine questions. I suggest that in such cases instead of simply dismissing the question, it would be more rational to point out that the question does not fall within the boundaries of science, and that fundamental philosophical questions arise regarding, first, whether these questions are meaningful and, second, if they might be meaningful, what kind of philosophical answers there might be.[13]

The materialist's suspicion of questions about the universe, taken as a whole, underlie the rejection of the ancient cosmological argument for the existence of God, a rejection that forms an important part of materialist philosophy in its typical form. This ancient argument, found for example in the first three of Aquinas' 'five ways', had argued that the very existence of the universe demanded a creator, called God. Both Hume and Kant produced what are generally regarded as classical refutations of the argument (although, according to Kant, there are other rational grounds for believing in God). As in the materialist position, there is no logical requirement, so it is claimed, that the universe has a source in a creative Mind. There is no reason why there could not be an *infinite* series of former states of the physical universe, each one leading to the next, with no 'beginning' that needs explanation. Moreover, modern materialists argue that even if the universe, and time along with it, go back to a 'big bang', there is still no way that an 'explanation' can be offered. The universe as a whole is 'brute fact', so why make it dependent on another 'brute fact' – that is, God. Surely this is an unnecessary complication, and reason, following the principle of Ockham's razor (which says that all unnecessary entities should be discarded),[14] must conclude that the God hypothesis should be rejected as redundant?

Behind this materialist position there lies an ambiguity with respect to what we mean by the 'whole universe'. This could be taken to mean simply the sum of all the physical events or 'things' in the universe, and some writers do seem to have meant just this. The 'whole' is then seen as merely a series of disconnected or 'discrete' events or 'things'. Hume's philosophy of impressions and ideas encourages this view of the universe as a jumble of discrete entities or events, any organizing principles being provided by our minds. When the universe is conceived in this way it may be true that there is no logical reason why it might not stretch back for ever, with no overall 'beginning'. However, this has never been the understanding of 'whole' in the theistic tradition, and now we find that contemporary science gives strong support to something akin to the older, richer conception. As one philosopher of science puts it: 'physicists have discovered the universe to be one, single, and indivisible whole.'[15] What this means is that not only does it appear that a particular set of laws describe all parts of the universe, but each part of the universe is causally connected with other parts. This applies not only to spatial relations, where gravitational and other fields make all sources of energy interdependent, but also to temporal relations. The past has led to what is now, and the future to a large extent is predictable as the outcome of the present.[16] More generally, no part of the universe can be fully understood except in the context of the whole of which it is part. In 1933, Whitehead (as so often ahead of his time) wrote: 'The whole environment participates in the nature of each of its occasions.'[17] One immediate result of this understanding of the universe is that reference to an 'infinite series' of past events or configurations misses the point of the ancient cosmological argument. The issue is whether or not the 'whole', seen as an integrated unity, is in need of explanation. Further reflections on the nature of the 'whole' will arise when we come to the section on the relationship of the physical universe to thought, and recent formulations of what is known as the 'anthropic principle' within science.

This deeper understanding of the universe does not necessarily mean that materialism must be abandoned, but it does entail that what 'materialism' *means* is something more subtle than a simple statement to the effect that 'material things' are all that can be said to exist. No individual 'material thing' can be understood except in the context of a cosmic whole, and while this may not entail the introduction of any kind of theology, it must entail an account of the *interrelationship* of things that goes far beyond the cruder forms of materialism.

The Explanation of Consciousness

If materialism is to be sustained, it must be able to give a convincing account of thought and consciousness within its own terms. In the last hundred years, two things have helped to make this seem a reasonable expectation. The first is the decline of Cartesian dualism. According to Descartes there is a radical divide between the world of the self-conscious I and the exterior world, which is the outside world of 'extension' in space and time, the world of things. Among the problems that beset this philosophy was the difficulty of seeing how the inner world of the self and the exterior world, which includes our physical bodies, interact, for interact they clearly do, for example, whenever we decide to move our bodies. Descartes and his followers searched for a particular location, such as the pineal gland, where the interaction might take place, and there are amusing accounts of how they got chased from one place to another as different bits of the brain were gradually found to have functions within the physical system. But the search was hopeless, given the Cartesian presuppositions, since if a location in the brain seemed to have no other function it still would not explain how the two disparate worlds were linked. Increasingly, both scientists and philosophers rejected this dualism, and sought a different relationship between thought and matter. The second support for materialist accounts came with advances in the science of the brain, including brain anatomy and scans which not only show that while we think neurological activities are going on in the brain, but which also show how particular kinds of thought and feeling are associated with certain parts of the brain and certain kinds of neurological activity. Here, it might be thought, is evidence for Hobbes' contention that thought is simply a special kind of interior motion.

However, if Cartesianism is abandoned, it does not follow that materialism is right. Also, the fact of neurological activity during thought does not mean that thought *is* neurological activity, which is called 'the identity hypothesis', and which is the view held by *some*, but not all, materialists. Prior to arguing against this form of materialism, let us speculate that in the case of human thought, not only does every thought have a corresponding brain activity that could, in principle, be monitored, but also that there *could not be* a human thought without a corresponding brain activity. (For now, let us leave aside the question of whether divine thoughts, if they exist, also have some corresponding physical activity.) If this speculation could be proved to be right, it would not require that I give up theism and accept materialism. It would not prove that thought *is* brain activity, and it would not even rule out the theoretical possibility of thoughtful life after death if there is any kind of resurrected body. I am not committing myself to the truth of this speculation (and some recent experiments with near-death experiences suggest it may be false), but even with this concession, materialism still faces the problems I am about to discuss. Leaving aside for now the issue of causation, there are major problems with the identification of brain activity with thought.

Prior to my main argument we need to be clearer about what should be held to count as 'consciousness'. There are at least three aspects of consciousness to consider. At the 'lowest' level there is simply the fact of awareness, an awareness which other animals, especially mammals with more complex nervous systems, certainly share to some degree. This basic awareness could itself be divided into different levels, for there is a world of difference between being 'aware', in the sense of merely not being 'unconscious' and, at the other extreme, in the sense of having an 'awareness' that one psychologist describes as being like 'a radiance from within'. The description continues: 'It is the registering of the massively important process of tuning in to what at this moment is the priority for the whole organism, the totality of you ... .'[18] It is possible that this level of awareness shades over into what I am describing as the next 'level' of consciousness, which begins to require new categories of language to describe. Here there is conscious *reflection*, in which possibilities as well as present realities are held before the mind, and perhaps this occurs in the process of 'tuning in' to the whole context of an awareness. As already suggested, primates appear to share some of this capacity for envisaging the possible. At another level there is *self-consciousness*, when we are aware of these inner reflections, and ponder our individual relationship to the outside world, including other people. (I am not aware of any evidence that other animals share in this capacity, but if they do the following argument is not materially affected.) There is massive controversy about how and when these different levels developed. For example, some writers, including Bruno Snell and Julian Jaynes[19] have argued that full self-consciousness came very late, probably during the Homeric period in Greece. I am highly sceptical of such a late emergence for what Snell calls 'the discovery of mind' in the light of thought and poetry in China, India and the fertile crescent before 1000 BCE. However it is important to stress that issues like this are only of peripheral importance for the purposes of this book. Whenever and however consciousness arose in the full-blown sense of reflective activity that is conscious of itself, this is a phenomenon that cries out for explanation. The 'lower' levels of consciousness also cry out for explanation, but in what follows I am primarily concerned with self-conscious reflection of the kind that anyone reading this book is certainly aware of.

There is a huge literature on this subject, including many papers by scientists and philosophers. A good starting-point for those wishing to pursue this literature is a set of twenty-nine papers from the MIT Press, entitled *Explaining Consciousness – The 'Hard Problem'*[20] (the 'hard problem' being the difficulty of explaining how any physical system can give rise to conscious experience). One of the things that emerges from a survey of this material is a fundamental disagreement among scientific experts in the field, first, about whether there really is a 'hard problem', and second (when a 'hard problem' is admitted), what kind of answer should be given. Some argue from and for a frankly materialist position. In one case the writer refers to her 'commitment' to a materialist position, and adds 'if we are materialists, we have to *believe* [emphasis added] that consciousness is something physical'.[21] Others take very different, and much more open approaches, arguing, for example, that there are systematic reasons why the reductive methods that work in other areas inevitably fail here, and using words such as 'mystery'.[22] The view that I shall argue for is that the identity hypothesis, which is the most robust form of materialism, is highly questionable, and that when we move to other views, then the sense in which the accounts are 'materialist' becomes less and less clear. At best (from a materialist standpoint), materialism is a *possible* philosophy, among other possibilities.

Let us suppose that I have a scanning machine set up so that I can monitor *all* brain activities while I am thinking. Of course, this cannot be done now, but I am assuming – as a concession to the materialists – that there is no reason, in principle, why it might not be possible for all of them to be monitored. Strictly speaking, I am not observing the activities, for they are within my head, but I am *monitoring* them in a way which gives me an exact picture of what is going on. Suppose that within this context I now start to think about whether my thoughts *are* the brain patterns, or whether the brain patterns are instead the physical *accompaniments* of my thoughts. The brain patterns I now observe, are, if the identity hypothesis is right, my present reflections on the issue of what brain patterns are. But this contention raises grave difficulties. It might seem plausible (though I think it is mistaken) to say that some thoughts *are* brain activities, but to say that reflection on whether or not thoughts are brain activities is itself just another, albeit more complicated, brain activity, seems not to capture what we mean by *reflecting on brain activity*. How can an account of brain waves describe what is going on when we reflect on whether or not reflection is purely a matter of having certain brain waves?

Let us pursue another thought experiment. I am reviewing a book on law, and I decide to find out how many times the book has referred to the principle that no criminal should benefit from a crime. I use a word finder or scanner to see how often words like 'benefit' have been used but I am aware that no such mechanical device can find *all* the instances, since the principle may be used or implied without any use of the words I search for, and the words may be present when the principle is not. To find my answer I have to read through the book again, using my *understanding* of the principle to detect all the instances. While I carry out this search someone monitors all my thoughts, as in the former thought experiment. If the identity hypothesis is right, then every time I recognize an instance of the principle, there will be some 'sameness', not only in my acts of recognition, but (and here lies my difficulty) in the pattern of ideas that I am reading. Since the principle could be referred to in any number of verbal ways, the sameness cannot be simply embedded in the *words* I read, but in what I take them to signify. The monitor, therefore, shows both the train of ideas that the words on the pages conjure up, and my reflection upon them. If I were briefed to defend the identity hypothesis I might suggest that this combination of two trains of thought is analogous to a complex auditory signal, behind which are two or more polyphonic sets of notes. But now suppose that someone says that I have got the answer wrong. Can the identity hypothesis make sense of *error* in this context? The error cannot be in failing to recognize a verbal pattern, for there is no finite set of verbal patterns that could identify when the principle was being referred to – it must be in a failure in *understanding* that a certain idea should be evoked by the word pattern. It seems to me that the identity hypothesis cannot explain what the nature of this understanding is.

At this point let me hazard why the more extreme materialists have felt forced to advocate the identity hypothesis, despite objections like those I have raised. There is, I suggest, a worry that any alternative account will force a return to a Cartesian philosophy in which there is a claim that is just as strange as that of the identity hypothesis, namely one that involves a duality in which 'thoughts' dwell in some quite mysterious zone, and yet (given our knowledge of brain scans) march exactly in step with neurological counterparts. Is not this a situation – it might be alleged – where a good scientist, following the principle of Ockham's razor, will simply ignore the ghostly counterpart of the neurological activities? The whole suggestion conjures up what Gilbert Ryle called 'the ghost in the machine', a perspective against which he formulated a series of powerful arguments.[23] Let us explore, therefore, another way of handling the issue, one which, for the present, leaves open the question of whether or not it should be classed as 'materialist'.

In conscious human thought (and perhaps in animal thought too, but let us leave this aside), it can be suggested that there is always an 'inner' and an 'outer' side to any adequate description of what is going on.[24] This is not to introduce the 'ghost in the machine' by the back door, for there is no suggestion that there are two distinct realities, or what Ryle calls 'different kinds of existence'.[25] The suggestion reflects the way in which light might be investigated as a stream or particles or as a wave motion, with no assumption of a duality in nature itself. Let us begin with the 'outer' side. A description of brain activity is an account of the 'outer side', or at least of part of it, for one might want to include activity within the whole nervous system and, perhaps too, observable behaviour which is intimately connected with movements within the brain. It is not essential to think of the brain as giving a command to a motor that then pulls a muscle that then results in observable behaviour. The neurological movements within the brain are part of a whole system that results, some of the time, in observable and measurable behaviour. I think it was an awareness of this linkage that led, in part, to the wild claims of the 'behaviourist' school. According to this, my so-called 'inner' sense of say, a tooth-ache, has no meaning except in so far as there is an exterior behaviour that other people can observe. The identity hypothesis is *not* committed to this (even more extreme) philosophy. When 'behaviourism' is used to mean an area of study in which observable data can be collected from human or animal movement, then I have no objection, even if the behaviourist then goes on to see how far behavioural explanations can be carried. But when this perfectly legitimate *methodology* becomes also a philosophy in which the meaningfulness or existence of non-behavioural aspects of human life is denied, then we have a case of a dogmatism in which it is insisted that reality must conform to the instrument we happen to be using. It is really a more subtle case of saying that if my telescope can't see it, it isn't there. Iris Murdoch has shown how the behaviourist programme makes it impossible to describe crucial aspects of human experience.[26]

Although human thought often leads to outward activity, there are many cases where it does not and in these cases I cannot see why we should not refer to a 'mental event'. For example, take the case of a great composer, let us say, called Drahms, who composes a new quartet, opus 100, entirely in her head, prior to any writing down on paper or humming of the melodies. (There is evidence that Mozart sometimes composed in this way.) She tells her husband that at last opus 100 is finished and that seeing[27] it as a whole has been a great experience. Then, just before putting it all on paper, she dies. One of the husband's friends says 'What a shame that the quartet was never experienced', and he replies, 'Oh but it was, by Drahms, the day before she died!' Here would be an example of an event that *did* have an 'outer' manifestation of a kind, namely the neurological activities that took place in Drahms' head while she experienced her opus 100, although no one was there to monitor them. However, the main thrust of the event was 'inner', and therefore it makes perfectly good sense to speak of it as primarily a mental event. (Ryle, while defending his quasi-behaviourist position,[28] makes his argument much easier by concentrating on cases of *known* tunes, which someone repeats in their head. Hence he can more plausibly say 'there are just things and events, people witnessing some of these things and events, and people fancying themselves witnessing things and events that they are not witnessing'.[29] In the case I describe, Drahms was not fancying that she was a witness to an event, for example, in a concert hall, although she may *also* have done this, she was actually experiencing a significant, although purely inner event. I cannot see why this should not be classed as a 'real' experience.) The only other reason I shall give here for rejecting a behaviouristic philosophy is its failure to account for its own philosophy of behaviourism. B.F. Skinner made an attempt to do so, but he was faced with trying to show how his behaviouristic view was itself a form of behaviour that could be totally explained on his principles.[30]

Let us turn to the 'inner' side, which a more modest materialism might allow one to speak of. This 'inner' side of thought can only be described, by its very nature, through references to personal experience. Much of the time we do not concentrate on our inner worlds, we simply think and act, and it is only in later reflection that we are conscious that all the time there was an 'inner' side to our activities. But when we keep still in active reflection about what we ought to do, or about how to go about solving a mathematical problem, or about whether my thoughts are totally caused by my bodily state, and so on, then we are acutely aware of this inner aspect. Notoriously, when we try to *focus* on it, it somehow eludes us, but I think we can see why. Focusing on the inner side means, in practice, trying to make it an *object* for our reflection, akin to the way in which a particular theorem might be an object that we focus on; but the whole point of the inner side is that it is not an object of reflection, but the inner side of reflection itself. This is why Hume could never, as it were, 'catch' himself in his reflections.[31]

This inner side is also crucial to our understanding of other people, but, of course, with the difference that we cannot directly observe it except, just possibly, in certain telepathic experiences, if these are genuine. However extrapolating from our own inner world, when we look sensitively at, say, a classroom of children, we are acutely aware that we are in the presence of individuals, each one of whom has his or her own inner world. Without this sensitivity much of our social life and language and moral sense would be unintelligible.

When we consider thoughts or ideas that we share with others, there is an interesting complication. Suppose I am thinking about Pythagoras' theorem. I know that countless others, including Pythagoras himself, have had 'the same thought'. Perhaps, the sameness of the thought, from the 'outer' point of view, might be apparent from brain scans. There is, in other words, a sense in which many of us have the 'same' thought, and the thought is not a kind of private property. Similarly, except in the extraordinarily rare circumstances when I think of something really original, all my thoughts about the world, or about philosophy, are shared by many others. Ideas therefore, from one aspect, consist of things that can be held in common, and described objectively. A thought is only unique to me in terms of its 'inner' aspect, and that means, I suggest, not simply that there was an 'outer' component that happened to be in *my* head, but that there was an 'inner' aspect that was essentially unique, because it was part of the experience of an individual, conscious subject.

If this combination of inner and outer is to form part of a *materialistic* account of consciousness, it must be combined with the claim that the outer, or physical, aspect is the cause, or foundation, of the inner. Sometimes this is put in the form of a claim that consciousness is an 'epiphenomenon', rooted in the material state of the brain. This, for example, was essentially the position of T.H. Huxley. An important, contemporary exponent of a similar view is the philosopher John Searle. In his writings there is a rejection of the identity hypothesis, and a genuine sensitivity to what I have called the 'inner' side of consciousness, but he maintains what is still a (more subtle) materialist position through his insistence that all mental phenomena are *caused* by 'processes in the brain'.[32]

The first point to make in response is that if such a view is accepted, it might still be possible to adopt a form of theism, since God could have designed a universe in which human consciousness arises when a certain kind of physical complexity is present, which is then the 'cause', at least in the sense of 'immediate cause' of each act of consciousness. (There would still remain questions about the 'cause' of the physical order as a whole.) However, there are strong grounds for not accepting Searle's analysis of the situation. When one asks what one means by 'cause' in this context his response is to say that physical brain processes cause mental phenomena *in the same way* as the micro properties of matter cause, for example, 'solidity'.[33] One of the problems with this view is that it does not take into account what I have already referred to as the 'transcending' nature of human consciousness, so that even if it is plausible to claim that – in some sense – physical processes are the 'cause' of mental events, it is not plausible to claim that mental events are caused *in the same way* as effects such as solidity.

Let us explore this matter further. Reflecting on materialism, the philosopher Karl Popper wrote: 'We can only wonder that matter can thus transcend itself, by producing mind, purpose, and a world of the products of the human mind.'[34] What

Popper suggests here about transcendence leads to further comments (built upon what was written in Chapter 2) concerning the 'transcending' nature of consciousness, whether or not it is in some way based in matter. Let us suppose I am listening to an account of how my thinking is claimed to be limited, first, by the genetic structure of my brain and, second, by my cultural conditioning. We are all aware that as soon as these conditioning factors are pointed out, we can, and often do, embark on a process of 'transcending' them, if we have not done so already. If I learn that the nature and limits of the langauge I use for reflection are determined by the way in which human brains are 'prewired' (which is the view of some of those within the science of linguistics), once I am aware of this prewiring and explore its nature, I can reflect upon this conditioning influence, and react creatively to it in a way that necessarily transcends the conditions I reflect upon. If I am told that my religious views are the result of x and y, I immediately start to reconsider x and y, as well as the more general claim *that* I am conditioned by these factors. If I am told that survival, either of my species or of myself or of my genes, is the driving force of my moral convictions, I can immediately contemplate various other ultimate sources for morality, and may choose to adopt one of them. We have already noted how psychoanalyists use their own psychoanalysis as a ground for what I call a measure of 'transcendence'. In general, the claim that there are *influencing* conditions (including genetic and environmental ones) is obviously true, but that these are *totally conditioning*, in any straightforward sense, is manifestly untrue, precisely because of what I have called this 'transcending' power of mind. Mind can reflect upon and react to the conditions which are said to condition it and therefore crude forms of determinism are manifestly false.[35] Moreover, hardline materialists who support strong forms of determinism tend to beg the central issue by asking 'What is it that *causes* an allegedly free agent to choose one action rather than another?'. However, they read into the word 'cause' a materialist philosophy, which simply does not take account of the claim that with the emergence of rational intelligence, something has come into being that cannot be adequately described in terms of materialist categories. This point is of a piece with the general discussion of the difference between a *via negativa*, in which we are able to say what something is not, and a *via positiva*, or way of analogy, whereby something positive can be said. Both in attempts to describe the nature of God (especially in Chapter 5) and in attempts to describe the nature of free will, the negative approach is much easier, while any positive approach can only proceed in a cautious way, with full awareness that God and freedom, if they are realities, are not 'things', but reflections of a 'spiritual' dimension. Indeed, any positive concept of freedom is intimately linked with the concept of God, through the notion of *creativity*. This observation does not prove the reality of 'free will', but it does show that many rejections of it are based on a circular argument that effectively assumes the truth of a materialistic philosophy, often, as in 'scientism', without an awareness of the dogmatism involved. There are, of course, limitations on the transcending power of the human mind, but (Kant's arguments notwithstanding) we cannot lay down in advance what these limitations will turn out to be.

Another version of the argument to the effect that rationality, when developed, transcends the conditions which give rise to it, looks at the necessary inadeqaucy of a 'natural history' of reason. There is an illuminating parallel here with the 'natural history' of ethics. In this latter case (in a way that parallels the case of rationality), it is perfectly possible to suggest a history of how some ethical standards and social rules developed within the history of our species, as the necessary preconditions of human survival. We can even see how the interiorizing of these social rules – in terms of inner feelings of shame or guilt – can help to make these rules more effective. However, once these social rules have developed, and reflective people like Socrates consider the variety of social rules, and ask which of them, if any, are morally 'better' than others, natural history cannot begin to answer this question, since the question is partly *about* the natural history. What is sometimes called 'positive morality' (the rules and values actually in operation) must be distinguished from 'critical morality' (the moral critique of positive morality). The superficial response is simply to say that any question about which moral rule is 'morally' better is meaningless (or, more technically, that there is no such thing as 'critical morality'). However this response misses the point of my argument. The question 'which, *if any*, of these moral rules that is actually observed, is *intrinsically better?*' is meaningful, even if one takes the sceptical position that the answer is that all rules are purely relative, and that nothing is 'intrinsically better'. (Hence the crucial inclusion of the words 'if any', which allows for the meaningfulness of the sceptical reply: 'None'.) In other words, my argument is not designed to prove that there is a critical morality (although I believe that there is), but to prove that the issue of whether or not there is a critical morality is a real issue. The reflective question about morality necessarily transcends the answers provided by natural history, because even if the answer is negative, it is recognized that whether or not the answer is negative is itself a crucial issue. Putting this another way, reflective questions about the possibility of a universal (or 'natural') morality prove that the *idea* of a universal morality exists, not of course in the sense of a Platonic Idea (*eidos*), existing in some 'real' world beyond the conceptual configurations of human minds – a matter which is left open by this argument – but in the sense that human beings have, and often share, the concept of a universal standard. The parallel argument with rationality is obvious. It may be perfectly possible to give a natural history of the development of the human capacity to reason in terms of the benefits of rationality for survival, and indeed my account of the possible origins of rationality in Chapter 1 actually encouraged such an explanation. But this explanation, which may succeed (up to a point[36]) in explaining the origins of the rational capacity, *cannot* be complete, because once we reflect upon this natural history (or alleged natural history), we can immediately raise questions both about this natural history, and about the rational capacity we recognize within ourselves, even if we believe that the natural history explains its origin. Is our logic sound? Do we have an appropriate attitude to the present authorities? Is our way of evaluating general positions adequate? Do the circumstances that have led to our reasoning capacities succeed in giving adequate grounds for 'objectivity'? What kinds of 'objectivity' can we hope to achieve? Do Rorty and Co. provide sufficient reasons for their positions? All these questions necessarily transcend any suggested natural history of rationality.

This argument concerning how reflective consciousness necessarily *transcends* materialistic accounts can be put in the form of a sort of theorem. When I examine, let us say, a text, the observation of the words and the figuring out of what they mean can be called a 'first order' process; when I sit back and reflect on my reading of the text, perhaps wondering whether the author is distorting the evidence, this can be called a 'second order' process; when I sit (even further) back and reflect on what I am doing when I reflect on my act of reading, perhaps by wondering whether all my reflections are simply expressions of unconscious drives, this can be called a 'third order' process. In theory, one might then posit fourth and higher levels, but – and here comes the crunch – these alleged 'higher' levels are, in reality, bogus, because they are already included in the third level. The act of reflection on reflection already includes an awareness of the possibility of an infinite series (like that of mirror images when I stare into a mirror that faces another mirror), and itself is able to ask and to comprehend questions about the whole series. Reflection on the nature of reflection is already to ask questions that are, in a significant sense, ultimate, because the possibilities and significance of all the other levels can be taken into account.[37]

Let us return to the thought experiment in which I observe the outer aspects of my thought on a monitor, and reflect on what the relationship of the inner aspect of my thought is to the (presently observed) outer aspect. I decide to make the monitor readings take on a special formation – which I have already discovered to arise when I do difficult mathematics – and, as I start a difficult calculation I observe that the monitored activity behaves as I anticipated. Here, not only is it odd to say that the observed activity *is* the thought, it is also odd to say that the observed activity *caused* the thought, along with the observed change in brain processes. In this case it is more natural to say that my thought caused the change in brain processes. Commenting on a similar case, Searle actually admits this, but then insists that when the mental is the cause of the physical, 'the top-down causation works only because the mental events are grounded in the neuro-physiology to start with'.[38] But this use of the word 'grounded' masks the difficulties. If it means that, as a matter of evolutionary development, the mental phenomena arose out of the neuro-logical, I have no problem. If it means that, when fully developed, mental phenom-ena are simply caused by the neurological *in the same way* as in his example of solidity, this, it seems to me, amounts to begging the crucial questions. However I do not propose to defend the reverse of Searle's claim, namely that an inner event simply causes the brain processes, rather my account of the inner and outer aspects of consciousness is designed to avoid the necessity of seeing either one as prior to, or causally dependent upon, the other. As a matter of history, I might believe that human consciousness is 'built upon' and 'dependent upon' a long process of physi-cal evolution. However this belief would not need to lead to a denial of the 'transcending' power consciousness, and it would not rule out reference to a Con-sciousness present at every stage of the universe's development. Therefore, to call such an historical account 'epiphenomenal', would be like challenging theism with a paper tiger. Now we have a fuzzy edge between what some would call a 'materi-alistic' account, and philosophies that are open to some forms of monism or theism.

Impressed by the phenomenon of consciousness, some philosophers have sug-gested that there is an element of consciousness in all matter, even at its most primitive level, a kind of 'panpsychism'. On this issue I prefer to be agnostic, for, as suggested above, there is also strong case for seeing various 'thresholds' emerge within evolution, when genuinely new aspects of the universe are manifest, and it may be that both the first intimations of consciousness and the full blown-consciousness that includes self-consciousness are things that involve a sort of quantum leap. If this is the case, even on a theistic view, there could be an important truth in the materialistic account, for it might be that, for human beings, consciousness could only *emerge* in the context of an animal *body* that, along with a thinking apparatus, has also the feelings and passions and drives that go along with being an animal organism. It is partly for this reason that I hesitate to adopt the view defended by the philosopher Popper and the neuroscientist Eccles in their joint book *The Self and its Brain*. Eccles claims to have an empirical, scientific basis for his defence of a 'radical dualist-interactionist' theory of the brain and the self-conscious mind.[39] My hesitation arises out of Eccles' insistence that 'In general terms there are two theories about the relationship of mental events to neural events', namely materialist ones (that make the mental *subsidiary* to the physical, and which *include* identity theories), and dualist-interactionist explanations (like his own).[40] The view that I am moving towards does not fit comfortably into either of Eccles' 'two [types of] theories'. Further, Eccles argues that 'there are at certain *sites* [emphasis added] of the cerebral hemisphere (the liaison areas) effective interactions with the self-conscious mind ...'[41] and this raises similar problems to that of the Cartesian vainly trying to find a (single) site for interaction, although Eccles does attempt some kind of explanation in terms of quantum mechanics. Maybe a case can be made for a 'dualist-interactionist' theory like that of Eccles, but such a theory is not essential in order to have a non-materialist view of consciousness.

Let us suppose that in our search for an adequate explanation of consciousness we are unhappy about materialistic accounts of the identity kind, and also of epiphenomenal accounts that simply see the neurological as the basis or cause of consciousness, because this still does not give an adequate account of the inner side and too easily assumes the causation of the mental by the physical. Let us also suppose that we are nervous about dualistic accounts, even of the kind proposed by Popper and Eccles, since we suspect that consciousness, at least in human form, *emerged* out of a certain kind of complexity, during the course of evolution. Where does this leave us?

The next paragraphs should not be dignified as a new 'theory' of consciousness, since a 'theory' needs to bring many things together in a more organized way. (Also, in the case of scientific theories, there needs to be predictive value.) It describes an approach to the central issues that is 'non-reductive', in that there is no claim that the 'outer' or physical side of consciousness will be able, in time, fully to explain consciousness. At the same time, it is not Cartesian, because it is suggested that in the case of human consciousness, the phenomenon emerged during the evolutionary process as a result of a certain type of complexity in the structure of the brain. It is certainly not 'materialist' in, say, Hobbes' sense, but for the moment we can leave open the possibility that it may be 'materialist' in some other ways. A lot will depend here on how much we think that the methodologies and assumptions of natural science are open to significant change.

In this search for a more adequate explanation of consciousness, help, I suggest, comes from recent discussions of what is often called 'the anthropic principle'. The principle is formulated in various ways: in what is called the 'weak' form it simply asserts that the universe has within it, from the beginning, the building blocks that can lead to the emergence of consciousness; in what is sometimes called the 'strong' form the principle states that 'the universe must have those properties which allow life to develop within it at some stage in its history'.[42] On first hearing of this recent interest in the anthropic principle one might well ask, 'But what is new, for surely nothing could be more obvious than that conscious life *has* arisen in the universe?' The appropriate response to this question is often overlooked. From the perspective of those who took a religious view of the matter (including a number of scientists), so long as the emergence of consciousness was seen as some kind of *miracle*, the result of an *external* creator, who chose to make human beings as a purely voluntary act, then there was no reason to look for anything *within* the physical universe that could explain human consciousness, freedom, creativity and love. The last thing I intend is to eliminate God from the creative work of our species, but instead of seeing this work as something that was, as it were, *imposed* on the physical universe, by introducing purely alien categories like thought into it, I propose, like many others, to see God's creative work as continuously working within the very structure of the universe. At the same time as this new approach has emerged within religious thinking, secular thinking, as we have seen, is also searching for some adequate explanation of consciousness that goes beyond the suggestions of materialists such as Hobbes.

It is worth pointing out that an understanding of the anthropic principle has similar implications for the emergence of living things. Let us suppose that in the next few years scientists are able to produce living beings (in the sense of biological, self-reproducing organisms) from inanimate materials – this ought not to produce shock waves in the religious community. If 'life' is produced in this way, an eventuality about which I am purely agnostic, it may in fact produce shock waves because so many people are still wedded to the view that both life in general, and consciousness in particular, must be manifestations of a miraculous *intervention* into the order of nature. But the most fundamental questions do not concern the steps that lead from atoms to life and then to consciousness (important as these questions are), but to how it is that nature has within itself, as it were, the potentiality to produce both life and consciousness. The metaphysical and religious questions, once again, are not scientific questions about how parts of the universe relate to each other, but questions about the processes and capacities of nature as a whole.

If we are to avoid assumptions about the truth of theism or the inadequacy of materialism, then our commitment to the anthropic principle needs to be stated with care. In its weak form it is inescapable, but the strong form goes beyond what we can observe, and makes an assumption that many materialists would not accept. *If* the strong form is accepted, then we can say that from the beginning, or from all eternity (if the physical universe is eternal), the universe has had the forces within it that were bound to lead to consciousness. These forces might then be referred to as Consciousness. For theists, this Consciousness has included an active awareness of the universe throughout its history; for materialists (if they will allow this use of the capital letter), it refers to an extraordinary potentiality, waiting for the occasion, which inevitably will come, to be manifested in actual form, at the very least in us.[43]

For those who feel that acceptance of the anthropic principle in its strong form is a step too far for a cautious rationalism, there is what John Polkinghorne describes as a 'moderate anthropic principle' which 'notes the contingent fruitfulness of the universe as being a fact of interest calling for an explanation', and this can be supported by a series of scientific claims about the narrowness of the conditions which allow for the development of our species.[44] In the rest of this section I propose to accept a combination of the weak and the moderate forms as certain, and to bear in mind the possibility of the strong form, without being committed to it at this stage of the argument.

What I am now suggesting is that not only do we have to take account of an 'inner' as well as an 'outer' side of consciousness, the 'inner' side can be seen actually at work in the very process of scientific thinking. We come to understand the universe (up to a point) by theorizing about it through inner acts of imagination and reflection. Here we interact with the universe, not as minds that have no intimate relationship with it, but as individual centres of consciousness that are products of the universe, and part of it. Moreover, the inner reflection ponders the 'outer' aspects of consciousness and can see the 'inner' and 'outer' accounts of thought not as rivals but as complementary. Both are needed in any adequate account of what a person is. As already suggested, the situation parallels seeing light as both wave and particle. One day a fuller account may emerge, but, as in the case of light, it will have to be one that allows for the insights of both. As we near this point, the approach that I am suggesting may be dignified with the word 'theory'.

What emerges is that, step by step, there is a tendency for more sophisticated materialists to take the sting out of materialism. The abandonment of matter for laws of motion was one such step, the introduction of 'fields' of influence, along with the capacity for 'material' entities to influence other entities at a distance was another. (It is instructive to recall the furious opposition among some scientists to the very concept of action 'at a distance'. However, this ability to influence at a distance is now a feature not only of gravitational and other field theories, but also, in a different form, of quantum mechanics in what is known as the Einstein-Podolsky-Rosen effect: 'Once two quantum entities have interacted with each other, the one retains a power to influence the other, however far apart they may subsequently separate.'[45]) More subtle accounts of consciousness provide yet another step in this process, especially when these accounts are dissociated from determinism as, for example, in the writings of Steven Rose.[46] Another step occurs in discussions of the relationship of computers to human minds, and the realization that if computers actually become the entities that some scientists envisage, the significant question will not be 'are humans really computers?', but 'are some computers really persons?'. In other words, recent work with artificial intelligence has tended to increase our respect for and amazement at the human mind, and *if* something like it could be simulated, to call this new thing that emerges a 'machine', akin to what machines have normally been, would be to beg all the crucial questions. The result of all this is that when we hear a scientist or a philosopher making a statement like 'mental events are physical events' (for example, in the work of Donald Davidson), it is impossible to evaluate the significance of this, and how much, if at all, there is a denial of the claims made by liberal theology, without examining how the word 'physical' is used, and what assumptions are read into this usage.

An appreciation of what I have here called mind's 'transcending' power, not only throws further doubt on both the identity hypothesis and any theory of a purely materialistic cause of thought, it also suggests that any account of a precise 'location' of thought in one particular place is mistaken. A location would suggest that I could not only know that a thought is actually 'there' (in a certain area of my brain), but that I could know that my thought *that* my thought is 'there' is 'here' ' (in another part of my brain). Then, in turn (given the transcending nature of thought), my thought that this is so (a kind of 'third order' thought) would have to be in yet another location, and so on indefinitely, until eventually one might run out of places in the brain. But there is no need to get sucked into this game of chasing around in the brain for the place where the thought of the thought of the thought (and so on) is to be found. This is another case of where we must avoid a 'bogus dichotomy' in which we are asked to choose one of two narrowly defined options, in this case, between the view that a thought is located in one special place and that it is totally independent of any physical object in space. Whereas the brain and the 'outer' aspects of thought (that can be monitored), have physical locations, pointing to any particular space and saying 'there is the mind' or 'there is that thought' is a mistake. On the other hand, to deny that the brain has a vital function in consciousness seems equally absurd. A third, and more hopeful, approach is to suggest that mind is analogous to (or perhaps a special case of) a *field* comprising patterns of electromagnetic energy. Such a field could then be said to be 'centred' on the brain, at least in this physical life. Thus thought can be said to have a special relationship to something in space, but need not have an exact spatial location.

Throughout this section, part of my argument has been based on the claim that 'materialism', in its modern dress, is rarely the narrowly conceived view that its critics imagine. A similar argument applies to the understanding of 'science', which is also a concept that has been evolving. Congruously, Roger Penrose denies that science, as presently constituted, *can* comprehend the phenomenon of consciousness (in humans or other animals), because there is a 'missing ingredient'; but instead of concluding that science will never be adequate, he suggests that (as often in the past) we are moving towards a 'new' and 'expanded' kind of science in which a full understanding of consciousness may be forthcoming.[47] If this is so, the word 'materialist' will be given a broader meaning in which there may not be an inevitable conflict with theism.

Yet another, although highly controversial, way in which science may be due for a reassessment of its nature arises from new developments in the area of parapsychology. The majority of scientists used to reject all of this, largely on the grounds that the alleged findings were not *repeatable*, and therefore not a proper object of scientific work. Also, at least some sceptics rejected the *possibility* of paranormal phenomena in principle because they were thought to endanger the very activity of scientific work, especially in terms of the detached observer.[48] Recent claims by scientists in this field to be able to generate repeatable experiments, along with a new assessment of what it means to be 'detached' have opened up the possibility that just as hypnotism changed from being seen as make-believe to being incorporated into orthodox science during the nineteenth century,[49] so some parts of the paranormal field may become incorporated into a broader view of what science is.[50] If this happens, a range of mental phenomena that fit very uneasily with old-fashioned materialism will become much more widely accepted.

Levels of Explanation

The suggestion that language about the inner and outer aspects of consciousness should be seen as giving complementary rather than rival accounts of what is going on can be strengthened by a consideration of different 'levels' of explanation.

Let us suppose I am walking down a street, casually looking at the shop windows, but primarily concentrating on a philosophical problem. One description of this event, which I shall refer to as an example of level one, is concerned with what is going on in the languages of physics, chemistry and biology. This level describes the neurological processes going on in my brain and, 'behind' this, the movement of the atoms and subatomic particles that are involved. A full account, at this level, would be almost if not literally infinite, since the material descriptions of what is going on in my brain need to be linked with a physical description of the rest of my body, and also of the environment in which I am walking – which stretches, ultimately, to the whole universe. The physical account, in other words, would be part of a huge description in terms of elementary particles, or still more ultimate 'strings', in constant motion and interaction. A second level, which concentrates on my experience as a walker, is in terms of the sensations that are received through the five senses. If the description at this level were to cover the sensations of all conscious beings, animal as well as human, then there is, once again, a quite enormous degree of complexity, and we would have to include sensations received by more than five senses – for example, sensations received by bats and dolphins in response to sonic signals. If I am considering only my physical sensations, the description is much more contained, but still complex enough. A third level would consider the train of thoughts that are going on in my mind (or – if we enlarge the context – in all the minds that are in the universe). A fourth level would consider my life story, and the way in which my present walk and sensations and thoughts fit into a narrative that could be written up as a biography (or – if we enlarge the context – a biographical account of the life stories of all the self-conscious beings in the universe). We can imagine other 'levels' of description – involving, for example, the life of institutions or communities – but let us stay with the four I have outlined. It should be stressed that, for the ordinary person, all of these levels are mutually compatible. To use the language, and to concentrate on the issues raised by any one of them, does not involve having to deny the legitimacy and usefulness of any of the others.

It would be a caricature of materialism to say that it is committed to denying the existence of the levels beyond the first, but – in its more robust form – materialism is committed to the belief that the other levels are 'reducible' to the first. But what does this term 'reducible' mean? If it means simply that without the material level the other levels I have listed[51] would not exist, this might be admitted by monists and theists with no sense of there being any challenge to their positions. If – as is more likely – it means that the further levels are ultimately to be identified with complex descriptions on the first level, as in the 'identity hypothesis' discussed earlier, then the argument presented in this chapter has shown why this claim can be challenged. For example, consider the level two experience of seeing a patch of red colour, perhaps as I look at a rose in a flower-shop window. References to the way in which the experience of colour is related to, or even produced by, the physical properties of a certain wavelength of light, the nature of my retina, the properties of the rose's surface, and so on, do not succeed in giving us an idea of the *sensation* of red. To say that the red sensation (as opposed to the red 'colour') *is* the wavelength, etc., is a category mistake which parallels the category mistake of saying that my thoughts *are* the neurological events that can be monitored. Sensitive to this problem, the more sophisticated materialist changes tack. 'Reducible' does not refer to the kind of reducibility claimed by the identity hypothesis, since it is appreciated that just as, in general, the whole is more than the sum of the parts, complex organisms like brains produce 'epiphenoma' that require new levels of description. However, so the more sophisticated materialist continues, these further levels are 'caused' by, or 'ultimately explained' by the first level.

The position I have argued for accepts that this kind of materialism reflects a *possible*, rational position, but that it is by no means the only candidate for rationality. Not only are other positions viable, the materialist position, thus described, presents significant problems. In the case of the 'causation' claim, this may be a plausible one with respect to the second level, but already by the third level (when we come to conscious reflection) the phenomenon of what I have called the 'transcending' nature of thought raises additional difficulties for all materialistic claims about causation. More generally, the more we appreciate how the individual event, even at the subatomic level, is interlinked with the way in which the whole universe functions, materialism is forced, more and more, away from explanations in terms of this or that set of events at the material level, towards an understanding of the web of relationships that connect all things. To call all these *relationships* aspects of 'matter' is highly misleading.

This concludes my basic critique of materialism. In view of the claim that the viability of a general position depends, rationally, on its overall internal and external coherence, the debate is not concluded, because the viability of alternatives (that is, monistic or theistic philosophies) cannot be properly judged until they are examined in terms of this twin criterion. This, in turn, will affect the rationality of opting for a materialist philosophy. However, the general thrust of the critique should now be clear. In its more extreme forms, I do not think that materialism is a rational option. As materialist philosophies become more and more sensitive to the issues I have raised, it becomes less and less clear that they have to be radical alternatives to all forms of monism or theism. In general, however, I prefer not to opt for materialism, because if the term is not to become exceedingly vague, it does imply the *priority* of physicalist accounts of what goes on to any other. Even within the context of a scientific debate this may lead to problems, for example, with the search for an adequate explanation of the direction that evolution has taken, but when materialist assumptions are systematically applied to areas like art or ethics, or religion, then the problems multiply.

Notes and References

1   See, for example, Rose, Steven (1997), *Lifelines*, London: Penguin Press, where reductionism is criticized.

2   In his *Economic and Philosophical Manuscripts* Marx writes 'alienated labor takes away the object of production from man, it also takes away his *species life*, his real objectivity as a species-being…' (original emphasis). See Fromm, Erich (1961), *Marx's Concept of Man* (with Marx's *Economic and Philosophical Manuscripts* trans, T.B. Bottomore) New York: Ungar, p. 102.

3   *Telos* is the Greek word for 'end' or 'purpose', and a 'teleology' is a system that attempts to explain things in terms of purpose. The purpose does not have to be that of an individual consciousness, like that of the Christian God, but can be something that is integral to a system, as in Aristotle's concept of nature. Sometimes contemporary scientists use a teleological concept, but in a very different way. When speaking as scientists they don't refer to what might be called an *external* teleology but rather to an *internal* teleology – for example, when the heart is said to have a purpose or function within the context of the human body.

4   I shall argue that theism does make a valuable contribution to ethics, but it is not its only possible foundation.

5   Hobbes, T., Introduction to *Leviathan*.

6   Ibid., ch. 3.

7   Ibid., ch. 12.

8   Dawkins, R. (1976), *The Selfish Gene*, Oxford: Oxford University Press, pp. 3 and 215.

9   Dawkins, R. (1995), *River out of Eden*, London: Phoenix, p. 155.

10 Dawkins, *The Selfish Gene*, pp. 3 and 207. In the second of these references Dawkins is writing of 'the survival value of the god meme in the meme pool'. A 'meme' is described as a unit of cultural transmission.

11 Dawkins, *River out of Eden*, p. 113.

12 My position here could easily be misunderstood. When Francis Bacon totally rejected any idea of 'final causality' in science, we do not necessarily have to follow him, for his idea of 'efficient causality', which he alone accepted, may be too narrow to account for some of the more complex explanations that contemporary scientists use. In particular, the influence of fields of different kinds may indicate the need to reintroduce something akin to the old idea of 'final cause'. There is also, I shall try to show, a case for seeing a theological principle as required for the *general* operation of evolution. However, the introduction of divine interventions to explain particular events within nature is quite another matter, and it is here that I find common cause with Dawkins.

13 There is a further complication because the 'boundaries' of science are not universally agreed.

14 Ockham did not state the principle in this form, but it is a popular phrasing of what can legitimately be seen as an implication of his principle.

15 Harris, E.E. (1992), *Cosmos and Theos*, New Jersey: Humanities Press, p. xiii.

16 Even without introducing the notion of human freedom, the future is not completely predictable because of the principle of uncertainty described in modern physics. The longer the view taken, the more the details are unpredictable in principle, but the general pattern or shape of the universe is predictable.

17 Whitehead, A.N. (1933), *Adventures of Ideas*, Cambridge: Cambridge University Press, p. 52.

18 Houston, G. (1995), *The New Red Book of Gestalt*, London: Gaie Houston, rev. edn p. 15.

19   Snell, B. (1953), *The Discovery of Mind*, trans. T.G. Rosenmeyer (1976), Oxford: Blackwell; Jaynes, J. (1982), *The Origin of Consciousness in the Breakdown of the Bicameral Mind*, New York: Penguin.

20   Shear, J., ed. (1997), *Explaining Consciousness – The 'Hard Problem'*, Cambridge, Mass.: MIT Press.

21   Hardcastle, Valerie G., 'The Why of Consciousness: A Non-issue for Materialists', in ibid., pp. 61–2.

22   Chalmers, D.J., 'Facing up to the Problem of Consciousness' in Ibid., pp. 13 and 18.

23   Ryle, G. (1949), *The Concept of Mind*, London: Hutchinson's University Library, e.g. pp. 15–16.

24   There is some counterpart to this in Spinoza's claim that the one order of reality can equally be described in terms of 'extension' or of 'idea' (*Ethics*, part 2, Prop. VII), but my reasons are different from those of Spinoza.

25   Ryle, *The Concept of Mind* p. 13.

26   Murdoch, I. (1970), 'The Idea of Perfection' in *The Sovereignty of Good*, London: Routledge and Kegan Paul, pp. 17 ff.

27   The experience may not have been at all like 'hearing' the work, bar by bar, seriatim, but a vision of the structure of the whole. Hence the word 'seeing' may be as appropriate as 'hearing'.

28   Ryle denied that he was a behaviourist, but some of his statements certainly come close to affirming the doctrine. See *The Concept of Mind*, pp. 327 ff.

29   Ibid., p. 249, cf. pp. 251, 256, 265, 268–9.

30   See Skinner, B.F. (1953), *Science and Human Behaviour*, New York: The Free Press, pp. 17–18.

31   Hume, D., *A Treatise of Human Nature*, Book 1, part 4, section 6.

32   Searle, J. (1989), *Mind, Brains and Science*, London: Penguin, p. 18.

33   'Just as the liquidity of the water is caused by the behaviour of elements at the micro-level, and yet at the same time it is a feature realised in the system of micro-elements, so in exactly that sense of "caused by" and "realised in" mental phenomena are caused by processes going on in the brain at the neuronal or modular level, and at the same time they are realised in the very system that consists of neurons'. Ibid., p. 22.

34   Popper, K.R. and Eccles, J.C. (1977), *The Self and its Brain*, New York: New York: Springer International, p. 11.

35   It is false that all human thought and action can be explained, even in principle, *in the way* that mechanical 'things' might be. There are more subtle forms of determinism that cannot so easily be dismissed. However, not only do these run into problems with the precise definition of 'determinism', many of them do not challenge the claim that humans have a significant freedom. An analysis of 'compatibility' theories would go beyond the scope of this book.

36   The issue of the total adequacy of any Darwinian or quasi-Darwinian explanation of the *origins* of rationality arises in the same way as in the parallel case of consciousness. It is one thing to explain the evolutionary advantage of each step in a process, it is another thing to explain how nature has within it the capacity to bring forth the whole process.

37   The point can be put in another way. We are familiar with series that can go to infinity, like '2, 4, 8, 16 …'. Such series not only have items within the series (in this case the numbers), but commas, or some other indication of the gaps between the items, and these commas represent some rule by which the next item is generated – in this case – a rule of doubling. At first sight we could schematize the series of reflections on the text as 't, rt, rrt, etc.' (where 't' stands for observation of the text and 'r' for reflection on the letter that follows). However, this representation overlooks the fact that at the third

stage (here signified by 'rrt'), reflection is *about* the 'comma' (because, in the case of this series, the generation of the next level is precisely reflection on the earlier level), so that the comma itself becomes the next item in the series. This means that the r and the comma become interchangeable, so that the series becomes a string of r's or of commas. Therefore the series disappears at the third step. There may be a parallel in the series of moves that are required for one person to know that another has received a message. When I receive a reply I know that my message got through, but I may have to send another message so that they know that I know. Then, perhaps another message is needed so that I know that they know that I know that the message is received. This series could go on for ever, but in fact it soon becomes pointless, because *intelligence* realizes that what is needed is simply 'mutual knowledge' that the original message is received, and this is achieved as soon as I know that they know that I have received the first reply – which is, once again, a *third* level of reflection.

38 *Mind, Brains and Science*, p. 93.
39 Popper and Eccles, *The Self and its Brain*. See also Eccles, J.C. (1979), *The Human Mystery*, New York: Springer International, pp. 226 ff.
40 Eccles, J.C. (1987), 'The Effects of Silent Thinking on the Cerebral Cortex' in *The Brain-Mind Problem*, ed. B. Gulyas, Maastricht: Leuven University Press, p. 44.
41 Popper and Eccles, *The Self and its Brain*, p. 359.
42 See Harris, E.E. (1991), *Cosmos and Anthropos*, New Jersey: The Humanities Press. Also Barrow J.D. and Tipler, F.J. (1988), *The Anthropic Cosmological Principle*, rev. edn, Oxford: Oxford University Press, ch. 1.
43 For different uses of the term 'miracle', see Langford, M.J. (1981), *Providence*, London: SCM Press, pp. 17–24.
44 Polkinghorne J. (1991), *Reason and Reality*, London: SPCK, pp. 77–8. A similar suggestion is made by Dorothy Emmet. While avoiding commitment to the strong form of the principle she advocates a 'strengthening' of the weak form in order to emphasize the extent to which we live in 'an enabling universe'. Emmet, D. (1996), *Philosophers and Friends*, Basingstoke: Macmillan, p. 119.
45 Polkinghorne, J., *Reason and Reality*, p. 94.
46 See Rose, *Lifelines*, ch. 1.
47 Penrose, R. (1995), *Shadows of the Mind*, London: Vintage, pp. 7, 12, 430.
48 See, for example, Hansel, C.E.M. (1966), *ESP: a Scientific Evaluation*, New York: Scribner, in which it is systematically assumed that a non-paranormal explanation for phenomena *must* be found.
49 The Austrian physician Franz Mesmer, 1734–1815, was the principal forerunner of hypnotic techniques in medicine but was branded a quack by the contemporary establishment. With respect to some of his ideas this attribution was not without foundation, but with hindsight it is clear that prejudice prevented an appreciation of a genuine discovery.
50 See especially Sheldrake, R. (1994), *Seven Experiments that Could Change the World*, London: Fourth Estate; and Radin, Dean, (1998), *The Conscious Universe*, San Francisco: Harper Collins.
51 This does not necessarily mean all the levels, for there could be spiritual (angelic) levels of reality that in no way depended on the material.

Chapter 4

Religious Experience and Monism

Monism

Monism (from the Greek *monos*, meaning 'alone' or 'solitary') can be considered as a philosophical approach to reality, but most of its exponents have thought of it in religious terms. Others, who have held to what most would class as monistic systems, have not *expounded* a system at all; rather, they have been people whose religious outlook is described, from outside, as monistic. Because of this generally religious context for monism, the argument of this book needs to take a new turn. Up to now the stress has been on the role of reason reflecting upon 'ordinary' human experience, such as the phenomenon of consciousness. We now have to look at the controversial field of religious experience, since without it neither monism nor theism can be understood, except in exceedingly vague and general ways. In making this switch we are not abandoning a rational approach, but it is a rational approach that now includes reflection on the data of religious experience. There will be no claims based upon sheer authority, and no claims about some kind of 'direct' knowledge which does not need to be questioned and analysed. Perhaps, as suggested earlier, some people do have what could be called direct or intuitive knowledge, but I am not proposing to rely on any such claim.

Many philosophers and theologians have made a distinction between 'natural theology', referring to arguments that have no direct reference to religious experience, and 'revealed theology', based on appeals to such experience. Aquinas, for example, held that natural reason could tell us that there was a God who was good, but it was only by revelation that we knew he was a Trinity. As the last paragraph will have indicated, the distinction is not a sharp one since both forms of theology, when properly pursued, use rational methods. If the line that divides ordinary and religious experience is not always sharp, then neither is there a sharp line dividing the two kinds of theology.

One consequence of this continuing, rational approach is that when we reflect on religious experience we are reflecting on it from an 'outer' perspective. This point must be expressed carefully for, of course, the whole point of religious experience is that the people who have it experience it in an 'inner' way. However, when we make *generalizations* about religious experience, especially that of others, we are looking at it from the outside. It is an inescapable *fact* that many kinds of people, in all kinds of cultures, have had psychological experiences that have been described both by them and by those outside the experiences as 'religious'. Anthropologists, sociologists and psychologists, both religious and non-religious, are among those who study such psychological experiences in an objective way. The controversial questions concern not their 'reality' (meaning simply the actual occurrence of these experiences), but their interpretation. Are they intimations of a divine reality, or are they the products purely and simply of the unconscious mind, or are they the result of low oxygen levels, produced perhaps by drugs or accident or the deliberate cultivation of certain bodily states, and so on? These questions are all open, at least in part, to rational inquiry. Furthermore, the question must be raised concerning how far, in this area, it is legitimate to make any distinction between experience and interpretation, an issue that will be considered later in this chapter.

In order for any useful generalizations in this field to be made, one of the claims that has to be investigated is that, despite a host of individual variations, certain common *patterns* can be found within the experiences classed as religious. This is a claim that is specially stressed in some of the studies of experiences described as 'mystical'. As one puts it: 'The more one tries to explore the writings of the mystics, the deeper one tries to delve into their meaning and significance, the more one finds a most impressive basic unanimity.'[1] As we shall soon see, this view of mystical experience has been sharply criticized, and in my discussion of this matter I shall suggest that many critics have gone too far, but the issue is one that cannot be decided only by reading 'secondary' material, such as this book. There is much to be said for the serious inquirer not only reading introductory books on religious experience but, better still, actually delving into some primary sources in this vast field.[2]

Putting aside a consideration of the sceptical response (concerning alleged patterns or unities in religious experience) until later, here are three suggested generalizations that may be helpul for the argument that is to be developed both in this chapter and in the following one on theism.

1   Some experiences are described as a contact with a 'wholly other', in which one feels (what can be described as) a sense of the 'numinous', the 'awe-inspiring', the 'fascinating'. Otto claimed that there was a *cognitive* component to this kind of experience and I shall comment on this matter later.[3]

2   Many experiences report a *union* or *unity* with either the whole universe (universal or 'cosmic' consciousness), or with what is believed to be God, or the Great Spirit. These experiences are described in a number of ways, including (a) a sense of being one with the whole of nature, (b) a sense of literal absorption into the being of a greater reality, or (c) being in a loving and intimate relationship with a greater reality, while remaining, in some degree, separate. All three fall within the range of what is often called 'mysticism', a term which has come to refer to an overpowering sense of unity: (a) is the language of nature mysticism, (b) of monism, and (c) of theism. R.C. Zaehner, in a classic study of mysticism, also makes a threefold division, although of a rather different sort.[4]

3   Many of these experiences include a sense of the smallness, or unworthiness, or sinfulness of the I, in the presence of the greater being.[5]

There are other ways of describing and of classifying different kinds of religious experience. Richard Swinburne, for example, divides the field into five kinds.[6] The particular classification I am using does not claim to be exhaustive or definitive, merely useful for the purposes of the subsequent argument. The three aspects of religious experience I have stressed may exist separately, or combined in various ways, and all of them admit of innumerable variations. The first two might be thought to be contradictory, but in practice when there is a sense of the 'wholly other', this may be a prelude to an experience of union in which the 'otherness' experienced comes to be viewed as other because of human sin, or a false dualism, or error, or illusion, which when overcome leads to an 'enlightened' experience in which there is a profound union. For the rational inquirer these generalizations raise a number of obvious questions, in addition to the overriding one concerning whether they represent a contact with 'true reality', as those who experience them usually suggest. For example, do very similar, or perhaps identical experiences underlie both monism and theism? Do the experiences tend to have certain cultural determinants which, while not wholly accounting for their content, account for the form in which they occur, and therefore, to a degree, whether they are seen in monistic or theistic terms? Are 'out-of-the-body experiences' and 'near-death experiences', which are often reported by people who do not see them as necessarily religious, of the same genre as 'religious experience'?

Taken together, the foregoing questions demonstrate the difficulty of defining exactly what should count as a 'religious experience'. If one describes them as 'an overpowering sense of being in the presence of another', the use of the word 'another' begs many questions, and may be unfair to monistic interpretations. If one describes them as involving a sense of the 'numinous', then this assumes that there is a special kind of religious 'fear' that binds all these experiences together, and this may rule out many experiences that ought to be included. Further, one can be religious without having ever had a 'religious experience', and one can be an atheist, and have had, and even claimed to have had, 'religious experiences'. I see no easy solution to this problem of definition and in consequence, as a starting-point, I shall include any experience that is regarded by the person having it as *significant* for their evaluation of questions about how to live, and what really matters.

The Content and Interpretation of Religious Experience

In order to make any rational assessment of these experiences, an important step must now be taken regarding the relationship of the content of the experiences and their interpretation. It is tempting to make a sharp division between the *content* of all the different experiences and their *interpretation*, but this division begs too many questions. Prior to the discussion of the sceptical position we should note that in many cases the content, as described, cannot adequately be expressed purely in terms of feelings. Alongside the feelings of awe and wonder there is often found the claim that words are heard and truth is imparted. For example, the content of some of Hildegard of Bingen's most powerful visions are expressed in this way. In such cases it is possible to admit the genuineness of an experience, and to believe that truth is disclosed, without being committed to the view that the actual words, as described, *are the essential content*. Evidence for this suggestion can be found in Hildegard herself, who when referring to angels (who are often the alleged intermediaries in revelation) contrasts their language, which is that of singing praise, to the rational language of humans.[7] (Also, it is hard to treat Hildegard's long statements of what were alleged to be divine *words* with the same seriousness as the images that she describes as seeing, especially when these words reproduce contemporary views of, for example, the pollution of women after childbirth, and the explanation of why stunted children are born.[8]) This suggests that the highest forms of contemplation transcend the limits of human language. In general, I must admit to considerable scepticism with regard to any verbal account of revelation, a scepticism that is grounded in part on the fact that the nature of the alleged content is rarely, if ever, clearly expressible in words, and in part on the observation that people who make specific claims about the content of revelatory experiences tend to make contradictory assertions about what has been revealed. It is logically possible that one set of consistent claims is the result of actual revelation, but my own view is that such specific claims are generally to be treated as part of the individual's contribution to an underlying experience. (I am not making the dogmatic claim that words could *never* be part of the content of a revelation.) In the case of the revelations that lie behind sacred scriptures there has long been debate about whether what was revealed were the 'words', or some vision of reality that the prophet or other recipient then put into their own words. When 'fundamentalism' is taken to mean belief in the 'verbal inspiration' of a sacred text, it is interesting to note here a tradition that has rejected this form of inspiration, claiming instead that God typically works through human beings in a way that respects their freedom and allows for their own, fallible interpretation of what they experience in some kind of vision. This, for example, was the view of the Cambridge Platonist, John Smith, in the 1650s, who supported his non-verbal account of revelation by reference to earlier rabbinical accounts of inspiration. The higher forms of prophecy, he claimed, made use of the human intellect and, further, 'it seems most agreeable' to the nature of prophecy that 'those words and phrases' in which the visions were expressed 'should be the prophet's own'.[9]

The rejection of verbal inspiration with respect to religious scriptures has many important consequences for religion, but for the present let us return to the more general issue of the relationship of content to interpretation in religious experience. Seeing the underlying content of all religious experience as feeling alone does not match the complexity of many of the accounts, and in the light of this a threefold classification can be suggested in which we distinguish, first, powerful feelings, second, a sense of 'presence' and, third, an interpretation. The third element, interpretation, is provided by the receiver, but often in ways they do not realize so that when they report actual words or actual doctrines they are not being dishonest. From the receiver's point of view the overall experience was a unity, but reflection can strongly suggest where individual and cultural elements have 'shaped' what is reported. This position cannot be proved, but it helps to make sense of the diversity of claims.

In a classical study of 'cosmic consciousness', Maurice Bucke claimed that in all cases the recipient knew that 'the Cosmos is not dead matter but a living Presence'.[10] What then is this 'presence' that is neither pure feeling nor interpretation, and provides (if my suggestion is warranted) a special kind of content to religious experiences? Once again I suggest that the reader look at some of the classical accounts of religious experience. Simply to write about them represents a *double* externalization. The experience itself is crucially 'inner', the account provided by the receiver is already to a degree an 'outer' one, and my generalizations are reflections on this outer account. It should at least be possible to move from my (third-hand) generalizations to reading some primary sources (which are second-hand accounts). Then the possibility could be entertained of actually trying some meditation techniques, especially those that do not necessitate prior acts of faith. Then it might be that first-hand experience arises. I stress the words 'it might be' since in first-hand experience there is often a sense of 'givenness', or of 'grace' breaking into one's life, as if from an initiative that does not come from within. Nevertheless, there is a good case for a 'taste and see' approach and this does not have to mean that one must make religious assumptions. I accept that materialist accounts of these experiences are perfectly possible, and (in the sense I have described earlier) can be 'rational'. (Shortly before his death the positivist philosopher A.J. Ayer described an extraordinary 'near-death' experience which he interpreted in naturalistic terms.) At the same time, *many* materialist accounts are *not* rational, precisely because there has been no serious attempt to assess the data that is available. A consistent theme of this book is that caricatures of religion frequently accompany the rejection of religion, and some of these caricatures are based on a lack of acquaintance with the nature of religious experience.

Fortunately there are some fairly common human experiences which can, up to a point, illuminate what I mean by 'presence', and may provide intimations of it. In typical cases, these experiences may not indicate the presence of a spiritual reality, but they include a sense of 'awareness' that it is often hard to express in words, and which illuminates the way in which we see our lives and the world around us.

First, when we are in a poetic mood (and surely many of us have had a shot at writing poetry), very often we have a sense of something we want to communicate. The content may include an emotion, like nostalgia, but very often it is more than that. We have a vague sense of a way of seeing things that adds to our *understanding*. We find it hard, or impossible, to express this in ordinary prose, so we resort to a kind of indirect rendering through the language of poetry. We try to express ourselves, or to evoke a response, that parallels our experience. More importantly, when we read the great poetry of others, we find that our understandings are enriched. In general, although there are important differences between mystical experience and what would normally be classed as 'poetic experience',[11] there can be a significant intimation of a reality that is beyond the reach of ordinary prose, an intimation that involves more than feelings. Music is another example. Again, there is emotion, often expressed by the composer and the performer and felt by the listener, but there is more. In this case language is never able adequately to express what is communicated in great music through the vast complexity of the structure. How many people (of those who are familiar with classical music) can listen attentively to, say, the slow movements of Beethoven's *Quartet in A Minor* or Schubert's *Death and the Maiden* quartet, without finding a new sense of awareness? For some this can happen just through the score, even without an outward listening. Further, while the score and the complexity provide a common, repeatable content, each individual performance, like each individual experience of the numinous, has a certain uniqueness and individuality. Karl Barth, in the context of a tribute to Mozart, gives us one clue to the illuminating power of music:

> There is in his music no light that does not also know shadow, no joy that does not include pain, but also no terror, anger, or complaint that peace does not accompany either closely or at a distance ... Those who hear it aright ... *understand* [emphasis added] themselves as the people they are ... as those who have fallen victim to death but who still live, and they feel themselves summoned to freedom.[12]

Other art forms could also be described in their 'revelatory' modes. Yet another, and perhaps surprising, example is provided by humour. Our human sense of the ridiculous, or comical, or (most significantly) the incongruous, is often rooted in an *understanding* of why something is incongruous that increases with greater insight into reality. The effective use of irony always depends on some unstated understanding. It is not by chance that 'wit' and intelligence are linked. There is an ancient tradition of Christ being represented by the 'fool' or jester who challenges conventional ways of seeing things. Writers in this field have pointed out how the 'holy fool' particularly works at the 'boundaries' of human categories – for example, of the sacred and the profane, and of the powerful and the powerless.[13] The character of Nasrudin represents a parallel tradition in Sufism. There is also the notion of the *power* of the fool (although not, of course, in the political sense), suggested, for example, in the role of the jester in the Tarot pack. Closely linked with all of this is an appreciation of certain states that are called 'madness', as in Plato's account of the four types of divine madness[14] which are not to be confused with a fifth type, that we might call 'clinical madness'.[15] In all these cases, there is not just feeling and interpretation, there is something else, which I am suggesting has something in common with the religious sense of 'presence', and that can claim to have a cognitive aspect. Only through such an approach, I suggest, can the full significance of religious experience be appreciated.

In his book on mysticism, F.C. Happold makes a suggestion that parallels my account of religious experience. 'The raw material of all religion' he writes, and 'the inspiration of much philosophy, poetry, art, and music, is a consciousness of a *beyond*, of something which, though it is interwoven with it, is not the external world of material phenomena ... .'[16] Further:

> ... the mystical element [that is, what we might call 'religious experience' of the full-blown kind, experienced by many of the saints] enters into the commoner forms of religious experience when religious feeling surpasses its rational content, that is, when the hidden, non-rational, unconscious elements predominate and determine the emotional life and the intellectual attitude.[17]

What I am calling a sense of 'presence' leaves open the question of whether this is an intimation of (1) God, or (2) a totality (that may be the universe as a whole), or (3) the inner core of one's own self, or (4) some unusual physiological state. These are all interpretations of a kind of experience that – so it is suggested – comes through as a kind of *pattern* in many of the first-hand accounts. The first interpretation is theistic, the second a kind of 'cosmic consciousness' that is compatible with theism or monism, the third monistic, and the last materialistic.

Let us concentrate on monist interpretations, which are of particular concern in this chapter. One of the things that suggests a monistic account of mystical experiences is the belief that underlies many (but not all) forms of monism to the effect that the knowledge given in them comes from within. When one learns to meditate properly, it is alleged, one finds within oneself layers of illusion that need to be stripped away. Typically, some monists describe enlightenment as peeling away the outer layers of an onion until one comes to the centre, which turns out to be both one's true, inner self, and the kernel of all reality. Here, just as a drop of water can return to the ocean from which it came, so the 'separated' but truly illusory self, becomes part of the great Self. The ultimate truth can then be simply expressed. The terms used will be different, depending on the culture and the outward form of the current religion, but the truth is (in the language of Vedanta) that Atman (the individual soul) *is* Brahman (ultimate reality). The whole meditation process is not so much a looking or listening to what is 'out there', as a retreat into the depths of one's own being, and discovering a truth that is already implicitly known. In other monistic traditions, the starting-point is not so much a looking within, as a growing awareness of a transcendent reality that calls one to a union of a more and more profound kind, so that the initial sense of transcendence is overtaken by a sense of immanence. However, as the climax approaches, the language parallels the inward approach, as the self becomes in some way merged, or even annihilated, within the absolute.

This picture of what religious experience is really about represents the underlying view within many forms of Hinduism, Buddhism and Daoism, despite important differences of detail. It is also the *language* (whether or not it is the philosophy) of some of the writings of a number of Muslim and Christian mystics, such as Meister Eckhart. This fact raises again the crucial question as to whether monism and theism represent different interpretations of essentially the same kinds of experience, or whether they relate to significantly different experiences. This question, in turn, is complicated by an important controversy concerning whether, in the case of mystical experience, it is legitimate to make a sharp distinction between experience and interpretation, and to this issue we must now turn.

Some Sceptical Responses to Religious Experience

In recent decades it has been argued not only that any *account* that is later given of what a religious experience was like is inevitably coloured by the cultural and linguistic context (which is certainly true), but that the experience itself must be coloured in an analogous way. In other words, the question arises as to whether it is meaningful at all to refer to experiences apart from the way they have been interpreted. This issue has led to a vast literature within the fields of both philosophy and theology.[18]

A natural response would be to suggest that behind the particular experiences of different mystics there lies what might be called a 'source' or 'root experience' which is universal. At this point the sceptical attack becomes more focused, with the claim that any reference to such a root experience, unless one can give some uninterpreted account of it, is like being asked to say what a chicken is like when one has taken all the feathers off.[19] In other words, the nature of this 'source' is left empty. A powerful variation on this kind of scepticism is provided by George Lindbeck in his *The Nature of Doctrine*. Instead of trying to explain the different forms of religion as the product of 'deep experiences of the divine (or the self, or the world) which most of us are accustomed to thinking of as peculiarly religious' he suggests a reversal in which the experiences are understood as products of a religion.[20] (Behind this lies Lindbeck's suggested approach to religion as 'cultural-linguistic' rather than either 'cognitive' – with an accompanying search for true, religious 'propositions' – or 'experiential-expressive'.[21] I shall return to this matter in Chapter 5.) Another version of scepticism with regard to the interpretation of (alleged) mystical experiences can be found in Denys Turner's *The Darkness of God*. In this interesting and provocative examination of how the medieval mystics have been read, he writes: 'At its boldest, my hypothesis is that modern interpretation has invented "mysticism" and that we persist in reading back the terms of that conception upon a stock of medieval authorities who knew no such thing – or, when they knew it, decisively rejected it.'[22]

An adequate response to these different forms of scepticism is impossible here, but I propose to suggest that there is a reasonable defence for there being a kind of 'root' experience – and that my suggestions about 'presence' lend support to this defence. The response that follows is not essential for the principal claims of this book, but I shall argue that there is more mileage to be got out of *patterns* of religious experience than the sceptical positions allow.

The response begins like this. Even if the detailed descriptions of religious experience turn out to be legitimate only at some 'lower level' of language (to anticipate a distinction made by Śankara that will be referred to later in this chapter), and even if the way in which a sense of 'presence' is actually 'experienced' (as opposed to being 'described'), is affected by the culture in which one is placed, there is the possibility that we may be able, in theory, to distinguish between a 'source' of a religious experience and the way it is 'felt' by individuals in their personal and cultural contexts. If this is so, then it is still legitimate to refer to an underlying source, which is then *both* experienced and described in a personal and cultural context. For this reason I do not think that we can rule out, in some *a priori* manner, the *possibility* that there may be an underlying source, or 'root experience', which may be the same in typical cases of both monistic and theistic mystical traditions.

Next, let us consider the objection that reference to an unknown and indescribable root experience is empty, on the analogy of the featherless chicken. An attack that uses this kind of analogy itself makes use of implicit assumptions that can be questioned, and may rely on significant ambiguities in the notion of 'emptiness'.[23] If I were forced to stay with the analogy of the chicken I might say that the true representation of the chicken was something like Plato's 'mathematical object',[24] which in modern dress might include an account of the DNA. More seriously, my reply to the criticism parallels my reply to the rejection of objectivity by many postmodernists. The denial that we can make a sure representation of something does not necessarily imply that there is no 'reality' behind it, nor that we may be able to have some glimpses as to its nature. For theists, the belief that we are made in the image of God, and can therefore participate in the divine intelligence, makes sense of such a belief. Also, there is a secular version of an equivalent belief based on Anaxagoras' insight into the intelligible nature of the universe which our minds can begin to comprehend, because they are part of the same universe. We cannot, of course, *know* that this is so, but nor can the sceptic *know* that this is not so, and therefore the acceptance of human limitations actually opens the door to the possibility of objective knowledge. The sceptical attack, whether coming from a postmodernist or from someone who denies the possibility of any insight into an ultimate source of religious experience, is just as much dependent on human language and the limitations of human reason as is the proponent of the bolder *via positiva*.

In addition to these reservations, I suspect that there is more of a common pattern in the experiences of those that have been called mystics than Denys Turner allows. Although he may well be right if we are thinking of *feelings*, as that term is normally used (although on this matter I reserve judgement), what I have called a sense of *presence* is something which may be implicit in both the writings of the classical 'mystics' of all the great religions and many more recent writings that discuss the experience of prayer. Moreover, Turner's account of the classical mystics is coloured by the emphasis on the *via negativa*, or 'apophatic' way, which he supports, and which he sees (perhaps rightly) as central to many medieval writers in the Neoplatonic tradition. Naturally enough, this emphasis tends to downplay both the possibility and the potential significance of common (and 'positive') experiences of the divine. But in support of a *via positiva* (to balance a perfectly acceptable role for the *via negativa*), consider what Aquinas says about natural law (bearing in mind that Aquinas was well versed in both the Aristotelian and Neoplatonic traditions, and that he too had powerful religious experiences). Human beings, in using their reason, and in working out what is providential for human life, *participate* in the Eternal Law of God.[25] This is a powerful claim, for it means that our thinking in the area of ethics – when it is well ordered – is not simply a pale reflection of the divine Providence, but actually partakes of it. According to Aquinas, at least in this area of human rationality, what I have called the transcending power of the human intellect is something that the *via negativa* fails to describe.

Let us return to the issue of whether it is plausible, within the realm of what has come to be called 'mystical experience', to see patterns of similar experience that are then interpreted differently. One pointer to the phenomenon of different interpretations of what may be identical or similar experiences can be found in the use of the analogy of water, in which unity with God or the absolute is likened to absorption into the ocean. Not only is this the language of some of the *Upaniṣads* (which are seminal writings within the Hindu tradition, probably written between 800 and 300 BCE),[26] it is also the language of many Christian mystics, notably Teresa of Avila. For example, after describing a state of union with God that can be likened to the joining of two candles, so that there is a common light, she *contrasts* this kind of union (in which one candle can later be separated from the other) with the kind of union experienced in the 'seventh Mansion'. This is 'like rain falling from heavens into a river or a spring: there is nothing but water there and it is impossible to divide or separate the water belonging to the river from that which fell from the heavens'.[27] This use of identical analogies strengthens the case for claiming that there is a continuum, or fuzzy line, between monistic and theistic philosophies, especially when they are expressed with subtlety. A stress on the immanence of God, coupled with a sense of the inadequacy of human language, tends to push one towards monistic language; a stress on the transcendence of God coupled with the way in which certain transforming experiences, such as that of love, are felt to give us some insight into the nature of God or the absolute, tends to push one towards theistic language.

The Claims of 'Perennial Philosophy'

It is important not to accept too readily the assumption that there is no significant distinction between monism and theism, particularly in the light of the popular attraction of the view that 'all religions are basically the same', a claim that is often made without a serious study of different traditions. For example, a monist philosophy is sometimes advocated in the context of claims about a 'perennial' philosophy that the careful student of religion, it is alleged, can find to be at the core of all world religions.[28] But here much caution is needed. Although I have so far stressed the possibility of common patterns in the religious experiences of different cultures, this can too easily lead to an *a priori* assumption that an identical experience underlies all religions, with a consequent disregard of significant differences. This is particularly important when we move from the feelings associated with religious experience, and from the sense of presence, to the way in which the content of the experiences is then *described*. The tendency to interpret religious experiences all over the world as 'one' (which fits very well with any monistic account of religion) has been much assisted by poor or tendentious translations of essential sacred texts that gloss over differences. A good example is *The Pocket World Bible* which, in a useful way, introduces readers to basic texts in the major religions, but at the expense of misleading inaccuracy in some places.[29]

The conclusion I am approaching needs to be stated with care. All over the world there *may be* common patterns in what is generally called 'religious experience', or more narrowly – when there is a powerful sense of union – 'mystical experience', and if these common patterns can be found, then this provides one ground for taking religion seriously, for it cries out for investigation and explanation, whether this explanation, in the end, be purely psychological or sociological or in terms of actual contact with a greater reality. However, any common patterns that can be found must not obscure essential differences that also exist, and the danger posed by the oversimplified views of those whom Zaehner calls 'indifferentists' – 'those generous but loose-minded persons who would have us believe that all religions are equally true ...'.[30]

In the light of the need to balance an awareness of similarities with an acknowledgement of differences, it is instructive to look at the context of attempts to translate the term 'God' into Chinese.[31] Here we see both the belief that there are common patterns in the religious experience of contrasting cultures and religions, and the pitfalls of failing to realize significant differences. The first Jesuit missionaries in China were generally men of major intellect and learning, and many of them, under the leadership of Matteo Ricci, made a serious attempt to read and understand some of the Chinese classics. They became convinced that hidden within the texts, especially the Confucian ones (which should not be classed as monistic), there lay fundamental truths of natural theology upon which Christian doctrine could be built. This, with hindsight, was partly a result of reading the texts without sufficient general background, and partly a result of a belief that God had revealed himself to an earlier generation of Chinese scholars at the time of the universal flood associated with Noah. After the death of Ricci in 1610, many missionaries became increasingly alarmed at the results of this blend of Chinese terms and Christian doctrine, claiming that it had led to distortion of the gospel by putting it into completely alien categories. At the same time, following a period of considerable respect for the first missionaries within the Chinese literati, there developed a deep suspicion, and claims that the Christians had systematically distorted and *used* the classical texts to their own ends. Conversions among the literati, which early on had been significant, almost completely dried up.[32]

A cynical response to this history would be to assert that any *exposition* of religion is so culturally and linguistically dependent, that no universal truths can be expressed. A more optimistic assessment holds that, despite differences of language and culture, the 'transcending' power of the human mind does enable some universal understanding. However, the understanding must be *achieved*, and this cannot be done by inaccurate translations or the glossing-over of fundamentally different categories of thought. Ricci was right to look for ways in which the God he knew had revealed himself within the context of Chinese culture but, as with many missionaries, there had not been enough 'homework' in really seeking to understand the complexities of a different culture.

The foregoing paragraphs have attempted to appreciate both the genuine patterns of similarity and the real differences that mark an understanding of the different religious traditions. This brings into focus the way in which we *interpret* foundational experiences, both within our own traditions, and – perhaps even more – in those of others. One consequence is that monism is not the 'given' of all religious experience, it is an *interpretation* of certain common patterns of experience in which both powerful feelings and a sense of 'presence' have been found. In favour of this kind of interpretation, in so far as one can make a rational assessment, two positive points emerge. First, monism is rooted in profound human experiences of *unity*. (Even in the Western tradition the third (and for the Neoplatonists, final) stage of the mystical way was described as 'the unitive way'.) Second, at the intellectual level, the search for unity, in some sense, is basic to rationality. Is not science, for example, built upon the attempt to bring a huge diversity into a few general laws or principles, and ultimately (at least for many scientists) to a unified field theory?

Problems with Monism

What is there to be said on the negative side – prior to a presentation of theism as an alternative style of religious philosophy? I shall suggest three things, but with the caveat that none of them is presented as a 'disproof' of monism. It is rather that anyone attracted to monism should seriously consider these three problem areas. As in the case of materialism, if – in the light of the problems I explore – a crude form of the basic philosophy is replaced by a more subtle and rational form, much will have been achieved.

The first negative comment has already been suggested. It is all too easy, especially within a cultural tradition that has a generally accepted interpretation, to assume that the given interpretation is the only right one. Experiences of a fundamental unity can be interpreted in non-monistic as well as monistic ways.

The second concerns how monism handles the apparent diversity that we experience. The term 'one' is notoriously difficult to define. If all things are literally one, then what account does one give of the *manifold*, whether of things in the world or of individual thoughts or of individual persons? If the stress is on the secondary or derivative nature of all these thing*s*, then we seem to have something akin to Aquinas' *analogia entis*, and we may be closer to theism than to classical monism. Once again, in these cases, a fuzzy edge is appearing. As I have suggested, by accentuating certain themes and certain passages, many thinkers who are classed as monists could also be classed as theists. In ordinary language, words like 'illusion' come from the need to *contrast* ordinary experience, say of a tree (which has a degree of stability even though we can see the tree move and change with the seasons), with a dream tree or hallucinatory tree (which tends to have little or no stability – and which we cannot correlate with the experience of others). If the monist claims that there is a corresponding contrast between the changlessness of the One, or of God, and the world of our ordinary experience, then a theist like Aquinas would be happy to agree. Only God has true changelessness (a claim which process theologians will wish to qualify), and this contrasts with the nature of the created order. This is precisely what the *analogia entis* describes. Only in some forms of monism is the more radical line taken that every apprehension of the manifold is *pure* illusion. It is then that the second criticism arises, for the illusory nature of everything in common experience certainly fits oddly with how we normally talk of the manifold, and respond to it. Sceptics, like myself, feel obliged to ask for a more coherent account of why this is all *pure* illusion if they are to be convinced. The fact that most, or perhaps all, items in the manifold are ephemeral, or changing, is not enough to show that they are pure illusion, unless one introduces assumptions about all reality being absolutely 'changeless'.

There is a standard reply to this problem, which it is important to outline. In the early ninth century CE, the great Indian philosopher, Śaṅkara, building on a tradition that goes back to the *Upaniṣads*,[33] advocated a two-level theory of truth. Lower, common-sense knowledge (*vyavaharika*) is legitimate until it is contradicted by the higher level in the experience of Brahman. At the lower level, not only is it legitimate to make the sort of distinctions between reality and illusion that we ordinarily make, it is also legitimate to think of the Absolute as a personal God. However, at the higher level, the experience of *identity* is held to be 'self-authenticating and not directly communicable', although it can be evoked, for example, by the Vedic texts.[34] An approach along these lines certainly makes sense of ordinary language about the world of sense experience and the distinctions we need to make, but when a justification is asked for acceptance of the 'higher' level, then the claim to 'self-authentification' makes it virtually impossible to enter into a rational dialogue. Here the critic of monism may feel that we have a special case of the impregnable castle, and that referring to theism as a 'lower level' of knowledge is patronizing. I am inclined to be less sharply critical, and to think that the mystical experience which (I suspect) partially accounts for Śaṅkara's theology leads him to express a special case of what the Western tradition calls the *via negativa*. Advaita (literally 'non-dualist') philosophy points to the inadequacy of any human language to describe the ultimate. Hence, within what I am calling 'monistic' thought, we find a preference for the negative term '*not*-dualistic', to a more positive term such as 'monistic', the latter representing a Western way of describing Śankara's theology (and being a term only introduced into Western thought by Christian Wolff in the eighteenth century). Seen in this way, I certainly do not rule out the possibility of monism being a rational position to take (given the earlier account of 'rational'), but I deny that it is the only rational position. A philosophy that includes a doctrine of the *Imago Dei* in all humans, and hence not only the possibility of an analogy of attribution, but also of a special case of the divine image in Christ, provides a genuine alternative. Moreover, this alternative (theistic) position need not deny the transcending quality of the experiences on which Śankara's whole position rests. Finally, the stress on 'self-authentification' makes it hard to distance *advaita* philosophy from other, less noble traditions which make similar claims.

The third problem area concerns the moral status of the person and, intimately linked with this, the nature of love. The link between a theistic belief in the creation of different, individual persons and their intrinsic value is clear, but it seems harder for a monistic philosophy to provide the same ground for individual rights and the same sense of the unique value of each individual, given the belief that all individuality is illusory. In practice, as we know, many monists, including the Buddha (whose original teaching should probably be described as monistic), have stressed compassion towards every person to a degree that shames many theists, but it is hard to see *why* the same value should be given to a temporary expression of Brahman as to an individual soul that has a particular significance for all eternity. Congruously, some people link the growth of human rights in the West to a *pluralistic* belief in both the reality and the value of all individuals, and suspect that the alleged smaller stress in the East has historical connections with monism. I am not sure of this, but I hold that monists do have an intellectual problem in explaining the compassion for the individual that they so often show.[35] The Christian mystic, Ruysbroeck, took this problem further, claiming that although for the monist there can be 'rest' (and, he claimed, a kind of dangerous self-absorption) there cannot be what he called 'love' of the kind that reaches its fulfilment in ecstatic union with God.[36] Love, in the monotheistic tradition (and often in the modern secular tradition), is a union of two or more beings. Unless some meaning is given to this idea of 'beings' (in the plural), the significance of love tends to evaporate.

My final comment on monism is more positive, and returns to the theme of the fuzzy edges that exist between the principal systems of thought, especially when more subtle variations are described. While it is easy to make a sharp contrast between monism and theism when these systems are described in a simple way, as soon as we get more sophisticated descriptions possibilities of compromise emerge. For example, some monists talk of the fulfilment of the self within the great Self rather than its annihilation, and many theists talk of how the selfish, egoistic self has to die, in order that the true self may be found. (Here we can recall the words of Jesus: 'Except a corn of wheat fall into the ground and die, it abideth alone: but if it die, it bringeth forth much fruit. He that loveth his life shall lose it … .'[37]) Already it is is clear that a crude distinction between the extinction of the self and its continuation needs to be made less sharply. In the case of the *Advaita* teaching, the essential difference between a typical monist and a typical Christian can only be

found by a subtle interpretation of words, not by a simple statement of the doctrines. This is why some people think that the two systems of thought, which may
seem to be in sharp disagreement, can come close to each other.[38]

Notes and References

1 Happold, F.C. (1963), *Mysticism*, London: Penguin, p. 118.
2 In addition to Happold, other useful introductory books include James, W. (1902), *The
   Varieties of Religious Experience*, London: Longman, Green, and Co.; Underhill, E.
   (1911), *Mysticism*, London: Methuen; and Zaehner, R.C. (1957), *Mysticism Sacred and
   Profane*, Oxford: Clarendon Press. The last-named includes a discussion on the relation of drug-induced states to 'genuine' mystical experience, and on the relation of
   monistic and theistic religious experiences, which the author distinguishes more sharply
   than I would.
3 Otto, R. (1932), *The Idea of the Holy*, trans. J.W. Harvey, Oxford: Oxford University
   Press. On p. 117 he claims that the numinous 'issues from the deepest foundation of
   cognitive apprehension'.
4 Zaehner, *Mysticism Sacred and Profane*, p. 168.
5 For example, Isa. 6.
6 Swinburne, R. (1979), *The Existence of God*, Oxford: Clarendon Press, pp. 245–51.
7 'The angels, who are spirits, cannot speak in comprehensible language. Language is
   therefore a particular mission for humanity.' Quoted in Fox M. and Sheldrake, R.
   (1996), *The Physics of Angels*, San Fransisco: Harper, p. 169. However, in one respect
   this is a misleading rendering of the Latin (from *Patrologia Latina*, Paris: Migne, 1844,
   ff., vol. 197, p. 1045). Part of the relevant passage reads *Angeli qui spiritus sunt, nisi
   propter hominem verbis rationalitatis non loquuntur; quoniam linguae eorum sonans
   laus sunt*. Thus, according to Hildegard, 'for the sake of humans' (*propter hominem*)
   the angels can use rational language.
8 See Hildegard's *Scivias* [*Scito vias domini*], Book 1, visions 2, 21 and 4, 15.
9 Smith, J. (1660), *Select Discourses*, London, pp. 180 and 273. Smith, Dean of Queens'
   College, Cambridge, was a Hebrew scholar, and this enabled him to benefit from little
   known rabbinic sources.
10 Bucke, R.M. (1901), *Cosmic Consciousness*, Philadelphia: Innes, p. 8.
11 See, for example, Maritain, J. (1953), *The Range of Reason*, London: Bles, pp. 24–6,
   on the differences between mystical and poetic experiences.
12 Erler R.J. and Marquard, R., eds (1986), *A Karl Barth Reader*, trans. G.W. Bromiley,
   Edinburgh: T and T Clark, pp. 94–5.
13 See Bastien, J.W. (1987), 'Humor and Satire' in *The Encyclopedia of Religion*, ed. M.
   Eliade, New York: Macmillan.
14 Plato, *Phaedrus*, 265b.
15 See Dodds, E.R. (1951), *The Greeks and the Irrational*, Berkeley: University of California Press, p. 64.
16 Happold, *Mysticism*, pp. 18–19, original emphasis.
17 Ibid., p. 19.
18 For an overview, see Payne, S. (1988), 'Mysticism', in *Routledge Encyclopedia of
   Philosophy*, ed. E. Craig, London and New York: Routledge, vol. 6. See also the
   discussion in Bell, D.N. (1981) 'A Doctrine of Ignorance: The Annihilation of Individuality in Christian and Muslim Mysticism', in E.R. Elder, ed., *Benedictus* (*Studies
   in Honor of St Bededict of Nursia*), Kalamazoo, Michigan: Cistercian Publications, pp.
   30–52.

19 Bell, D.N., 'A Doctrine of Ignorance', p. 31.

20 Lindbeck, G.L. (1984), *The Nature of Doctrine*, London: SPCK, p. 30.

21 He views Bernard Lonergan as an exponent of a third way, which seeks to combine the cognitive and the experiential-expressive. Ibid., pp. 17, 31 ff.

22 Turner, D. (1995), *The Darkness of God*, Cambridge: Cambridge University Press, p. 7.

23 Consider the case of a scientist who says that although they are sure there is a true answer to a certain problem, they have no idea what it is. Here, it might be claimed that the claim is not 'empty' since a positive assertion is being made, namely that a true answer 'exists', but the content of the unknown truth is, as it were, 'empty' with respect to us (although a typical postmodernist would say that the claim itself is 'empty', because no representation can be given). Congruously, there may be a claim that there is a 'reality' that lies behind mystical experience, even if no account of it can be given. For the postmodernist this claim is empty in two senses – that is, in terms both of the claim that there is a 'reality', and in the sense that no account of the nature of this reality can be given. My position is, first, that even if no account could be given, the claim that there is a 'reality' is not empty in the full sense, but only with respect to content; second, that given the possibility of a *via positiva*, the claim is not empty in either sense. The situation is further complicated by the possibility that the aforementioned scientist might mean (i) that no answer could ever be found by humans, given our intellectual capacities, or (ii) that some partial answer might one day be forthcoming. Having had the intelligence to formulate the problem, I question whether we could ever truly know that the former situation was the case.

24 Plato, *Republic*, 510–11.

25 Aquinas, *ST*, 1a 2ae Q. 91, 2 (*participatio legis aeternae in rationali creatura lex naturalis dicitur*).

26 See, for example, *Katha Upaniṣad*, II, 1, 14–15 and *Mundaka Upaniṣad*, III, 2, 8 in Radhakrishnan, S. (1953), *The Principal Upaniṣads*, London: Allen and Unwin, pp. 635 and 691.

27 St Teresa of Avila (Teresa of Jesus), *Interior Castle* (*Las Moradas*), VII, ii; *The Complete Works*, trans. E.A. Peers (1978), London: Sheed and Ward, vol. 2, p. 335.

28 See Huxley, A.L. (1956), *The Perennial Philosophy*, London: Chatto and Windus. In the introduction Huxley refers to 'the highest common factor' in all the great religions.

29 Ballou, R.O. ed. (1948), *The Pocket World Bible*, London: Routledge and Kegan Paul. Under the section on Daoism [the translation uses the old form 'Taoist'], occurs a passage: 'He who knows what God is, and who knows what man is, has attained' (p. 528). A better translation reads: 'He who knows what it is that Heaven does, and knows what it is that man does, has reached the peak'. *Chuang Tzu – Basic Writings*, trans. B. Watson (1964), New York: Columbia University Press, p. 73.

30 Zaehner, *Mysticism Sacred and Profane*, p. 198.

31 What actually happened is that after a period of considerable controversy, the Roman Catholic church opted to use one word, *tianzhu* (literally 'heavenly master'), while the Protestant churches nearly always use another, *shangdi* (literally 'supreme emperor'), but sometimes a third term, *shen* (literally 'spirit'). All of these terms leave much to be desired, the first two because of the political images they conjure up, the third because it can mean one of many gods as well as 'God'. Moreover, all three terms are used in a variety of senses within classical Chinese literature.

32 The story is told by Gernet, J. (1985) in *China and the Christian Impact*, trans. J. Lloyd, Cambridge: Cambridge University Press, ch. 1.

33 See, for example, the *Mundaka Upaniṣad*, I, 1, 4–5; Radhakrishnan, *The Principal Upaniṣads*, p. 672.

34   Smart, N. (1967), 'Ṣankara' in *The Encyclopedia of Philosophy*, ed. P. Edwards, London: Macmillan, vol. 7, p. 280.
35   We may recall a corresponding paradox within extreme Calvinism, where doctrines of the 'elect', coupled with the 'assurance' that one was numbered among the elect, might suggest that virtuous behaviour was not necessary. In practice, many Calvinists were scrupulous in the observance of (what they held to be) righteous conduct.
36   See Zaehner, *Mysticism, Sacred and Profane*, p. 172.
37   John 12: 24–5.
38   See Ward, K. (1991), 'Christian Vedanta' in *A Vision to Pursue*, London: SCM Press, ch. 16.

Chapter 5

The Meaning of Theism

Essential Characteristics of Theism

Theism (taken from the Greek word for God, *theos*), refers to the philosophy that the physical universe is a *created* whole, and God is the author or creator of this whole. In 'classical theism' this creator God is not, in any sense, a part of this created whole, and there is therefore a fundamental dualism involved, since there is an absolute divide between the creator and what is created. Aquinas' 'analogy of being' was a way of expressing such a classical theism, since, as we have seen, only God has true 'existence' and all created things have 'derivative' existence. I do not propose to make this classical and dualist account a *defining* characteristic of theism, since many thinkers who wish to call themselves theists either reject this dualism, or wish to describe it in different ways. However there are some characteristics of the concept of God that can be described as *defining* characteristics, on the grounds that in their absence it would be misleading to speak of 'God' in the same sense as that used within the major forms of monotheism. In this section I shall list three such essential characteristics. It must be stressed that throughout the following discussion the primary concern is with the meaning of the concept of God, and therefore the *religious* power of the idea of God is not in the foreground. At the same time, without this religious power, and the overwhelming sense of 'presence' which 'God' implies within the religious life, the importance of the concept would be hugely diminished. Moreover, I shall return to the 'faith' context of the idea of God at the end of the chapter.

The first essential characteristic of theism is its identification with monotheism – meaning that there is only *one* God. This does not rule out some polytheistic language for the following reason. When religions talk of 'gods', in the plural, they can mean many different things. The early strata of the Old Testament, for example, clearly implies that there are many 'gods', meaning powerful and usually evil, unseen forces, but they are not the source of creation. Later on, the writers preferred not to use the word 'god' for such entities, even though their existence was not always denied.[1] A similar problem arises with Hindu polytheism. No doubt, for some worshippers it is accurate to say that there is a multitude of gods, but many sophisticated Hindus have a more subtle interpretation that can take two basic forms. What is probably the more original form is a version of monism in which the language of many gods is seen as a way in which more primitive people can appreciate different aspects of one spiritual reality; the other, a version of monotheism, in which the lesser, non-creative powers are similar to the Old Testament 'gods', except that they are usually benign, while Brahman is the one supreme God. We then find a Hindu version of theism.

Whether the Christian doctrine of the Trinity is consistent with a strict monotheism will be discussed in Chapter 7.

The second essential characteristic of theism has already been indicated; it is belief in the creative role of God. However this does not necessarily mean that the universe started, along with time, at a particular moment. Aquinas, for example, insisted that it was perfectly possible for the creator God to be the eternal source of a universe that had no beginning. He claimed that we only know that it actually had a beginning from revelation (that is, from the book of Genesis), but that from the point of view of natural reason we could only know that the universe depended on a creative source.[2] Thus whether or not the physical universe is eternal is not a matter that is settled by this defining characteristic of theism. Another matter not settled is whether God made the universe as a *purely* voluntary act of love, implying that he might have chosen never to make any universe. Classical theism has asserted the purely voluntary nature of creation, but many theists see a kind of necessity in God's making of a universe, although allowing freedom to make one kind of universe rather than another.[3] This last view, however, does not entail that God can make *any* universe, since God's commitment to the law of non-contradiction rules out all kinds of speculative possibilities (and robs the objection to theism based on the presence of suffering of much of its force). The creative activity is nearly always linked with monotheism, but in rare cases it is not. In Marcion, for example, creation is seen as the product of two creative powers.[4]

The third essential characteristic of theism is the presence of *some* 'personal' aspects to God, so that – in typical cases of theism – God can be said both to know and to love individual people and, indeed, other individual animals. The suggestion that this is mere anthropomorphism has already been argued against in the discussion of analogy and of the doctrine of the *Imago Dei*. Creativity, in so far as it involves a *decision* to make this rather than that, is another essential aspect of a 'personal' God. Deism is a special and somewhat borderline example of theism. It was popular in the eighteenth century, and its extreme form alleged that a creator God acted in making everything that exists but then abstained from interference, leaving it as a clock that simply runs itself and never needs rewinding. Such ideas were given impetus by Isaac Newton's mechanical view of the heavenly bodies, along with an explanation of how gravity kept them in position. Newton himself, however, was not a deist, for not only did he believe that God had to make occasional *adjustments* to the heavenly order,[5] God was also held to have personal qualities.[6] If the Deist God is thought of as not being aware of individuals, or caring about them, then it is significantly different from theism, and has some things in common with monism. It is for similar reasons that the systems of Plato and Aristotle do not fit comfortably into the monism/theism division. In both cases 'God', when used for the supreme principle, cannot be aware of individual humans. However, already another fuzzy edge emerges in any attempt to classify deism and the views of either Plato or Aristotle. In the case of Aristotle, God is, in a sense, part of the universal system, since he is the being that is *situated* beyond the outermost celestial sphere. At the same time, God (Aristotle's 'first unmoved mover') is qualitatively different from all the other celestial forces, since he alone influences all beneath him by 'final causality' alone. That is to say, instead of 'pushing or pulling', like all other ('efficient') causes in the great system of Nature, he simply draws things to himself as a persuasive object of love. He is personal in that he is supremely happy, but impersonal in that he is blissfully unaware of the rest of Nature.

When we start to go beyond a very general account of what theism means, rooted in these three characteristics, we soon run into both difficulties and controversies. In the next seven subsections I shall supplement the initial description (in terms of a God who is One, Creative and Personal), with a fuller account, summarized under seven further characteristics of the concept of God as it can be found in its developed form within the Western tradition. This sequence of characteristics (three, followed by seven), should not be taken as either definitive or exhaustive. It is merely my own attempt to summarize the most important aspects of the concept of God. Moreover, the seven characteristics that follow are not central in quite the way that the first three are, since whereas anyone who denied the appropriateness of one of the first three would not be able to claim that they were 'theists' as that term is normally used, anyone who denies one or more of the following seven characteristics might still claim to be a 'theist', although one who disagrees with most monotheists on how the concept of God should be understood.

In each case I shall include some statement of what God is *not*, since within any rational account of theism this *via negativa* is the easier part. I shall also try to give some positive account of what can be said about the nature of God. Throughout this chapter, I am not assuming that the God of theism is a reality; rather, I am attempting to clarify the meaning of the concept. My argument that there is such a reality will be pursued in the next chapter. (Despite my criticism of positivism in Chapter 1, the movement was right to point out the ambiguity in the use of the term 'God', and this chapter is, in part, a response to this positivist challenge.) A further general comment concerns the relationship of the different characteristics or 'attributes' of God that are explored in this chapter. I indicated in Chapter 1 that there are many places where the issues have been oversimplified in order to write in a way that is more accessible to the general reader, and the question of the relationship of the attributes is one of these. The great theologians have always stressed that although we can refer to the attributes of God, the plurality involved is a matter of our limited vision, and that a complete understanding would see the 'simplicity' of God, meaning that what are to us different attributes would be understood as a unity.[7]

God and Providence

According to more sophisticated theists, God is not providential in that he *directly* governs all things. For example, the indirect form of governance is emphasized in Aquinas' account of God's activity, where he repeatedly insists that when we seek the causes of events within the world, we should look first at what he calls the 'secondary' or 'proximate' cause. God is 'first cause' of all things, because he is creator of the order of nature, but, as Austin Farrer put it, 'God makes the world make itself'.[8] If the tree falls down in a storm it is not helpful or relevant (except in special circumstances) to say that God caused it to fall. The 'proximate' causes would probably be the wind, the age of the tree, the condition of the soil, and so on.

God does not, as it were, pull billions of strings to make things happen. He sets up an order in which things happen 'naturally'. It is this which makes possible ordinary human prediction, responsible action, and the whole exercise of natural science. This is a matter which tends to be misunderstood by many of those who have no religious faith who think that all theists are committed to a quite extraordinary and improbable belief in a God who is *directly* responsible for all that happens.

How then is God 'providential', other than in setting up the whole order of nature? Some theists hold that he is active, in part, through miraculous *interventions* in the natural order. Other theists, especially in recent times, are doubtful about whether this is a typical mode of God's activity, or even whether it is ever employed. We have already seen that in Aquinas' sense of miracle, neither creation nor redemption were miracles in the strict sense, and I have argued that this applies equally to the fundamental claims regarding the incarnation and resurrection, although *ancillary* events usually associated with these things, on a traditional view, would be miraculous. Whether God *ever* intervenes by the suspension or overriding of the natural order is a matter which theists disagree about. The reason why some insist that this seldom or never happens is not, contrary to what might be expected, primarily a worry about the strength of the evidence. It is linked with the claim that any human and natural order which can be the context for human responsibility and the development of love *must* have its own autonomy. Once it is claimed that God has intervened in a miraculous way on any particular occasion, then the obvious question is why does he not intervene in others – for example, to stop someone like Hitler back in 1933? If a condition of having a responsible and generally predictable order is that nature is allowed to run its course and that human freedom is given its rein, then the claim that God never intervenes by 'miracle' is at least understandable. Obviously theists disagree amongst themselves on this, but a rational theism either severely limits, or altogether avoids reference to miracle, except when the term is used loosely – that is, to mean an event that is wonderful to behold, or a source of inspiration.

Those theists who hold that God does, on rare occasions, act through the miraculous (in Aquinas' sense of the term) face a difficulty, in that unless there is some principle which governs when such rare events occur, it looks rather as if the theist is bringing in the notion of miracle in an essentially arbitrary way whenever it is convenient to do so. In Appendix 1 I shall attempt a fuller analysis of the general problem, but at this stage I will offer the following suggestion. Given the reasons for *not* believing that God continually intervenes through miracles, in either natural events or human affairs, then if a miracle (in the sense being discussed) is to occur, there needs to be from the divine perspective, some special reason for a miracle, while, from the human perspective, the event must have a certain ambiguity, so that we could not *know* that a miracle has occurred. Without this ambiguity the principle that we need to live in an ordered world, in which we can look for causal connections, and in which we can maintain human responsibility, would be in jeopardy. For this reason, the theist cannot properly bring in the notion of miracle as a general explanatory device. Moreover, although a theist might come to believe that a miracle has taken place, this belief could not form part of a sound argument directed at a non-believer. This involves a significant change in the way in which miracles have often been used in the history of monotheistic religions, for claims about miracles have often been cited as alleged demonstrations of divine power. Theists may very properly refer to their personal experiences of what they believe to be divine grace, and to the experiences of others, even when these experiences sound 'extraordinary', but this is quite different from claiming that certain public events *prove* the reality of God. I do not think that this latter defence of theism can be rationally supported, and it is utterly congruous with this suggestion to note how Jesus continually played down the evidential power of his acts of healing, asking those who were healed not to spread the matter abroad, and refusing to provide dramatic signs of power. He wanted the disciples to be attracted to his message because it was recognized as 'light'.

If God is actively involved in human affairs, but not (or rarely) through the miraculous, then his activity must be described in other, providential terms, and indeed most theologians have claimed that there is a providential activity that is not, in the strict sense, miraculous. The most obvious way in which this may happen is through mental or moral influence on people, who in turn influence both history and nature. If we accept that friends can influence each other for good without destroying their autonomy in any way, then once it is accepted that a personal God has an analogous relationship with us, there is no reason, in principle, why his influence should jeopardize our autonomy. In addition to an influence through our relationship with God in prayer and through other people, many theologians have believed that there can be a gradual influence on nature itself through the equivalent of a kind of 'pressure' to evolve in one direction rather than another. This too is something that theists have different views about, but the notion should not be too easily dismissed in the context of new understandings of the complexity of natural forces. If human minds can interact with nature in ways that we are only beginning to understand, *a fortiori*, if there is a divine mind, nature may be under its guidance without a denial of an appropriate autonomy. The indeterminism of many things in nature, while not in any way providing a proof for the work of freedom, may indicate one of the contexts in which the freedom of humans or of God may operate.[9]

Even with these emphases on God working through people, and (indirectly) through a subtle influence on nature, this account of providence may sound anaemic to some theists in comparison with the 'full-blooded' belief in God's direct involvement in the everyday affairs of the faithful that typifies much religious literature. The following suggestion may help: the more we come to understand the complexity of the natural order and the way in which the mental and the physical interact with each other (for example, in the healing process), then if theism is a correct interpretation of reality, the less we can lay down limits to what life can be like when people live in harmony with God, with others, with nature, and within themselves. Thus, without any commitment to the verbal inerrancy of the Bible, a Christian can read the Acts of the Apostles and find a saga of life under the direction of Spirit, which can be paralleled in other accounts of those who live by faith. Similarly, a 'saga of the Holy Spirit' can be found in the gospels, the diaries of Christians like George Fox, John Woolman and John Wesley, and in the lives of holy people in a variety of traditions, including Muhammad. Only in a relatively few passages is something corresponding to 'miracle' (in Aquinas' sense of the term) required to make sense of all these sagas of life with the Spirit. Then, as now, people who live with a sense of the living presence of God, and who are open to a much greater range of possibilities than the ordinary person, seem to find their lives surrounded by signs of grace.

God as Omnipotent and Omniscient

When God is said to be omnipotent or omniscient, we have already seen that this does not necessarily mean that God can do literally anything, or know every detail of the future. Medieval theologians were familiar with the 'paradox of omnipotence', which emerges when you ask a question like 'Could God make something that was too heavy for him to lift?'. Whatever answer you give to this, God seems to be limited. The logical conclusion is not that God cannot be omnipotent, but that the term, when applied to *everything*, is incoherent. Any coherent claim has to mean that God can do (or know) whatever it is logically possible to do (or know).[10] Anselm put the matter like this: if omnipotence includes the power to do or experience what is not for one's own good, then 'impotence' is understood within the word 'power'.[11] We have already noted how Aquinas argued that God was bound by the law of non-contradiction – or more strictly, that it was meaningless to talk of God being able to break the law of non-contradiction – and this denial that it makes sense to talk of God doing literally anything is one of many things that was implied. Even William of Ockham, who is often described (wrongly) as an *extreme* voluntarist, argued that God could not do anything that involves a manifest contradiction.[12] This view of omnipotence runs through the liberal approach to a number of issues, but it must include a cautionary note if it is not to depart from a genuine theism. The 'paradox of omnipotence' does show that a careless use of references to God's *absolute* power can lead us to speak nonsense, but the danger on the other side is to assume that *we* are always in a position to know what is *logically* impossible. This point can be illustrated by considering the case of someone who insists that the angles of a triangle *must* add up to 180 degrees, and that this is an analytic truth, based on the meaning of the terms. Faced with a better mathematician they may be startled to find that this is only true when we deal with triangles on a plane surface. This should provide a salutary warning, especially when we try to apply our logic to a God who must, if he be a reality, transcend the ways in which we live in a whole range of ways. This does not mean that we should withdraw the claim that there must be (what we misleadingly call) 'limitations' on the divine power, but that we cannot appreciate exactly how these apply. It is for this reason that I have argued that among the rational options should be included the claim of classical theism to the effect that God does know the whole future, even though I have indicated a preference for a more radical approach. This argument also lies behind my suggestion, in Chapter 1, that a liberal theology need not deny the legitimacy, within the circle of believers, of a 'mystical' or other forms of theology. Within such theologies there should still be the demand that what God does is ultimately in accordance with reason, but there might be less insistence that we should begin to make sense of this reason, except in the way in which – within these theologies – they accord with particular kinds of experience. However (to repeat my point) such theologies cannot have a significant role either in the way in which the faith is presented to non-believers, or in the way in which believers debate among themselves how the fundamentals of the faith should be interpreted.

One of the important consequences of a better understanding of omnipotence is that there are strong grounds for saying that God *could not* make John Doe good. Assuming that freedom is an essential part of John Doe's nature, if this freedom were so overridden that he became morally good, this would no longer be John Doe. God could, in principle, enforce a certain outward behaviour, but not the inner person, without destroying an autonomy that is part of the nature of a person. At the same time God can influence John Doe in a way that parallels and extends the influence of friends. Providence (and, for Whitehead, the whole work of God) works through the persuasive power of love. Another consequence of this understanding of omnipotence has a major impact on materialist arguments about the ruthlessness of nature – 'red in tooth and claw'. If anything recognizable as humankind is to be created, with the extraordinary 'median' nature of being rooted in physical and animal nature while, at the same time, having a transcending mind and a capacity to love, it may be *logically* demanded that this creature *evolve* through a long process. There may be various possibilities about the details of this evolution (as, perhaps, will be found on other planets), but the claim that God, if there be a God, *could* have done it so differently that there would be, for example, no competition for survival, may be logically absurd. Among the many intriguing suggestions that are relevant here is that of the neuroscientist, Irene Tracey, that human pain and consciousness may be inextricably linked.[13] I do not think we can *know* this kind of thing for certain, but nor do I think that the materialist can know, for certain, that there is any logical option, other than evolution, for a God who chooses to create a universe in which something corresponding to human life would exist. In this context, Voltaire's famous polemic on Leibniz's claim about the 'best of all possible worlds' turns out to be superficial.[14] With regard to omniscience, I have already outlined an argument against the view that it is logically possible for an infinite intelligence that is actively involved in human affairs (even if only at the mental and moral level) to know all the details of the future, given the reality of human freedom.

The understanding of both omnipotence and omniscience within the more recent liberal tradition has important implications not only for the traditional problem of suffering, but also for that of 'predestination'. This term, as normally used, implies more than the claim that God, in some way, 'foreknows' all that will happen – it suggests that, as sovereign Lord, God also directs or determines all that will happen. The huge literature on this issue centres on the obvious problem of how any such doctrine can be combined with the notions of human freedom and responsibility.

It is often claimed that those who upheld a strong doctrine of predestination, especially Calvin, felt themselves forced to do so by the 'remorseless logic' of any adequate account of God's sovereignty. The liberal response to this should now be clear. Classical accounts of predestination do not follow 'remorseless' logic, but a completely 'false' logic, because they begin with a flawed, and indeed contradictory, notion of what omnipotence means. The Thomistic doctrine of God's commitment to the law of non-contradiction, once again, has more implications that are often realized – even by many Thomists, who themselves have sometimes advocated strong accounts of predestination. There is no need for the Christian to say that God 'determines' everything that will happen. Indeed, the amazing nature of God's sovereignty is that in creating free agents (and also perhaps, in creating a natural order with its own inherent autonomy), God himself *chose* to give up total control. The Calvinist position introduces the new (and unnecessary) paradox, that a sovereign God *could not*, while being God, choose so to limit his sovereignty! At the same time, it does not follow that the whole debate on predestination was a matter of foolishness, and still less that the primary biblical texts on which the doctrine has been based (such as Romans 8: 29 and 1 Corinthians 15: 10) have nothing important to say. There is, once again, an important 'paradox' behind the debate, a paradox that arises out of human attempts to understand many things, both in science and in theology, from within the limited perspective of the human intellect. As in all the serious cases of such paradox, one can point to the insights that must be held in tension. In this case there is, on the one hand, the religious sense that God is 'sovereign Lord', and the conviction of the saints that 'by the grace of God I am what I am'; on the other hand, there is the equally religious sense that humans have responsibility and creative freedom. The famous debates on predestination, although leading in many cases to doctrines that, in my view, should be firmly rejected, have frequently been undertaken as a result of a commitment to take seriously both of these insights.

Creator 'Out of Nothing'

As we have seen, the claim that God is a creator does not necessarily mean that the universe started at a particular time, or more strictly, with time as we know it. Nor does it mean that God *directly* controls each new happening. On the positive side, an analogy with the way we as humans experience creativity, whether we are thinking of art, mechanical inventions, human relationships or political and social organizations, gives considerable substance to the idea of creativity *until* we come to the idea of creation *ex nihilo* – 'out of nothing' – for which there seems no human analogue. Here moderns theists can, I think, be divided into two groups. Some claim that here is something totally incomprehensible that just has to be accepted as a *necessary* consequence of there being a created order. The impossibility of any human analogue renders this act simply beyond our understanding. Others, within the general movement known as 'panentheism', do not see the need to speak of an act of creation *in this way*, on the grounds that it is a mistake to think of a God existing without a created order, and *deciding* to make an order. Rather they see the universe as a necessarily existing whole, and God as the being who is totally immanent within it, and responsible for its creative power. Whereas 'pantheism' (at least in its cruder forms) meant that God simply was 'everything'; 'panentheism' – literally 'God in everything' – says something more subtle. It denies that an account of all the items in the physical universe provides an account of God. Just as, in general, the whole is more than the sum of its parts, and just as, with any complex organism, a description of the parts leaves out the organizing principle (or 'soul' – in something like the sense used by Aristotle), so the God of panentheism, though immanent within the universe, also *transcends* it.

An interesting version of panentheism can be found in the writings of John Macquarrie, although he prefers the term 'dialectical theism' because of the way in which he sees any adequate description of thinking about God as involving two sides of the divine nature that need to be kept in balance.[15] Two examples of these dynamic tensions are transcendence and immanence, and impassibility (meaning inability to experience any change) and passibility.[16] Macquarrie tries to be fair to both classical theism and more recent, Whiteheadean ideas, but in many places his position ends up as sharply critical of the classical exposition. Another important thinker who adopts *some* aspects of the panentheist position is Keith Ward. For example, on the issue of divine suffering – which is closely related to the doctrine of creation – he sees value in the traditional teaching about the impassibility of God, while at the same time he criticizes its one-sidedness: 'For while God, being acquainted with my suffering, does truly suffer, nevertheless, God's appropriation of this suffering as part of the divine infinite knowledge is wholly different from mine. God knows exactly what my suffering is like; but God's infinite bliss cannot be destroyed by that experience.'[17] I do not propose to settle the debate on impassibility in these few pages! My point is simply that theism, once again, covers a range of options within it, and that although creativity is one of the essential characteristics of theism, there are different accounts of what this implies.[18]

The Goodness of God

The God of theism is described, at least within the major religions, as being both good and loving. This might seem an obvious point, but in fact the claim that a monotheistic God was 'good', in any sense that related to what humans mean by moral goodness, came comparatively late. The God described in the early strata of the Old Testament was certainly not loving to all people,[19] and by the standards of the great prophets his justice was questionable. The most serious problem with fundamentalism (when this is taken to mean belief in the verbal inspiration of the original scriptures) is the difficulty of interpreting passages where God, according to a literal reading of the text, commands the slaughter of women, children and animals, especially throughout the book of Joshua. Obviously, these commands to slaughter are connected with a primitive belief in 'solidarity', so that, for them, there was not the same problem of justice that faces those who believe in *individual* moral responsibility. One of the fascinating things about the Old Testament is to see the emergence of this belief in individual responsibility, especially in Jeremiah, and, at the same time, the belief that God is concerned with questions of human justice, for example, in Isaiah, Amos and Micah. Then, as a climax to this moral development, especially in Hosea, comes the idea that God is not only just, but loving. The Christian view is that Jesus represents the culmination and fulfilment of this process of development, already – like the golden rule – to be found in the Hebrew scriptures.

The following texts express three important advances in moral development:

> In those days they shall say no more, The fathers have eaten a sour grape, and the children's teeth are set on edge. But every one shall die for his own iniquity: every man that eateth the sour grape, his teeth shall be set on edge. (Jeremiah 31: 29–30)[20]

The old proverb, here rejected, powerfully expressed a belief in the appropriate effects of solidarity, along with the Mosaic belief that the sins of the fathers deserved punishment until the fourth generation. (Exodus 20: 5). Jesus went further, insisting that calamity need not be the result either of the sins of the fathers, or of one's own sin. (Luke 13: 4; John 9: 2–3).

> Woe unto them that join house to house, that lay field to field, till there be no place, that they may be placed alone in the midst of the earth! (Isaiah 5: 8)

Acts of enclosure have always raised problems of justice. Consider the problem of settlements today in the Holy Land.

> When Israel was a child, then I loved him, and called my son out of Egypt. (Hosea 11: 1)

This love is powerfully symbolized in Hosea's acceptance of, and marriage to, an unfaithful person.

Many scholars have pointed to a similar 'moralization of the gods' in other regions of the world at about the same time as these Hebrew sources, and it is this which has led to suggestions of a sort of world-wide spiritual movement during the fifth and sixth centuries BCE. Unless one holds that there was more physical communication than is so far known, here is one of the stronger bases for a Jungian account of the 'collective unconscious'.

One consequence of this moral development is that although goodness and love might *now* be called defining characteristics of theism, they could not always be described as such, because they were *discovered* to be attributes of God that replaced earlier ideas in which holiness was described in terms of dangerous power and purely *ritual* purity.[21] Indeed, the three passages just quoted would have been startling to many of those who first heard them.

Once the link between holiness and goodness is made, some new questions emerge. In particular, is goodness something that God creates, or is it something 'intrinsic', akin to the law of non-contradiction, which God recognizes? Plato, who discusses this issue in a classic passage,[22] solves the problem by identifying goodness with his non-personal God (the Idea of the Good), and by placing this God above the gods – who, being good, recognize, but do not invent, what is good. Other thinkers, including fourteenth-century Nominalists like Ockham, took the opposite tack, and made the will of a personal God the sole arbiter of what was to count as goodness.[23] Mainstream Christianity has tried to steer a course between these two positions, recognizing that Plato's solution of there being a Good that is 'above' God could not simply be taken over wholesale. Aquinas, for example, accepting the kernel of Plato's position, argued that God's *will* is necessarily in accordance with his good and loving nature. Therefore, arbitrary will does not determine morality; rather, it is determined by 'natural law', which humans can begin to grasp as they participate in the divine thinking about what will make for true human happiness and flourishing. Consistently, in Chapter 2 we noted *two* areas where, for the Thomist, God's sovereignty must be described in less than absolute terms. The first results from God's commitment to logical necessity, the second results from the direction of God's will by what is truly good. For Thomists, this does not place anything above God, since intrinsic and loving goodness are identified with the nature of God. However, this has not gone down well with all monotheists, for some hold that this Platonic-Thomistic compromise is at variance with the total sovereignty of God, to which one must submit. This is the case in some Islamic circles (bearing in mind that 'Islam' can be taken to mean 'submission'). But Islam is not monochrome on this matter, and within its history there has been a rationalist tradition, especially in the ninth and tenth centuries CE, within the movement known as the *Mu'tazila*, which adopted a version of Plato's solution. According to 'Abd al-Jabbar, for example, there is always an intelligible reason for the things prohibited or commanded in revelation.[24] Also, many Muslims point out how in the Qur'an the divine compassion and mercy are stressed alongside the divine transcendence, and this certainly invites a position which parallels that of Aquinas. In contemporary, popular Islam, however, there is a tendency to place no restrictions on the divine will.[25]

In the twentieth century, some sceptical thinkers, especially within the positivist tradition, reintroduced the ancient question of the relationship of God to goodness by asking whether 'God is good' is an analytic or synthetic statement.[26] If it is analytic (that is, based simply on an analysis of the meaning of the terms), then 'God is good' is true merely by definition, in which case there can be no sense of *discovering* a truth about reality. If it is synthetic (that is, not simply based on analysis), we only discover, as a matter of fact, that God is good, and therefore it is possible, in principle, that God might not be good. Either way, so the sceptic may continue, theists have a problem, since they want to say *both* – that 'God is good' is a meaningful statement, and that God is *necessarily* good.

The theist's reply to this challenge should begin with an awareness of the general assumptions that underlie positivism, as explored in Chapter 2. In particular, the sceptic's question assumes that all meaningful statements must be slotted into the frames of the analytic and the synthetic *as these are defined* within positivism. Moreover, even if these frames are adequate for ordinary statements about the world, it is assumed that there could be no room, in an overall philosophy, for a transcending concept like that of God, which could not be fitted into the categories that are appropriate for the world of 'things' in the universe.[27] Following this observation, a wise theist might continue as follows. In terms of the *history* of the human understanding of God (Aquinas' *via inventionis*), 'God is good' was a discovery, so that, in a way, the statement was 'synthetic'. However, the more God is understood (in Aquinas' *via judicii*),[28] the more it becomes clear that the reality that created the universe could not be other than 'good' – even though the nature of 'good' is first discovered, not by a definition of what God wills, but by the human experience of what makes for happiness and harmony and justice. Thus 'God is good' is not analytic in the simple sense of being true by analysing what the *word* 'God' means; it is however suspected to be necessarily true (by those who reflect on the divine nature) because of the kind of experience we have of God, and because of the kind of world which we experience as his creation. As a result, theists are certain that what God wills is good, not because his will simply defines the meaning of good, but because we have discovered that God's nature is in complete harmony with the human vision of the good. Moreover, we find that the human vision of the good needs to be enriched and made fuller, as we discover new dimensions of the good as God comes to be more understood (as in Hosea's revelations about the *love* of God). Thus as people moved forward from the first, faint understanding of God, manifested, for example, in the early strata of the Old Testament, the God whom they worshipped was *discovered* to be good in terms of a concept of good that was *initially* learned in a human context. However, this human context turned out to be what it was because of the loving nature of God. A consequence is that when an early religious narrative presents an account of God that seems to fall below our understanding of goodness, theists are perfectly entitled to question the accuracy of the narrative. This is not a simple case of judging God by human standards – as many fundamentalists insist – but of 'honouring' God, by recognizing, first, that our best insights into the nature of goodness must be applied to God and, second, that these insights have been assisted by God's own teaching as it unfolds in the later prophetic tradition, and in the life of Jesus.

The following consideration may add to our understanding of the relationship of God to the concept of 'good'. Any exposition of what the word 'good' signifies must include a sense of 'personal good' which comprises not only the things we strive for in the present, which are therefore regarded as objects of immediate desire, but also the things which have the capacity to fulfil our long-term hopes and needs and aspirations. In the light of this, it is virtually inevitable that if there is an intelligent, creative source of the universe, then these latter, more substantial 'goods' will be intimately linked with the nature and purposes of this creative source, since what will truly allow us to flourish must be related to fundamental aspects of our given natures. Within the mystical tradition, for example, to the writer known as Pseudo-Dionysius (about 500 CE), 'good' is one of the essential names of God, and the explanation given is in terms of the relationship of Creator to creation.[29]

The relation of God to goodness can now be summarized as follows. As with the other attributes of God a *via negativa* can be stated more easily. God is *not* good in the sense that good is *simply* the product of what he wills. A positive account of the good and loving nature that determines the divine will can only be stated hesitatingly and analogically, based on what is believed to be a narrative of God's dealings with humans (in the Scriptures) and the belief that when we see human persons acting justly and lovingly, they begin to reflect something of the loving nature of God.

God as the Source of Grace

We have already seen that one of the defining characteristics of God, within theism, is that he is personal. However, as we have also seen, this does not mean that we simply build God in our image: it arises out of the belief that at our best we are already reflections of God. Hence the term 'anthropomorphic', when applied to God, is ambiguous. When a child brought up in a monotheist family first learns to pray, it is almost inevitable that there will be features in the child's picture of God that are too human. Later, it would be natural to say that this anthropomorphic picture must give way to something more subtle. Much the same may need to be said to many adults, whose picture of God is so immature that when they abandon belief in God, they are rightly abandoning something that, for them, it is irrational to hold on to. Sadly, however, the concept of God that is appropriate for a more mature belief may never have developed so that the rejection of theism is actually the rejection of a caricature. When theism does mature, it does not, for the theist, mean the total abandonment of all elements of the anthropomorphic, because of the idea of the 'image of God'. What has been claimed about consciousness has strengthened this claim and given added grounds for a rational belief in theism. If it were inevitable that human consciousness evolve, then our little centres of consciousness may be a product of what might be called Consciousness. This suggestion already implies a God of some kind, although not necessarily a God who is aware of individuals. The claim that God is an infinite consciousness that (unlike Aristotle's God) knows and loves individuals is not, in my view, demonstrable by rational means, but it is perfectly consistent with rationality. Moreover, when we also take into account the phenomena of religious experience, additional rational grounds for a fully personal God can be developed.

The claim that God is in some way 'personal' leads naturally to the idea of 'grace'. Although this is a term most frequently used by Christians to refer to the way in which God assists and strengthens us, especially in the work of Christ and in the presence of the Holy Spirit, there are parallel notions of divine assistance and help that can also be called 'grace' in all the great monotheistic systems. Even in the case of philosophies that speak of God in non-personal ways, there can be an analogue of the idea of grace, but, in such cases, not in the sense of a personal God's direct concern with an individual. Plato, for example, gives a powerful picture of ultimate goodness and beauty (although unaware of us) *drawing* us by the power of love, and Aristotle's first mover draws all below him by an equivalent love. In both cases, however, it is not God's love for us that stirs this enabling grace, but our love of the beautiful.[30]

God as Ultimate Reality or Infinite 'Substance'

For those unfamiliar with traditional theological language, one of the most difficult aspects of the divine concerns the use of the word 'substance'. God, it is often said, is 'infinite substance', and in classical Christian theology Jesus, it is alleged, is of 'one substance' with the father. Clearly, 'substance' here does not mean 'stuff'. The closest English word to the original Greek, from which the term (*ousia*) is taken, is probably 'reality'. I am not suggesting that we return to the use of the word 'substance', but if we are to capture what traditional teaching about God has claimed we need to give equivalent force to some word such as 'reality'. It is partly for this reason that I was anxious, in Chapter 2, to argue against both the postmodernist position and that of Don Cupitt. Similarly, when religious people have talked about 'spirit', they have not meant some sort of rather thin or mental material, but something that is more *real* than anything experienced through the senses. Thus expressions like 'God is being' or 'God is spirit', as with 'God is substance', are all ways of making a claim about the reality of God, and all sound equally strange to someone brought up in a materialistic culture, who has been taught that what cannot be seen or touched or measured is suspect, except as some kind of phantasm of the mind. The assumptions built into this materialistic culture must be recognized for what they are. They *may* be justified, but they need to be justified. Theism (outside its presentations in writers like Cupitt) uses words like 'reality' to refer to an infinite being that, in principle, could not be seen with our eyes, or touched with our hands, or measured in any way. Once again, therefore, it is relatively easy to say what this reality is *not*. God is not a 'thing' or a 'being' just like other things or beings within the universe. This point has sometimes been made by saying, first, that God is 'no thing', and then by contracting this to 'God is nothing'. When the point of this statement is understood it can be a powerful way of pointing us away from some kind of idolatry but, of course, to the ordinary person it tends to be misunderstood as a claim that there is no God. Another way of stressing the way in which God's reality is essentially different from all 'derivative' reality, of the kind that belongs to creatures, is to deny that the word 'Being' can be properly used of God. Plotinus, in the fifth *Ennead* writes: 'In order that being be, The One must be not being but being's begetter.'[31] One can sympathize with this strain of thinking in the Neoplatonic tradition, but still think that the ordinary person is less likely to be misled if, like Aquinas, we think of God as 'Being' in some absolute sense, or as ultimate Reality. It should also be remembered that the Neoplatonic language has often been associated with an 'emanationist' doctrine that sits unhappily with the Christian idea of creation.

Within the Biblical tradition, this emphasis on the reality of God is intimately linked with the passage in the book of Exodus where Moses is told God's name: 'I am that I am.'[32] There is a scholarly debate concerning whether or not this was a teaching that actually goes back to Moses, perhaps around 1200 BCE, or whether it was a later interpretation, perhaps turning some more prosaic name into a variation of the verb 'to be'. However, this debate is of secondary importance, since even if the teaching came after Moses, it is an *astonishing* teaching, in the context of the history of world religions. Early in the Judaic tradition, it was either revealed or understood that a God who is truly the creative source of the whole universe, cannot have a name *like* the names we give to things, or even people. Moreover, the source of the world that we normally call 'reality' must have a nature that is superior to this reality, since it is the very source of all the 'being' that we know. This can be contrasted with a whole range of superstitious and magical traditions in which some secret name for God is revealed to the initiated, with the idea that by the use of this name some kind of power will be given to people. Instead of God being truly our sovereign Lord, he becomes an object to be manipulated to our convenience. As in superficial understandings of prayer, this is a terrible reversal of the true order of things.

With regard to a further account of what the divine reality (or substance) is, there are, I hold, three basic approaches open to those who are seeking to understand religion within the limits open to the human mind. The first is to stay, strictly, with the *via negativa*, and say that the nature of the divine reality is for ever 'incomprehensible', except in so far as we can use other terms that raise equivalent difficulties, such as spirit, or universal Mind. We can say what God's nature is not, but we cannot hope to give any positive account. This approach may be defended in terms of the general problem of attempting, from *within* the universe, to give an explanation for the ultimate source of the universe. There may still be a kind of natural theology that defends the need to claim that we must posit the reality of such an incomprehensible being, and there can also be claims that certain religious experiences point to the existence of such a reality, but there cannot be any rational exploration of the nature of the deity. However, the consistent use of this approach makes it very hard to give a coherent meaning to a statement such as 'God is love'. Even if this is a truth that depends purely on revelation, if it is a truth, then *something* positive is being asserted about the nature of God.

The second approach begins with the *via negativa*, but, as in Aquinas, allows *some* place for an analogy of attribution, and therefore does make it possible to claim that 'God is love' expresses a 'truth'. This approach also allows some positive meaning to claims that God is ultimate 'reality', or that (in traditional scholastic language), in God, 'essence' and 'existence' come together. This is the version of classical theism for which I have sympathy, and certainly do not rule out. However there is another approach that may claim to say something more about the divine nature.

This third (and very speculative) approach builds upon the link between human consciousness and the concept of a universal source of this consciousness that has already been made. It also builds upon the doctrine of the *Imago Dei*, but stretches this doctrine further. Let us suppose, as has already been suggested as a possibility, that human consciousness can best be described either as a field of energy, or as something that is analogous to a field of energy. This field is associated with the brain, but is not, strictly speaking, located in one, identifiable place. Within such a view there are a range of possible beliefs. For example, just possibly this field of energy pre-existed the particular body we have, but such reincarnational views are in no way demanded by this suggestion. The field might gradually emerge as conscious activity develops in the foetus or baby. Equally, this suggestion leaves open the question of life after physical death. At death the field might vanish, or gradually wither away, or continue indefinitely as a field with a unique identity. Yet another possibility is that there is no sharp division between humans and other animals, but rather a sharp distinction between the human *level*, which is characterized by a special kind of complexity within the field (that can then be the context for consciousness, creativity and love), and the purely animal *level*, with many humans tending to live, at least some of the time, on an animal or even a vegetable level. (The term 'couch potato' may be more significant than people realize!) Meanwhile, some non-human animals may have flashes of consciousness that intimate a 'human' level. On this view, there is no need to see human beings as emerging suddenly within the evolutionary process, either by a special act of creation or through a highly original mutation. The human *level* is really distinct from the animal level, but individual primates and proto-humans could live in a kind of hinterland, with periodic glimpses of the truly human level. An analogy for this situation that has been suggested is that of the first fish-like creatures who ventured on to dry ground, and who (after an interim period of evolution) were able to survive in two realms (the land and the sea), but without total comfort in either. The parable of Adam tells of the emergence of a new level of being (born on a physical level, but with potential on the spiritual), not the instant creation of a particular individual. In sum, with respect to an understanding of the human species, and the final significance of individual persons, there are many options within theism, although at the end of Chapter 7 I shall give rational grounds for believing in human immortality.

Within such a 'field' theory of consciousness, if God is real, and if God can properly be said to have thoughts, and a consciousness of which our thoughts and consciousnessess are pale imitations, then perhaps God has a quasi-material aspect, as in the case of human minds. Once again, the divine consciousness could either be seen as a vast, or infinite field of energy, or as something analogous to such a vast field of energy. This would be one way of interpreting a panentheist version of theism. In cruder versions of panentheism, the physical universe is sometimes said to be God's 'body', although God, in his totality, transcends the physical universe. A more cautious form of panentheism would not wish to use the word 'body', because this invites misunderstanding, and suggests something analogous to a 'composite' view of the divine nature, but it does stress the immanence of God within the universe, not simply as an exterior being that loves it, but as a heart and mind (once again, using the language of analogy) that is found within the context of the network of interrelationships that the universe truly is. If this is one way that God's reality can be conceived, his creative relationship to us can be *partially* understood. We know how fields of energy interact with other fields of energy and interpenetrate them without losing their identity. In this way we can conceive how human (or other intelligent) minds could be aware of each other, and influence each other, and, on the model I am putting forward, God's influence is of the same kind, only magnified and exalted. Some of the ways in which the divine Mind works must be beyond our understanding, but once it is admitted that we can have some knowledge of God, like dim reflections in a mirror, based on a genuine resemblance between our consciousnesses and his, then there is no need to insist on *total* incomprehensibility. Both in science, and elsewhere, I have already argued, the rational approach to all mysteries is not only to seek for some evidence of what is, but also to search for some explanation that makes for comprehension. Later on, I shall indicate how this approach enables some progress to be made in two problems that are otherwise, for the theist, total mysteries. The first is the teaching of the Christian version of theism to the effect that Jesus was the unique Son of God. The second is the problem of explaining the criterion of identity, if it is held that the immortality of individual persons is a consequence of the divine love of a personal God.

God as 'Necessary Being'

The last feature of theism I shall discuss also raises many difficulties. It is the idea that God, in some way, exists *necessarily* rather than *contingently*. Sometimes this characteristic of God is called 'aseity', which means 'self-caused'. When this word is used, the claim is being made that God is totally different from every 'contingent' thing in the universe or from the universe taken a whole. This forms one of the essential steps in the traditional cosmological argument. This phase of the argument can be summarized thus: whereas it makes sense to ask for an explanation of any 'thing' within the universe, and whereas it may make sense to ask for an explanation of the universe itself when it is seen as an integrated whole, it makes no sense to ask for an explanation of God, once his nature is understood. Referring to a being with this self-caused nature, the philosopher Richard Taylor wrote: 'Now whether such a being in fact exists or not, there is in any case no absurdity in the idea. We have found, in fact, that the principle of sufficient reason seems to point to the existence of such a being, as that upon which the world, with everything in it, must ultimately depend for its existence.'[33]

This argument, I have found, is unconvincing to many people, and I suspect that the chief reason is that they are not sure about Taylor's claim that there is 'no absurdity in the idea' of a self-caused being, namely God, about whose existence no explanation can meaningfully be asked. It is important, therefore, to examine further this idea of a 'necessary' being.

One of the standard objections to this idea goes as follows: 'necessary' suggests 'logical necessity', and this is a term that can properly be applied to some logical or mathematical *relations*, but not to *beings*. For example, the conclusion of a valid syllogism follows *necessarily*, if the premises are true. However, to transfer this word to an entity, it is often alleged, is to render it incoherent. On the other side, if God is real, then he is not a being, like other beings, that might or might not be – that is to say, that is characterized by 'contingency'. So the word 'necessary' has been used for this unique being in order to distinguish God from *all* contingent entities that might or might not exist. The word 'necessary', it is suggested, is the most natural one to use as a contrast with the word 'contingent', even though a necessary *relation* is not being referred to. (Richard Swinburne has distinguished six senses of the term 'necessary being' and those wanting to pursue this issue further could begin by considering his discussion.[34]) Once again, therefore, we can combine a *via negativa* with a more positive approach. God is not 'necessary' in the sense that some mathematical and logical *relations* are necessary. On the positive side, the word 'necessary' carries a sense of 'not by chance', or 'not-contingent' that points to a fundamental aspect of the way in which God, it is believed, has a reality that is different from that of any created thing. Put in this way, it can be seen that God as creator, God as ultimate reality, and God as necessary being are interrelated.

But now another difficulty arises. If God, to be God, must be 'necessary' in the sense of 'non-contingent', then it follows that imagining his non-existence does not make sense, and this in turn, suggests either that we should be able to prove the existence of God as absolutely certain, or that the term 'God' is incoherent, so that God *cannot* possibly exist. This is, in fact, how the issue is sometimes seen.[35] Yet again, however, one of Aquinas' insights can help us see the issue differently. If we could see God as he really is, and as he sees himself, then we would see that God must be, and must be as he is. Thus 'God exists' is self-evident 'in itself' but not 'to us'. To put this in another way, from God's point of view, but not from ours, the ontological argument (that is, an argument based purely on an understanding of the idea of 'God') is valid.[36] We only see God dimly. What we do see is that *if* God is real, then he must exist and must be as he is. His existence, and his nature, properly understood, would be seen to be 'self-explanatory' in a way that could not apply to any other being. Hence we can say that there is no necessary proof, *for us*, of the existence of God, and yet, at the same time, if there is a God of the kind referred to in the theistic traditions, then at this point the search for explanation has to stop. Referring to the being that comprises this stopping point Keith Ward writes: 'its simple description would have to provide the reason for its being as it is.'[37] We then have something that corresponds to what Swinburne calls an 'ultimate explanation'.[38] The importance of this characteristic of God – that is, as 'necessary being' – will be further explored in the next chapter, when it will be seen as an element within the cosmological argument, when that argument is properly understood.

This concludes the aspects of deity that I have picked out in order to bring out what theism entails. The first three 'essential' or 'defining' characteristics are (1) unity, (2) creativity, (3) a 'personal' nature that allows one to say that God *loves*. The seven additional characteristics comprise: (4) God as providential governor of the universe; (5) God as omnipotent and omniscient power; (6) God as creative source of the *whole* universe; (7) God as good (an insight that eventually leads to the realization that God is love); (8) God as the personal source of grace; (9) God as ultimate reality; (10) God as necessary being. In each case a *via negativa* can say, in a certain manner, what God is not, but also I have claimed that something positive about the nature of God can be asserted by way of analogy.

God and Mystery

In the rest of this chapter I propose to focus on three concepts to round off the discussion of the meaning of theism. The first concerns the concept of mystery, the second that of revelation, the third that of personal faith.

Sometimes the word 'mystery' is used, very superficially, to refer to a puzzle, or something that is simply not yet known. At other times, it is used for things that are either unknown, or partially unknown, as a way of referring to an idea of profundity, or deep importance, the result of which is that any answer given cannot 'plumb the depths'. One critic of the cosmological argument, Milton Munitz, in a generally perceptive book, argues that a problem with theism is that in giving an answer to the 'mystery' of existence, it then (for theists) removes the mystery. However, he claims, the whole point of the mystery of existence is that there is not, and could not be an 'answer'.[39] This is a mistake, because when a partial answer is offered to the kinds of question I am concerned with, the sense of mystery may not, and perhaps should not, disappear, whether we are thinking of science or religion. When Roger Penrose thinks about a fundamental question in science, he refers to 'the *mysterious* relationship between the Platonic mathematical world and the world of physical objects',[40] but this does not mean that he has no understanding of the matter. Similarly, when typically religious people look up at the stars and marvel at them and feel a profound mystery concerning them, this does not mean that they have no sense of what they are. Even though they may know a lot about the physics of stars, and may be convinced that they are the product of a creative intelligence, and that they are part of a great purposive and evolutionary scheme, this partial understanding does not remove the sense of mystery – if anything, it deepens it. The sense of mystery surrounds things or events that inspire awe, and whether or not we believe that we have some insights into what they are, and why they are, this sense of mystery remains.

Theism and Revelation

The idea of 'revelation' is intimately related to that of religious experience since it is often claimed that some kind of knowledge or insight, that would not otherwise be available, has resulted from such experience. In a broad sense, revelation is something that arises in all the major religions, since none of them is without a history of religious experience of one kind or another, but it is typically in the context of theism that revelation is most often referred to. In all the major versions of monotheism, truth is alleged to be given by God, sometimes in the form of words, sometimes in the form of a prophetic vision that then must be put into words, and sometimes in the form of an event that then must be interpreted. The discussion of the relationship of experience to interpretation is of fundamental importance here, for any rational evaluation of the great religions must ponder the questions of how far each one depends upon some specific claim to revelation, and how far such claims are justified – especially in view of the fact that, superficially at least, some of the claims seem to be in tension with each other.

The position that is implicit in the foregoing sections can be summarized like this: although it is not denied that God may, on occasions, have revealed actual words to a human being, in general, the revelatory experiences that are central to the major religions do not need to be seen as verbal, but rather as events that are charged with meaning, or as inner personal experiences that are later found to be charged with meaning. Examples of revelatory events would include the Jewish deliverance from Egypt and the central events of the life of Jesus, namely his birth, teaching, death and the disciples' experience of his presence at Easter. Examples of inner experiences might include Moses' reception of the Ten Commandments on Sinai and Muhammad's reception of what later was recorded in the Qur'an, although how far these were purely *inner* experiences is clearly controversial.

If this view is accepted, it follows that revelation has frequently been both misunderstood by followers of the great forms of monotheism, and unfairly caricatured by sceptics. Acceptance of revelation is not, or at least should not be, the blind acceptance of some alien authority, for one's personal interpretation and personal experience enter into the way revelation is received. In the case of revelatory *events*, then the mature believer must interpret what happened, or is alleged to have happened, in their own way and, in the case of the revelatory *inner experiences* of others, then these too have little significance until they have gone through a process of reflection, and very often a linking with one's own personal experience. For example, Christians may be taught about the experience of being 'in Christ', which emerges from the testimony of Paul and other first-generation Christians and which forms part of the theology of the church, but until a contemporary Christian has some personal experience, either of fellowship within the Christian community, or of what they believe to be a personal experience of the presence of Christ, or both, then this alleged 'revelation' will have little meaning. Thus in the case of both events and experiences, revelation is not, within the liberal tradition, some kind of absolute authority that is independent of personal evaluation. Of course, if a theist believes in a personal God, he or she then believes that God has some kind of absolute authority, but this does not mean that any specific *claim* to represent this authority must be accepted without question. Moreover, it can be argued that only when the concept of God is integrated with the concept of the Good (as it is within this chapter), is any doctrine of God's absolute sovereignty to be welcomed. The evidence for this is precisely the atrocities that have so frequently been justified in the name of religion, when what were believed to be God's commands, and therefore worthy of absolute obedience, were totally divorced from rational evaluations of the good. In contrast, even the most anti-religious zealot, if they have any moral agenda, believes in the absolute sovereignty of Good, meaning that in so far as we believe that we can discern the good, this is the object of a compelling moral obligation. In this regard it is also significant to note that the God revealed in the Christian tradition seems to eschew reliance on any blind obedience. When asked a question, Jesus typically asked a more searching question in return, and usually taught in parables that leave us to interpret in a way that respects our autonomy. By implication, God wants disciples, but not fanatical zealots.

Secular caricatures which fail, in an adequate way, to distinguish between fundamentalist and more rational views of revelation abound. An interesting example is in Ernest Gellner's *Postmodernism, Reason and Religion*,[41] and in this case the context illuminates the unfortunate results of misunderstanding. In essence, Gellner sees three and only three strong candidates for a world-view. Religious fundamentalism he rejects for reasons that parallel several of my arguments. The kind of relativism that goes with postmodernism he also rejects for reasons similar to my own. The 'third' way, which he espouses, is called 'Enlightenment Rationalist Fundamentalism', and attempts to provide a rational basis for a programme of political and moral reform. However, he does not see that many religious people (Christians and others) could make common cause with him here – with respect to his moral agenda – because he rejects the 'very possibility' of revelation on the grounds that his third option 'does not allow any cultures to validate a part of itself with final authority, to decree some substantive affirmation to be privileged and exempt from scrutiny'.[42] In at least two ways this is a misunderstanding of what revelation stands for. First, for reflective theists, 'final authority' only arises when the alleged revelation has been sifted and reflected upon, and concluded to be the expression of a God who is good. It then parallels the way in which a good secular humanist will regard the moral imperative to attempt to reduce suffering as a kind of 'final authority'. Second, the liberal tradition never defends exemption from scrutiny.

The foregoing suggests the kind of response that should be made to George Lindbeck's approach to religion, briefly introduced in Chapter 4. To see revelation *primarily* as 'propositional', reflecting a 'cognitive' approach to religion, is mistaken, in view of the existential dimension of faith. However, at least for historical religions such as Christianity, *some* religious assertions need to be made if one is to have a faithful continuation of the tradition. One might support these fundamental assertions by saying that they represent 'propositions', but I would prefer to phrase the claim differently. To call an assertion like 'God is love' a 'proposition' is misleading, not because it looks like a truth claim (which, in my view, it is), but because it is so unlike what we normally think of as a 'propositional truth', like 'Edinburgh is the capital of Scotland'. In contrast, a fundamental Christian assertion like 'God is love', represents the claim to a truth that must be both sought after (because we only dimly see what the truth is), and responded to in the way that one lives.

In some passages, Lindbeck allows for the possibility of some 'ontologically true affirmations' within his own 'cultural-linguistic' approach, but when one looks closely at why he allows this, misgivings arise: 'Propositional truth and falsity [within Lindbeck's approach] characterize ordinary religious language when it is used to mould lives through prayer, praise, preaching, and exhortation. It is only on this level that human beings linguistically exhibit their truth or falsity … .'[43] My problem is not with the prayer, praise, preaching and exhortation, it is with the 'only at this level'. Despite the many insights that come from Lindbeck's analogy of the 'grammar' of religion with the grammar of a language, something important is left out. The traditional Christian, including the traditional liberal Christian, believes that behind and beyond the physical universe there is a loving creator who is reaching down to us in love, and that this would be true even if no person realized it and no religious grammar presently recognized it. Behind all human constructions, there is a discovery, a truth waiting to be revealed.

God and Personal Faith

An understanding of the roles of mystery and of religious experience leads naturally to a consideration of personal faith. In the discussion of monism I referred to the living reality of certain experiences, and the same point must be made about theism. Indeed, I have suggested that very often the root experiences may be the same in monism and theism. Without an awareness of the power and nature of these experiences the foregoing account of the major characteristics of the God of theism are like the proverbial 'dry bones'.[44] For only a few very cerebral individuals has theism been primarily a philosophical idea. Thus we can sympathize with Pascal's outburst, when recording a profound religious experience:

> God of Abraham, God of Isaac, God of Jacob,
> Not the God of philosophers and scholars …[45]

For the vast majority of theists, religion has been a living faith, and even if most of them have not had religious experiences of a dramatic kind, such as those recorded in the writings of the famous mystics, they have had religious experience of a less dramatic nature. For example, they have tried to pray, and sometimes *felt* what they believed to be the presence of God; they have tried – at least some of the time – to live a religious life, and have sometimes felt upheld by grace. Moreover, when we try to appreciate this 'common-or-garden' religious experience that forms part of the life-blood of all the great religions, it may be artificial to draw a sharp line between religious experience and purely secular reflection on the mystery of consciousness. There does not have to be a sharp division between 'ordinary experience' in all its richness, and 'religious experience'. In this regard the writings of Heidegger, despite monumental obscurity, especially in his earlier works, bear witness. His reiterated starting-point is the awareness, within the consciousness of the reflective individual, of 'Being'. Thus in typical language, that is at the same time both mystifying and compelling, he writes to one student: 'To think "Being" means: to respond to the appeal of its presencing.'[46]

In the next chapter we shall review the issue of how far the faith of theists can be supported by rational argument.

Notes and References

1 The term 'henotheism' is sometimes used to describe a view in which there is a supreme God but also a number of lesser beings who share enough divine characteristics to be called 'gods'. It may then be said that in the Old Testament we see henotheism gradually being replaced by monotheism.

2 Aquinas, *ST* 1a, Q. 46 and *De Potentia*, 3, 17.

3 See, for example, Harris, E.E. (1992), *Cosmos and Theos*, New Jersey: Humanities Press, p. 186.

4 From the fragments of his writings that remain (from the second century CE), it seems that the physical world we know was created by a lesser, somewhat imperfect God, while the perfect heavens were the product of a superior God, of whom Jesus was the true representative.

5 See Hurlbutt III, R.H. (1965), *Hume, Newton, and the Design Argument*, Lincoln: University of Nebraska Press, p. 7.

6 Manuel, F.E. (1974), *The Religion of Isaac Newton*, Oxford: Clarendon, pp. 17 ff.

7 See Aquinas, *ST* 1a, Qs. 3–4. Several ideas combine to bring about the teaching about divine simplicity. One is the realization that God is in no way 'composite', because he is not made of 'matter'. This, in turn, relates to the way in which in God, unlike the case of creatures, there can be no distinction between the nature or 'essence' and actual existence. This, in turn, is linked with the understanding that in God there is no unrealized potential (as in creatures), or, in Scholastic language, that God is 'pure act'. My defence of some aspects of process theology need not involve a denial of any of these claims, but it does involve a controversial interpretation of them. God, in his freedom, has chosen to create creatures 'in his image', thereby accepting certain 'limitations' upon his freedom. In this context, while the divine nature cannot be changed in itself (it is fully 'realized' within what Whitehead calls God's 'primordial nature') his relationship to us (which involves God's 'consequential nature') is subject to a certain kind of change.

8 Farrer, A.M. (1966), *A Science of God?*, London: Geoffrey Bles, p. 90.

9 See Langford, M.J. (1981), *Providence*, London: SCM Press.

10 cf. *Omnipotens vero est non quid possit omnia facere, sed quia potest efficere quidquid vult. Epitome Theologiae Christianae*. (Omnipotence, truly, is not being able to do all things, but being able to bring about whatever one wishes.) V, *PL* vol. 178, 1700. The *Epitome* has been ascribed to Abelard but may be by one of his pupils. In the same passage, the author approves Augustine's claim that God cannot do injustice (*non potest facere injusta*) because he is himself the highest justice and the highest good.

11 Anselm, *Proslogium*, ch. 7.

12 William of Ockham, *Quodlibet* VI, q. 6.

13 See *Oxford Today* (The University Magazine) **12** (1), 1999, p. 24.

14 The term 'best' in this context is highly ambiguous. One can easily imagine a world where there was no suffering, but the issue is whether one could conceive, in all its details, a world containing free agents, capable of love, who were the product of an evolutionary process, in which there was no suffering.

15 Macquarrie, J. (1984), *In Search of Deity*, London: SCM Press, p. 15.

16 Ibid. pp. 178–81.

17 Ward, K. (1991), *A Vision to Pursue*, London: SCM Press, p. 96.

18 For an introduction to panentheism, see the writings of Charles Hartshorne, including (1967), *A Natural Theology for our Time*, La Salle, Illinois: Open Court.

19 For example, in the case of the children who died in the great flood and the innocent children of Canaan. It is not clear that God was loving to the adults, but here their destruction can at least be related to the claim that they were sinners.

20 cf. Ezekiel 18: 2–4 where, at a later date, the same proverb is again referred to and rejected.

21 cf. Isa. 5: 16, where, perhaps for the first time, holiness is defined in terms of righteousness.

22 Plato, *Euthyphro*, 10a.

23 Ockham's position is not the extreme 'voluntarism' often attributed to him. In the famous passage where he says that if God willed us to hate him this would be good, it needs to be pointed out that obeying God, in such circumstances would be, in a sense, showing our love for God. On this issue see his commentary on the sentences (of Peter Lombard), [*Reportatio*] II, Q. 15 (vol. 5 pp. 342 ff. in the Bonaventura edn, New York, 1981). Further, his references to the generosity of God do not make sense if what constitutes 'generosity' is purely what God decides to count as such. Also, in his discussion of ethics he makes several references to the need to have 'right reason' (*recta ratio*). For an overview see Copleston, F. (1953), *A History of Philosophy*, London: Burns and Oates, vol. 3, pp. 104–10.

24 Hourani, G.F. (1971), *Islamic Rationalism – The Ethics of 'Abd al-Jabbar*, Oxford: Clarendon Press, p. 57.

25 Genuine dialogue on moral issues between those who believe in verbal inspiration (be they Christian, Jewish or Muslim) and others can be very difficult. For a Thomist any claim that God wills something that is moral should be able to be backed up, in principle, with the *reasons* why this thing is good. Moreover, these reasons should be seen to be reasons by all people of intelligence and good will. This is why, on this view, St Paul talked about the moral law being written in the hearts of all people (Rom. 2: 14–15). However, the more moral goodness is defined purely in terms of what God wills, the harder it is to get hold of any 'reasons' for a position that one could discuss. Furthermore, with the stress on God's will tends to come a belief that certain human authorities have a unique right to interpret this will. Then, when these authorities disagree, there seems to be no possibility of a rational forum for discussion.

26 See, for example, Nielson, K. (1973), *Ethics without God*, London: Pemberton Books, pp. 5 ff.

27 A similar problem arises with the positivist's question: 'Is "God" a name or a description?' The theist cannot readily fit the concept of God into either of these categories. However, the demand that the concept must fit into one or the other is a special case of *assuming* that theism is meaningless.

28 Aquinas, *ST* 1a. Q. 79, 8 and 9.

29 Pseudo-Dionysius Areopagite, *The Divine Names* 693A–701B.

30 See Plato's *Symposium*, especially at 200, where there is a moving account of love as a kind of emptiness or poverty, striving for a beauty that it does not yet possess.

31 Plotinus, *Enneads*, V, 2, 1, in *The Essential Plotinus*, trans. E. O'Brien (1964), Toronto: Mentor, p. 107.

32 Ex. 3: 14.

33 Taylor, R. (1963), *Metaphysics*, Englewood Cliffs, NJ: Prentice Hall, reprinted in D.R. Burrill, ed. (1967), *The Cosmological Arguments*, New York: Doubleday, p. 293.

34 Swinburne, R. (1993), *The Coherence of Theism*, Oxford: Clarendon Press, chs 13 and 14.

35 In a famous article the philosopher J.N. Findlay argued that since God, if he existed, had to be a necessary existent, and since this concept was self-contradictory, his existence could be *disproved*. Later, after discussions with Hartshorne, he changed his mind, and argued that if God is in any way *possible*, then his existence must be *necessary*. See Plantinga, A., ed. (1968), *The Ontological Argument*, London: Macmillan, pp. 111–22.

36   Aquinas, *ST* 1a, Q 2, 1.
37   Ward, K. (1982), *Rational Theology and the Creativity of God*, Oxford: Blackwell, p. 6.
38   Swinburne, R. (1979), *The Existence of God*, Oxford: Clarendon Press, pp. 76–7.
39   Munitz, M.K. (1965), *The Mystery of Existence*, New York: Appleton-Century-Crofts.
40   Penrose, R. (1995), *Shadows of the Mind*, London: Vintage, 1995, p. 416. See also Searle, J. (1989), *Mind, Brains and Science*, London: Penguin, p. 24 who wants us to maintain 'our sense of the mysteries of nature'.
41   Gellner, E. (1992), *Postmodernism, Reason and Religion*, New York: Routledge.
42   Ibid., p. 76. On p. 4, Gellner suggests that non-fundamentalist religious people reduce their teachings to 'doctrinal vacuity'. In the case of moral teachings this misses the point that it is not only the content of ethics that is at stake, but the status of moral values.
43   Lindbeck, G. (1984), *The Nature of Doctrine*, London: SPCK, p. 68.
44   See Ez. 37.
45   Translated from the paper found sewn up in Pascal's doublet after his death. In a way this outburst is misleading since many religious philosophers have had equally profound experiences of God, but it does express very well the difference between a merely philosophical idea of God and the experience of a living presence.
46   Heidegger, M., *Poetry, Language, Thought*, trans. A. Hofstadter (1975), New York: Harper and Row, p. 183.

Chapter 6

The Traditional Arguments for the Existence of God

The Cosmological Argument Revisited

Several steps have been taken which prepare the way for a reconsideration of the ancient cosmological argument for the existence of God. First, over against Logical Positivism, a case has been made for the meaningfulness of language about God. Not only have the general assumptions that underlie positivism been questioned, an attempt has been made, especially in Chapter 5, to indicate what the word 'God' means, notably within the context of religious narratives. Second, over and against postmodernism, a case has been made for some universal aspects of reason, in terms of which an argument can be held to support a universally true conclusion. In particular, the attack on postmodernism has suggested the way in which reason can respond to the search for some general philosophy, both through the criterion of finding a position that is internally and externally coherent, and in terms of seeking an 'organizing idea' of the kind that Keith Ward describes. Third, it has been argued that the universe needs to be seen as a 'whole', rather than as a collection of discrete events or things. Fourth, although both materialism and monism have been presented as possible candidates for a general philosophy of life, it is clear that neither is free of problems. Also, when these world-views are presented with some sensitivity to these problems, it is not certain that they are necessarily in conflict with all forms of theism. Fifth, the sense in which God can be thought of as a 'necessary' being has been explored, and the significance of this will be taken up shortly. Finally, the account of the concept of God given in Chapter 5 makes it clear that any demand for a 'proof' of the reality of God, corresponding to the way in which the word 'proof' is used in contexts like those of mathematics, science and law, indicates a failure to *understand* the concept of God. The concept of a reality that both undergirds the physical universe and transcends it could not possibly be demonstrated in a manner that is appropriate for items within the universe. What we might hope to find is (i) a demonstration of the shallowness of any philosophy that reckons to explain the richness of our experience without reference to the divine, and (ii) a demonstration of how a theistic philosophy enriches and enhances our understanding of human experience. These things can provide the rational context for faith, but there is a systematic absurdity in claiming that what religious people mean by 'faith' could ever be achieved simply by reflection, and without an existential dimension. Faith can, and I argue, should, avoid any acceptance of the *irrational* but, by its very nature, faith must go beyond the rational and involve a commitment of the person.

The way is now clear for a consideration of the rational claims of theism. We shall begin with the ancient cosmological argument, a form of argument that goes back at least as far as Plato's *Laws*.[1]

Those who reject the cosmological argument rarely quote, or indeed are aware of, the more recent formulations of it as found, for example, in the writings of Richard Swinburne, Keith Ward and Errol Harris. I shall argue that, properly understood, the argument does carry weight, and helps to render theism a viable option.

In order to appreciate the force of the cosmological argument, in addition to the preparatory steps mentioned above, the argument needs to be reformulated in order to link it with two of the other arguments that past theologians have used, realizing that they are all aspects of the same argument. In the past some theologians have offered the 'ontological' argument, based merely on the implications of the idea of God,[2] the 'cosmological' argument, based on the very existence of the universe, and the 'teleological' argument that stressed the alleged 'design' manifested in the universe. When the three are combined, the structure of the argument goes like this: when the nature of the universe is appreciated, as a complex whole, then an explanation for it is demanded that goes beyond anything that materialism can offer. What must be explained is not only the bare existence of the universe (as in the cosmological argument), but the complex structure that has led to the emergence of consciousness. This is a teleological argument, but not in the old form that proceeded, unconvincingly, from the need to explain individual things in the universe by an exterior designer (formulations of the argument that were rightly rejected by Hume), but an acknowledgement of the complex structure, as a whole, that has led to consciousness and the capacity to love. This is the form of the argument that is essentially unaffected by Darwinian explanations, for the fundamental 'mystery' does not consist in an understanding of how one thing changes into another (which is the proper subject of the empirical sciences), but in an appreciation of the extraordinary nature of the cosmic whole, which has, from the beginning of time, the capacity to bring forth 'the myriad of things'. The explanation that is then suggested is not an 'explanation' in the scientific sense, that would be couched in terms of how different elements within the universe are related to each other, but an 'explanation' that addresses the question of how the 'whole' can be accounted for. The suggestion made by the cosmological argument is that the universe is dependent on an infinite consciousness that exists by some kind of necessity (as formulated by the ontological argument), rather than by chance, a consciousness which acts as a creative force throughout the universe, and of which our minds are either parts or reflections.[3] Expressed in this way it can be seen how the ontological, cosmological and teleological arguments are all part of a larger response to the mystery of existence.

The importance of the ontological argument within the larger argument needs to be further explored. As I have indicated, when it is used by itself, for the reasons I have given, it does not demonstrate the existence of God to the unbeliever, despite its forceful presentation by St Anselm. Its importance lies elsewhere, namely in pointing to the *nature* of the being with which all the theological arguments are concerned. The materialist, as we have seen, cannot see why questions of explanation should stop at any point – why not go on asking them for ever, or why not simply admit that some questions cannot meaningfully be asked? But behind this materialism lie one or two basic assumptions. Either it is assumed (often in an unexamined borrowing from a controversial positivist philosophy), that all non-scientific questions about reality must be meaningless; or it is assumed that the Being referred to in the theological arguments is just another 'being' of the kind explored by the sciences. However, unlike the 'objects' explored by the sciences, the concept of God is, we have seen, that of a 'necessary' being, about whom it does not make sense to ask for a cause.

Here I can indicate two additional reasons for taking very seriously the possibility of there being an ultimate explanation of the universe that does not, in its turn, need to be explained. One refers back to religious experience. While the feelings and the sense of 'presence' do not themselves provide an intellectual description of what is experienced, the sense of the 'wholly other' and of the 'numinous' is utterly congruous with a claim that one is in relation to a being that transcends all contingent existence, and upon whom everything depends. The other reason refers back to the scientific search for intelligibility. We cannot prove that the world is 'intelligible', but its intelligibility is something that has undergirded science from the time of Anaxagoras to the search for a unified field theory. But *if* the universe is ultimately intelligible, then it must make sense to go on asking for explanations *until* there is a reason why the explanation that is offered is 'ultimate'. This idea of an ultimate explanation is suggested by the theistic doctrine of God, and this is why some philosophers hold that contemporary science actually points to theism. It points, rather than proves, since there is no proof that everything is ultimately intelligible, but it may turn out that a crucial assumption that undergirds theology is one that also undergirds science.

A reconsideration of the anthropic principle can strengthen the case for seeing God as the 'ultimate' explanation. I suggested earlier that it makes sense to ask for an explanation of the integrated whole that comprises the universe, but I also think that when we include consciousness in our account of the universe the situation changes. In practice, however, one cannot exclude consciousness from the universe, because for a question about the universe to be posed at all, it must be posed by a conscious mind that is – by definition – part of the universe.[4] However, any explanation when applied to a conscious mind is subtly different from the explanation of non-conscious 'things'. When we ask for an explanation of how a particular consciousness arises, such as my own, only *part* of the answer is in terms of my immediate ancestors. Another part of the answer lies in the potentiality within the universe to produce consciousness. If we consider the possibility of taking the anthropic principle in its strong sense, and if, in line with this, we explore the possibility that Consciousness has been there all the time, waiting to be exemplified in all these different individual consciousnesses, then the explanation of particular consciousnesses refers back to something (Consciousness) that is not time-related to the emergence of my particular consciousness. This Consciousness is indeed prior to *any* individual consciousness. This does not provide a proof of theism, for the argument at this point assumes both the strong anthropic principle and the actual presence of Consciousness in the universe from all eternity, but it provides an explanation of individual consciousnesses that is congruous, and fits in, with the idea of a necessary being.

Theism is a rational interpretation of the universe, especially when the phenomenon of consciousness is taken into account.

Strictly, however, (as before) theism is not *one* rational option, for there are at
least two theistic views of this matter, and we can be agnostic about which is the
better. On one (classical) view, the Consciousness that is the ultimate source of my
consciousness lies in an eternal Mind that exists outside the physical universe, but
that is nevertheless in an intimate relationship with it. On the other (panentheist)
view, Consciousness arises out of the complexity of the physical universe itself,
when it is seen as a whole. In either case, while the question 'What is the explanation of this individual consciousness?' is perfectly clear, and we can begin to
answer it, the question 'What is the explanation of Consciousness?' is a different
kind of question. The suggestion that it has always been there, and that, unlike
particular minds, Mind is eternal, is perfectly coherent. The Consciousness to
which the anthropic principle points stands, as it were, behind the physical universe
as it evolves, influencing the development towards individual consciousnesses.
Therefore the suggestion that Consciousness is 'self-caused', or has 'aseity', even
if not provable, is understandable. However if this is so, the concept of God as an
eternal entity, about which it cannot (meaningfully) be asked 'Why is he there?', is
also coherent. Therefore, when the cosmological argument ends with the suggestion that God is the creative source of the whole universe, it is perfectly reasonable
to say that this is the ultimate explanation of the universe, in so far as any general
explanation can be given.

An analogy may be helpful here. In the legal system of any state there are
thousands of what are technically called 'positive laws' – because they have been
put in 'position' as laws through a constitutional process. In the case of the United
Kingdom, they have been passed by Parliament and then given the royal assent.
The 'explanation' of each of these laws, or the whole collection, seen as a kind of
collectivity, is in terms of constitutional laws. But constitutional laws themselves
are different, except in so far as these constitutional laws themselves allow for
amendment. Constitutional laws do have a beginning in time – and this is where the
analogy I am building up breaks down – but in typical cases they are not explained,
from a *legal perspective* in terms of other laws. (Any 'explanation' that could be
given would be non-legal, in terms of revolutions, foreign invasions, mythological
prehistory, and so on.) The constitutional law, from a legal perspective is 'ultimate'.
Whereas it always makes sense to ask for an explanation of a positive law (that is,
in terms of how this particular law passes the constitutional criteria), it just does not
make sense to ask for a legal explanation of constitutional law (except when it
arises from an amendment). From a legal perspective, it just *is*. In a parallel way,
for the theist, God is not part of the system of the universe, he is either outside it (as
in classical theism) or transcends it, even though totally immanent within it (as in
panentheism). The appreciation of why constitutional law is, in a legal sense,
ultimate, depends on *understanding* the difference between ordinary law and constitutional law. Similarly an appreciation of why God is, in a metaphysical sense,
the ultimate explanation, depends on an *understanding* of the difference between
ordinary things and the kind of reality that is God.

I am tempted to push this analogy one stage further. As I have just indicated,
constitutional law is not necessarily altogether unchangeable. Whether or not there

are provisions for change depends on the particular nature of the constitution concerned.[5] Similarly, although all theists regard God as the ultimate source of the universe, some (that is, classical theists) see him as totally changeless in himself, others (that is, panentheists), see God as totally changeless in his moral character, but subject to change in terms of his relationship to us. For the former, God cannot suffer – only (for classical Christian theism) Jesus in his human aspect can suffer; for the latter there is no reason why God himself cannot be said to suffer, and the prescription on this, it is held, comes not from the Bible, but from too much reverence for Aristotle.[6]

The Cosmological Argument and Probability

One of the reasons why the cosmological argument has not been taken seriously enough by the sceptic is that it does not fit comfortably into the kinds of argument that are most familiar elsewhere. Although some theists still consider it a 'deductive' argument, meaning that the conclusion follows necessarily, one of the major objections to this view is that it seems absurd to say that all those who do not agree with it have an intellectual failing, since they cannot follow a necessary argument. However, if we call it an 'inductive' argument, akin to those we meet in the empirical sciences, we must note that in science we are often able, after the event, to see whether the argument succeeded in giving us the correct answer. There is no parallel way, certainly in this life, of checking the results of the cosmological argument. Also, as we have seen, the cosmological argument does not use *bits* of evidence, in a way that is typical of inductive arguments, but relies on a way of interpreting *all* the evidence. Similar problems arise if the cosmological argument is offered as one of 'probability', although a number of theologians have suggested this approach.[7] Normally it only makes sense to say that something is 'probable' when one could hazard a guess as to how probable – say, twenty, fifty or seventy-five per cent and so on. But to reflect on any one of the traditional cosmological arguments, or on the combined argument I have outlined, and then to hazard a guess as to the *degree* of probability of there being a God, seems very odd. Psychologically, it might make sense for a particular individual to say, 'I think the probability is over fifty per cent', or something like that, but for anyone to give reasons for putting a particular figure on the probability would be strange. The reason is clear. There is no benchmark against which we can check how often the reasoning has proved right or wrong. In contrast, if I say that a horse has a fifty per cent chance of winning a race, I can look at how often horses with similar statistics have won in the past, and this gives meaning to a figure, such as fifty per cent.

So what kind of argument is the cosmological argument? It may be helpful here to recall one of the problems associated with positivism. Behind the positivist critique of religion is a demand that religious language, if it is to be meaningful language about reality, has to 'fit' into the requirements or category of scientific language. But to make this demand is to beg all the vital questions, for if the God of theism is a reality he is certainly not a 'thing', or a scientific 'law', or any concept that the empirical sciences, by their very nature, could demonstrate to be real. Once again, however, this *via negativa*, about what the cosmological argument is not like can be followed by a more positive account of what kind of argument it is, because when people make fundamental decisions in the areas of morality and politics similar criteria are appropriate. In ethics and politics, I do not have in mind particular decisions, such as whether or not to vote for a certain candidate, but decisions about one's general orientation, which will, in turn, affect many individual decisions. A realistic example, for some people, would be pondering the decision to join a political party. Here, several factors parallel very closely pondering a decision regarding a religious position. First, there is (or should be) a rational element, corresponding to the criteria for adopting a general position taken from Raphael, namely internal and external coherency. Second, there is (or should be) the awareness that intelligent and honest people can opt for different positions. Third, there is an existential element, since the decision will affect how I act and, very likely, how I feel about many things. Fourth, once we are dealing with a range of (rationally acceptable) 'living options', there is the matter of what we feel 'drawn' towards. This is one of the places where it is hard to draw a sharp line between the purely cognitive and the emotional or aesthetic sides to our consciousness. In ethics, politics and religion, the attractiveness of the overall philosophy, the attractiveness of its presentation and the attractiveness of the human exemplars we meet, all have a huge influence on our decision, and there is nothing wrong or irrational in this being so, *provided* we are considering a 'living option'. Fifth, in this case, someone might say: 'I think that party x is *probably* has the best policies', but it would be odd to say 'I think party x has a fifty-five per cent chance of having the best policies'. Particularly after the choice has been made, the commitment that almost certainly goes with the decision would make this language inappropriate. Also, as in the case of religion, it is very unclear how a figure like fifty-five would be arrived at.

In sum, the cosmological argument is neither a deductive nor an inductive argument of the kind used, respectively, in mathematics, and in law and science, but it is a kind of argument that is appropriate, and which most of us probably use, whenever some *general* position is being entertained. Perhaps we need a new word to characterize this kind of argument. Prior to the decision to adopt a general position one can see that the position is a rational option, and that the argument for it has persuasive force; after the decision, the position may be held with a certain 'assurance', given the experience of *living* with the option taken. This approach to the nature of the argument also allows, from within a theistic perspective, for the workings of grace. The sense that belief and faith are in some way 'gifts', even though there has been a voluntary and conscious decision, fits in well with the way in which one can be *attracted* to an option in the ways I have indicated.[8]

There is one more thing to be said about the *kind* of argument we are concerned with. I have argued that the ontological, cosmological and teleological arguments are all, when properly understood, part of *one* argument. I have also suggested that the argument from religious experience bears upon the issues, because not only does a claim of some common content to religious experience in all the world's great religions make the overall case more plausible, but the sense of the numinous that is commonly found begins to give a new level of meaning to the notion of a 'self-caused' being, which is, without this, a very dry and purely philosophical category. The new thing to say is that there is also a subtle link with the 'moral' argument (which, as we shall see in the next section, comes in two forms). The link is subtle, because it will not do to say that the more moral a person is, the more they will be persuaded by the argument for the existence of God. Such a suggestion would cast a slur on all non-believers, which we can see to be unwarranted. It may or may not be the case that after adopting theism people tend to become better (I personally think they usually do), but it is quite unfair to suggest to an honest and sceptical thinker that what they require is simply more honesty. But, at the same time, if God is ultimate goodness, there must be some interconnection between our belief and our vision of the good. The link, I suggest, is provided by what I have referred to above as the 'attractiveness' of a general position. Once a great religion is seen as a living option (from a rational point of view), its attractiveness may be a crucial factor in a decision to look at it more closely and, later perhaps, adopt it. This, in turn, has obvious implications for the kind of evangelism that a theist should consider warranted. It is clear that many searchers for a spiritual approach are put off, and rightly put off, both by the intellectual presentation of many religious positions, and by the narrow-mindedness and bigotry of many religious people. The best reasons for a person to take a close and personal interest in a religious position is because it is attractive, either as a coherent and challenging general position, or as something that has attractive insights, or as a belief system that has attractive exemplars. Whether a gospel should be preached in any other way I shall not discuss, but clearly, the mere living of a good life in conformity with a religious position should provide the key element in any attempt to spread the message.

The Moral Arguments

So far there has been little mention of a genuinely 'agnostic' approach to religion, in the popular sense of the term. Here there is no particular philosophy to describe – such as in the cases of positivism, secular humanism and materialism, all of which expound reasons for rejecting theism. In the case of agnosticism, however, there is no adoption of a positive alternative to theism and, at the same time, a refusal or an inability to make a decision with respect to any overall philosophy of life. Is there anything wrong in simply being undecided, and in not being prepared to opt for materialism or monism or theism? I certainly have no grounds to criticize people in this position, especially since I cannot see their thinking from the 'inside', but although there is the clear possibility of a rational position that falls under the umbrella of agnosticism, this is a context in which the traditional moral arguments for theism need to be considered.

Let us suppose that one is an agnostic, in the sense defined, but wants to affirm at least some of the moral values that theists have, and in particular, the claim that 'people matter'. In this context we can consider two forms of the moral argument, both of which should be distanced from certain popular versions of the moral argument that cannot be supported by reason. Just as there are naive presentations of the cosmological argument that cannot hold up to rigorous criticism (for example, because they take no account of Darwinian principles), so there are naive presentations of the moral argument that can diminish rather than support the case for theism. These are examples of the *caricatures* that religious people are often responsible for that parallel the caricatures that the non-religious often present.

One common, and false, presentation of the moral argument alleges that religion is essential for morality, in that without it individual people cannot be moral, or can have no reason to be moral. John Locke, for example, claimed that 'promises, covenants, and oaths, which are the bonds of human society, can have no hold upon an atheist'.[9] This is manifestly false: not only have many atheists been highly moral, they are sometimes able to say *why* they act morally, in terms of a general philosophy of life which, even if a theist like myself may think mistaken, can certainly be 'rational' in the sense defined earlier. More sophisticated versions of the moral argument tend to take one of two approaches. In the first, the argument goes that even though *individuals* may be both atheistic and moral, a *society* that is atheistic will tend to lose a general sense of moral values that is essential for its long-term well-being. There is a case for this claim, in line with the Biblical insight 'Where there is no vision, the people perish',[10] but I do not propose to follow it here, since even if a version of this argument is agreed to have force, it is essentially a pragmatic argument that points to the usefulness of religion, rather than to its truth, and it is the latter that I am concerned with in this book. In the second approach, the argument goes that even though an ethical atheist can offer reasons of a kind, these are not fully adequate for supporting the seriousness of moral endeavour, and especially the idea that there can be moral *discoveries*. The two arguments that I shall outline shortly fall into this category, but before giving them, some more background may be helpful.

Although I shall argue that theism does help to support the seriousness of moral endeavour, I do not propose to argue that the philosophical puzzles that surround the whole question of morality are simply *solved* within a religious philosophy. There are a series of interesting and difficult problems that philosophers face when they try to define moral terms, and in particular when they try to show how these terms are related to descriptive terms about the world. These problems do not just go away when the concept of God is introduced, they reappear in questions about the sense in which God can be called morally good. However I shall not pursue these problems in this book beyond the comments made in Chapter 5 concerning the nature of the divine goodness. On a more positive note, a religious ethic can claim to offer *reasons* for there being moral discovery, that many (but not all[11]) secular theories cannot. For example, Rorty's general position forces him to admit that we can give no ultimate 'reason' why cruelty, for example, is wrong[12] (although elsewhere he says that there is such as thing as 'moral progress').[13] We can – on a Rortian view – give reasons of a kind. For example, we can show how cruelty conflicts with other things we happen to seek, including the happiness of others, but any suggestion that there is something 'objectively right', in the classical sense of 'objectively', in seeking the happiness of others is simply 'empty'. In Chapter 2 , this fact helped us to see why many writers within the Frankfurt School, Marxism, and feminism, especially those who have strong moral agendas and are concerned with the global search for human rights, find this postmodernist position extremely unsatisfactory, even if they have no religious beliefs. While not able to solve all moral dilemmas, a religiously-based account of ethics provides one of the ways in which we can offer a 'reason' why cruelty is wrong.

The problem of finding an adequate grounding for moral values – a grounding that would allow one to refer to the word 'reason' for a moral belief – becomes more evident when we examine practical areas of morality, such as medical ethics. An interesting secularist approach to the issues is offered by H. Tristam Engelhardt. Following a claim that the postmodern age brings into question any hope of a canonical, humanistic account of health and medicine, he argues that 'if one cannot discover who is *in* authority or *a* moral authority by appeal to God or reason, then authority will need to be derived from the consent of those participating in an endeavor'.[14] In terms of finding a practical way forward when those engaged in the debate cannot agree about foundations, there is much to be said for this suggestion, but as a philosophy of what practical ethics is about it has serious shortcomings. These go back to reflection on contract theories, where the issue was continually raised (for example, in the seventeenth century) concerning what *moral* ground there is for keeping one's contract – that is, in Engelhardt's case, for honouring an obligation arising out of one's consent, when it is in one's personal interest not to do so. (It is like the issue of whether Hobbes can give an adequate answer to the 'free-rider' who really believes that – as an exceptionally clever person – he can get away with a secret breaking of the contract, even though it is essential that others generally keep the contract.) Probably, the best way of trying to fill the 'moral void', when it is asked *why* I should keep my agreement, is offered by Hume, in terms of shared passions of sympathy that can nearly always be appealed to. However, this only provides a 'reason' for acting morally in so far as one can tap into an actual sentiment of sympathy within the person one is in disagreement with.

An alternative approach, and one that, in my view, is implicit in the traditional moral arguments for the existence of God, is to challenge the basic *assumptions* that lie behind the philosophy of empiricist philosophers, from Hobbes (despite his avowed belief in God), through Hume, to contemporary postmodernists (despite their disavowal of empiricism in its old form). Just as Freud and Leuba, in their examination of religious experiences, had 'insulated' themselves from being open to the possibility that there could be a spiritual reality that their methodologies could not reach, so there is often found a more general set of assumptions that a basically materialistic philosophy *must* be the only one for a rational person to assume. Here we may recall the parable of the castle, expounded in Chapter 1.

In the light of this discussion, let us return to the two forms of the moral argument that the agnostic may do well to ponder. In the first – *roughly* corresponding to the fourth of Aquinas' 'five ways' – the agnostic is asked whether the value that ought to be given to human life is a value that is just felt, perhaps as a result of childhood conditioning, or whether it is something that corresponds to a *discovery* about what human life is really about. Even if the claim that it is a discovery – as, for example, for some of those who first listened to the great Hebrew prophets – cannot be demonstrated, the suggestion that it is a discovery gives a new sense of significance, and one might say *élan*, or excitement, to the moral life. It is not only something one may just opt for, for reasons that are acknowledged to be ultimately psychological, it is an option that one believes puts one in tune with the universe, because one is discovering what life is 'really' about. But if values, like that of love and of the intrinsic value of every human life, are embraced as discoveries, then the suggestion that they are discoveries because they are grounded in a loving and purposive created order begins to make sense. God provides an ultimate ground for the significance of values such as love and justice. Moreover, in the Christian version of this suggestion, we can see something of the moral character of the creative source of the universe in a distinct and unique image, namely Christ. To put this another way: a theistic position allows one to use the word 'real' in relation to what are said to be moral discoveries, since this term is not always linked with the physical world explored by the five senses. For this reason, a theistic position allows one to use a term such as 'moral discovery' in a richer sense than secular philosophies can allow. As with the cosmological argument, this is not a 'proof' in the deductive or strictly inductive sense, but it can form a persuasive ground for belief in a God who would not be God if he could be directly apprehended.

In the second form – *roughly* corresponding to the argument in Kant's second critique – the agnostic is asked whether the objectivity of moral values is something they really wish to affirm. If they say yes, then the suggestion is made that one ought also to affirm a general philosophy that makes sense of this objectivity. In the case of human rights, for example, we often find people who fervently espouse human rights and make great sacrifices in order to promote them, but who, when asked where these rights come from, or in what they are grounded, have virtually no reply. But if we affirm the God of theism, then we affirm belief in a creator who has made individuals with an eternal, individual significance, and the whole created universe is designed, at least in part, to make the lives and the well-being[15] of these people possible. Here is a philosophy that might, when fully developed, be adequate for the moral ideals we have adopted. Again, this is not a 'proof' akin to what we know in science or law, but it is an appropriate ground, or 'reason' for belief in a supreme good. Somewhat paradoxically, there is ammunition for this argument in Rorty, whose position on objectivity I have strongly criticized. Commenting on questions such as 'Why not be cruel?', he writes: 'Anybody who thinks that there are well-grounded theoretical answers to this sort of question – algorithms for resolving moral dilemmas of this sort – is still, in his heart, a theologian or a metaphysician.'[16] I endorse this claim, but draw the opposite conclusion, namely that we *need* some kind of theology or metaphysics to give our moral claims the status they require if they are to be taken with utter seriousness.

Finally, what might be said to an agnostic who cannot feel any sense of commitment to a moral order that they would want to characterize as 'objective', perhaps after taking a dose of positivism or postmodernism? Clearly, the foregoing moral arguments can have little weight. Here I do not have an *argument*, but I do have a proposal.

Let us suppose that I am trying to persuade someone who has no love of music that (as I fervently believe), if only they will really listen, they may begin to discover something of immense value. I can try to encourage them to *attend*. I might, as part of the process, persuade them to observe a typical non-attender at a concert. The 'listener' pays attention for a few seconds, then is clearly preoccupied with something else, for the effort of actually focusing on the music itself for more than a few seconds is too hard. One can observe the same phenomenon with a poor student reading a difficult book, and similar phenomena in many other contexts. I am not morally criticizing people who only half-listen for on some occasions there is much to be said for simply letting the music, as it were, 'flow' around while one relaxes and thinks of other things. My point is that one cannot hope to appreciate, and then really enter into an experience, without making oneself, *on some occasions*, really *attend*.

The issue here should not be confused with the problem of the short 'attention span' that plagues modern society, a problem which may be a result of the way in which entertainment is now packaged. It is true that many people find it extremely hard to concentrate on any one thing, such as a lecture, a play, a symphony or a church service that lasts longer than twenty minutes, but this is a different problem from that of being able fully to attend *at all*, unless there is an element of love. Once there is a love, then attention comes naturally, but prior to developing this love, full attention must be freely given, often with a considerable effort of the will. (There are some illuminating remarks on 'attention' in the writings of Iris Murdoch.[17]) Just as a genuine theist 'attends' on God in prayer, so anyone else can be encouraged to 'attend' to something of worth, whether it be something good or beautiful or true, and they are encouraged to do so, in many cases, by example. Part of what it means to have faith is to believe that when anyone really attends to, let us say, something beautiful, or something worthy of true value (like the well-being of a person), they will be drawn to value it in a new way, and then to love it, and then, perhaps, to see the implications of the value they have invested with love. It is not by chance that many people experience a kind of conversion experience while being caught up in the beauty of a musical encounter, and then find that the whole orientation of their lives is turned round. This, I suggest, indicates one way in which the moral argument works.

Four Other Arguments for the Reality of God

Among the other arguments that have frequently been used to demonstrate the reality of God, two, it seems to me, are clearly fallacious. One of these, the argument from miracles, I have already referred to. The argument, to be effective as a proof, must establish the virtual certainty of miracles *in the sense* defined by Aquinas. I have stressed that, for a believer, it might be rational to believe that such a miracle has occurred, but for a non-believer any evidence would always be open to alternative explanation – including the possibility that one is suffering from illusion or hypnotism. (Under hypnosis, completely sceptical people can come to believe they are seeing ghosts.) At the same time, I have stressed that extraordinary events, in one's own life or those of others, may properly *shake* someone to a re-evaluation of their philosophy of life. If this is what is meant by the 'argument from miracle' it can be accepted, but this is not the 'proof' which the typical form of the argument has claimed in the past.

Within the context of a liberal theology, similarly negative things need to be said about the 'argument from prophecy' – still found among many sects. This is not an attack on 'prophecy' as this is found in the Scriptures, which is a 'forthtelling' of the nature and purposes of God, rather than a 'foretelling' of the future, akin to looking into a crystal ball. Sometimes this 'forthtelling' has implications for the future, but this is not because the future is fixed in all its details. For example, when Jesus saw how the zealots were preparing for an uprising against Rome, he could see more clearly than anyone where this was leading, and how it would involve the destruction of the temple: 'There shall not be left one stone upon another.'[18] In the argument from prophecy, however, a series of events are claimed to have been predicted in detail within certain Biblical passages. The problem for a rational evaluation of this claim is that *after* the event an ingenious manipulation of a text can always make it seem that it referred to what happened. The situation is clearer when the interpretations refer to events that are yet to come. In such cases, the predictions, like those of most astrologers, are usually couched in such vague terms that a true believer can always see a fulfilment. However when more specific claims are made, occasionally, as one would expect, the event happens, but when, as is more usual, it does not (as in the Adventist predictions concerning 1844, made by the Millerites), then one observes among true believers a process of reinterpretation. In the 1880s Charles Taze Russell, the principal founder of the Jehovah's Witnesses, claimed that the second coming had actually come, invisibly, in 1874, and that 1914 was to be the great occasion when there would be the end of 'gentile rule' and 'the appearance of the kingdom of heaven'. Since 1914 the story has been redescribed, making 1914 the time of the 'invisible' coming, and quietly dropping the references to 1874. Such adjustments to prophetic claims are typical of the way in which true believers can rarely be persuaded that prophets have got it wrong.[19] (In this case, another factor concerns how 1914 is reached, which involves a series of *interpretations* of events and numbers, especially in the book of Daniel.) In general, even when a specific and surprising prediction is made, for reasons that parallel the alleged proof from miracles, there cannot be a *proof*, for alternative explanations can always be made. In addition, the treatment of Daniel in the Old Testament and Revelation in the New Testament (the principal quarries for Biblical predictions) depends upon reading them as strict prophecy rather than as allegory, although the latter is much more plausible. There is the further problem that some ancient churches[20] deny that Revelation ought to be in the Christian canon at all because of its late inclusion, along with arguments within the early church about its status.

A similar point emerges when one tries to investigate astrological predictions. For example, a mixture of vagueness and sympathetic interpretation by true believers typifies the predictions of Nostradamus.[21] In 1991, two of his admirers published an interpretation of the prophecies, using a key of heroic ingenuity, which made it seem that a whole series of detailed predictions had been fulfilled. Then they made the tactical error of making some specific predictions for the future, based on the same key, including the death of the present pope (John Paul II) in 1995![22]

More seriously, all these attempts at detailed prophecy, especially those based on interpretations of obscure passages in the Bible, are based on an idea of God's Providence that needs to be questioned. I have argued that if human freedom and responsibility are to be taken seriously, there must be a large measure of contingency in the world. The general shape of history may be inevitable, and it may be part of the divine plan that some very specific things will happen, but that these specific happenings will take place at a certain time, or that all the general details of history could be known in advance, depend on a view of history that is strictly opposed to the freedom of people and the necessary contingency of most events.

An argument that has more force than the two foregoing ones, despite severe limitations, is based on Pascal's 'wager'. In its original form this alleged that all people were faced with the choice of believing in God or not. However, if God actually existed and one chose not to believe, one would have lost eternal life, whereas if one chose to believe and it turned out that God did not exist, one would have lost little. Therefore it made sense to 'wager' on the existence of God. In this form the wager argument contains at least two fallacies. First, since belief is more than *saying* 'I believe', it is not clear that someone who went with Pascal's wager could be called a 'believer'. At the very least, if real belief is to be found, we must combine Pascal's argument with William James' insight that one can only legitimately choose to believe from among what one regards (from a rational point of view) as 'living options'. Another problem arises when we reject the implied claim that a non-believer is necessarily going to lose eternal life. This point will be further explored in the section on 'exclusivity' in Chapter 7. However, in a more modest form the argument has something in common with the second form of the moral argument described above. If one believes that God might be a reality, and if one is attracted to the idea of belief, either because of the evidence that believers tend to be happier,[23] or because one believes that morality will be given a firmer grounding, then there may be an element of *choice* with respect to belief, at least for some people. If a certain world-view is, for me, a living option, I may make a decision 'to hitch my horse to this wagon'. Initially, for a Christian, this might simply mean that someone is going to try to follow the example of Jesus, but this personal commitment may gradually lead to some or all of the credal beliefs.

The final argument that I shall refer to is the 'the argument from religious experience'. I do not think that the phenomenon of religious experience provides a 'proof' of a kind that must lead the honest sceptic to belief. However, I have tried to show how an awareness of certain kinds of experience enters into the rational evaluation of a philosophy of life. For example, the similarity of certain experiences from all over the world, if established, is something that cries out for explanation. Also, in this chapter, we have seen how the initially dry concept of a 'necessary being' is given new significance in the context of certain experiences. As these two examples illustrate, an appreciation of the nature and power of religious experiences enters into the valuation of the living options in a whole variety of ways.

The Problem of Suffering

Since the expositions of materialism and monism have concluded with criticism, at this juncture there ought to be a corresponding critique of theism. However, most of the more obvious objections have been discussed, including the attacks from positivists and postmodernists and attacks that are based on misunderstandings of doctrines such as providence or omnipotence. I have taken the position that many rejections of theism are in fact legitimate rejections of caricatures, and not of theism at its best. There is one problem, however, that dominates most people's objections to monotheistic religion, namely the 'problem of suffering', and although this has been referred to several times, more needs now to be said. What has been argued is that when it is seen that any coherent account of God cannot have a 'limitless' doctrine of either omnipotence or omniscience, then the implications of this – in terms of what is actually involved in the commitment to logical possibility – are more far-reaching than is commonly understood. For example, the idea of an 'instant' Adam, made without an evolutionary and social context, may not be just a practical impossibility that would limit a human inventor, but a logical one as well, that must 'limit' what God could do.

One difficulty with this defence of theism is the tension, perhaps conflict, with the living faith of some of the most ardent followers of theism who feel that God is really 'in charge' of the daily happenings in their lives, not to speak of the sweep of history. For example, I listened recently to someone who had a child born with a major handicap. After an initial period of despair she turned to Christianity and not only found her life suddenly full of meaning, but declared that the handicap was a particular sign of God's grace for which she was now thankful. In the presence of such belief I am reluctant to express any disagreement, not because I share the belief that the handicap was deliberately sent from God (which I certainly do not believe), but for two other reasons. First, I could very easily be misunderstood. My own belief is that such events can always be *used* by God, not that they are actually intended by him. Therefore – in the case in question – the event actually was a source of grace, but not because this was, as it were, planned to happen in this way. Second, it is presumptuous for someone who has two healthy children, like myself, to tell someone who has a handicapped child what it is appropriate for them to believe. In fact, I never ceased to be amazed at the courage and devotion of the vast majority of parents I meet who are faced with problems of this kind, and I feel that I should be the one listening to them.

A similar objection to the rationalist approach I have adopted can be expressed from the side of the non-believer. Apologists like myself, it can be claimed, may succeed in making theism 'reasonable', but at the expense of 'taking all the stuffing out of it'! God is no longer the one who lovingly directs all our footsteps, he is rather a universal Consciousness that we may be in contact with only on a purely mental level.

I do not have a complete answer to such a criticism of 'watering down' theism, whether it comes from an ardent theist or from a sceptical non-theist. However my remarks about the experience of those who live with a daily expectation of the work of Spirit are certainly relevant. There is also this to be said: when theism is limited to a philosophical position, then the criticism is just. A purely philosophical theism, for many, is not an *attractive* option by which to live, and for which to make great sacrifices. However, I have insisted that religious experience, both in terms of the dramatic sense of unity felt by the few, and the more prosaic sense of grace felt by the many, is the life-blood of religion, and that it is grotesque to look only at the philosophical options if we are to understand what the choices are about. To this general point I want to add one particular aspect of religious experience that bears directly on the objection I have just raised. It will be presented in Christian terms, but analogous experiences may be present in other forms of theism.

In descriptions of Christian experience, especially in times of suffering, one of the recurrent themes is the sense that one is not alone. The general sense of 'presence' I attempted to describe in Chapter 4 becomes a particular sense of personal presence. Sometimes this is expressed through the doctrine of the 'communion of saints', which is an aspect of 'solidarity' that does not have to be jettisoned when Jeremiah's insight into individual responsibility is taken on board. There is both a belief and a powerful feeling that one suffers (and rejoices) as part of a great company. However, the more specific experience I want to refer to is the sense that Christ is with one, sharing in the suffering. A powerful description of this experience can be found in a book written by a professional Cambridge historian, Margaret Spufford, who had to face both her own brittle bone disease, and the fatal sickness of a child. During her account she quotes a book by Hubert Vanstone in which he writes: 'The artist fails not when he confronts a problem but when he abandons it: and he proves his greatness when he leaves no problem abandoned. Our faith in the Creator is that he leaves no problem abandoned and no evil unredeemed.' She then goes on to say: 'One of the most helpful things that was ever said to me was "The definition of 'Almighty' means that there is no evil out of which good cannot be brought".'[24] It is in this context that the experiences described in the book, in which an extraordinary sense of the crucified Christ is felt at moments of extreme suffering, are of the utmost relevance. To believe that God frequently interferes in a direct and physical manner may be a naive view that the searcher for a rational faith must abandon, but what remains is not a cold philosophy, but the option to experience a living faith in which everything is indeed made *different* through the way in which it is shared 'in Christ'. Along with this sense of Christ sharing our experiences is a sense of extraordinary value placed in each individual, leading to a sense of being loved as if we were the only object of love. When we fall in love, the object of our love is endowed with an amazing majesty, and here, in this human experience (that can be at the same time a transcending experience), we can glimpse something of the loving care that is felt for each person within the profoundest experiences of God's love. Recalling the discussion of positivism in Chapter 2, here we can see one of the places where religious belief can 'make a difference'.

Notes and References

1 Plato, *Laws*, 893 ff.
2 This was rejected by Aquinas prior to Kant's famous argument against it. However, a case has been made for its re-establishment when stated in ways that neither Aquinas nor Kant really considered. See Plantinga, A., ed. (1968), *The Ontological Argument*, London: Macmillan.
3 If the human mind is seen as a 'part' of the universal Mind, then we have a form of theism that overlaps with monism.
4 There is a similar problem with the ontological argument. In the abstract one might consider the question of what follows from the mere idea of God, but in the concrete the idea does not arise unless there is a conscious human mind to pose it. Immediately, we are no longer in the world of pure *a priori* ideas, but in the world of existing minds. Therefore I do not believe that the ontological argument can be totally separated from the cosmological.
5 See Hart, H.L.A. (1961), *Concept of Law*, Oxford: Oxford University Press, pp. 71–2.

6   I have oversimplified the issue here. Aristotle did say that, in the case of God, any change or mutation would be for the worse, but quite apart from Aristotle there are genuine religious and philosophical reasons for holding that God must be essentially changeless.

7   For example, F.R. Tennant. For a summary of the problems with this approach see Hick, J.H. (1983), *Philosophy of Religion*, 3rd edn, London: Prentice-Hall, pp. 26–8.

8   For a discussion of the way in which faith is related to the notions of reason, will and a gift of God, see Castellio, S. (1563), *De arte dubitandi et confidendi ignorandi et sciendi*, ed. H.F. Hirsch, (1981), Leiden: Brill, pp. 7–8.

9   Locke, J., *A Letter Concerning Toleration*.

10 Proverbs 19: 18.

11 For example, secular versions of utilitarianism can claim to discover that the pursuit of certain moral principles, like toleration, can be shown to increase the greatest happiness of the greatest number.

12 Rorty, R. (1989), *Contingency, Irony, and Solidarity*, Cambridge: Cambridge University Press, pp. xv, 173, 184–5.

13 Ibid., p. 192 . This 'moral progress' can only be in terms of a greater sense of 'human solidarity'. It is clear, however, that Rorty's philosophy demands that this progress cannot relate to any 'objective' standard, outside his chosen pragmatism.

14 Englehardt, H. Trinstam Jr (1991), *Bioethics and Secular Humanism*, London: SCM Press, pp. 111 and 119. Emphases are in the text.

15 In this context the term 'well-being' is better than 'happiness', since although the eventual destiny of people must be one of happiness, if we are to believe that God is good, the immediate purpose may be the building of a moral character that is essential for the experience of the higher forms of happiness. In the present we should always seek the 'well-being' of another, but not in all cases (for example, the criminal about to be sentenced) their immediate happiness.

16 Rorty, *Contingency, Irony, and Solidarity*, p. xv.

17 Murdoch, I. (1970), 'The Idea of Perfection' in *The Sovereignty of Good*, London: Routledge and Kegan Paul, pp. 36–7, 55.

18 Mark 13: 2.

19 See Harris, D. (1998), *The Jehovah's Witnesses*, London: Gazelle Books, pp. 19–21, 147–52; and Cole, M. (1956), *Jehovah's Witnesses*, London: Allen and Unwin, p. 91.

20 Including the Coptic church and the ancient church of Southern India that claims descent from St Thomas.

21 The sixteenth-century Frenchman known as Nostradamus is probably the most famous of all astrologers. Most of his predictions are couched in exceedingly vague terms. Perhaps the best example of a prediction that has been regarded as accurate (among a huge number that are too vague to assess, or that are inaccurate) is one [V, 33] concerning a disaster at Nantes, in 1793.

22 Hewitt, V.J. and Lorie, P. (1991), *Nostradamus*, London: Bloomsbury, p. 201.

23 On this matter see the psychological investigation carried out by Myers, D.G. (1992), *The Pursuit of Happiness: What Makes a Person Happy – and Why*, New York: Morrow.

24 Spufford, M. (1989), *Celebration*, London: Fount Paperbacks, p. 80; Vanstone, W.H. (1977), *Love's Endeavour, Love's Expense*, London: Darton, Longman and Todd.

Chapter 7

The Trinitarian Option

Forms of Theism

In the previous chapters there have been several references to 'classical' theism, in contrast with 'non-classical' theism, which include panentheism. This is a very crude distinction because there are a number of very different issues within the debate between classical and non-classical views, and many people who hold a 'classical' position on one issue may hold a more radical, non-classical view on another. Among the issues that relate to the adequacy of classical theism is the question of 'passibility', which refers to the debate concerning whether God can be said to experience change or suffering, and if he can, in what way.[1] Another issue concerns the nature of omnipotence, and (for example) the claim that God's power can and does allow for the 'miraculous', in Aquinas' strict sense of the term. 'Classical' theism allows for such miracles while some forms of theism either reject their possibility, or their occurrence, or are generally much more cautious about them. Among the other issues are questions relating to omniscience and predestination. Also, while all theists are likely to use the terms 'immanence' and 'transcendence', the way in which they are described as essential characteristics of God varies considerably, and this has major implications for matters such as an analogical knowledge of God that goes beyond a pure *via negativa*. Behind all of these issues lies a general debate as to the extent to which older, 'monarchical' and 'patriarchal' pictures of God needs to be modified or rejected. There are also many other issues that are not discussed in this book.

Since this book does not attempt to provide a systematic theology, from now on I am going to make few references to any of the foregoing issues. Instead, within this chapter, I propose to concentrate on one particular option that will probably determine how the next stage of a rational quest will go. However, the following point needs to be stressed. Although I have supported a 'rational and liberal' tradition throughout this book, on one central issue the position I have defended has been very 'classical'. I have claimed that we can properly speak of God as an objective reality. Moreover, within this chapter I shall proceed to defend a number of other claims that are part of the classical Christian tradition, including the belief that Jesus, by his life and death, brought about a unique work of redemption; that Jesus was the 'express image of God' in a way that is consistent with traditional teaching on the incarnation; that we can speak of the Holy Spirit as the third member of the Trinity, and that we can believe in personal immortality. In all these central concerns, the 'liberalism' is a feature of the *method* by which the doctrines are presented. Further, when I have shown a preference for a 'non-classical' theism' – for example, with respect to divine foreknowledge, divine suffering and reliance on miracles – I have not claimed that the 'non-classical' view was the only rational option for a Christian, only that these non-classical views are legitimate options.

In this chapter, the one option I shall discuss in any detail is that of a Trinitarian versus a non-Trinitarian version of theism, although this inevitably involves a discussion of the doctrines of redemption and incarnation, with which Trinitarianism is entwined. However contrary to what might be expected, the Trinitarian/non-Trinitarian distinction is not the same as the Christian/non-Christian distinction, although much of the time this will be in the background. Behind this important point lie two claims that I shall attempt to justify; first, that there are non-Trinitarian forms of Christianity and, second, that there are at least intimations of a Trinitarian view in many accounts of God in non-Christian religions.

With respect to 'non-Trinitarian Christianity', we need to begin with the New Testament and in particular the account of the life and witness of the early churches described in the Acts of the Apostles. For the present discussion we can assume that the account given of the early church is basically accurate since, even if it is not, it represents the way the church viewed its early days, and this is all we need for the present argument. Within this book it is clear that, in the first decades of the church's life, in order to become a Christian only three interrelated things were required. The first was to repent of one's sins, the second to be baptized 'in the name of the Lord', and the third was to profess what might be called the first 'creed'. This creed appears to have been quite simply 'Jesus is the Christ', or variants such as 'Jesus is Lord' or 'Christ is Lord'.[2] It is well known that no developed doctrine of the Trinity can be found in the earliest requirements for baptism, or anywhere else in the New Testament, although there are many separate references to Father, Son and Holy Spirit, many dual references to Father and Son, and at least two in which the three are named together.[3] The general view of church historians is that the doctrine of the Trinity developed gradually, based upon interpretations of the New Testament, and reached its final form in a succession of grand councils, most notably those of Nicaea in 325 CE and Chalcedon in 451. Later in this chapter I shall discuss the extent to which this development can be justified, but for the present the conclusion that is inescapable is that many or all of those who were baptized in the first years of the church, immediately following the events at Pentecost, did not have to profess anything that could be called a Trinitarian formula. They were required to acknowledge Jesus as Lord (*kurios*). This certainly included taking Jesus as the model by which to live, both in respect to manner of life and manner of prayer, but it clearly left *undefined* any precise account of how Jesus was related to the Father or to the Holy Spirit. However, if these first converts could properly be called 'Christians' (as they were at Antioch[4]), despite the absence of a Trinitarian creed, it is hard to say to see why a modern-day theist *must* be a Trinitarian in order to be a Christian. Even if one believes that a doctrine of the Trinity was a legitimate development (as I shall argue), and that Christianity is correct to make the doctrine an important part of its standard teaching (a view which I shall defend), to insist on this test for *every* Christian, in the light of the early history of Christianity, is hard to justify. Surely, to be a Christian, it should be enough to profess what the first Christians professed.[5] Different churches may quite reasonably demand more for the holding of office within their denominations given the traditions that have developed, traditions which help to define what these denominations are, but this is quite a different matter from laying down the demands of what it is to be a baptized Christian. At present, the norm in the churches is to baptize in the name of the Trinity, and the chief reason for this is the command to do so recorded right at the end of St Matthew's gospel. This, almost certainly, represented general practice by the time this gospel was written, probably around 80–90 CE (although the use of this formula does not demonstrate that most Christians then held 'the doctrine of the Trinity' as this would later be understood). My suggestion is that in the light of Christian tradition the Trinitarian formula should be maintained as the norm, but those who wish to be baptized with the simple formula used by the first Christians should have this request granted.[6] It is worth stressing that there have always been many individuals who have considered themselves to be Christians but who have rejected the doctrine of the Trinity. Isaac Newton was one of these.[7]

With respect to intimations of Trinitarianism in non-Christian religions, a good example is provided by the (female) notion of Wisdom in the Old Testament. In a number of passages, Wisdom seems to be what is sometimes called a 'hypostasis', meaning an entity with the same essence or substance as God, and yet, at the same time, not simply another word for God in his fullness.[8] A similar point can be made with respect to the Old Testament use of the word 'spirit', which sometimes refers to an aspect of an individual human person, but is on many occasions a hypostasis for God, as when God is held to say (through Joel) 'I will pour out my spirit upon all flesh; and your sons and your daughters shall prophesy', words which the first Christians believed to have been fulfilled at Pentecost.[9] Another important example of a hypostasis within Judaism occurs after the completion of the Old Testament in the thinking about the concept of *logos*, especially in Philo, who wrote early in the first century CE, and for whom the term represented the *intelligible* aspect of a transcendent God.

In Zoroastrianism a concept approaching that of a hypostasis occurs in the seven 'beneficent immortals', who are both divine and human, and act as mediators between the transcendent God, Ahura Mazda, and humans.[10] Again, in those versions of Hinduism that are monotheistic (like that of the philosopher Mahdva, who flourished in the thirteenth century CE) or that tend towards monotheism, Vishnu has incarnations in beings such as Rama and Krishna. Similar remarks can be made with respect to some schools of Mahayana Buddhism where the Bodhisattvas, who operate as mediators between the divine and human levels, represent another 'intimation' of Trinitarianism in that, once again, there is a search for some aspect of divinity that is more approachable than the totally transcendent. (It is also interesting to note Indian schools which, against the general trend, give a *permanent* place for the individual soul – for example, in Buddhism and in the Mahaparinirvana Sutra.)

Islam provides an interesting special case, since given the emphasis on the transcendence of God one would look in vain for a 'hypostasis' for God in the pages of the Qur'an (or Koran). However, at least implicitly, an issue is raised that has implications for Trinitarian thinking. God's transcendence is so much stressed that there is felt to be a problem with the idea of God's *direct* communication with prophets, even of the stature of Muhammad, and therefore the revelation recorded in the Qur'an (or provided by the very existence of the Qur'an) is believed to have been through the intermediary work of the angel Gabriel, sometimes identified with the 'Holy Spirit'.[11] (The exception is Moses, who in both Jewish and Islamic tradition had some kind of 'direct' contact with God.[12]) However, this raises the obvious problem of how a *totally* transcendent God communicated with Gabriel, assuming that Gabriel in no sense shares the divine nature. If Gabriel saw the Qur'an recorded on heavenly tablets (which is one tradition within Islam), the issue simply reappears in another form, for the question is now how an eternal and totally transcendent God wrote these particular verses. I suggest that it may have been an awareness of this problem that lead to the teaching of some Islamic schools that the Qur'an is 'uncreated', which implies that it has no temporal beginning, and which parallels, in an interesting way, Christian teaching on the 'uncreated' nature of Christ. But the questions still return around the general issue of how a transcendent God reveals the content of the Qur'an at a particular time and place. These observations are not meant to imply any criticism of Islam, the point is rather that *all* forms of theism face a profound issue when they combine a transcendent God with an immanent God who has relationships with individual people, manifested in particular events. One consequence of this issue is that the absolute 'oneness' of God cries out for some explanation regarding what *kind* of unity God has, and this explanation must make sense of a transcendent deity conveying *specific* revelations either directly to Moses, or for Gabriel to pass on to Muhammad.

As I have just intimated, the issue raised here faces any version of monotheism that stresses transcendence, for as soon as God is said to do a specific action, including the creation of the world at a moment in time (or, more strictly, at the moment in which time as we know it began), or to convey a specific message, or, in general, to be 'personal' in the sense of being aware of individual persons, then the transcendence of God can appear to be compromised, for he is now, as it were, stepping into space and time. Indeed, this problem helps to explain the attraction of monism for many religious people, for here the problem does not appear, at least in the same form. Moreover, the more the transcendence of God is stressed, the more there is a tendency to look for a mediating figure with a human face who somehow, it is thought, begins to fill the infinite gap. In both Orthodoxy and Roman Catholicism, the virgin Mary is the subject of devotion, in part, because she fulfils this role.[13] Logically, however, if God is infinite, and a human being finite, no amount of mediators can actually *begin* to fill the void. This consideration provides one of the contexts in which a certain logic can be seen in the Christian doctrine of the Trinity, for if Christ is, in some extraordinary way, both human and divine, then the gulf is indeed bridged.

Reviewing these different approaches to the unity of God in non-Christian religions, my conclusion is not that non-Christian monotheists are often crypto-Trinitarians, but that any claim that God is 'one' is not fully explanatory, and allows for a number of interpretations. Within many of these interpretations there is a claim that God is experienced in different ways (sometimes corresponding to the different 'names' of God). For example, within the context of profound mystical experience, Julian of Norwich describes the characteristics of God as life, love and light, and then builds up an account of the Trinity experienced as creative, redemptive and enabling. But now comes a crucial distinction. These different 'ways' can be 'different' in a superficial sense, analogous to the different ways in which I might see a house according to the position from which I am observing it. Here the differences are only in respect to the particular observer. At the other extreme, the differences may mark 'real' distinctions within the thing observed, analogous to the different rooms within a house, when a house is seen as a unity that comprises a number of integrated parts (that is, the rooms). For reasons that will become clear, any doctrine that corresponds to a traditional Christian account of the Trinity has to avoid *both* of these analogies, and assert something in between them.

Here it may be helpful to recall the account of paradox given in Chapter 2. If we take the lines from John Henry Newman's hymn that asserts 'Firmly I believe and truly, God is three and God is one', we are certainly presented with a paradoxical claim. For those not familiar with the Trinitarian tradition there is a paradox in sense one (a claim that is unorthodox) and in sense two (one that is surprising). However, a Trinitarian who accepts the general theme of this book will *deny* that here is a paradox in sense four (an actual, logical contradiction), and will want to argue that the doctrine of the Trinity is a paradox in sense three (the assertion of something that *appears* contradictory, given our limited ability to understand). The discussion of this matter must begin by asserting that the words of Newman's hymn should not be taken in the most straightforward (univocal) sense, but are poetic or metaphorical. This does not mean that no 'truth' is being expressed, or (as a positivist might say) that Newman's words merely express an emotive utterance, but that the truth is one that cannot, for us, be expressed other than through metaphor. It is not that somehow one really equals three, but that 'one', when used to refer to the being of God, refers to a 'unity', not a mathematical number, and the nature of this unity is something we glimpse, at best, 'in a glass, darkly'. I shall argue that given the belief that human persons are made in the image of God, the closest analogy we can find for the kind of unity the Trinity points to is to be found in the way in which the human psyche is a blend of different elements, all of which are crucial to the complex unity that makes us what we are. A liberal Christian can perfectly well express belief in the Trinity, but in the context of a claim that the doctrine attempts to express a fundamental truth about the nature of the divine unity, and that the paradox is a classic, or *the* classic example, of a paradox in what I have called sense three. The task of presenting this view is made more difficult by the fact that the Trinity is often represented by outsiders, and sometimes by fellow Trinitarians, as a crude Tritheism, corresponding to the previous analogy of separate and distinct rooms within a house.

Let us begin a search for an account that falls somewhere between the two house analogies that I have rejected by suggesting that there is a strong case to be made for the view that while the one God is experienced in many different ways, some of these ways fall into certain groups or patterns, so that there is a sameness in the quality of the experience on each occasion. This observation can lead to two different approaches to the way in which the experiences of God are linked together.

The first approach starts with the realization that a *human* experience of the whole depends upon the whole manifesting itself in forms which are (to some degree) comprehensible to us. For example, when God is experienced as creative power, people may use the term 'Father', and there may be a multitude of such experiences, all of which sense a creative aspect of God, but they may have sufficient sameness of quality to be classed as one 'way' of experiencing God.

Modifying my analogy, it is as if we were thinking of the *visual* views of the house as some kind of collectivity (as opposed to auditory or tactile perceptions), wherein all the visual views have a common pattern. Then we might conclude that there were three general ways of experiencing the house, the visual, the auditory and the tactile. (For the sake of the illustration, we can forget the senses of smell and taste.) This is to say something much more significant than that there are different ways of seeing the house (as in the first analogy); it is saying that given our human nature, the way the house is represented to *all* humans, and not just particular ones, necessarily comprises these three modes of presentation. However, this analogy (based on the similarity of all the visual experiences) does not necessitate any inherent distinction within God himself. One way of bringing this point out is to refer to the 'three attributes of God' described by the Jewish philosopher Saadya Gaon, who wrote in the tenth century CE. 'The very idea that God is the Creator', he writes, 'involves the attribution to Him of Life, Power, and Wisdom.' Taken out of context we might seem to have here an intimation of the Trinity that parallels suggestions in Augustine and Julian of Norwich, but Saadya goes on to insist that it is *we* who must use these three words, while 'Reason conceived them as one single idea'. Moreover, 'Let nobody assume that the Eternal (blessed be He) contains a plurality of attributes'.[14]

As this reference to Saadya indicates, so long as accounts of the Trinity are described as continuing aspects of God that are plural *with respect to us*, then it is not certain there must be any real challenge to the monotheism of orthodox Judaism or Islam. It is worth remarking, however, that many Christian sermons on the Trinity do not, in fact, assert anything more than this. We have experienced God, they say, in three ways. As a typical Quaker book puts it: 'in order to adopt the needful revelation of Himself to the nature of man, the Most High has manifested Himself in nature, in history, and in the human heart.'[15] An approach to the Trinity along these lines has the attraction of making the differences between the main forms of monotheism one of emphasis and certainly invites a constructive dialogue. However, for reasons that will appear, traditional Christian theologians would not be happy to leave the matter there, and I shall give reasons to suggest that they may well be right in their insistence that more needs to be said.

The second approach to the way in which the different experiences of God are linked together takes us into difficult waters. It suggests that the different 'modes' in which the unified whole that is God is experienced is not only a matter of how the presentations have to be made *to us*, given the limitations of human nature. The additional suggestion is made that there is something 'intrinsic', within the very nature of the united whole, to which these modes point. However, they are not modes or aspects (or whatever other unsatisfactory words one comes up with) that could possibly exist by themselves, outside the unity concerned; they are rather ways of beginning to understand what the 'unity' is all about. (In contrast, a particular room within a house, could exist by itself.) An analogy used by Augustine can help here. As an illustration for his belief that there are really existing *relationships* within God, he described the three modes of memory, understanding and will in which the human mind is present for itself.[16] This, and other analogies from within the human experience of itself, are sometimes called *Vestigia Trinitatis* (that is, 'traces of the Trinity'), and their force as anything more than suggestive analogies depends on the degree to which one takes seriously the doctrine of the *Imago Dei*, as already discussed.

The difference between an account of the Trinity rooted in the way that God appears to (all) humans, and an account in which it is suggested that there are 'real' distinctions within the Godhead, reintroduces the important distinction that is stressed by Ṣankara, and briefly discussed in the discussion of monism. On one view, Trinitarian language is perfectly legitimate provided it is always seen as language that is either (1a) *demanded* or (1b) *permitted* by the 'lower' level at which we are forced to operate, given the limitations of the human condition. If it is 'demanded', then the implication is that all humans should find some acceptable form of Trinitarian language, but nevertheless there could be some mutual understanding with non-Trinitarian theologies, since there would be a recognition that the Trinitarian language is a staging-post towards a more sublime language in which the Oneness of God would be equally appreciated by those coming from different traditions. If the Trinitarian language is 'permitted', then there could more clearly be mutual dialogue and respect between the major systems of both monotheism and monism. In contrast, within the view (2) that Trinitarian language can begin to capture 'real' insights into the divine nature, based on some glimpse of the actual nature of the divine unity, Trinitarian language can itself be seen as the beginnings of a 'higher' language. The position that I am moving towards accepts that all three positions (1a, 1b and 2) can be rationally defended. If I am right, then Trinitarianism is a rational option, but it is a mistake to think that there is only one rational form of this option.

However, whichever version of Trinitarian teaching we prefer, the doctrine needs to include a consideration of three primal experiences of the first Christians. As in the more general discussion of theism and monism in earlier chapters, without a sensitivity to these we will be dealing only with 'dry bones', and the huge and often acrimonious history of the debate on the Trinity will be incomprehensible. The three root experiences are: first, the sense of being forgiven, redeemed and transformed by what Christ has done; second, the sense of living in a totally new kind of fellowship, in the communion of saints, and 'in Christ'; third, the Pentecostal experience, in which Christians felt what they called the Spirit at work within them. Whether these experiences have been properly described by Christians, and (still more) whether they actually justify a doctrine of the Trinity (as inherent within the Godhead), are questions I am leaving completely open at this stage of the discussion. My point is that without an exploration of these matters we cannot hope to evaluate, and perhaps develop, any meaningful Trinitarian account of God. The debate leading up to Chalcedon will appear as so much triviality and nonsense, as it did, in the main, for Edward Gibbon, who pointedly describes the furious Christian debate over an iota.[17] In contrast, with a sensitivity to these underlying experiences the history, for some, may read like a heroic epic in which the truth is fought for (as in Prestige's *Fathers and Heretics*).[18] For others, including myself, it is neither of these, but rather an all-too-human endeavour to understand some real and transforming experiences. Behind Prestige's epic there is genuine quest but, as with Arthur's knights, the quest was marred, again and again, by human frailty.

The Accuracy of Scripture

Since this whole book attempts to be a rational quest, in the sense described earlier, whenever the truth or accuracy of the Bible is important for an argument to be sound, this truth or accuracy must be argued for rather than merely assumed. Thus, in the references to the Acts of the Apostles I was careful to point out that the argument depended on how the early church viewed its beginnings, and this the book certainly does, leaving aside the question of its literal accuracy. However, in the next section questions of truth and accuracy of the Bible become important, in part because of claims about what Jesus said and did, and in part because of claims about some primal experiences of the first Christians, as described in the Acts of the Apostles and some of the letters, which are alleged to be illustrative of what Christians have experienced throughout the church's history.

The need to face this problem of accuracy can be illustrated from a fault in some of C.S. Lewis' writings. For example, both directly and indirectly he poses the dilemma that Jesus must have been bad or mad or what he claimed to be.'[19] Much as I respect Lewis, and end up by sharing most of his beliefs, there are two rational problems with an approach in which one is forced to choose between these three options. The first is that Jesus' claims, for example, about being the 'Son of God' can be subject to many interpretations. The other, from a logical point of view, is prior, since an evaluation of the claims assumes that he made them, and many of those who reject Christianity simply deny that we have an accurate historical picture of what Jesus said and did.

The first point to make in response to this problem is that the essential religious claims require neither a belief in the verbal inerrancy of the Bible, nor a belief that all of the allegedly historical material is accurate. In the case of the Old Testament, the only thing that is absolutely essential as background for the New Testament is an appreciation of a Hebrew culture that had certain teachings about the nature of God, teachings that emerge in a long narrative that does not depend (for an understanding of the meaning of the key terms) on it being, at all times, an *historical* narrative. (At the same time, it is hard to make much sense of this narrative unless *some* of the events have *some* historical foundation.) Within this narrative we find a prophetic tradition in which a 'Messiah' was expected. In the case of the New Testament, it is not required that all the details, including those of the apparently miraculous events be accepted, but it *is* necessary, for purposes of the following argument, that the general outline of Jesus' life be correct, and also the basic account of the stories he told in order to express his teaching. A rational approach to this is elaborated in the rest of this section.

In fact there is good case for a considerable historical core in some books, even in the case of the Old Testament, in particular, both books of Samuel and of Kings. If we take R.G. Collingwood's criteria for what constitutes scientific, humanistic history, then the court history of David and Solomon (which portrays the heroes with at least some of their 'warts'), probably dating, at least in oral form from around 1000 BCE, may be the earliest humanistic history that we have.[20] Also, there is a good case to be made for the claim that oral tradition tended to be accurate in respect to a number of matters, such as the age of ancestors. If we divide the earliest ages by twelve or thirteen (taking account of the ancient lunar calendar), the Abrahamic period ages by two (taking account of an ancient custom of dividing our year into two seasons) and take the Davidic period as using twelve-month years (following more contact with Northerners who were more exposed to the changing seasons) all but a few of the Biblical ages make sense. Sarah, for example, was forty-five of *our* years (or ninety seasons) when she became pregnant. Further, I think it is very hard to explain the extraordinary tenacity of the Jewish people if they were not forged by some overwhelming communal experience, as in the story of the Exodus. However the relatively conservative opinions I hold on Scriptural accuracy are not essential to the argument of this chapter.

The next point is that a rational approach to any controversial claim about an event in the past, especially when the event appears surprising or extraordinary, demands that we look at both the nature of the claim, and the context in which it is made, prior to any weighing of the alleged evidence. Suppose I hear rumours to the effect that a winged horse has been seen flying over Dorset. Of course, I do not believe the story. Suppose I go to Dorset and meet twelve people who describe, in very similar terms, seeing the alleged flying horse. I still do not believe the story, but as I probe further, and (let us say) rule out the effects of alcohol or drugs, I begin to wonder whether something extraordinary may have happened. I still would not believe that there was a flying *horse*, because I believe that horses *can't* fly, but I might start to believe either that there was some kind of group hallucination, or that some weird machine that looked like a horse had passed overhead. Putting all this together, the point is that such claims are not evaluated simply by hearing the evidence, but by considering what kind of claim is being made in what kind of context. Some things, like flying horses, it is virtually impossible to believe in, whatever the evidence, because they conflict with some basic assumptions we have about what is possible.

However, faced with this realization, a truly rational personal should have some misgivings, because ruling out certain possibilities on *a priori* grounds (that is, on grounds that are not related to physical evidence concerning the events in question) sounds like a form of irrationality and prejudice. Perhaps some of the things we think are impossible are not really impossible at all. Indeed the history of science is full of discoveries about things that were wrongly thought to be impossible. This point is not made in order to suggest that it would be right to start believing in flying horses, but to underline how dangerous it is to read a sacred text and assume *either* that it is accurate *or*, like the dogmatic atheist, assume that it describes impossibilities.

Let us take a different scenario that does not deal with an alleged 'physical' object, like a flying horse. I hear that three people claim to have seen the ghost of a man in armour standing in the corner of a medieval window. I am sceptical, but then I meet all three, and again I establish beyond reasonable doubt that at the time of the alleged sightings they were not under the influence of alcohol or drugs. I also establish (and this is crucial) not only that the descriptions are very similar, but that none of the three had heard about the sightings from the others, or from any other source, so that the power of suggestion does not provide an easy explanation. I go to the room and can find no evidence of strange effects of light or mirrors or pictures and so forth. I spend some nights in the same room but experience nothing peculiar. All this, in actual fact, represents the kind of situation that pertains in a number of allegedly 'paranormal' happenings and, as we know, the result is that some relatively rational people think that a paranormal event occurred, and others do not. My argument is that both reactions can be defended rationally. On the naturalistic side, it can be pointed out that it is *always possible* to find explanations that are either 'natural' or that only stretch the existing view of what is natural a little. There could be a complex case of fraud; there could be an unexplained effect of the light; there could be some suggestion at the unconscious level, in Jungian terms, which the second two witnesses picked up, and so on. Those who accept the paranormal would again have a range of possible explanations. This could be a 'psychic footprint', because (it is alleged) people can sometimes pick up on an event in the past; it could be a telepathic experience, transferred from either one witness to the other or from someone departed; it could be an experience of a departed person's spirit, that was somehow earthbound. The view one opts for will be determined to a large extent, not only by the immediate evidence, but by one's views of what is possible and what is likely, in the context. Also, as this example shows, there is some overlap between what would generally be called naturalistic interpretations and paranormal ones, for the Jungian account in the first set, and the telepathic one in the second, can obviously be seen as two ways of describing the same view. This is really a special case of the fuzzy edge between materialist and non-materialist philosophies.

With the realization that materialistic explanations of alleged paranormal events or spiritual experiences are always possible, if they are made complex enough, the charge that many materialists tend to be (unscientifically) dogmatic can be better understood. One of the responses I have met from the materialist camp goes as follows: given Ockham's razor as an appropriate methodological device, the 'simpler' explanation of events or experiences should always be accepted. However, it is always simpler to assume some naturalistic interpretation (even if we don't yet have it) than one that brings in a new or alien 'category', such as a ghost or God. Hume's rejection of miracles comprises a more sophisticated version of exactly this claim. There are two irrational aspects of this argument. The first is that a legitimate *methodological* device, within the scientific enterprise, cannot properly be used as a means to evaluate fundamental questions about the boundaries of science itself. The second is that the criterion of 'simplicity', while clear in some contexts,[21] is not at all clear in others. It may be claimed that it is much 'simpler' to introduce a paranormal or spiritual explanation for some events.

These examples set the scene for a consideration of the gospel narratives. If I were to read them 'out of the blue' I would see them as interesting fable or allegory, and almost certainly as some kind of fiction. However, if I read them in the context of what I know, first of the Old Testament, and then of ancient history generally, the rational evaluation becomes much more complex. It includes both what I think is 'possible' in the light of my general experience and philosophy of life, and what significance I give to the Old Testament expectations. This is what makes a rational evaluation of the gospels very different from, let us say, *The Book of Mormon*.[22] A conservative Christian might argue like this: 'I believe, on all kinds of grounds, prior to reading the gospels, that the world is the product of a creative intelligence that seeks to draw us by love. Further, I see within Israel a tradition of the longing for a Messiah that will fulfil the hopes for a new understanding of God, one intimated in the picture of the suffering servant in Isaiah. Then I read the gospels and I discover a perfect congruence between my expectations and what I find. I see no reason why any of the stories, miracles and all, are not possible in this context.' At the other end of the spectrum a materialist might see a fabulous account, largely created by the rumour and legends abounding in church circles some thirty to seventy years after the actual events (whatever these may be) that gave rise to the stories. My own suggestion, which is more cautious than the first and less dogmatic than the second, lies between these two and proceeds in a number of *rationally justified* steps. One thing that is immediately obvious, however, is that the apostles' experiences of the living Christ cannot be likened to the twelve witnesses to the alleged flying horse, since the contexts of the claims are quite different.

Step A1

The following historical events seem to be required in order to make sense of the development of Christianity. A man of extraordinary spiritual talent, known as Jesus of Nazareth, lived in Palestine and told a series of stories, the parables, which it was relatively easy to remember. These stories indicate that he saw his own coming as representing a crisis in history and the fulfilment of the expectations of the great prophets. He ran into trouble with the authorities and was crucified, somewhere around 30 CE. Shortly afterwards some of his followers claimed to have seen him and founded the first Christian communities. The new religion spread, and around the period 65–90 CE, or possibly earlier, what came to be called the four gospels were written by members of these communities. It is very likely they were written precisely because the Christians who actually remembered Jesus were dying out.

The grounds for each of these claims are very strong, although I would not use the word 'proof'. They include pagan references to the first Christians – for example, in Pliny the Younger, in a letter written around 106–112 CE to the emperor Trajan, asking advice on how to deal with the Christians. There is almost certain evidence for the existence of the early Christian community and their essential beliefs in Tacitus, shortly after Pliny, and certain reference in Suetonius from around 125 CE.[23] There is also the manuscript evidence relating to the gospels, with many ancient manuscripts, at least one of which probably dates from before 150 CE, and with large portions dating from around 200.[24] In the circumstances of a small, persecuted community, this represents a very short gap between the events and the surviving manuscripts. There is also a mass of scholarly material on the content of the gospels and the styles of writing. There are surviving letters from Christians such as Iranaeus, from before 200 CE. Most importantly, there is the actual existence of the first Christians and their essential message. At this, step one, the *truth* of the Christian message is not assumed, only the bare facts just listed. Nevertheless, the rational grounds for insisting on our knowledge of these 'bare facts' needs to be stressed. After a period of unwarranted suspicion of any data relating to the historical Jesus, contemporary scholarship is returning to an acceptance of the certainty, not only of the existence of Jesus, but also of several salient aspects of his life, for which we have, for example, much better evidence than we do for the life of Alexander the Great.[25]

The following consideration may help some readers to be confident in an historical core to the Christian gospels, at the very least with respect to the minimum claims I am making at this stage. In one of his surviving letters, Iranaeus reminisces with an old friend, Florinus, about their student days together, recalling the lectures of the aged Polycarp, who we know was martyred in about 155 or 156. Polycarp, he remembers, used to tell stories about John, 'the disciple of the Lord', who was either the man we know as John the Apostle, or some other personal associate of Jesus. The scholarly C.H. Dodd summed up the situation like this: 'Iranaeus, then, in France shortly before AD 200, was able to recall at only one remove a man who had known Jesus intimately.'[26] This recalls personal memories of my aged grandmother, describing, in the 1940s, her life as the daughter of a Northumbrian farmer when she was a girl in the 1870s, along with vivid accounts of her father riding forth in his carriage. The timescale (roughly 130 years) is the same. Such anecdotes are not 'proof', in any sense, but they can support rational conviction in certain historical events. For example, take the case of the Last Supper, with its institution of the Christian 'Holy Communion' or 'breaking of the bread'. St Paul, writing in the 50s CE, describes this central communal memory (1 Corinthians 11), as do the gospels of Mark, Matthew and Luke. The author of the gospel of John, possibly writing a little later than the other gospels, was clearly sensitive to pagan caricatures of the event (which alleged that Christians actually drank blood), and therefore deliberately describes the communion in symbolic terms (throughout John 6). Meanwhile, Luke's Acts of the Apostles (probably written in the 70s or 80s) makes it clear that the 'breaking of the bread' was the principal act of Christian worship. Then, with utter congruity, we find that Pliny's account of the Christians (in his letter to Trajan) refers to them coming together for food. No doubt, when a host of individual memories (like those of Polycarp) become subsumed under a 'communal memory', various details can get added or obscured, but this practice, which we can sometimes observe happening, provides no ground for doubting the reality of an historical core.

Step A2

Whereas step A1, in my view, should be taken by *any* rational agent who reflects on the evidence, step A2 is a rational step for someone who is prepared to go somewhat further (while not yet as far as step A3, which is where I would go). With regard to the Old Testament what is accepted is i) that there *may* indeed be a loving, purposive intelligence that is reaching out to human beings; ii) that the Jews were justified in looking forward to a Messiah who would come to fulfil their prophets' expectations. Moreover, within the prophetic messages we can see a fascinating development, as what was at first seen as a political saviour is increasingly seen in spiritual terms. In the greatest prophets the extraordinary perception is found that the coming Messiah will demonstrate the kind of love that will make him vulnerable, a man 'despised and rejected of men'.[27] With regard to the New Testament, the story of Jesus now takes on a richer meaning. Not only does his teaching become filled with echoes of a long expectation and the fulfilment of a great tradition, many things now become much more believable. If there may indeed be a God, whose representative in some sense Jesus is, then the scope of what it is *reasonable* to believe now widens. Certainly (congruent with what we find today in the area of psychosomatic illness), Jesus could indeed be a healer as well as a teacher. While the verbal accuracy of every verse is not required, and there can still be no certainty regarding the miraculous, the gospels are now seen as a believable presentation of a person of huge spiritual power.

Step A3

This step is taken by anyone committed to a recognizable form of Christianity. As we have seen, this can take many forms, from a conservative literalism that accepts every verse and every miracle to a much more guarded approach, that at the historical or factual level *may not go beyond step A2*. However what is common to all those who take this third step is a *commitment* to try and follow the 'way' of Jesus, however this is interpreted, regarding manner of life and manner of prayer. In other words, we have reached at least the first creed, as described in the Acts of the Apostles. It is of the utmost importance to recognize that this step involves more than belief, in the sense of believing that x and y are the case. A personal, existential decision is made. Congruously, a perceptive Roman Catholic writer describes the talent of both Kierkegaard and Lonergan 'for forcing us out of the neutral stance of, say, the student of religions, and challenging us to our own personal commitment'.[28]

This existential dimension to Christian faith is crucially important during periods of doubt. As already indicated, there is nothing wrong, at all times, with an appropriate use of doubt, but when Christians go through a long period of serious doubt about the very reality of God, let alone specific doctrines, they often wonder whether they are still within the Christian fold. Typical of this doubt, it should be noted, is not a rejection of the *notion* of a God who can be said to be 'real' (as in Don Cupitt), but doubt about whether the God one is seeking is 'real'. My suggestion is that so long as these seekers feel committed to attempting to follow the lifestyle of Jesus, however they interpret this, and remain committed to trying to say the Lord's Prayer (even if it is to 'Our Father, if you are there'), then the Christianity is genuine. This is a variation on step A3, a step that brings one into the community of believing and worshipping Christians.

The Experience and Interpretation of Redemption

Serious debate on the doctrine of redemption needs to start with a distinction, made by Dean Matthews among others, between a basic experience and the human interpretation of this experience – a theme that is already familiar from the discussion of monism and theism. Matthews writes: 'We need to get clear on the point that no *doctrine* of the Atonement is part of the Christian faith and that many different views are possible concerning the manner of the Divine forgiveness.'[29] In this section I shall seek to explore the experiential side of two of the three root experiences referred to earlier in this chapter, namely: first, the sense of being, forgiven, redeemed, and transformed by what Christ has done; second, being so renewed that one experiences being a 'new creature', 'in Christ'.[30] Only in the context of these experiences can the Christian doctrines of redemption and incarnation be understood.

Many contemporary people have no strong sense of being sinful, or of being in some crucial way 'alienated' – that is 'separated' – from other people or from their true selves or from God. Earlier I described a sense of personal sin or inadequacy as one of three typical kinds of religious experience, but although this is true, I believe, with respect to the history of religions, the secular or semi-secular cultures in which many of us now live means that this sense of sin or inadequacy is either less felt, or is felt in ways that are not connected by many people with religion. Yet without a sense of sin, or at least of 'alienation' (which, in so far as it results from our own shortcomings, is a consequence of sin), it is very hard to enter into the mind-set of the first Christians. Some people find Karl Marx's account of human alienation a useful stepping-stone to a mature understanding of the human condition and the way in which it needs to be redeemed and transformed. In Marx's account, the materialistic culture we have been brought up in, particularly under capitalism, has distorted our true natures which are to be 'species beings' who find both their fulfilment and their true happiness and freedom in cooperation with others. Presently, typical humans are alienated from each other (for example, in the class struggle), from nature (which we exploit), from the work of our own hands (because of the distorted economic relationships many people have) and, ultimately, from our own selves.[31] When such views are combined with a passionate concern to liberate the poor and the oppressed, one can well understand much of the driving force for those 'liberation theologies' that have found common ground in Marx and the gospels. However, this is a step I am wary of since, despite Marx's acute analysis of the human condition, there are serious flaws in his overall picture.[32] Nevertheless, if Marx had had a place in his philosophy for alienation from God we would have had an almost complete account of the human condition; what would still have been lacking is a *solution* that is adequate to our nature, not only as 'species-beings', but as spiritual persons, made in the image of God.

The suggestion I am leading up to is that when we take a realistic view of what we are, and at the same time, if we have a sense of moral responsibility, then it is utterly *appropriate* for a rational person to feel guilt. However, let it be clear that, in the view I am promoting, 'guilt' can be, and often is, an extremely unhealthy feeling that we ought to shed. Indeed, there are many situations in which one of the first tasks of a therapist is to try and remove an inappropriate sense of guilt. My claim is that there is an appropriate form of guilt, not that it has usually been felt in a healthy form. Until recently many children passing through puberty were encouraged to feel guilty about having certain feelings, and about the way these feelings were typically relieved in private, both of which were either completely or relatively innocent. At the same time bullying, in either physical or non-physical forms, was pretty well accepted as 'normal' behaviour. But it is the latter, and not the former, for which a sense of guilt, I am suggesting, is perfectly appropriate. It goes along with any notion of personal responsibility. The other part of my suggestion is that guilt is unhealthy if there is not a means of getting rid of it, so that it does not lead one to a morose depression. But there are appropriate ways of getting rid of it, namely through acts of repentance, forgiveness and (when possible) restitution.

Once it is admitted that there is an appropriate place for guilt, then the sense of sin, which is a religious term for an awareness of failure in the context of an overriding responsibility towards our creator, becomes not only understandable, but rational. (The New Testament word translated as 'sin' (*hamartia*), literally means, 'falling short of the mark'.) This, in turn, is the context in which the Christian experience of redemption or atonement can begin to make sense. The first Christians experienced an overwhelming sense of rebirth when they felt forgiven, reconciled and born into a new community, as a result of what Jesus had done.

This is one of many places where a narrative can enhance our understanding. Hauerwas has a powerful passage where he talks of 'learning to be a sinner', by which be means learning to be aware of our actual state. As a person reads the New Testament story and begins to identify with the characters, then they begin to see the implications of those actions that hurt others, directly or indirectly. Frequently, these actions result from our failure to take responsibilities seriously rather than through deliberate acts of wrongdoing. In the context of the New Testament narrative, read not only as history but also as a living parable, the sensitive reader increasingly identifies with the crucifiers.[33] This ancient insight is nowhere more powerfully evident than when an actively involved audience, listening to Bach's *St Matthew Passion*, comes to the place where the soloists pose the question 'Is it I?', and then joins (vocally or silently) in the chorale 'It is I whose sin now binds Thee'.[34]

I do not want to suggest that there cannot be forgiveness in other than Christian settings, or that, say, Muslims cannot really feel reconciled to God when they repent. Later on I shall directly address how a rational Christian philosophy must make sense of such experiences, along with the more general issue of the extent to which it is appropriate for any religion, including Christianity, to claim any 'exclusiveness'. For the present I simply want to unpack the nature of the typical Christian experience, and see how it led to ways of thinking about the relation of Jesus to God.

Much Christian language that expresses an overwhelming sense of reconciliation centres on the cross, and the way in which this is felt to have opened up a new relationship with God. This is the point at which the difference between the felt experience and the *theory* about what has taken place needs to made in its strongest terms, since, quite frankly, much of traditional Christian theory about the cross is simply unacceptable on either rational or moral grounds, or both. Here a brief review and critique of the principal theories must be attempted. A famous study by Gustaf Aulen puts them into three categories although, as we shall see, these categories are not exhaustive.[35]

One of these is specially associated with Peter Abelard (although he did not see redemption entirely in terms of it), and is often called the 'exemplary theory'. The loving example of Jesus, both in his life and death, is such that people can be *drawn* to repentance and a new vision of life in a way that would otherwise be impossible. Abelard describes how in redemption we acquire true liberty 'so that we should fulfil all things not so much through fear as through our love for him who shewed towards us a favour than which, as he himself says, none greater can be found: "Greater love hath no man that this, that a man lay down his life for his friends."'[36] Similarly, Jesus is reported as saying: 'If I be lifted up from the earth, I will draw all men to me.'[37] This is a theory of the atonement that few Christians have any difficulty with until and unless it is made the *whole* story, in which case it is alleged that it is too much based in psychology and not enough in 'ontology' – meaning the effecting of a 'real' change in the divine-human relationship. Another way of making this point is to claim that an exemplary theory is 'subjective', and does not allow for any substantial difference between what Jesus did, and any other person who truly demonstrated the love of God. Some more 'objective' account of what took place, it is alleged, needs to be provided. I shall suggest that this theory can be amplified in a way that counters this objection.

A second theory is especially associated with Luther although he was representing an ancient way of thinking and, as in the case of Abelard, he did not see redemption exclusively in terms of one theory. Aulen calls it the 'Christus Victor' theory and it capitalizes on certain Biblical passages where God or the Messiah is seen as triumphing over the devil. In a colourful image, Luther suggests that God trapped the devil into arranging the death of Jesus, concealing his divinity from him, so that when he had 'taken the bait' he had – using Luther's own fishing analogy – taken on a prey that he could not digest.[38] If we do not concentrate on such fanciful analogies, there are some positive things to say about this theory, for it does tap into a profound sense of the cosmic conflict between good and evil which characterizes so much imaginative literature; Luther himself 'distinguishes explicitly between the idea itself and the imagery in which it is clothed'.[39] Also, it can be expressed in ways which avoid any literal belief in a personal devil – a topic on which I suggest that we remain agnostic for present purposes. However, although the New Testament does refer to Christ's victory over sin and death, as an explanation of *how* the human person is forgiven and transformed it is hard to find any understanding from this imagery unless it is linked with the suggestions I shall be making.

The third theory is specially associated with Anselm, and is the one most familiar in the Western church's evangelical preaching, both Catholic and Protestant. It is often called the 'substitution' theory, for reasons that will be apparent. In its typical form it goes like this. The justice of God demanded that human sin could only be forgiven if there were a suitable sacrifice, while such is the enormity of human sin that we could not pay the price. However, Jesus, in his humanity, as a perfect representative of us all, himself paid the price – the enormous price that only his death could provide – when, as St Paul put it, 'he was made sin for us' on the cross.[40] Thus God's perfect justice was satisfied and it was possible for man to be forgiven and redeemed. Hence the special devotion awarded to the crucified Jesus and the language of many evangelical hymns in which 'Christ dies in my place'. Sometimes we find the theory put even more crudely, to include the following claims for example. First, since God is infinite, *any* sin deserves eternal punishment, since it is an offence against the infinite love of God. (Anselm uses a variation on this argument, as does Calvin, who uses it to reject the distinction between mortal and venial sin. However this claim tends to remove all moral distinctions, while both the Scriptures, and ordinary moral sense, regard some faults as greater than others.[41]) Second, the *anger* of God had to be appeased by an offering of suffering. Third, there is an original guilt (not just original sin – a distinction we shall explore later in this chapter), passed on to all Adam's heirs, which makes us deserving from birth of a terrible punishment which was only remedied by the death of Jesus. Fourth, God changed his mind in response to what Jesus did (a claim which Anselm never made).

Justice demands that we evaluate the theory without accretions such as these that it tends to attract. It must be admitted, for example, that much Biblical language suggests a 'juristic' account of the atonement, with references to Jesus paying a 'ransom' and being our 'advocate' who makes 'propitiation' for our sins.[42] However, there has been a host of criticisms from Christians of many persuasions, including Quakers,[43] which it is hard to answer *if* the juristic language is taken literally. As a 1995 Church of England report put the problem: 'In addition to the moral difficulties of the notion of substitution, there is also the question how we are involved in Christ's atonement and how we benefit from it.'[44] When the notion of substitution is a symbolic way of referring to the basic *experience* of redemption that I have mentioned, the objections can be handled, but when it claims (as probably in Anselm himself) to be a rational account of *how* we are redeemed, then there are major problems, both intellectual and moral. It is very important to be clear about this distinction between symbolic language and rational explanation. When I go to a Good Friday service, like many liberal Christians I have no trouble joining sincerely in hymns which express thanksgiving for what Jesus did on the cross, because, for reasons that I shall soon express, I believe that if he had not acted as he did, my life would not be what it is. I can say, in all sincerity, that I depend on the cross of Christ, and that if Christ had not died in obedience to his mission to accept the human condition, I would not have experienced the forgiveness that I now have. But when I am asked to accept the typical evangelical *explanation* of how Jesus saved us, then I face the following problem.

Although, in a variety of ways, we can actually share other people's burdens, we cannot meaningfully share their guilt, except when we have been party to some communal sin. We may be 'responsible' for what others have done in the sense of inheriting a duty to try to correct the wrongs, say, our parents did, especially if we are now benefiting in some way from these wrongs, but we cannot be 'responsible' in the sense of inheriting their *guilt*. As we have seen, from Jeremiah onwards, it was realized that justice demands that people carry their individual responsibility so far as guilt is concerned. This does not involve an unbridled individualism since we are relational beings who only find true happiness and fulfilment in the context of a community. The Christian gloss on this universal realization is the recognition that we are only complete within the communion of saints, and 'in Christ'. However, this insight into our communal or relational nature is not to be confused with a doctrine of collective guilt. Therefore, although I shall be giving a powerful meaning to the idea that 'Christ died for me', from both a logical and a moral point of view this cannot be that he *literally* 'bore my sins' in the way that many Christian preachers have expressed the matter. Here, there has been a kind of teaching (like the total rejection of evolutionary theory) that tends to drive away from Christianity many a thoughtful inquirer. There are also important moral implications, for doctrines of collective guilt have been used to justify the most inhuman treatment of innocent people. In all of this there is a link with the danger of searching for a spiritual guru who will so take over our minds and wills that our individual responsibility to think and to choose is taken away. There are, of course, very different gurus, in both East and West, who seek to enhance our responsibility, and Jesus was such. When asked a question he typically responded with another question, forcing people to think, and to follow him not blindly but because he was seen to represent the light. Any guru, or any representation of a Christ who wants to 'take over', is morally dangerous. As in so many instances, the really evil can be a distortion of something really good. The link between the false guru and literal 'substitution' theories of the atonement is in the similar disregard for the very uniqueness of each person that makes them truly precious, a uniqueness that includes their individual freedom and responsibility.

A similar distortion of Christian teaching on forgiveness arises when the work of Christ is seen to remove human sinfulness in some automatic, or quasi-mechanical way, which does not involve the active cooperation of the sinner. An early, rational approach to this issue can be found in William Chillingworth, mentioned in Chapter 1, writing in the 1600s. Remission of sins, he argues, does depend on the work of grace, but it is not 'immediate', for it depends on repentance and 'serious conversion'.[45]

As in other places where my passion for reason leads me to what some will consider to be radical positions (although positions shared with many other theists),[46] many readers will feel uncomfortable with this critique of cherished beliefs that have had a great sustaining power. Let me therefore move on to a more positive approach to the work of Christ that does not pose the same intellectual and moral dilemmas. I shall try to show that the Anselmian theory points to a great insight, but that this insight must be expressed much more carefully than it often is.

In loving human relationships there is frequently a tension between love and justice, and in particular between *mercy* (which is one of the implications of love) and justice. This tension is powerfully portrayed, not only in the Biblical drama, but in many great works of creative fiction. Suppose I have greatly wronged C, and that the effects of this have been to cause loss and hurt to C, but that (in this relatively simple case), no one else is hurt.[47] C, as an act of mercy, comes to me and offers to forgive me and to be reconciled. Sometimes, even in human relationships, this is the only way in which the relationship can be remade, given the nature of my fault. Here, C does not share my guilt, but C may, in human terms, 'share my burden' and feel pain. They have also suffered the effects of my fault. If reconciliation is achieved, where is *my* suffering? It consists, first, in the pain of admitting my fault; second (more subtly), in the cost of undoing the character traits that this fault has engendered – that is, in Biblical terms – in 'dying to the old man'; and, third, in the cost of making any reparations that I can.

In this perfectly realistic account, wherein does the problem of justice lie? It is not, at least primarily, in the fact, taken by itself, that the penalties I suffer may seem to be light in comparison to the pain and suffering I have caused; it is in the fact that justice, in its primary sense, is a matter of being 'fair and equal' to all. But suppose that my fault is great, while my friend B's is much less, and that B too is forgiven by C in circumstances that are identical except for the relative smallness of B's fault. But here there seems a great unfairness, for (apart from the issue of reparations, which in many cases it may be impossible for me to make), my much greater fault does not seem to have been matched by greater pain borne by me. In human terms, it is as if I were to give the whole gang the same sentence, even though one member was far more guilty than the others. The same sense of injustice arises when it is announced that the blessedness of the kingdom of heaven will be given equally to new converts and to those 'which have borne the burden and heat of the day', as in Jesus' parable of the workers who are all paid one penny, regardless of how long they have worked.[48] Here there does seem to be a paradox, and mercy and justice to be in tension. The crude version of the Anselmian model is an attempt to resolve this paradox by making the demands of justice completely satisfied by putting the burden on Jesus. But instead of satisfying the demands of justice this compounds them, for justice – as we normally understand it – demands that punishment be proportional to guilt. Therefore, since Jesus *cannot* share our *guilt*, it would seem that we should pay penalties that are proportional to our guilt.

This suggestion can be fortified if one accepts Kant's argument to the effect that a moral person who recognizes their guilt must will that the appropriate punishment be forthcoming. In fact, not to provide the appropriate punishment, on this view, amounts to failing to respect perpetrators as autonomous persons, and as ends in themselves. Kant here writes of 'respect to humanity in the person of the miscreant'.[49] We may not follow Kant in the accompanying argument that capital punishment is the only acceptable penalty for murder, because it alone fully respects the moral integrity of the murderer (I think that he is mistaken here), but still think that he has put his finger on an important consideration. Something within us finds it hard to feel free of guilt, and that we have been treated with the respect due to our true humanity, until and unless we pay the appropriate penalty.

How then is this sense of justice to be squared with mercy – that marvellous act of generosity that seems, superficially at least, to depend on a violation of justice:

> The quality of mercy is not strain'd;
> It droppeth, as the gentle rain from heaven
> Upon the place beneath ...
> It is an attribute of God himself;
> And earthly power doth then show likest God's
> When mercy seasons justice.[50]

In the Christian context, God's mercy and God's grace are here intertwined. God reaches out to us (an act of grace) and offers to accept us as we are (an act of mercy) – 'Just as I am' – and not as we ought to be. Every parent understands the human analogue when they reach out to their children, not as they would like them to be, but as they are. From the children's perspective, knowing that they are loved and accepted as they are is part of the essential background for a stable home. Here then, as in all important paradoxes, we have once again experiential grounds for the two truths that are set in tension – an awareness of the need for justice and an awareness of the need for mercy. Can we, once again, see at least the beginnings of a resolution to the tension?

Indeed we can, for we are not concerned here with human justice as it is often found, in which there is a vengeful desire to cause suffering that is at least proportional to the offence, but with a higher form of justice which – because it is centred in love – does not seek a penalty for its own sake, but only the penalty that can lead a person to be restored. Here Kant is both right and wrong. He is right to see that we cannot truly respect persons, and treat them as ends in themselves, if we simply 'let them off'. To do this is to prevent them being the kinds of person who can grow and flourish. Moreover, the *lex talionis* (the demand for an equivalent punishment) does point to a truth – namely, that there must be some proportion between the degree of guilt and the pain of the healing process – but it is misleading to see the *lex talionis* (as Kant appears to have done) as a principle that must be fulfilled in order to satisfy some abstract principle of justice. God reaches out to us, and offers us a forgiveness that is free (in that he does not want any recompense for the pain he has suffered), but which does demand that as responsible agents we go through the process that enables us truly to receive forgiveness and benefit from it. Here, let us recall the three kinds of pain that the one receiving forgiveness has to endure. If I have sinned greatly, there will be much greater consequences for my process of healing than there will be for person B, in the previous example. The pain of admitting my mistake will be greater. The pain of 'dying to the old man' – in a process that may take years – will be greater. In addition, part of this process must involve an appropriate reparation. Let us suppose, unlike my example, that others have been hurt, and that I cannot make significant reparations to them, perhaps because they are dead. It seems to me that the healing process will inevitably involve making 'vicarious' reparations. For example, if while acting as a doctor, I have sinned greatly against innocent people, I might join *Medicins Sans Frontières* and in this way, work out my reparation before God. Everyone, with a little imagination, can find their own equivalent for this. It is not at all the same thing as the medieval 'treasury of merit', which Luther rightly criticized, because it is not a case of earning good points, or of being granted good points by the church, so that God will reward us. It is a case, for the sinner, of going through a process which so changes us that we are *enabled* to receive the mercy that is offered. Moreover, in addition to these three kinds of pain, in the context of Christianity there is a fourth, namely the pain involved in forgiving others their trespasses against us. In the teaching of Jesus, this is one of the conditions for our being in a state to receive forgiveness. Here too an element of proportion comes in, not concerning the extent of God's forgiveness, but through the fact that the greater our sinfulness, the harder it is for us to forgive others from the heart. Putting all this together, for the sinner, redemption does involve a suffering that has a relationship to the degree of fault.

One consequence of the need to be able to *receive* forgiveness is that Christians should take the idea of purgatory seriously. At death, all but a few of us have not finished either the process of purgation that is needed for full reconciliation, or the similar process of 'sanctification' that would make us ready to receive or appreciate the higher forms of life with God. The claim made by many Protestants that God's forgiveness is complete is true (for the repentant person), but misses the point. It is a matter of what can prepare a human person, for whom responsibility is part of their very nature, for the higher stages of happiness. (Whether this purgation is in a special place, or a special state, or whether it takes place in 'lower' strata of a heaven, remembering Jesus' words 'in my Father's house are many mansions',[51] is another question, and one about which I am agnostic.)

Let us return to the attempt to understand more fully the way in which what Jesus did, in both his life and death, enables forgiveness to be offered in a new way.

Suppose that we have taken step A2 in the process of the rational evaluation of Scripture, as described in the last section, and that we see Jesus as a Messiah who, as part of his mission to bring about a new order – 'The Kingdom of Heaven' – seeks a new means of reconciling people to God, one anticipated by the great prophets.[52] Although endowed with extraordinary gifts he chooses to *identify* with the life of the ordinary person, just as the good Samaritan in his most famous story identified with the victim, 'going where he was'. He refuses to use any special powers to make bread or display wonders to the crowd. When the situation gets dangerous he refuses to call angelic powers to his aid. He fully accepts the human condition, 'being in all ways tempted [or tested] as we are'.[53] When it is necessary he sets his face to go to Jerusalem, knowing the virtually inevitable result, and finally he accepts the predicted outcome, a painful and ignominious death. (The result was virtually inevitable, not because every detail was preordained, but because, given human nature, sooner or later the authorities would have to respond, either by acceptance of his message or by taking the active steps that Jesus expected. We can recall here Plato's prediction that a truly good man will cause a reaction that will lead to his suffering or death.[54])

The idea of moral heroes having to share human vulnerability if they are to be an inspiration to us needs special emphasis here. In fantasy literature, a hero who turns out to be an alien with extraordinary powers that human beings do not have fails to be an *example* for us to follow. The image of 'superman' only takes on significant human interest when his creators find it necessary to introduce vulnerability – for example, in his response to a strange metal. Tolkein's Gandalf only begins to be a *human* exemplar when he is tempted to take and use the ring of power.[55] In great literature, the heroes that inspire always share our humanity. Moreover, a key to the moral life for all of us is an acceptance of our common humanity, so that we are prepared to apply to ourselves the rules that we would have others apply to themselves. As Kant rightly saw, the essence of wrongdoing is treating ourselves as *exceptions*. Thus if God were to inspire us through a demonstration of a perfect life, it had to be in the context of a Messiah that shared our vulnerability. This is what Isaiah had come realize.

Since Jesus was clearly seen by himself and his followers as a special representative of God (leaving aside until the next section the question of his exact status), then here, in this acceptance of vulnerability, was an extraordinary demonstration and acted parable of God's love for us. Not only is Jesus acting with total love, he represents the love and mercy of God. As the New Testament puts it, 'Being in the form of God' Jesus 'made himself of no reputation [literally, in the Greek, 'he emptied himself'], and took upon him the form of a servant, and was made in the likeness of men: And being found in fashion as a man, he humbled himself, and became obedient unto death … .'[56] God, in his mercy, wishes to forgive and seeks reconciliation, demanding only those things from us that make it possible for us to *receive* forgiveness and *achieve* reconciliation. However, to this *demonstration* of love (which might be thought to limit one to an Abelardian or 'subjective' account of redemption), there is the need to add a further element, one that draws on the powerful experience of being 'in Christ' in a new kind of union that simply would not have been possible if Jesus had not 'taken on humanity' and been known as a person, living among us. Throughout the New Testament the baptism experience is described in these terms: a dying and a rising with and in Jesus. One even shares, in some degree, with the work of his redeeming love, marked by many references to sharing the sufferings not only of fellow Christians but of Christ himself,[57] and one reference which suggests that we can even extend the redemptive sufferings of Christ through our own sufferings in him.[58]

Let us suppose that in the context of the special demonstration of God's love, undertaken by a divine representative, someone returns to the old question: 'Was the work of Christ ultimately a "subjective" one, in which what matters is *only* how *we* respond, or was it an "objective" one which depends not only on our response, but on some actual change in the divine-human relationship?' My response would be that this question is badly framed (it is a *question mal posée,*) because it suggests that true objectivity cannot be a feature of something that is 'only' a powerful symbol. But the very existence of certain symbols changes what is possible. Although God's forgiveness is available to all who truly repent, in the Old Testament, for example, many people *could not* truly repent if it were not for the symbol that is seen to be acted out, in history, in both the life and death of Jesus. If we add to this the possibility of a new relationship 'in Christ', which only became possible because Jesus lived among us as a human person, then there can be an 'objective' doctrine of the atonement, without having to resort to the dubious logic that goes with the *literal* acceptance of either the Christus Victor or the substitution theory.

A good example of how a 'symbol' may actually change what happens in the real world, is provided by the Christian Eucharist. The Eucharistic experience is of a symbolic supper in which there is a new experience of being with the living Christ, made known in the 'breaking of the bread'.[59] For a long time there has been a dispute between conservative evangelicals who claim that the Eucharist is not a sacrifice, but (according to some) *only* a 'memorial' and conservative catholics (within several denominations) who insist that it is a 'sacrifice' in which (according to the more extreme version), the events of Jesus' passion are in some way re-enacted. However, neither of the extreme views seems adequate, for although there is clearly a memorial of some kind, typical Christian experience of the Eucharist points to the way in which the worshipper begins to enter into a transforming experience that somehow stands outside the ordinary sequences of time. Christ is felt to be present, as at Emmaus,[60] in such a way that participating in this powerful symbolic act involves participating in all the Eucharists that have ever taken place,[61] and in the very life of Jesus. It isn't a case of the events being 're-enacted', but of being 'entered into'. It is a mistake, therefore, to make a sharp contrast between the 'objective' and the 'symbolic' when we deal with those symbols that are embued with transforming power.

There is certainly much to be said for an account of the work of Christ which permits the Christian to use 'objective' language. Thus Leonard Hodgson wrote 'we need to maintain at the heart of the doctrine of the atonement the message of an objective achievement wrought once for all by God in the history of this world', for if we have only a 'moral influence theory', then salvation 'is only relevant to that small selection of mankind which has heard the gospel preached… .'[62] Further, expressions such as 'he died for me' become perfectly acceptable, since (on the approach I am advocating), if Jesus had not offered himself in this way, as part of a life of complete obedience and love, then I would not have had this effective symbol, nor the possibility of the 'in Christ' relationship. In this regard there is a useful passage in H.A. Hodges' *The Pattern of the Atonement*. After discussing the serious flaws in legalist accounts of the atonement, he too finds meaning in the context of a union in which we become 'in Christ'. Outside this context, the claim that Christ died 'on our behalf' is completely unacceptable, but in this context the language can take on new meaning, 'for the things which Christ is said by this doctrine to do on our behalf are things which we also do in him'.[63]

The foregoing reflections on the atonement can help us to respond to a more recent objection that has been raised against the Abelardian approach (the first objection being its alleged 'subjectivity'). There are two prongs to this recent objection: the former claims that any 'moral influence' theory of salvation, based on the example of the cross, tends to promote the idea of suffering being *in itself* redemptive; the latter, that this idea, in turn, tends to promote a passive rather than an active response to the plight of those who suffer. In their joint paper 'For God so loved the world?', Joanne Brown and Rebecca Parker write 'The moral influence theory is founded on the belief that an innocent, suffering victim and only an innocent, suffering victim for whose sufferings we are in some way responsible has the power to confront us with our guilt and move us to a new decision.' And, in a similar vein: 'We must do away with the atonement, this idea of a blood sin upon the whole human race which can be washed away only by the blood of the lamb.'[64]

One of the major misunderstandings that these quotations reveal concerns the view that Christians are committed to belief in 'original guilt', a topic that will be more fully addressed later in this chapter, but even in Chapter 1 we noted – significantly – that Abelard did not share this belief. The more immediate misunderstanding concerns what the authors say about suffering. No doubt, there have been Christians who thought that suffering is redemptive *in itself*, but the more accurate description, at least within the liberal tradition, is to say that it is *love* that is redemptive *in itself*, and that suffering is always, *in itself*, an evil. The point is that, in order to love, suffering may have to be endured. This is the price of interdependence, empathy and vulnerability, the last-named being a theme that runs through this book (and the importance of which is stressed by another feminist author in the same volume of papers).[65] Further, while in no way belittling other examples of love, the significance of Jesus' love is that for the Christian it expresses not only the love of one person, but also the loving nature of the creative source of the whole universe. This is why, as we shall see in the next section, the whole issue of redemption or atonement cannot be separated from that of the incarnation. Hence the powerful symbolism of 'the lamb of God'. Finally, none of this affords any ground for denying the need to fight against suffering – although in the light of the passivity towards cruelty and oppresstion that has characterized many Christians, the fault for this misunderstanding must lie, in large measure, with Christians.

I shall conclude this section with a reflection on an interesting ambiguity in Anselm's writings. Early on in his exposition of the atonement, in accordance with his general theme of 'faith seeking understanding', Anselm indicates that he is concerned to bring understanding to someone who *already* has faith, but elsewhere he writes as if he is also seeking to show how reason should lead unbelievers to an understanding of God's work in Christ.[66] I am sympathetic to Anslem's dilemma since I suspect that serious attempts to discuss the atonement are often trying to do two rather different things at the same time. The first is to help unbelievers have some understanding of the Christian teaching in the context of their own moral understanding. Here I think that Anselm is generally unsuccessful, especially when he stresses the *infinite* gravity of human sin and the need for redeemed humans to make up for the number of fallen angels. The second is to give a much fuller understanding of the work of Christ in the context of how a believer is likely to see things. Here I think Anselm may have much to teach someone who is sensitive to the holiness of God. Abelard's suggestions about the moral influence of God's love in Jesus is an example of successful teaching in the first context – aimed at both believers and unbelievers; while bringing out the implications of a relationship 'in Christ' is an example of the second, for this is a relationship that is consequent to an experience of commitment.

Redemption and Incarnation

The three theories of the atonement discussed all link the doctrine to that of the incarnation, that is, the doctrine that in Jesus the word was made 'flesh' [from the Latin *caro, carnis*], and they are right to do so, since what is achieved is intimately connected with the question of who is doing the achieving. The issue must now be raised of what a rational inquiry can say about the nature of Jesus' relationship to the creative source, called 'Father'.

Once again, we can take a step-by-step approach. Let us assume that we have already taken step A2 regarding the accuracy of the Bible, and also, without as yet any Christian commitment, we have some empathy with the experience of redemption and of a new life 'in Christ' as described in the last section. In this context, what can be said about the nature of Christ?

In step B1, we note some of the things which it is virtually certain that Jesus said about himself. The parables, again and again, show that he saw himself as the 'bridegroom', the long-awaited son or heir, the Lord of the harvest, and in short, the expected Messiah or Christ. ('Messiah' is the Hebrew, and 'Christ' the Greek for the term 'anointed one'.) Most significant is the parable of the vineyard, in which the Lord sends his servants the prophets to receive the fruits of the vineyard, only to have them beaten and rejected. Eventually he sends his 'son', saying 'They will reverence my son.' But instead, he is killed.[67] Another pointer to the way Jesus saw himself can be found in his many references to 'the Son of Man',[68] a term that occurs in the book of Daniel and also in the book of Enoch, written in the first or second century BCE, and which we know was the source of much contemporary interest at the time of Jesus. Although we cannot be certain if Jesus was making use of these sources, there was probably a reference (as Vincent Taylor suggests) to the kind of Messiahship that he claimed.[69] Also relevant is the way in which he was felt to teach 'with authority'.[70] Finally, we may underline the way in which, according to the gospels, Jesus did not hesitate to proclaim that people's sins were forgiven, in a way that shocked many bystanders.[71] Despite my criticism of C.S. Lewis' argument, he was right to stress the importance of this claim, and the challenge it involves for how we think about the nature of Jesus. Given the negative reaction, I think it unlikely that this aspect of Jesus' ministry was invented by Christian commentators.

In the foregoing I am deliberately omitting many other claims which the gospels ascribe to Jesus, not because I reject them, but because there can be legitimate doubt (particularly at this step B1), regarding whether Jesus actually made the claims or whether the writers of the gospels were recording pious tradition. These include references by Jesus,[72] or others, including demons that were about to be cast out claiming him to be the 'Son of God'.[73] Also omitted are all the 'I am' expressions, allegedly used by Jesus in St John's gospel, which are clearly meant to echo the Mosaic name of God, 'I am that I am', for example, 'Before Abraham was, I am.'[74] At this stage I am also omitting three important claims made about Jesus by the first Christians, that is to say, that he was the *logos*, eternally involved in the creative process,[75] the image (*eikon*) of the invisible God,[76] and, using a similar term, the 'express image' (*charakter*) of God.[77] Also, put on the sidelines, as it were, is the evidence that he felt no personal sense of sin.[78] Omitting all of the above as 'not proven', for stage B1, what can be said about the status of Jesus? My first conclusion is that no *single* view can be proved to be correct, even within the range of what might be called Christian options. However at the least, it must be said that if we accept the expectation of a Messiah, then seeing Jesus as the Messiah is utterly congruous with the record we have. If, taking an existential step of commitment, we accept that he was the Messiah, and that we wish to call him Lord, we have moved into the range of *Christian* options (as in the case of those who take what I described earlier as step A3), even if we do not espouse a Trinitarian formula. Moreover, within this limited context, the least that could be claimed is that Jesus is a prophet of a very special kind, for not all prophets came as the fulfilment of a whole tradition. This, I suggest, is sufficient, along with what has been argued before, to make this 'minimalist' type of Christianity, a rational option, although by no means the only possible rational option.

Most of those who call themselves Christians would now want to take a second or a third step. In step B2, it is not enough to see Jesus only as an exceptionally good man and a very special kind of prophet. He was, in some extraordinary way, the 'Son of God', as claimed in many of the gospel passages. However, for reasons that will appear, this does not necessarily entail speaking of the 'divinity' of Jesus. The language of divinity arises within step B3, which represents acceptance of most, or all of the traditional Nicean language of the Trinity, especially the part in which Jesus is said to be 'of one substance' with the Father.

How, if at all, can some rational evaluation of steps B2 and B3 be made? As always, we must look for internal and external coherence. In the light of this I shall first indicate the grounds on which step B2 can be supported and then move on to a consideration of step B3.

If someone accepts the claim that Jesus was the 'Son of God' and very likely, with this, the suggestion that some of the Biblical references to this claim represent the actual language used by Jesus, this does not necessarily entail that Jesus was 'divine' in the sense claimed by the orthodoxy of the Nicean and Chalcedonian formulae. There is a well-known claim, in both Christianity and other forms of monotheism, that all human persons are potentially 'sons and daughters of God'. As we have seen, in Christian theology we are all born in the image of God, and what we have to achieve is the 'likeness'. When we do achieve this likeness, then a special kind of sonship and daughtership has been reached. Prior to this, we might be called 'sons and daughters of God', but more because of our potential than because of what we are actually like. As Paul wrote in one of his more poetic moods: 'For as many as are led by the Spirit of God, they are the sons of God. For we have not received the spirit of bondage again to fear; but ye have received the Spirit of adoption, whereby we cry, Abba, Father.'[79] This theme is especially strong in the Orthodox Christian tradition where it is frequently asserted that the divine became man so that man could become divine. Building on this usage and this insight, step 2B sees Jesus as the 'Son of God' in a very special sense, because he had a unique relationship of closeness to the Father that 'blazed a trail' for his followers. If this step is taken, then (as before) more things become reasonable to believe with respect to the Bible, because they are now seen in a new and richer context. Some or all of the passages that I deliberately did not rely on for step B1 may now be rationally acceptable.

Here then we find another form of a theism that is recognizably Christian, but which already goes some way beyond the 'minimalist' acceptance of the first creed. This richer form of Christianity is happy with much of the language which the church uses about Jesus, however, it still falls short of the Trinitarian orthodoxy of most of the mainstream churches where what I have called step 3B is the expectation. In this third step both the oneness and the 'simplicity' of God are affirmed, but at the same time it is claimed that the oneness involves an eternal unity of three persons. Can rational grounds be provided for this step B3, or are we now entering a realm of the purely non-rational (or, as some would allege, of the irrational)? While, in the debate over this issue, I am much more hesitant about what can be classed as 'rational', I think that there are rational considerations that lie behind step B3, even though it may often be the case that obedience to a tradition rather than a consideration of these rational grounds is what has brought about the faith of the typical Christian.

Rational Consideration 1

For human beings, moral goodness is an *achievement*. (Aristotle saw that 'moral virtue' as opposed to 'natural virtue' is an *acquired* disposition.)[80] As a result it only makes sense to say that a baby or very young child is morally good if we believe in reincarnation. Babies, of course (if we put aside the question of reincarnation), are 'innocent', but this is not the same as morally good, which, for humans, involves overcoming temptation and passing through a certain moral struggle. However, if Jesus, *during* his early life, achieved moral goodness, or moral perfection, and then *became* a special representative of God, we have a version of what is sometimes called 'adoptionism'. It is possible that a coherent account of the work of Christ can be built upon this foundation, but it does involve serious difficulties. The work of Christ can no longer be seen as a divine *initiative*, in the fullest sense, from the very birth of the baby in the manger, or from the annunciation to Mary. Moreover, the divine plan would be contingent on Jesus actually achieving the required status. If we do believe in reincarnation and if we think that Jesus was specially sent as a divine representative because of what he had already achieved (rather like a Bodhisattva), then an initiative of a kind can be taken to be present from the moment of Jesus' birth or conception, but there is still a serious difficulty, because it is not a *divine* initiative in the full sense of the term. There is a difference between the initiative involved in sending a representative, and in the initiative involved in coming *oneself*. Of course, it would be extraordinary to say that the Father, in his fullness and transcendence, became a mortal person, although there have been Christian 'heresies', such as Sabellianism, which have said something like this. It is clear, for example, that Jesus continually prayed *to* the Father. What would have to happen is that God, *in so far as he could be experienced in space and time* would have to come, like the good Samaritan, to the location of the person needing help. In other words, a divine initiative, in the fullest sense that can be conceived, and in accordance with the identifying love portrayed in Jesus' parable, would have, in some extraordinary way, to be 'divine', without being the Father. This is one of three grounds that I want to indicate which point towards a more traditional (step B3) account of the Trinity, and which have a rational, reflective element. On such an account, the 'aspects' or 'persons' of the Trinity are not only 'with respect to us' (recalling the distinction made in the first section of this chapter), but point to relationships within the very being of the unity of God.

Rational Consideration 2

As we have seen, any account of the incarnation that is rooted in the primitive Christian experience must link it with the idea of redemption. However, a more traditional account of the incarnation, along the lines suggested in the last paragraph, enriches the account of redemption in at least two ways.

First, the example of love is provided by God himself – so that it can truly be said: 'In Jesus, we see in time, the character of God in eternity.' It is not a case of seeing a perfect *copy* of divine love, but of actually seeing an *example* of divine love. This makes much more significant the New Testament verse that most powerfully expresses a belief in the redemptive work of Christ: 'God was in Christ, reconciling the world unto himself.'[81] A forceful way of bringing out the significance of this view of the incarnation is to appreciate the extraordinary moral power that it conveys. In Bach's *Christmas Oratorio* there is a passage in which both the words and the music juxtapose the mighty king (*Grosser Herr und starker König*) with the baby in the manger (*Liebster Heiland ... Muss in harten Krippen schlafen*). When the two are identified, not only is there a new insight into the nature of divine love, there is manifest the total absurdity of all human pomposity.

Second, if the result of this living symbol is that a new relationship becomes possible (the 'in Christ' relationship), and if this is a new relationship with *God*, it makes much more sense if Christ is, in some way, intrinsically divine.

One of the objections to this argument is that any idea of a change in the divine-human relationship, as suggested either by a traditional account of the atonement or of the incarnation (opening the way to a new relationship with God 'in Christ'), can be taken to imply some kind of change in God himself. For many monotheists this is simply ruled out by the nature of the divine transcendence. Any Christian holding to what I have called 'classical theism' must interpret any suggestion of a change in the divine-human relationship as something that only involves change with respect to us. In reflecting on this matter the following consideration should be taken into account. All monotheists who hold a doctrine of creation that involves an actual beginning of time have already committed themselves to some kind of change in the relationship of the divine to the created order as a whole. The form of mono- theism known as Sikhism is specially sensitive to this point, even though Sikhs generally describe God as ineffable. 'According to Nanak [the founding guru of Sikhism], God changed his own nature and function after the creation of the word.'[82] Most Christians would not describe the implications of creation in these terms, but it is obvious that with creation there is opened up a whole set of new possibilities with respect to God's relationship with 'creatures'. Christians might add this comment: if creation is in some special way achieved 'through the Son', then there was already implicit in the very act of creation, the possibility of a new and special kind of relationship with God once the Son became incarnate. More orthodox Christians would describe this change purely in terms of *our* relationship to God (and no doubt, some Sikhs would explain the matter in this way), while others might be happier to speak of change, of a kind, in the relationship of God to us. In any case, the issues that are raised with respect to the way in which God is related to creatures are not first *introduced* by a Christian doctrine of incarnation, they are already there within a traditional doctrine of creation.

Rational Consideration 3

When we try to describe what is involved in 'love', there is always a relationship involved. This can be cast into a threefold description because there must be (1) the one who loves, (2) the one who is loved, and then, in this context, it makes sense to speak of (3) the love that is between them. Thus Augustine writes that even in the case of humans 'when I, who conduct this inquiry, love something, then three things are found: I, what I love, and the love itself. For I do not love love, except I love a lover, for there is no love where nothing is loved. There are, therefore, three: the lover, the beloved, and the love.'[83] Interestingly, this claim about the threefold nature of any experience of love has both an intellectual and an experiential base. The intellectual base is rooted in an attempt to analyse the constituents of any act of love; the experiential base can be found not only in the writings of Christian mystics, like Ruysbroeck, but also in others. Zaehner draws attention to the words of a famous Muslim mystic, Abu Yazid (or possibly, one of his followers): 'I looked and saw that Lover, Love, and Beloved are all one, for in the world of union all must be One', and gives other examples of the same theme from the Sufi and Jewish mystical traditions.[84] This Trinitarian approach to the act of love has led to numerous attempts to build up a 'social' account of the Trinity, which I suggest can be helpful so long as we continually recall that any likening of the eternal God to a set of social relations can only be by analogy. When the unity of God is likened too closely to that of a community,[85] we are in danger of stressing a separate or quasi- independent picture of each of the three persons, since any genuine *human* commu- nity of persons consists of individuals, who although relational beings, do have a significant independence. I prefer to stress analogies for the unity of the Trinity based, as in Augustine, on the complex unity that comprises one single human person. Another example can be gleaned from Abelard, with his analogy of power, wisdom and goodness, representing Father, Son and Holy Spirit within a fundamental unity.[86] Such analogies are sometimes referred to as 'psychological', in contrast with 'social' ones. In any case, I suggest that the concept of 'one' is not simple, and is capable of different accounts, in which a search for the nature of 'oneness' is a search for a *unity* of elements that are not absolutely identical.

Considerations such as these can pave the way to a doctrine of the Trinity of a traditional kind that has a basis in rational reflection, although within the discussion of the Holy Spirit I shall again raise the issue of the adequacy of human language. In regard to the other considerations that should be explored in a more complete study I shall here make only one further comment. There is a rational case to be made for the view that a certain triadic or trinitarian logic underlies everything in the universe (here the small 't' in 'trinitarian' is deliberate). Part of the importance of Hegel lies in his suggestion that the triadic logic of the dialectical process of thesis, antithesis, synthesis (or action, reaction, resultant motion) is not only a matter of abstract logic, concerning a manner of argument, but also relates to how things or events can be understood in the context of the whole of which they are part. Here we should recall the claim that part of the problem with old-style materialism is its failure to think in terms of the whole which the universe turns out to be, and the dangerous tendency to concentrate on 'discrete' events, as if these could be understood in isolation. In Chapter 3, I argued that contemporary science was forcing us away from a Humean model of discrete events, only unified within the human understanding. This new insight may not demand what I have called a trinitarian logic, but we may find that it encourages or supports it. Moreover, an analogous understanding of the dynamics of the creative process may be hinted at in non-Christian thought. Consider, for example, the account given by Zhou Dunyi (or Chou Tun-i), 1017–73 CE, of the relation between the Great Ultimate (*taiji*), the cosmic forces (*yin* and *yang*) and the 'myriad things' that the interaction of these forces bring forth. In order to appreciate the possible relevance of this account, we should recall the distinction made in Chapter 2 between an analogy of attribution and an analogy of proportionality. Although there might be some resemblance between the concept of the Great Ultimate and that of the creative Father, if, following a proposed analogy of attribution, one were to liken the *yin* and *yang* to the Son, one would be falling into the trap of misrepresentation, caused by the ardent desire to seek convenient similarities which, on analysis, turn out to be false, or at least far-fetched. However if, following a proposed analogy of proportionality, one suggests an analogy between the dynamic *relationships* involved in the Chinese and Christian versions of the creative process, then a legitimate resemblance might be found. There are many other suggestive examples of how trinitarianism may indicate a universal, creative process.[87] If these suggestions can be adequately supported, then a Trinitarian philosophy can be seen as an ultimate reflection on a more general principle of trinitarianism. In this ultimate reflection, the creative source of all (the eternal Father) eternally brings forth an object of his love (the eternal Son), and the bond between them is manifested in the eternal Spirit.

However, it must be admitted that there are genuine difficulties associated with Christian Trinitarianism, and in the light of the particular difficulties that I shall now turn to, I propose, within the context of this book, to make a step B3 account of theism a possible option (and one that I take, along with many other Christians), not *the* option that all rational persons must take, even within the context of a Christian faith.

Problems with the Divinity of Christ

The claim that Jesus is both human, and divine, in a way that is more than that in which we can all become 'divine' as redeemed sons and daughters of God, has been rejected by many thoughtful people. One difficult aspect of the claim is this: if Jesus is to be seen as truly human, in the way demanded by traditional accounts of redemption, then he had to have no special 'advantage' when it came to resisting temptation. But if he faced temptation in exactly the way that we do, then, it would seem, he might have sinned. But does it make sense to say that a divine being might sin? The more we say he might have sinned, but by overcoming temptation he fought the good fight and won over the powers of evil, the harder it is to make sense of Jesus being truly of the divine substance. However, the more we say that Jesus *could not* sin, because he was morally perfect, the more we distance him from what humanity is all about. An equivalent problem arises over the issue of whether the virgin Mary had some special grace, indicated by an immaculate conception, in which she, *unlike* the rest of us, was born without original sin. If this is a correct account it becomes much less clear how she can be a true example of a human perfection that we should copy – since she was born with an extraordinary advantage which ordinary men and women do not possess.

To clarify the situation we need to explore what the term 'original sin' means. The evidence suggests that for most of Christian history no significant distinction was made between original sin (*peccatum originale*) and original guilt (*culpa originalis*), since the full implications of Jeremiah's acceptance of individual responsibility were not realized. The situation has been complicated by an unfortunate mistranslation of a key passage in St Paul (Romans 5: 12), for where the Latin of St Jerome says that we all sin 'in Adam' (*in quo omnes peccaverunt*), the Greek can more naturally be translated as saying that we all sinned 'like', or 'in the manner of' Adam.[88] This may sound like a pedantic point, but it is of great importance, for there is a long, and thoroughly unhappy tradition in which we have been held to be born 'guilty' and under a *deserved* condemnation, because of our participation in Adam's sin, and the fact that many Western theologians used Jerome's Vulgate rather than the original Greek assisted this error.[89] This belief in an inherited guilt can be found in Roman Catholic, Protestant and Anglican sources. An example of the last is a statement made by the Elizabethan bishops to a Convocation in 1563: 'Original Sin standeth not in the following of Adam ... but is the fault and corruption of every man that is naturally ingendred of the offspring of Adam ...' and consequently everyone 'deserveth God's wrath and damnation'.[90] But given Jeremiah's insight, not to mention the logic of ordinary moral terms, this makes no sense (unless, once again, we introduce reincarnation). In the seventeenth century, one of the few Christians to dissent from the general view was the Quaker, Robert Barclay, who insisted that our corrupted state 'is not imputed to infants, until by transgression they actually joyn themselves therewith'. Interestingly, he follows this claim with an analysis of the Greek text of Romans 5: 12.[91] Chillingworth had not been quite so explicit, but he strongly suggests that there is no guilt attributable to infants,[92] while Jeremy Taylor explicitly denies the attribution, basing his argument on the Greek text of Romans 5: 12 (*Unum Necessarium*, 1655, and *Deus Justificatus*, 1656). Although there had been some earlier Christian writers who had denied infant guilt – for example, Julian, a fifth-century bishop of Eclanum who was exiled for Pelagian beliefs – the extent to which Barclay, Chillingworth and Taylor were ahead of their time in this matter can be seen from the way in which only for the last hundred years have large numbers of theologians distinguished 'original sin' and 'original guilt'. The former refers to an inherent weakness that is involved in being part of the human species, and which leads us to sin, in the manner of Adam. This is one of many places where psychoanalysis may offer insights – for example in the findings of Melanie Klein on the role of aggression in the layers of a child's mind that are laid down at a very early age. However original *guilt* should be rejected as a mistake.[93] This, for example, was the clear statement of the 1922 Commission on Doctrine in the Church of England.[94] On this view, no one is born with original guilt, but original sin is simply part of the human condition, a condition that does not absolutely necessitate that we sin, but which – given the fact that we are relational beings – encourages us to do so, and entails that nearly all do. The doctrine of original sin, seen in this way and distinguished from original guilt, points to an important truth, and should not be jettisoned by liberal theology. John Wesley argued that it was possible for the Christian, with the means of grace that were available, to live completely without sin.[95] There is a good case for going beyond this and claiming that it must be *possible* for every person, with the grace that is available to them – and not just to Christians – to live without sin. Without such a claim it is hard to see how *guilt* can be deserved. It would not follow, of course, that 'enlightenment' was not needed, even by such rare individuals. Moreover, if we bear in mind the strict meaning of sin (the New Testament *hamartia*), namely 'missing the mark', in practice it is always safe for a preacher to say to any congregation: 'I am a sinner, you are sinners, we are all sinners, in need of God's forgiveness.'

This discussion suggests how a liberal Christian is likely to respond to the traditional doctrine of the Fall. Just as it is possible to consider the doctrine of original sin to contain an important truth, provided it is separated from errors, such as the doctrine of inherited guilt, so it is possible, and I think essential, to preserve a truth which the doctrine of the Fall has always pointed towards. The human race is indeed 'fallen', in the sense that there is a *collective* problem of human frailty and sin which nearly always drags both individuals and institutions downwards, unless they are specially open to the work of the Holy Spirit. The story of the fall of Adam is a powerful way of expressing, in myth or parable, an essential truth about the human condition, a truth which can also be expressed in the term 'original sin'. Taken literally, the story becomes connected with historical claims about actually existing individuals called Adam and Eve, and then the intelligent inquirer is likely to be turned away. Seen as a myth, it can be held not only to illuminate human nature, but to teach this spiritual truth: when, like Adam, people try to put themselves in the centre, and to be 'like God',[96] then we are especially vulnerable to the effects of pride. In sum, a realistic approach to human problems has to include the perspective symbolized by the Fall.

In the light of this discussion of original sin I do not think that the problem of how Jesus can be truly human, and yet be unable to sin, is much assisted by references to original sin. He had no original guilt, and neither do we. (Similarly, Mary had no original guilt, and so I have no problem with the claim that Mary was born 'immaculate', because I think that with respect to guilt we all are!) If 'original sin' only describes an aspect of the human condition, then Jesus too was party to this – although I realize that it sounds strange to say this because of the tradition that he and Mary were born in special ways. (Due to an unfortunate aspect of the thinking of Augustine, the presence of original sin was often associated with the lust that accompanied conception, and this is part of the context for the doctrines of the virgin birth for one, and of the immaculate conception for the other.[97]) If 'original sin' means something else – perhaps a feature of the human condition as found in the world as it is now, as opposed to the world as it could be – then it might be true to say that Jesus was born 'without original sin', but it needs to be explained in what ways Jesus did not feel the pressures that all other humans feel.

What then can be said in defence of a teaching that Jesus was both truly human and truly divine, bearing in mind, on the positive side, the way in which adequate accounts of redemption and incarnation may point in this direction, and on the negative side, the problem I have just raised concerning Jesus' humanity if he had any special advantage when it came to temptation? Recalling the argument of Chapter 2, is this another paradox that we need to live with, or is it one that we should learn to live without by abandoning one horn of the dilemma?

I have no easy answer, but here are five options, and intelligent readers may come up with others. First, we can simply say that this is a mystery that defies any attempt to find a rational understanding, but that we are justified in believing in it, nevertheless, by the experiential need to say both that Jesus is human and that he is divine. As readers will expect, I am loath to take this way out, unless at least some beginnings of insight can be offered, analogous to the way in which scientists theorize about ways out of dilemmas that their experiential evidence points to. Second, we can, as may have done, qualify the humanity of Jesus, by admitting that although he could *feel* temptations, as we do, he could not succumb to them, so that he was not, strictly speaking, tested in quite the way that we are. Third, we can qualify the divinity of Jesus, as many have done, saying (perhaps) that he only became truly divine when he achieved moral perfection. Fourth, we could make the suggestion, outrageous as it may seem to some, that God took an incredible risk in Jesus, in that although he really shared the divine substance, there was the theoretical possibility that he might choose something less than the highest good. Here, the goodness of Jesus and (in the context under consideration) of God himself, at least under one aspect, becomes, in a sense, a contingent matter. Fifth, we might insist that any perfectly good person is incapable of sin, and that although with all other humans this perfection is an *achievement*, in the unique case of Jesus, he represented perfect humanity from his birth, or conception. This may look rather like the second option, and perhaps suffers from the same drawback, but it involves less of a qualification than most versions of the second option, since the advantage that Jesus is alleged to have would be the same as the advantage, in respect of temptation, that any truly good human can develop. As one writer on this subject puts it: 'The capacity to sin does not belong to human nature as such.'[98] Here it is interesting to recall that in the Confucian tradition the true sage has reached a perfection from which a moral fall becomes impossible.[99] In the case of Jesus the difference refers only to the stages in which the ordinary human develops this perfection.

Among all these options my personal preference is for the fifth, but this is one of the many places where I tread cautiously, and make no suggestion that this is the only rational option for others to take. However it is the option which fits most comfortably with a doctrine of the pre-existence of Christ, which is certainly taught in the New Testament,[100] and which is implicit in any developed account of the Trinity. Also, the following considerations may help to make the fifth option more attractive. Earlier in this chapter, I referred to the difficulties Trinitarian Christians face when they speak of God 'taking on humanity' in the context of the incarnation, since this implies that with the birth of Jesus there was some kind of change in the relationship of the eternal God to creation. I suggested that this problem was not *introduced* by the doctrine of the incarnation, but that it was already latent in *any* form of monotheism that speaks of the universe beginning at some specific time – or more strictly – that speaks of time beginning with the created order. In other words, the Christian's problem of relating a timeless God to a specific event, within history, is a special case of a more general issue that confronts all monotheists who believe in an original act of creation. My suggestion here is of a similar kind. The problem of how Jesus could be both perfectly human, and 'unable' to sin, is a special case of a problem that faces any reflection on the possibility of a human perfection in which the good person becomes more and more 'unable' to do evil. This in turn is a special case of an issue that faces all reflective persons, be they religious or secular, as they try to understand the nature of human freedom. At a primitive level of development, humans are able to choose to do good or to do evil, but – if we have any doctrine of moral growth – as they become more and more developed the nature of human freedom must be understood more subtly. It becomes more and more certain that truly good persons will choose to do what is good, but it seems absurd to conclude that as a result they have less freedom than the evil person. Instead, we should say that the nature of a developed freedom is one that involves, not a return to evil, but more and more *creative* options within the range of good things that are possible. If God is good, his freedom must be analogous to this creative freedom, as experienced by the saint. In consequence, the problem that faces Christian theology, in seeking to understand a perfect human life that could have *human* experience, and yet be 'unable' to sin, is, once again, not simply a problem, as it were, invented by Christian theology; it is a special case of a problem that is implicit in any serious attempt to understand the nature of human goodness and its relationship to human freedom. In the fifth century, there was a furious debate concerning the issues involved in the 'monophysite' (literally 'one nature') movement, centred on the question of whether Christ had a human or divine nature or both. While we may properly condemn the tone and manner of this debate, it is completely wrong to see it, as Edward Gibbon did, as a 'dispute on so trifling a difference'.[101] The issue involved was a special case of a genuine problem that faces truly reflective people, and the resolution of the issue must be concerned (as Confucius saw), with the harmony that develops within the truly integrated person. In a similar vein, Anselm argued that we can say that Jesus 'could' lie, 'if he willed it', but at the same time we must say that, given his goodness, he could not *will* to lie.[102] This must always be true of moral perfection. Once again, it is all too easy to caricature the Christian tradition.[103]

The nature of Jesus' moral perfection is only one aspect of the overall problem of what it means to say that Jesus is divine, or that he had a 'hypostatic union' with the Father. In this regard, I want to make one further suggestion about how a certain beginning to understanding can be attempted in an area where, if God is a reality, there must be mystery, and yet where (in line with what I have argued elsewhere) we should not be forced into the acceptance of paradoxes unless there is both strong experiential evidence for two or more claims that must be held in tension, *and* some glimmerings of understanding.

One of the ways in which I have simplified complex issues is by talking of persons as if they were minds, somehow encased in bodies. There is much to be said for a more complex model in which each person is a unity of body (*soma*), mind and spirit. Some people make a further distinction between spirit and soul, corresponding to the difference between *pneuma* and *psyche* in the New Testament. When distinctions like this are made, then 'mind' tends to refer to consciousness, and to cognitive operations of this consciousness, while 'spirit' or 'soul' incorporates drives, attitudes, virtuous dispositions and (arguably at least) some feelings. Feelings are sometimes thought of as entirely 'bodily', but this is misleading. It might be the case that without a body (either a physical body, as in this life, or a quasi-physical body in some form of resurrected life) feelings could not be experienced, but this is not to say that feelings are part of the bodily aspect of us in the way that, say, our muscular strength is. The spiritual, or soul, aspect of what we think of as a person is intimately linked with our feelings – and especially the feelings that are associated with love – and these are *constitutive* of the persons we are in a way that our muscular strength is not. (Kant, I suggest, was mistaken when he tried to divorce the love that we are commanded to cultivate from every kind of feeling or inclination.[104])

This is the context for a further suggestion concerning what it might mean for Jesus to have a divine, as well as a human nature. I suggested earlier that a human mind could be seen as either a special case of a field of energy, or as something analogous to this. This field would have a regular shape or pattern, as well as a particular identity, an identity constituted by being *this particular* field – even if the same pattern were to be found in another individual. (Similarly, even if identical twins – in addition to identical DNA – had identical brain patterns, which they don't, they would still be different centres of consciousness.) God, I suggested, may also be conceived as a special case of an (infinite) energy field (panentheism), or something analogous to it (classical theism). Now the *pattern* that makes this field unique can be more or less copied in other examples. Indeed, to say that humans are made in the image of God refers to an element of similarity, and when the moral 'likeness' is achieved, there is another kind of copying. Perhaps, Jesus, at birth or at conception, had a unique, miniaturized 'copy' of the divine field, which not only made his spirit *resonate* with the divine in the most powerful way possible, but that actually made him *participate* in the divine in a manner that was unique to him. (A comparable suggestion can be found in the thought of Schleimacher when he writes: 'To ascribe to Christ an absolutely powerful God-consciousness, and to attribute to Him an existence of God in Him, are exactly the same thing.'[105])

Moreover, when we become 'in Christ' we too begin to share this special kind of resonance. Here, whether we are talking of Jesus' mind, or soul, or spirit (distinctions that may be legitimate, but which I do not propose to elaborate on here) there could be some glimmering of understanding when we speak of Jesus being 'the express image of God'.

I shall end this section with a parable which may make the student of religion specially sensitive to the difficulties of dealing fairly with claims about the unique status of Jesus. Suppose that I live on a planet where, despite many similarities with planet earth, no one has ever witnessed thunder and lightning because the atmospheric conditions for these things simply have not arisen during human history. Then one day, for the first time, the conditions that are necessary for an electrical storm are present, and some people witness a flash of lightning, while others who do not actually witness it see some of the effects. The extraordinary release of energy is totally mysterious and wonderful, as are some of the effects, but this does not mean that *after the event* some kind of understanding cannot occur. In the light of this understanding some people suggest that there could, one day, be a 'second' strike.

The parallel that arises goes like this. If, in Jesus, there were a resonance with the divine that was of a kind that had not been witnessed before on this planet, then there could be a discharge of spiritual energy and power of an unprecedented kind. However, after the event, some understanding could be reached, especially as one considered the growing context for the event (the Old Testament expectations paralleling the changing atmospheric conditions), and the new understanding that the event revealed (the experiences of being 'in Christ' paralleling the lessons about electric charges that emerged). The analogy breaks down when the 'relational' is seen purely in non-personal terms, but something of the significance of events that are, for us, *unique*, can be appreciated from the parable. In my story it would make sense for someone to say: 'Here, in the lightning, we had for the first time a glimpse of that cosmic energy that lies behind all that is. Here was not just a picture, but an actual spark of this energy.' Similarly, a Christian might affirm: 'Here was a glimpse of the true character of the divine. Here was not just a copy, but an actual spark of the divine fire and a concrete experience of the divine love.'

The Problem of Exclusivity

When Christianity is of the 'minimalist' strain, in which 'Jesus is Lord' is the only affirmation, then there is no need for Christianity to claim exclusivity unless there is the additional claim that only those who acknowledge Jesus in this way are on the path to salvation. As one moves towards a more traditional account of the incarnation, whether with the relatively small step of claiming that Jesus was, in a special sense, the 'Son of God', or whether with the larger step of adopting something close to the Nicene creed, then the tendency to an exclusive claim is likely to get stronger. Not only is Jesus seen as the true 'way', there is the claim that only Christians are articulating certain fundamental truths, and holding to these truths, it has been alleged, is necessary for salvation.

Claims to exclusivity, in any of these forms, face strong and understandable objections both from followers of other ways (some but not all of whom have similarly exclusive views), and from materialists – who hold such claims to be intellectually absurd and morally evil. On the other hand, if the truth is important, and if one believes that one has insight into a certain aspect of truth, does not this entail some kind of exclusive claim, whether we are talking of science or history or religion? The response to this, of course, is that the *kind* of exclusivity involved in saying that only x is the way to salvation, is different from simply claiming that one has perceived something to be true. The objections to this *kind* of exclusivity are of two basic kinds. The first is intellectual, for given the great diversity of beliefs held by people of comparable intellect and integrity, how can anyone be so (justifiably) sure that x is the only path? The second is moral, for is it not a very strange God who would only save those who by luck, or some other factor – which in many cases seems to be contingent on happenstance of birth and opportunity – have been led to follow the x path? Doctrines of God's 'elect', especially when God is said to have foreknown and predestined the elect to eternal life, and not others,[106] add to a sense of moral outrage. Sometimes the outrage is intensified by the view that the elect are such only because of God's special gifts of grace.

Faced with this issue, many Christians feel unsure of what stand to take, for they feel the force of the objections just raised, and yet there seem to be many things in the Biblical tradition that call for some kind of exclusivity. If we have moved beyond level A1 in our estimation of the accuracy of Scripture, did not Jesus claim to be 'the way', and to say that only those who hear his word have eternal life, and that no one comes to the Father except through him?[107]

One way of handling this issue is simply to deny that Jesus ever made such claims, and the fact that most sayings of this kind, including the three just referred to, occur in St John's gospel, might be taken to support this view, for that gospel is often seen more as an early Christian meditation on the life of Jesus than as an exact historical record. However, leaving aside the historical accuracy of St John, an account of the incarnation that approaches a traditional one, as described in this chapter, raises the same questions. So the question of exclusivity returns in this form: 'If a traditional view of the incarnation is along the correct lines, what does this say about those who do not hold it?'

The response that follows is not invented by me, but typifies a liberal approach that has been popular for at least a century, and that is built on an ancient Christian tradition, a tradition found especially in the writings of Justin Martyr, around 150 CE, and in the school of Alexandria – although it goes beyond what any members if this school actually said. Justin Martyr writes: 'He [that is Christ] is the logos of whom every race of men and women were partakers. And they who lived with the logos are Christians, even though they have been thought atheists … .' He goes on to include both Socrates and Abraham among those who had responded to the logos.[108] The most exciting figure in the Alexandrine tradition was probably Origen, who died in 253 or 254 CE, and who was strongly influenced by Justin. He too saw a continuity between the searching spirit of the great philosophers and the Christian faith, in contrast with an alternative Christian tradition that tended to distance itself from the 'contamination' of all philosophical speculation. For example, referring to one of Plato's comments on 'the Maker and Father of this universe', Origen writes: 'These words are noble and admirable.'[109] Although Origen continually stressed the crucial impact of Jesus, according to his more positive approach to all human search for truth 'the logos called the human soul to recognize God, and, to a large extent, the philosophers had obeyed this call.'[110]

The implication of this tradition is that whenever men and women respond to God's word, or logos, they are responding to what Christ represents, even if they do not realize this. This is how Chillingworth could maintain (as we saw in Chapter 1) that Turks and heretics could be saved, while at the same time maintaining his commitment to the Christian faith. In a similar vein he claims that God will be satisfied 'if we receive any degree of light which makes us leave the *works of darkness, and walk as children of light*'.[111] The extreme position on this matter is taken by the Quaker apologist, Robert Barclay, referred to earlier in this chapter. In 1678, after arguing that the one 'Catholick Church' is made up, in reality, of all who are 'obedient to the holy light' he concludes: 'There may be members therefore of the Catholick Church both among the Heathens, Turks, Jews, and all the several sorts of Christians, men and women of integrity and simplicity of heart ... .'[112] However this is a position which most of those who call themselves 'liberal Christians', including myself, would *not* take. It is one thing to say (like Chillingworth) that all who truly endeavour to follow the light that comes from God are really responding to God's word; another thing to say that all such people are really members of the Catholic church! This disagreement with Barclay helps to stake out one of the limits regarding what the liberal Christian tradition I am supporting stands for. In a similar vein, in what follows I shall be supporting Justin's suggestion that Socrates and Abraham (as well as a host of others) genuinely responded to the logos, but I think it is highly misleading to say that they were really 'Christians'. This term, I have argued, should be used to refer to those who take Jesus as the model for how to live and how to pray, and who *articulate* the creed 'Jesus is Lord', and who – at least in typical cases – knowingly enter a community that seeks to be 'in Christ'.

In the spirit of the Alexandrine tradition, a good example of a nineteenth-century openness to the goodness of humans who are not within the Christian fold, but who can be said to have responded to the logos, can be found in the Biblical scholar F.J.A. Hort. In 1886, commenting on Article 13 of the 39 Articles (which alleges that good works done without faith have the nature of sin) he writes: '... faith itself, not being an intellectual assent to propositions, but an attitude of heart and mind, is present in a more or less rudimentary state in every upward effort and aspiration of men.'[113] A similar openness can be found in the Roman Catholic philosopher, Jacques Maritain. In 1945 he wrote of the person who believes he is an atheist but who, in an act of freedom, turns towards the moral good, and therefore, without knowing it, turns to the true God. Such a person both knows and does not know God (*qu'il connait du même coup sans le savoir*). Without knowing it, he continues, this person has both faith, of a kind, and charity.[114]

A contemporary way of summarizing the spirit of this whole tradition is to say that God's logos, or word, is continuously reaching out to men and women in what is seen to be good, or true or beautiful – Plato's three aspects of God. In so far as anyone responds to any of these, they are responding to God's word, whether they know this or not. Good persons by their actions, sincere scientists or scholars by their search for truth, and all artists who seek what is beautiful, to some degree and in their own way will find that they have sought God by responding to his logos.

Such a view leads inevitably to a denial that only Christians or only monotheists have a place in the heart of God or in the glory of the world to come. No one comes to the Father, except through the way that involves a response to what is seen as good or true or beautiful, because this is the way in which God's eternal word touches every person. This view can be perfectly well combined with an *appropriate* Christian truth claim. What distinguishes the Christian from the non-Christian, on this view, is not that only the Christian is saved, but that only the Christian *articulates* the *truth* that the logos was made flesh, and dwelt among us.[115] This gives a special challenge and opportunity to the Christian, and it enables the Christian to begin the experience of life 'in Christ' during this life in the fellowship of other believers. There is a unique responsibility, but not a unique destiny. This also allows for an appropriate 'assurance' of the kind I have described. It also leaves intact the stern warnings to all those who do not seek what is good, be they Christian or not. In sum, there is an appropriate uniqueness to Christianity, one that centres on the claim that 'the Word was made flesh.' This central claim has both moral implications for how people should live, and belief implications that lead (so I argue) to the viability of the doctrines of redemption, incarnation and Trinity.

One consequence of this approach to exclusivity is that when followers of a religion believe that their religion is, in some sense, 'true', this does not always mean that they are committed to the belief that other religions are 'false'. 'False' might be an appropriate term to apply to a whole religion in which there is systematic and manifest idolatry, or the cruel exploitation of people in sacrificial rituals, but not, I suggest, to the world-views that we commonly call the great religions of the world.[116] In the case of Christianity, a follower who adopts the minimum creed is committed to taking Jesus as the model for life and prayer, but this need not involve any negative comments on those who follow another way. In the case of more traditional Christians, including myself, in addition to this commitment, belief in the incarnation does lead to the view that there is a truth expressed in Christian teaching that is not found, at least explicitly, elsewhere. However, this need not involve a claim that all other ways are 'false'. I might hold that some particular, traditional beliefs, say of Hinduism, are false (such as those that are used to justify the caste system), or at best misleading, but I also hold that some traditional Christian beliefs (such as that in original guilt) are false, or at best misleading. Hinduism, and all the other great religions, at their best, represent ways which I can profoundly respect and hope to learn from, even though I hold that they do not articulate what I hold to be an important truth. This is quite different from saying that they are false.

The Holy Spirit

Previous sections have prepared the way for what needs to be said about the third person of the Christian Trinity. The idea of a collection of experiences which reflect an intrinsic differentiation within the Godhead has been raised with respect to the idea of incarnation. The idea of there being three, no more and no less essential 'persons' within the unity of the Godhead has been suggested by a consideration of what is implicit in both the understanding and the experience of love. Behind both of these ideas lies the claim that 'oneness' can best be understood as a kind of unity, in which – to use a musical analogy – there is the harmony of a single chord (a triad), rather than a single, undifferentiated tone. The next requirement is to indicate the primal religious experience that led to the Holy Spirit being called the third person of the Trinity.

The concept of God as Father points to belief in, and some experience of, creative and loving power. The concept of God the Son, for a traditional Christian, points to belief in, and experience of an eternal logos or word, glimpsed by humans in what is seen to be good or true or beautiful, and incarnate in a particular historical person. The concept of God the Spirit points to belief in, and experience of the active power of God, at work in nature, and in particular, at work within people. The Pentecostal experience, described in the second chapter of the Acts of the Apostles and in many other passages (especially associated with baptism) is the climax of a series of descriptions in both Old and New Testaments in which the work and power of the Spirit are described.

The actual words used to denote theological terms can be seen as secondary, since they can never capture adequately the divine reality that they are attempting to describe. Moreover, it is important to bear in mind that when the church developed the traditional language associated with its principal doctrines it did so in the context of the missionary needs of the church within a particular historical context. Thus, in the crucial period of the third and fourth centuries, it tended to react to the thought forms of Neoplatonism. (For example, typical of Neoplatonist thought is the view that everything other than the ultimate 'One' is the result of a kind of 'overflowing' or emanation from the ultimate. In this context, Christians wished to avoid any suggestion that Christ represented a 'subordinate' emanation and that the world was other than a voluntary act of creation – a matter which has hugely important consequences for the later history of science.[117]) There is therefore a serious question regarding how far the language developed then is appropriate for quite different historical and cultural contexts. However, more positively, an awareness of why particular words have been used, and of the history that led to their adoption, can be illuminating. The word 'aspect' has been used to refer to the ways in which God is experienced, but it can be seen that this word is inadequate, at least for someone who accepts a more traditional teaching along the lines I have defended, since it suggests that the Trinity is only threefold with respect to the way *we* see it. Similarly, although I have used the word 'modes', this word too is inadequate, especially since it has been associated with a view in which a single God presented himself in three modes, as it were, one after the other.[118] One advantage of using the word 'person', from the Latin *persona*, is that it does not imply either of these suggestions – although the literal translation of 'mask' would be equally inappropriate.

In the case of the Holy Spirit, part of the traditional language is to say that the Spirit is the person who 'proceeds' from the Father. In a parallel way, the Son is said not to be 'made' or 'created' by the Father, but to be 'eternally begotten'. Both terms ('procession' and 'eternally begotten') are attempts to indicate a combination of two beliefs, the first, that the Father is most appropriately thought of as the creative source of all things; the second, that neither the Son nor the Spirit should be thought of as aspects of God that came into being *after* the Father. They are rather essential elements in a unity in which the different persons 'coinhere' (corresponding to the Greek *perichoresis*), or abide in eternal communion with each other. (This is one reason why, earlier in this chapter, I was anxious to dismiss the suggestion that the relationships of the persons of the Trinity were like the relationships of different rooms in a house, for this analogy does not capture the 'coinhering' of the persons. This also explains why I am nervous about the contemporary emphasis on a 'social' doctrine of the Trinity, and prefer analogies based on the unity of a person.) In the case of the 'procession' of the Spirit, a word is sought which suggests a movement of flow without suggesting any *temporal* priority. In the Western church, the Spirit is said to proceed from and Father *and the Son* (*filioque*), while in the Eastern church the procession is said to be from the Father alone. Behind this stands a long historical and theological dispute which I shall not enter. However, this is certain: the Western church, without benefit of a general council, added the term 'and the Son', and later – for a long time – failed to realize that this was an *addition*, made without universal agreement. In recognition of this dubious procedure, and in respect for the Orthodox tradition, the Anglican church in Canada has returned to the older formula, pending a general church council on the matter.

An important issue with respect to the Holy Spirit concerns the sense in which it relates to *Christian* experience. The experience of the Spirit cannot be unique to Christianity, since at the least, according to the Christian tradition, the Holy Spirit was at work in creation and in the inspiration of Old Testament prophets. However, most Christians have felt that there was something unique about the 'seal of the Spirit' given in baptism. My suggestion, in this very controversial matter, parallels my suggestion in the section on exclusivity regarding the way in which Christ, as logos, is not only the property of Christians, and yet Christians have a unique relationship with the logos because of the acknowledgement that the logos was made flesh, and because of the 'in Christ' relationship that this makes possible. Similarly, I see no grounds for claiming that the Holy Spirit only works in Christians and Old Testament prophets. It is much more in line with our understanding both of the nature of God's love, and of our knowledge of people's lives – whatever religion, if any, they adopt – to see God's work *within* the hearts and minds of all who respond to the logos. Indeed, this is part of what it must mean to say that the Son and the Spirit 'coinhere'. At the same time, there is no need to deny a special gift of the Holy Spirit, a special anticipation of the resurrection life, anticipated in the event of baptism. As Geoffrey Lampe put it in a famous study, 'the indwelling presence of the Spirit is simply an aspect of the sharing of the resurrection life of Christ which is begun in Baptism'.[119]

Theism and Immortality

For some theists, personal immortality is not a realistic belief; it smacks for them too much of wishful thinking, even though there is also a commonly found wish that there should *not* be any after-life in which one is judged for one's transgressions. Surveys of church-goers, for example, show that a significant number of active Christians, who at the very least are committed to the creed used by the first

Christians, are either doubtful of any personal after-life, or positively reject it as a serious possibility. While these may well be rational options, my own view is that *within the context of theism*, and even more within the context of Christian theism, belief in the possibility of personal immortality is a more rational option. The reasons for this will follow shortly. However, it must first be pointed out that the issue is not simply that of after-life versus extinction, but, *if* there is an after-life, of what kind it is. Views on this matter have varied enormously, including belief in (i) a purely physical resurrection that is to last for ever (as in Hobbes); (ii) a physical resurrection that will last for one thousand years (as suggested by some passages in the book of Revelation), to be followed by some different state of affairs; (iii) a quasi-physical resurrection in which there will be no physical planet on which one lives, but space and perhaps time as well are experienced in ways we cannot imagine; (iv) the gradual absorption into the Godhead (in what may become a version of monism); (v) a gradual growth into a kind of unity with God which involves a complete transformation of the egoistic self, but not its annihilation. Some of these views, along with other options, may be combined. Reincarnation (vi) is accepted by a number of Christians, and was part of the standard teaching of the Cathars, although in its more plausible form, found, for example, in many of the Cambridge Platonists, the circle of lives ends as soon as a person became 'in Christ', so that this option (vi) is combined with option (v). As with the general belief in immortality, belief in reincarnation can mean a variety of things. For some, following a Platonic model, it is as if a soul simply changes its body, rather like a person may change clothes. At the other extreme, there is a Buddhist model in which reincarnation is more like a case of one candle being lit by another. Here, although the first candle is essential for the light of the second, there is – one might say – no continuity of 'substance'. Reflecting on all of these options, it is clear that several of them allow for a period of spiritual growth in a 'purgatory' that is seen either as a special place or a special state of being. With respect to all these, and other possibilities, I recommend a reverend agnosticism, although my personal preference is for a version of suggestion (v). Such a view, while not the only rational one, is consistent with an eternal divine love for a particular person, and consistent with a sense of justice, in which there is some ultimate balance between virtue and happiness, even though – as we shall see in the next chapter – this does not entail that happiness is the *motive* for virtue.

There are three kinds of argument for the existence of an after-life, within the context of theism. The first are philosophical arguments, including those found in Plato's *Phaedo* (although, as remarked earlier, Plato is not a typical theist). These I shall not discuss, except to say that, like most philosophers, I find them quite unconvincing apart from one suggestion that I shall refer to later. The second are sometimes called 'proofs positive', and are based on the alleged experience of contact with the departed. Here a rational evaluation is extremely difficult, and while I certainly reject the claim that there is any 'proof' here, there are, I hold, a number of extraordinary cases, reasonably well attested, which *suggest* or intimate the possibility that genuine contact has been experienced. However, although I give some references to this area of speculation, I do not want to stress it, since it is the third type of argument that I hold to be much the most important.[120] It should also be pointed out that personal experiences that are believed to represent actual contact with the departed might well be strong evidence for those who have them, but not for others.

The third argument is a matter of seeing what is consistent with a theism in which a loving God is acknowledged, a God who is personal in that he knows and loves individual persons. In other words, belief in a personal after-life is consequent upon another belief for which one has rational grounds. The nearest thing we get to an argument for immortality from the recorded words of Jesus come into this category. The Sadducees (who rejected resurrection, and therefore, in the context of the Judaism of the time, any personal immortality) came up with a standard objection to resurrection which centred on the imagined case of a man who had a series of wives each of which died, leaving the question of who would be his wife in the next life. Jesus responded:

> Ye do err, not knowing the scriptures, nor the power of God. For in the resurrection they neither marry, nor are given in marriage ... But as touching the resurrection of the dead, have ye not read that which was spoken to you by God, saying, 'I am the God of Abraham, and the God of Isaac, and the God of Jacob'? God is not the God of the dead, but of the living.[121]

This argument, it should be noted, is not rooted in any aspect of the human mind or spirit, as if this accorded some automatic right to a future life, but points to a consequence of accepting another truth – in this case, the power and the loving nature of God. Abraham lives, because God loves him and, by implication, we shall all live, *because* God loves us.

There are two interesting variations on this kind of argument, based in a person's relation to some eternal principle. One, which led to the first serious belief in immortality in the Hebrew tradition,[122] at the time of the Maccabees, was rooted in the demands of justice once the implications of Jeremiah's teaching on individual responsibility were worked out. When the righteous were cut down (as in the Maccabean revolt), justice demanded a future state for the righteous individuals, although prior to this it was generally felt that justice was served provided only that one's descendants were rewarded (or punished) appropriately.[123] This argument reminds us of a Kantian argument. If we are to support a belief in inherent justice, then we have to posit the truth of an after-life in order to make sense of any universal system of justice, and we find just this argument in Kant's second critique, echoing the belief of the Maccabees. The other takes up the reference to Plato, whose best argument, in my view, is not based on the nature of the soul as such, but on the implications of a state of knowledge in which a person *participates* in the eternal Idea of the Good.[124]

There are, however, several difficulties associated with belief in a personal life after death, whether or not this be eternal. In line with the rational approach taken throughout this book, I shall now respond to the two of these that I regard as most serious.

The first concerns the fact that the self that is to be granted eternal life does not seem to be static, but rather to be for ever changing as the brain grows and develops, leading, in many cases, to a final state of senile dementia. What then is the 'real' self that is to live again? It must be admitted that at first sight this problem appears to lend weight to a materialist account of the self and of consciousness.

William James, in his essay 'Human Immortality' gives a response that may serve as a starting-point. In addition to the idea of a 'productive' function of the brain, he writes, *'we are entitled also to consider permissive or transmissive function*, and this the ordinary psychologist leaves out of account.'[125] He goes on to defend the rationality of a 'transmission' theory of consciousness, in which, at the end of life, the mind is having to transmit through a more and more inadequate instrument, akin (we might now say) to the way in which a poor radio cannot properly transmit the incoming signal to the hearer (an analogy actually used by the philosopher C.D. Broad, who regarded the possibility of survival after death as a real option, although he rejected belief in a personal God).[126] Even if we think that the brain has a 'productive' function in the development of consciousness, as I do, this is entirely compatible with the view that once a field of consciousness has developed, its ability to function in the context of the human body depends, in part, on the physiological condition of the brain. Therefore our observation of human decay, while frequently tragic, does not necessarily entail that there is not a real self waiting for release. Plato's picture of the body as a tomb or prison (*sema*) may not be altogether wrong in such cases.

A problem with this suggestion is that if it is represented in a crude fashion, we seem to have relied, implicitly, on a Cartesian dualism which I have been careful to avoid. It isn't that 'thought' is trying, as it were, to 'break through' a damaged instrument, for clearly the inner side of a demented person's thinking is just as much affected as the outer, but the idea that a 'mind' is imprisoned by a defective instrument certainly invites dualism. In the light of this, I think it is important to stress William James' word 'permissive' rather than 'transmissive'. It is not a case of an independently existing mind (or radio signal) trying to express itself, so much as a field of energy that is not able (or 'permitted') to function normally. Seen in this way, this problem merges with the second, and greater, problem regarding a future life, which concerns the issue of finding a criterion in terms of which the *identity* of the person whose earthly body has been destroyed can be the *same* person as before. Without any indication of how such a criterion might be possible we may seen to be taking too much on sheer trust. If the field that constitutes our minds cannot express itself because of a defective body, we must ask what would allow, or permit, this mind to be itself again? If we say that it has been given a new body then we face this dilemma: if the mind is the real person and it can simply be *given* a new body, we are back to a form of Cartesian dualism; but if the body is in part constitutive of what we are, and that makes us *this* person, then what is the criterion that can let us call this new body the *same* person?

In what follows I shall indicate four of the ways in which this problem might be handled. The list is not exhaustive. For example, it has been argued that memory by itself might provide a criterion of identity, but this suggestion, like the others I do not discuss, all run into major difficulties.[127]

The most obvious way of handling the problem is to suggest that the same *matter* is present in the resurrected body as in the former body. There is an extraordinary passage in Augustine in which God is described as bringing the original pieces that made up someone's body from the far corners of the universe. He even discusses what is to happen if one is eaten by a starving cannibal, so that a piece of flesh might seem to belong to more than one person! His reply is that the flesh of the man that was eaten 'shall return to the first owner, of whom the famished man does but as it were borrow it ... .'[128] Although this is official teaching in some Christian circles,[129] it faces grave difficulties. First, apart from our brain cells, the other parts of our body are continually being replaced. Second, it is not at all certain that atoms have a continuing individuality of the kind demanded for the literal use of this criterion of identity. When atoms are split up into various charged particles, each of which is more like a mathematical formula than a solid entity, it is not clear what it would *mean* to say that the *same* atom has been remade. It seems unwise to make a theological doctrine a hostage to a particular view of the science of atoms.

A second suggestion is to make the *pattern* of material particles the criterion of identity. Here, the logical difficulty is that although within this life the pattern has a unique set of spatio-temporal coordinates, at death, if we imagine the exact pattern being remade, there is the problem that there could be any number of identical patterns made in this way, and since none of them would have the unique spatio-temporal coordinates that could identify our individuality in this life, it is not clear *which* individual (if any) would be the true me. A similar dilemma arises in some of the thought experiments devised along the lines of the *Star Trek* fantasies of people being 'beamed' from one location to another. Derek Parfit's book *Reasons and Persons* makes use of such thought experiments, imagining, for example, that as a variation on having myself beamed up to another location, my 'replica' is sent to another location while I am left behind.[130] Here we might say that the real 'me' is certainly the one left behind (because of the continuity of spatio-temporal coordinates), but if I am beamed to two different locations, and not left behind at all, *which* is the real me? Parfit, in his discussion of such cases, shows sensitivity to the issue of whether any beamed 'replica' could really be 'me', and held responsible, for example, for the evils I have done prior to replication. (John Locke raised similar questions in the seventeenth century through his thought experiment of a prince finding himself in the body of a cobbler.[131]) However, Parfit's thought experiments, in my view, suffer from a fundamental problem, for they *assume* that this 'beaming' by a total copying of my pattern (with or without its consequent destruction), followed by its reconstruction in another place, is logically or 'naturally' possible. But if the human person has at its core a special kind of energy field, or something analogous to such a field, then *even if* the physical pattern could be reproduced, the 'person' might not be. There might be some lifeless body, but not a person. To imagine a person being beamed, is to *assume* that certain things are possible, and if we then ask questions like 'Which is the real me?', what we may well have is another example of a *question mal posée*. Similarly, a recent writer on the use of thought experiments in science has written: 'The reason that thought experiments so often can be misleading is that behind almost every thought experiment will lie a large number of unquestioned auxiliary assumptions, assumptions which are assumed to be true but which, if false, would overturn the result in question.'[132] (Teleportation, in which the whole person is moved to another location, may or may not be a logical or natural possibility, but it does not raise the same dilemma, because there is no possibility of a 'replica', and it is not a case of the person being disintegrated and then remade, but, as it were, of being moved lock, stock and barrel.)

A third suggestion is to revert to a Cartesian soul, an essentially spiritual self that just temporally resides within, or in the context of a particular physical body. In its extreme form – in which the real self is a pure spirit with no material counterpart – this may solve the problem of the criterion of identity, but at the price of raising all the difficulties associated with Cartesian dualism, some of which have been discussed in Chapter 2. There is a more moderate form of this dualism, canvassed, for example, by C.D. Broad, in which the true self is a kind of 'field' (which is a term Broad uses) with quasi-physical properties. Suggestions along these lines clearly overlap with my own (fourth) suggestion, and whether or not one calls them 'dualistic' or 'monist' depends on the emphasis put on the relation of the field to the physical body.[133]

A fourth suggestion, and my own preference, is based on the idea already presented in which, either prior to birth (if we believe in reincarnation) or during the development of the embryo and foetus, a new kind of energy field develops which is the context for our consciousness. Not only does this energy field have a unique pattern, and not only – at least in this physical life – is it uniquely related to a particular body, it also has a unique resonance with its creative source – that is, God. It has often been suggested that what makes us unique is our set of relationships with other people, but this suggestion, standing by itself, cannot explain a life after death, since there must be some kind of 'entity' to which these relationships attach if the 'I' has any substance, and *a fortiori* if the 'I' can continue to have the same identity at the dissolution of the body. Nevertheless, the suggestion is on the right lines, for our unique relationship with God and with others, *when combined with* the notion that our consciousness arises out of a particular field of energy, can give a coherent criterion of identity. Our unique *resonance* in and with the divine consciousness is the essential factor. Once again, on this view, our immortality does not depend on what we are in ourselves, but on what we are in relation to God. On a Christian view, life outside the context of the redeeming work of Christ, and of the new creation 'in Christ', might well be a curse rather than a blessing, a case of going on and on and on for ever, rather than experiencing 'eternal life' as a new mode of being.

(This suggestion about the resonance of a personal field with the divine field, also allows for some insight into the nature of an infinite divine knowledge. An infinite field that interpenetrates all other fields, including human ones, would be in a unique position to know the entire state of the universe at any moment, including the inner thoughts and feelings of people.)

On this fourth view, it could still be maintained that whenever there is conscious thought, there is an 'inner' and an 'outer' aspect to thought, recalling the discussion of this matter in Chapter 3. If life after death is seen as involving a 'body' of some kind, in which there is an analogue for the neurological activity we now witness in the brain, then the sense in which there would be an 'outer' aspect that could in principle be monitored is fairly clear. If the claim is made that life after death can be 'purely spiritual', because the 'field' can simply continue to exist, then there are indeed problems – both in terms of the meaning of this 'purely spiritual field', and in terms of providing the 'outer' context for something analogous to thought as we know it now. Perhaps there are ways around these difficulties, but I certainly prefer the suggestion that either a significant future life must *wait* until a resurrection body is provided (which is a typical Protestant view), or that some kind of resurrection body is given at death (which is a typical Catholic view). In both options, the criterion of identity is given by the identity of a field that has a unique resonance with the divine Mind. Given this criterion, it is not essential that the person actually persists immediately after death, except within the divine Mind. Whether or not there is a 'waiting period' (from the human perspective) is yet another of the issues about which I prefer to be agnostic.

Notes and References

1   For a discussion of these issues that is sympathetic to non-classical views, see Fiddes, P.S. (1988), *The Creative Suffering of God*, Oxford: Clarendon Press.
2   Acts 2: 38; 8: 16; 10: 48; 19: 5; 22: 16.
3   Matt. 28: 19; 2 Cor. 13: 14 (where, strictly speaking, the reference is to 'God' rather than 'Father'). 1 John 5: 7 is probably a later addition.
4   Acts 11: 26.
5   Weatherhead, L.D. (1965), *The Christian Agnostic*, Abingdon: Hodder and Stoughton, p. 250.
6   This approach should also help to resolve some divisive issues concerning who should be accepted into bodies such as the World Council of Churches. A number of communities that have traditionally considered themselves to be Christian do not insist on any belief in the Trinity, although individual members may often have this belief. The best-known examples are the Society of Friends and the Unitarians. My suggestion is that evidence of a sincere acceptance of the creed used in the Acts of the Apostles is all that should be demanded. The issue is complicated by the fact that some bodies do not have a traditional form of baptism that includes an outward sign. However, if a believer chooses to interpret baptism as a spiritual rite that need have no outer form, can we justified in denying that they have had a 'baptism of the Spirit'?
7   See Manuel, F.E. (1974), *The Religion of Isaac Newton*, Oxford: Clarendon, p. 61.
8   For example, in Proverbs 8: 1–10.
9   Joel 2: 28; Acts 2: 17.
10   See the article by Groli, G. trans. U.F. Lubi, (1987) in *The Encyclopedia of Religion*, ed. M. Eliade, New York: Macmillan, vol. 15, p. 583.
11   The Qur'an, Sura XVI, 104; II, 81 and 254.
12   Sura IV, 164; Ex. 33: 11.
13   Strictly speaking, Mary is not meant to be an object of *worship* (which is reserved for God), but rather of honour, and prayers are meant to be directed through her, rather than to her. However, for many ordinary Christians these distinctions easily get blurred.
14   Saadya, Gaon, *Book of Doctrines and Beliefs*, trans. A. Altmann, (1965) in *Three Jewish Philosophers*, New York: Harper Torchbooks, pp. 82–3.
15   'Three Friends' (1884), *A Reasonable Faith*, London: Macmillan, pp. 26–7.
16   Augustine, *De Trinitate*, X, ch. 11. Elsewhere he uses the triad of memory, understanding and love, e.g. in XIV, ch. 8.
17   Gibbon, E., *The History of the Decline and Fall of the Roman Empire*, ch. 21. The debate he refers to was between those who argued for a 'same substance' (*homoousios*) doctrine of the relation of Father to Son, and those who argued for a 'like substance' (*homoiousios*) doctrine. Gibbon's remark is clever rather than insightful, since the

addition of a single letter (like *a*, when it relates to the Greek negative), can be of crucial importance.

18 Prestige, G.L. (1954), *Fathers and Heretics*, London: SPCK.

19 See Lewis, C.S. (1952), *Mere Christianity*, London: Collins, p. 53 for a direct use of this argument, and (1950), *The Lion, the Witch and the Wardrobe*, New York: Macmillan, (1970), p. 45 for an indirect use.

20 See Collingwood, R.G. (1946), *The Idea of History* , New York: Galaxy (1956), pp. 9–10. Collingwood claims that Herodotus invented 'scientific' history (p. 19), and here I disagree with him.

21 For example, one could lay down that any formula that had no mathematical term that used a higher power than 3, as in x^3, was 'simpler' than any formula that has a power of 4 or more.

22 The evaluation also depends on a detailed examination of the text in which one looks, first, for some collaborative evidence in other sources – for example, in references to people such as Pilate outside the gospels; second, to the quality of the material in terms of factors such as originality, spiritual significance and the *development* of themes.

23 The references in Josephus, allegedly from around 93 CE, are almost certainly later additions. Given the political insignificance of Christianity in its first hundred years, what we have is as much as could be expected to have survived.

24 See Metzger, B.M. (1992), *The Text of the New Testament*, 3rd edn, Oxford: Oxford University Press, pp. 36–40. P (Papyrus) 52, a fragment of St John, is probably before 150 CE, certainly no later than 200. Another Chester Beatty papyrus contains most of the Pauline epistles, and is from around 200. A fragment from outside the Beatty collection, P 66, has a section from St John that is variously put from 150 to 200.

25 See Sanders, E.P. (1993), *The Historical Figure of Jesus*, London: Penguin, e.g. pp. 3, 10–11.

26 Dodd, C.H. (1973), *The Founder of Christianity*, London: Fontana, p. 27.

27 Isa. 53: 3.

28 Crowe, F.E. (1980), *The Lonergan Enterprise*, USA: Cowley, p. 90.

29 Matthews, W.R. (1933), *Seven Words*, London: Hodder and Stoughton, p. 29. The emphasis is mine. Cf. Lewis, C.S. (1952), *Mere Christianity*, London: Collins p. 54, where he makes the same point.

30 2 Cor. 5: 17.

31 See especially Marx's *Economic and Philosophical Manuscripts*, trans. T.B. Bottomore, in Fromm, E. (1961), *Marx's Concept of Man*, New York: Ungar. Here is one sample: '*Communism* is the *positive* abolition of *private property*, of *human self-alienation*, and thus the real *appropriation* of *human* nature through and for man. It is, therefore, the return of man himself as a *social*, i.e., really human, being ...', p. 127 (emphases in the text).

32 These include: i) An extraordinary blindness to many aspects of the spiritual side of people, and with this, a one-sided view of what religion has meant. ii) A failure to see that human nastiness is not *only* the product of our environment, but that our animal nature inevitably leads many people to a lust for power, however ideal their upbringing. Here is a truth in the old doctrine of 'original sin' (provided it is distinguished from the false doctrine of 'original guilt'), and a naivety in the belief that once true communism is established, state and law could simply 'wither away'. iii) A failure to see that his view of history and economics is not the one, true, 'scientific' view, that he believed it to be. iv) A failure to see the danger in giving the elite, who (allegedly) *know* the true science of history and economics, the moral right to lay down the path for all. (In Lenin, there is the added problem that the elite are justified in using force in order to obtain the required end.)

33   Hauerwas, S. (1984), *The Peacable Kingdom*, Paris: University of Notre Dame Press, pp. 30–4.
34   In meditating on the events of the passion, the sensitive reader can identify with *all* the participants in turn, in each case viewing the events from a different perspective – including the perspective of Christ – especially for a Christian meditation which seeks to see the events 'in him'.
35   See Aulen, G., trans. A.G. Hebert (1931), *Christus Victor*, London: SPCK .
36   See Abelard, *Expositio in Epistolam ad Romanos*, ch. 3, *PL,* vol. 178, 836, trans. in Sikes, J.G. (1932), *Peter Abailard*, Cambridge: Cambridge University Press, p. 208.
37   John 12: 32.
38   See Aulen, *Chrislus Victor*, p. 119, where he dissociates the theory from any 'purely rational scheme'.
39   Ibid., p. 125.
40   2 Cor. 5: 21.
41   Anselm, *Cur Deus Homo*, I, ch. 21. Calvin, J. *Institutes*, II, ch. 8, 58–9; III, ch. 14, 3. However, elsewhere, Calvin does make a distinction between light and grave sins: see IV, ch. 12, 4. Cf. Luke 12: 47–48 (where some sinners deserve many, and others, fewer stripes).
42   For example, Mark 10: 45; 1 John 2: 1–2.
43   See, for example, 'Three Friends' (1884), *A Reasonable Faith*, London: Macmillan, where terms like 'ransom' are interpreted in terms of the effect of the Saviour's work on our souls, and where the 'figurative language' is said to be 'downgraded' when the atonement is made into 'a commercial transaction between the Father and the Son', pp. 52–60.
44   Doctrine Commission of the General Synod of the Church of England, (1995), *The Mystery of Salvation*, London: Church House, p. 212.
45   Chillingworth, W., (1838) *Works*, Oxford: University Press, vol. III, p. 121 (Sermon V).
46   See, for example, Leslie Weatherhead's similar rejection of the substitution theory in *The Christian Agnostic*, (1965), Abingdon: Hodder and Stoughton, pp. 68–74. There are hosts of similar criticisms.
47   This kind of simplicity is virtually impossible in practice since third parties are almost inevitably going to be hurt indirectly – in part because the fractured relationship will affect my character, and therefore, the kind of person that I am.
48   Matt. 20: 12. Part of the meaning of this parable lies in the implicit reference to those orthodox Jews who resented the way in which Jesus embraced sinners. Those who by long devotion had born the burden and heat of the day felt that their piety was not properly recognized. The problem lay in the nature of their piety. Given this context it would be a mistake to interpret the parable as negating all aspects of justice.
49   See, for example, Kant, ed. and trans. J. Ladd, (1965), *The Metaphysical Elements of Justice*, New York: Bobbs-Merrill, pp. 362–3, cf. 331–7.
50   Shakespeare, *The Merchant of Venice*, IV, i.
51   John 14: 2.
52   For example, in Jer. 31: 31–34.
53   Heb. 4: 15, cf. 2: 16–18.
54   Plato, *Apology* 28a, *Republic* 361 and 364. In the *Republic*, where the prediction is more explicit, it is made by Plato's brothers. However, in view of Plato's reworking of whatever the original dialogues were, he can be considered the principal author of the suggestion.
55   It is interesting to contrast this episode with the legend of the ring of Gyges, where a human being is tempted to accept superhuman powers, and becomes evil as a result.

56 Phil. 2: 6–8.
57 For example, 2 Cor. 1: 5–8.
58 Col. 1: 24.
59 For example, Acts 2: 46.
60 Luke 24: 13–32.
61 To add a personal note: one of the few religious experiences I have had was when as an undergraduate I took part in a Eucharist at the University Church in Oxford. At the moment of communion, I had an extraordinary sense that the communion rail did not stop at the chancel walls but extended infinitely, with countless worshippers joining in the communion. Whether this experience was the result of an idea in my mind, or an awareness of 'presence' (or both), I do not know.
62 Hodgson, L. (1951), *The Doctrine of the Atonement*, London: Nisbet, pp. 149–50.
63 Hodges, H.A. (1955), *The Pattern of the Atonement*, London: SCM Press, p. 56.
64 Brown J.C. and Parker, R. (1989), 'For God so loved the world?' in *Christianity, Patriarchy, and Abuse*, ed. by the same, Cleveland, Ohio: Pilgrim Press, pp. 11 and 26.
65 Brock, Rita N. (1989), 'And a little child shall lead us: Christology and child abuse', in ibid., p. 57.
66 Compare Book I, ch. 2 of Anselm's *Cur Deus Homo* with the Preface and other passages which seem to be directed at unbelievers.
67 Mark 12: 1–8.
68 For example, Mark 2: 10.
69 On different interpretations of the term 'son of man' see Taylor, V. (1957), *The Gospel According to St. Mark*, London: Macmillan, pp. 197–200.
70 For example, Mark 1: 22.
71 For example, Mark 2: 5–7. cf. Taylor, *The Gospel According to St Mark*, p. 201.
72 For example, John 10: 36.
73 For example, Mark 3: 11.
74 John 8: 58, cf. Ex. 3: 14.
75 For example, John 1: 14.
76 Col. 1: 15 and 2 Cor. 4: 4.
77 Heb. 1: 3.
78 John 8: 46.
79 Rom. 8: 14–15, cf. Gal. 4: 6; 'Abba' is the Aramaic term for Father, and was evidently used by Jesus himself in his prayers (Mark 14: 36).
80 Aristotle, *Nicomachean Ethics*, 1103a, 1144b.
81 2 Cor. 5: 19.
82 Singh S.K. (1987), 'Sikhism' in *The Encyclopedia of Religion*, ed. M. Eliade, New York: Macmillan, 1987, vol. 13, 316b. See also Cole, W.O. and Sambhi, P.S. (1995), *The Sikhs* (2nd edn), Brighton: Sussex Academic Press, p. 72.
83 Augustine, *De Trinitate*, IX, ch. 2, trans. S. McKenna, (1963), Washington, DC: Catholic University of America Press.
84 Zaehner, R.C. (1957), *Mysticism Sacred and Profane*, Oxford: Clarendon Press, pp. 196, 196n, 197.
85 See Moltmann, J., trans. M. Kohl (1981), *The Trinity and the Kingdom of God*, London: SCM Press, where this approach may be taken too far.
86 Abelard, *Intr. Ad Theologiam* I, 8–9. *PL*, vol. 178, 989.
87 Apart from issues regarding Trinitariansim, an interesting connection with Neo-Confucianism may lie in the subtle ways in which *ren*, the principle of humanity or humanness, is seen as a reflection of heavenly principles, including that of love. See Wing-Tsit Chan's comments on Zhu Xi (Chu Hsi) (1963), *A Source Book in Chinese Philosophy*,

Princeton, NJ: Princeton University Press, pp. 596–7. The Christian analogue lies in the way in which men and women are said to be made 'in the image of God'.
88   Rom. 5: 12.
89   See Calvin, J. *Institutes*, II, ch. 1, 7–8.
90   Quoted in Spellman, W.M. (1988), *John Locke and the Problem of Depravity*, Oxford: Clarendon Press, p. 8; cf. the similar language of Article 9 of the 39 Articles.
91   Barclay, R. (1678), *An Apology for the True Christian Divinity*, London (?), the 'fourth proposition' (in the unpaginated preface) and pp. 63–5 (p.65 is wrongly paginated as 56). The work first appeared in Latin, Amsterdam, 1676.
92   Chillingworth, W., *The Religion of Protestants*, vii, 7.
93   See Hort, A.F. (1896), *Life and Letters of F.J.A. Hort*, London: Macmillan, vol. 2, p. 329.
94   The Commission on Christian doctrine appointed by the Archbishops of Canterbury and York (1922), *Doctrine in the Church of England*, London: SPCK, (1938), pp. 63–4. The report goes on to mention several possible uses of the word 'guilt', but rejects any account of inherited individual culpability.
95   Wesley, J., *Forty-Four Sermons*, London: Epworth Press (1944 edn), XI, 15–16; XXXV, 14.
96   NB Genesis 3: 5.
97   It is only *part* of the context, because teachings about the nature and role of Mary often see her as a counterpart to Eve. When this is seen in a mythological rather than a literal way, a liberal Christian philosophy may find a range of insights within Catholic and Orthodox teachings about Mary.
98   Owen, H.P. (1989), 'The Sinlessness of Jesus' in *Religion, Reason and the Self*, Cardiff: University of Wales Press, p. 122. cf. Anselm, *De libertate arbitrii*, ch. 1. If one believes (as I do not) in an historical Adam and Eve, then one might argue that there was a certain kind of moral perfection in our first state, a perfection that was given rather than achieved. I have problems with this idea because (questions of the nature of Jesus apart), anything that we would now recognize as moral goodness in people involves a process of struggle. In contrast, the divine goodness cannot be an achievement, since this would involve a process in God that would contradict any idea of his eternal nature. (In process theology, God may 'change' with respect to the content of his experience as it relates to creatures, but he cannot change in respect to his essential or 'primordial' nature.) If Jesus *could* not sin, and had from all time the moral goodness which for all others is an achievement, then this is part of what it means to speak of his divinity.
99   Confucius, *Analects*, 17, 3. In this passage the others who are said to be incapable of change are the most stupid, and this would fit a theory that holds that people can become so low as to become unreformable. I prefer the view (as in Origen) that no one can fall so low as to be incapable of responding to God's grace. In another passage Confucius relates the wisdom of the sage (at seventy years of age) to the harmony beween desire and right (*Analects*, 2, 4.)
100 For example, Phil. 2: 1–11.
101 Gibbon, *The Decline and Fall of the Roman Empire*, ch. 47.
102 Anselm, *Cur Deus Homo*, II, ch. 10.
103 In 1964, Christians representing the ancient monophysite tradition met with those who held the more commonly accepted 'dyophysite' (literally 'two natures') tradition, and there was general agreement that both traditions held the same essential truth concerning the nature of Christ. Thus the extent to which terminology had led to misunderstandings was recognized. See Bell, D.N. (1989), *A Cloud of Witnesses*, Kalamazoo, Michigan: Cistercian Publications, pp. 138–9.

104 See Kant's comments on 'pathological' as opposed to 'practical' love, in his *The Moral Law* (*Groundwork of the Metaphysic of Morals*), trans. Paton, H.J. (1948), London: Hutchinson University Library, ch. 1, p. 65. Kant's ground for this is that 'pathological' love cannot be commanded. But although we cannot make ourselves love someone right away (with a love that includes feelings), we can begin a process – that includes action and attention and prayer – in which the appropriate feelings can grow.

105 Schleimacher, F. (1830), *Der christliche Glaube*, 2nd edn, translated as *The Christian Faith*, H.R. Mackintosh and J.S. Stewart, eds (1999), Edinburgh: T and T Clark, p. 387.

106 The doctrine of predestination can be held to point towards an important truth without involving these kinds of exclusivity. It is rooted in a sense of grace which leads Christians to stress not only the help which God gives us every day, but a grace which somehow 'goes before' us, prompting and assisting even the way in which we reach out to God. The New Testament word translated as 'predestined' (*proorisen*), for example, in Rom. 8: 29, can be seen as pointing to a truth along these lines.

107 John 14: 6; 5: 24; 14: 6.

108 Justin Martyr, *First Apology*, xlvi, trans. Barnard, L.W. (1997), in *St Justin Martyr and the First and Second Apologies*, New York: Paulist Press. Justin writes of the 'seeds' of truth (*logos spermatikos*) that are present in all true thinkers.

109 Origen, *Contra Celsum*, VII, 42. The Platonic reference is from the *Timaeus*.

110 Lietzmann, H., trans. B.L. Woolf, 3rd edn (1953), *The Founding of the Church Universal*, London: Lutterworth, p. 308.

111 Chillingworth, W., *The Religion of Protestants*, i, 8, original emphasis.

112 Barclay, *An Apology for the True Christian Divinity*, p. 182.

113 Hort, A.F. (1896), *Life and Letters of F.J.A. Hort*, London: Macmillan, vol. 2, p. 337. Hort goes on to criticize the language of the article.

114 Maritain, J. (1990), 'Raison et Raisons' in *Oeuvres Complètes*, Fribourg: Editions universitaires, vol. IX, p. 348. Maritain adds that such a person suffers from an inner division and frailty.

115 John 1.

116 I recognize some circularity here, since what we call a 'great' religion is likely to be determined, in part, by the absence of matters such as idolatry and cruelty.

117 The more the physical universe is seen as an 'overflowing' from the ultimate, the more a mathematical model is suggested, in which every detail of the universe is *necessitated*, and if only one had enough knowledge, or *gnosis*, then it could be worked out why everything has to be as it is; the more the physical universe is seen as the result of a voluntary act, with the consequence that God could have chosen to make things differently, the more an empirical model is suggested, in which one has to 'taste and see' what kind of world God has chosen to make. In due course, this was to have major implications in terms of the motivation for developing the empirical sciences (for example, in Roger Bacon at Oxford in the thirteenth century). Contemporary science clearly fits neither of these models in their pure form, for the search for intelligible theories, and especially a 'unified field theory', suggest something akin to a mathematical model in which 'harmony' is stressed, while the emphases on indeterminism and contingency indicate the continuing need for some kind of empiricism.

118 For this reason, the term 'modalism' is used to designate a heresy, associated with Sabellius.

119 Lampe, G.W.H. (1967), *The Seal of the Spirit* 2nd edn, London: SPCK, p. 318. He goes on to say that in the case of infant baptism the benefits are conferred 'to some extent proleptically'.

120 See Weatherhead, *The Christian Agnostic*, pp. 181–6; Broad, C.D. (1962), *Lectures on Psychical Research*, London: Routledge and Kegan Paul, especially in relation to 'cross-correspondence'; Stevenson, I. (1975), *Cases of the Reincarnation Type*, Virginia: University Press of Virginia, 1975; 'The Scole Report' (1999) in *Proceedings*, London: Society of Psychical Research, 58, Pt 220.

121 Matt. 22: 29–32.

122 The earlier Hebrew tradition believed in *Sheol*, a kind of underworld from which shades of the departed might be summoned by witchcraft (often translated – misleadingly – as either hell or Hades), but this was not the kind of after-life to which one looked forward, nor was it a place of either reward or punishment. It was more like a place for lingering shadows. In Hebrew thought, prior to the Maccabees, rewards and punishments were meted out to one's offspring on earth in accordance with a principle of solidarity.

123 2 Macc. 12: 43–5.

124 Plato, *Phaedo*, e.g. 100d.

125 James, W. (1956), 'Human Immortality' in *The Will to Believe and Other Essays*, New York: Dover Publications, p. 15, original emphasis.

126 Broad, C.D. (1958), *Personal Identity and Survival*, London: Society for Psychical Research, p.19.

127 On the memory theory see Penelhum, T. (1970), *Survival and Disembodied Existence*, London: Routledge and Kegan Paul, ch. 5.

128 Augustine, *De Civitate Dei* (*The City of God*), trans. E.B. Pusey (1945), London: Dent and Sons, XXII, 20. cf. The Qur'an, Sura 40, 1–9. Quite apart from cannibalism, it is perfectly possible that many atoms are 'recycled' through many human bodies.

129 One reason for the persistence of the claim that our resurrected bodies must contain essentially the same *matter* is the Thomistic teaching that in the case of human beings, it is our bodies which make us *individuals* (whereas angelic beings do not have this need, since, strictly speaking, each one is a separate species). My provisional response is that there are good grounds for the claim that we need bodies of some kind if we are to be truly existing individuals, but that it is not necessary for these bodies to have *the same matter* as our present bodies, provided there can be a criterion of identity along the lines of the fourth suggestion.

130 Parfit, D. (1986), *Reasons and Persons*, Oxford: Oxford University Press, pp. 200–201.

131 Locke, J., *An Essay Concerning Human Understanding*, II, ch. 27, 15.

132 Irvine, A.D. (1991), 'Thought Experiments in Scientific Reasoning' in T. Horowitz and G.J. Massey, eds, *Thought Experiments in Science and Philosophy*, Maryland: Rowman and Littlefield, pp. 160–61; cf. Gale, R.M., 'On Some Pernicious Thought-Experiments' in the same volume, pp. 297–303 .

133 Broad, *Lectures on Psychical Research*, pp. 19–20. Broad holds that some kind of quasi-physical body is essential if the 'dispositional basis', crucial for any significant identity of a person, is to be possible. I hold that an energy field, with a unique resonance in the divine, could provide such a basis.

Chapter 8

Some Personal Options

Recapitulation

If anyone has a passion for reason, and if they wish to address fundamental questions, it has been argued that although there is no indubitable starting point, a rational approach is possible, and there is a logic to the order in which the quest for answers should be described. First, we need to establish that the questions are meaningful, or coherent. Then we must establish that reason is a tool that can be used with some hope of reaching at least provisional, universal answers. Next, we must review the range of general positions that intelligent people have come up with. After that, the quest has taken a new turn, because it has proceeded on the assumption that theism is a possible option, and has then looked at a range of options within theism. In this context, I defended the plausibility of a form of Christianity that is traditional in some respects – for example, in holding a doctrine of the Trinity. Later in this chapter, I shall take the Trinitarian position as a starting-point and pursue the quest for rational options just one step further, considering the grounds on which a narrower choice, perhaps involving a particular denomination, might properly be made. In this context liberal Anglicanism will be presented as a rational choice, but not the only rational choice.

The order which I have just described refers to the way in which a liberal philosophy of religion needs to be *presented*. As already stated, this does not have to be the order in which an individual person comes to a position of faith. Just as an intellectual inquiry can begin in many places and then proceed in a series of circles, so a search for faith can begin in many places. In fact, for the individual believer, the order may often be the very reverse of the order in the systematic presentation. Someone may begin by being attracted to a particular religious community because of the quality of its life or because of the way they feel valued as an individual within it. Only later may there be a reflection on the philosophy which lies behind this community. For many people, 'belonging' comes before 'believing', and this is of crucial importance for those who seek to build faith within a generation of young people most of whom feel completely alienated from traditional beliefs. Alternatively, someone may simply be attracted to the person of the Buddha or Muhammad or Jesus Christ, and seek to be a follower of a way of life. Again, it may only be later that the philosophy that lies behind this way of life is explored. As in science, we must not confuse the logic of discovery with the logic of presentation.

Returning to the theme of rational presentation, I have reiterated that the Christian position presented in Chapter 7 was within the context of agreement that there are other rational positions, both outside and inside theism. However, it was also in the more provocative context of the claim that most people have irrational elements within their general positions. Also, many people have *overall* positions that cannot be rationally defended, both outside and inside theism, and one of the things this book hopes to do is to challenge all readers to consider whether this might be the case for them.

The way in which general positions tend to merge or overlap, especially when they are expressed in more subtle ways, is another of the conclusions that needs stressing. This is obviously true when we come to Christian denominations, where, for example, a typical Roman Catholic and a typical Anglican might well have much more in common in terms of an overall system of beliefs than two members of the same denomination. In other words, the boundaries that determine which denomination one is in are only partly a matter of the standard teachings of denominations; they are at least equally a matter of individual circumstances. Very understandably, many people do not wish to change denominations (which may involve hurt to family members and friends), until or unless personal disagreement with the standard teaching becomes fairly extreme, or until, as an official of some kind, one is expected to support a position one fundamentally disagrees with. As stressed in Chapter 1, there is also considerable overlapping across the boundaries of the main religions. Also, some of those who consider themselves 'secular' want to stress a 'spiritual' dimension to human life.

It could be argued that a special case of a secular system that is open to the spiritual dimension of human life is provided by Confucianism, which – especially in its classical form – does not fit comfortably into the categories of materialism, monism and theism. If forced to classify Confucianism under one of these headings, I would suggest that it was 'a form of materialism with a strong spiritual and moral emphasis'. However, this description is misleading, among other reasons because Confucianism does not so much assert a philosophy of materialism (as that term has normally been understood in the West), as claim that our attention should be focused on our duties and responsibilities in this life, seen as part of a universal *order* that encompasses heaven (*tian*) and earth. Thus what we might call a 'metaphysics' is implied, even though it is not asserted. Here we have an extreme example of the 'fuzzy edge' that I have frequently referred to.

Exclusiveness and Caricature

Every religion has its special doctrines, and in the light of this it is naive for followers of any religion or philosophy to deny all exclusivity. As stressed in Chapter 7, there is an objectionable *kind* of exclusivity which implies that only a small group of people have God's favour, or are destined for heaven, or have a right to force others to their view. Classical Marxism had its own secular version of this kind of exclusive claim, which was used, as it has been by many religions, to persecute those who disagreed. Indeed, this is one of the grounds which has led some thinkers to classify Marxism as a kind of religion.

The reference to persecution needs amplification. Several of the great religions have a questionable history in regard to this matter, and it is interesting to see how an almost identical argument has been used to persecute quite different sets of beliefs. In the case of Islam, although the Qur'an says explicitly, 'Let there be no compulsion in religion',[1] Muslim commentators on this passage frequently except followers of religions that are thought to be offensive to Islam – for example, because they are alleged to practice idolatry or because, as in the case of the Bahais, there is alleged to be a great prophet who comes *after* Muhammad. In the case of 'people of the book' or other monotheists, including Zoroastrians, Jews and Christians, some toleration is normally permitted, but typically, within an Islamic country, not only is proselytizing of Muslims not allowed, it is simply illegal for a Muslim to adopt an alternative religion. A recent Muslim work by the leader of a major Sufi order[2] includes the comment: 'In Islam, religion and politics are not separated: nor can the government be divorced from the official religion. Hence any propaganda for another religion must be prohibited as being contrary both to Canon and to State Law.' In a significant passage he then goes on to give the reason for forbidding apostasy: 'Anyone who penetrates beneath the surface to the inner essence of Islam is bound to recognise its superiority over the other religions. A man, therefore, who deserts Islam, by that act betrays the fact that he must have played truant to its moral and spiritual truth in his heart.' For this reason, the appropriate penalty is death, if he has been brought up as a Muslim, and two opportunities to recant if he was a convert to Islam, followed by death if he continues in his apostasy.[3] Interestingly, this whole argument parallels almost exactly much traditional thinking within Roman Catholicism prior to its official rejection in 1963, with John XXIII's encyclical *Pacem in terris*, where the rights of persons are claimed to include the worshipping of God according to conscience, 'privately and publicly'.[4] Aquinas, while approving the toleration of certain beliefs and practices, notably Judaism, approves the handing-over to the secular arm for punishment, including death, both heretics who refuse to repent and apostates from Catholicism. Moreover, his argument parallels the Muslim argument just cited, in that the grounds refer to infidelity and sinful stubbornness.[5] There is also a similar recommendation to receive a repentant heretic back after a lapse, but after a second admonition, even if admitted to do penance, the heretic should be executed.[6] This teaching lies behind Pius IX's *condemnation*, in 1864, of the views (i) that 'In the present day it is no longer necessary that the Catholic religion shall be held as the only religion of the State, to the exclusion of all other modes of worship', and (ii) that 'it has been wisely provided by the law, in some countries called Catholic, that persons coming to reside therein shall enjoy the free exercise of their worship'.[7] In a similar vein, the eminent Dominican theologian, Fr Garrigou-Lagrange, writing in the 1920s, asserts: 'The Church claims that the truth alone has the right to be protected. Since therefore it is certain that she alone possesses the whole truth, she alone has the right to protection.'[8] Similar views can be found in conservative Protestant thought, especially in its early days.

Obviously, these views do not express the views of all Muslims or Christians, particularly in more recent times and, as in so many other matters, we need to distinguish both religions and denominations as they are at their best and as they are represented in distorted forms. I argue in this book that honest and rational persons can adopt versions of Islam, Roman Catholicism and Protestantism, among other options. However, I also argue that the kind of exclusivity that justifies the intolerance indicated by the foregoing quotations is *irrational*, in that there is a failure to recognize the possibility of other, coherent options. All kinds of people can argue, and have argued, that *if only* you will really examine what they believe, you will see that it is the only truth. But the very awareness of this sea of competing views, often held by intelligent and honest people, should help us to see that one's own sincere belief and commitment cannot justify the persecution of alternative beliefs. Such intolerance is not only irrational, but – as the history of religious conflict demonstrates – pernicious. It also transpires that, in the modern world, Islam must rethink the question of the relation of religion to politics, just as the papacy had been forced to do, with an extraordinary contrast between the encyclicals of 1864 and 1963. (The toleration of *actions* is another matter, since no one can approve allowing people deliberately to hurt other people. However, the appropriate limits to the toleration of actions, and the complex way in which some actions may be related to beliefs, as in the case of racism, raise many questions that lie beyond the scope of this book.[9])

In contrast to this strong form of exclusivity, one of the happier aspects of recent decades has been a general growth in understanding across religious boundaries – at least by liberal elements within all the major religions – and within Christianity, the growth of the ecumenical movement. It is now rare to find Christians claiming that only members of their own denomination will be found in heaven. However, claims to a particular insight still imply exclusivity of a kind since it is asserted that here is a truth that is not found elsewhere, or that is only found elsewhere as a result of this insight, and this is true for all religions in their typical form. It is particularly evident in what are sometimes called the 'historical' religions, referring to those for whom particular events in history, or particular historical figures are of intrinsic importance. I shall proceed to indicate some of these exclusive doctrines. In each case the concern is to distinguish a claim that lies at the root of a religious tradition from accidentals which can easily be made a false target for those who wish to attack a religion. All religions can be, and often are, caricatured through a failure to make this distinction. I shall begin by taking four versions of monotheism, in historical order. All four of these, I hold, can be held by rational people, provided that the central claims are interpreted in ways that do no violence to reason.

Judaism, in anything like its traditional form, is committed not only to monotheism, but to the belief that Israel was, in a quite special way, the 'chosen' people of God, delivered from Egypt, and then provided with God's law or Torah. Further, the prophetic tradition firmly believes in a coming Messiah, who the majority of Jews believe has yet to come. Unfair caricatures of Judaism abound, perhaps the most important of which arises when Judaism is confused with Zionism, which is a political movement within Judaism about which many Jews have grave misgivings. Another unfair criticism, often found among Christians, is the assumption that the kind of Pharisaism criticized in the New Testament – in which there is a legalistic approach to all moral questions – is typical of Judaism in all its forms, which it certainly is not. Modern Jewry exists in a multitude of forms, and some of the reformed synagogues allow for equal status for women. Similarly, fundamentalism, in the sense of the verbal inspiration of Scripture, has been abandoned by many, but not all, religious Jews.

The particular emphasis of traditional Christianity has already been explored. It is the claim that in Jesus we see not only a prophet, but the Messiah who was in some quite special and unique sense 'the image of God'. I have argued that there is a rational basis for this belief, but it cannot be denied that it involves a controversial claim. I have also mentioned some of the most common caricatures that are levelled against Christianity, often by people who should know better. Examples are naive accounts of omnipotence and omniscience, crude versions of tritheism, predestination, verbal inspiration, original guilt, and so on – all of which can be found in the mouths of Christians at different times and places, but are caricatures of the way Christianity is portrayed in the liberal tradition.

Islam makes that claim that Muhammad was the 'seal' of the prophets, which means, according to Muslims, that he is the last great prophet. Here is the principal Muslim example of a particular claim. Most, if not all, of the other controversial issues associated with Islam are matters of how Islam is currently interpreted. All traditional Muslims insist on a doctrine of the *verbal* inspiration of the Qur'an, and this makes it very difficult to debate some of the more controversial questions, like the marriage rules, and other aspects of law (*shari'ah*). Although only a small part of this law is actually to be found in the Qur'an, those parts of it which have a Qur'anic base are seen as unalterable, and there is also a tendency to give early, non-Qur'anic sources of *shari'ah* a reverence which makes liberal interpretations difficult. However, I cannot see why this is any different from an equivalent issue in the history of Christianity. In the sixteenth century there were few, if any, places in Europe where belief in the *indirect* inspiration of the foundational, Christian texts could have been advocated without threat to life and limb. Gradually a more rational approach has gained ground, which reveres the Christian Scriptures without a commitment to *verbal* inspiration. I have no doubt that the same thing will happen, and is discreetly beginning to happen now, within Islam. At present, it is simply unsafe, in many Muslim countries, publicly to espouse this kind of liberalism – but this is no more a criticism of Islam itself than a criticism of sixteenth-century Christian Biblical views is a criticism of Christianity itself. With the rise of less literal interpretations of the Qur'an, many things that have already begun to change may change further – for example, concerning the status of women, the applicability of *shari'ah* in contemporary societies, and the belief that every event is directly planned by God ('It's the will of God' being a frequent response to every evil that occurs). Another problem relates to those Muslim apologists who use the so-called gospel of Barnabas as an historical source, when this book is well known in the scholarly world to be a forgery, almost certainly written in Italian in the late sixteenth century CE.[10] Once again, this is not a problem about Islam as such, which in many instances has a fine record of scholarship. Finally, the earlier point concerning toleration needs to be repeated. The intolerance shown by many Muslims, just like the intolerance shown by many Jews and many Christians, is not an indication of what Islam is really about, but an indication of the caricature that *any* religion can become when it is distorted by fanatical followers. At present, in many countries where there is a large Muslim majority, it is illegal or dangerous to promote the Christian faith, whereas in formerly Christian countries, such as England, Muslims are perfectly free to promote their faith. There is certainly a completely unjustifiable imbalance here, but it must be remembered that, prior to the eighteenth century, the same intolerance was manifest within most Western nations.

The Bahai faith is a tolerant, monotheistic religion that strives for universal peace with a special emphasis on the need for world unity. However, here too there are particular claims, for Bahais assert, i) that Baha'u'llah was *the* prophet of the nineteenth century, and ii) that there will not be another prophet of his stature for one thousand years. Regarding the first of these claims we might recall the prophetic work of Nakayama Miki, the founding woman prophet of Tenrikyo in Japan, whose primal religious experience took place in 1838, just fifteen years before that of Baha'u'llah. One reason for the importance of Tenrikyo is its espousal of complete equality between men and women,[11] so that the claim of Abdu'l-Baha that this equality is peculiar to the teachings of Baha'u'llah is inaccurate.[12] (Abdu'l-Baha was the eldest son of Baha'u'llah – and according to his will – the infallible interpreter of his writings.) We should also recall that Christianity in its Quaker form has made this claim since the seventeenth century.[13] As we shall see later in this chapter, on this issue much depends upon what one means by 'equality'.[14] Also, difficult questions arise about a claim that covers the next thousand years if there is the kind of contingency in history that (so I have argued) freedom requires. My general point is simply this: the Bahai faith, like the other great versions of monotheism, has its particular doctrines or 'dogmas' which invite a liberal rather than a literal interpretation. An additional observation concerns public worship. Observers of the Bahai faith may be surprised to find that in its original form no public prayers are provided except in the context of services for the dead. There is no close equivalent to the Eucharistic experience of Christians or the communal prayers of the mosque.

In the case of the non-historical religions, particular or exclusive doctrines are harder to highlight precisely because they do not depend upon alleged historical events, but upon timeless spiritual truths which are harder to define with precision. This is why, as we saw in Chapter 4, it is difficult to pinpoint exact differences between, for example, the *Advaita* (Hindu) doctrine that 'Atman is Brahman', and the Christian doctrine that we must lose ourselves in order to find ourselves.

I shall give just one other example from the non-historical religions. According to many (but not all) of its followers, Buddhism is not an historical religion in the sense that the typical monotheistic religions are, since the existence of the historical life of Gautama (one of the names given to the original Buddha) is not important, only the teaching. Whereas a disproof of the existence of Jesus would cause major problems for Christianity as we know it, an equivalent disproof of the actual existence of Gautama would not disturb most Buddhists. (There probably was an actual, historical Gautama of some kind, but this is not essential for the viability of Buddhism.) However, as with *Advaita* Hinduism, there are central teachings which can appear to be 'exclusive'. For example, suffering is only to be avoided, and enlightenment achieved, by a process of *detachment* (a teaching that comprises the third 'noble truth'). This seems to be in opposition, for example, to Christian views of love, which includes an emotional *attachment* that led Jesus to weep over Jerusalem, and to weep for his friend.[15] Once again, however, what appears to be a plain contradiction, based on a particular claim, turns out to be a much more difficult question of interpretation. There is, for Buddhists, a right kind of 'desire' (which is part of the 'eightfold path'), and an appropriate 'compassion', so although there may still be an important difference of emphasis, and different connotations given to the idea of love, it is not immediately obvious how far these are misunderstandings of each other's language based on problems of translating key words, and how far they express genuine differences in the ideal to be sought. The danger of caricature comes in oversimplifying the difficulties in a dialogue across different languages and different cultures. At the same time, Buddhism does face an important issue here that raises difficulties (parallel to the difficulties faced by all the great religions). The normal presentation of the ideal of detachment certainly seems to be in tension with a conception of love in which there is empathy for the sufferer, and an acceptance of vulnerability symbolized by the cross.

In addition to these recurrent caricatures, there are hosts of individual ones, often presented within the context of a generally rational discussion, and in a way these are more dangerous, since one can too easily assume that a dubious picture is of the same quality as the rest of the presentation. An unexpected example of this kind occurs in Rorty. He writes: 'From a Christian standpoint this tendency to feel closer to those with whom imaginative identification is easier is deplorable ... For Christians, sanctity is not achieved as long as obligation is felt more strongly to one child of God than to another ... .'[16] This is a classic example of error being a distortion of an important truth. What Christianity is committed to is the belief that God loves all people with an equal love, and that Christians are morally bound to seek to love all people. However, the view that we should *feel* the same love to all is *not* the typical Christian view. Aelred of Rievaulx, for example, argued strongly that it was appropriate for the Christian to rejoice in the *special friendship* of a small circle of friends (just as Jesus seems to have done). If we would learn to love all, it is much better to begin by loving a few, intimately.[17] True friendship is a sort of school for universal charity. Not all Christians have followed Aelred in this matter (and Kant seems to support the kind of view that Rorty ascribes to Christianity), but Aelred's popularity and canonization are indications of support for another view. Moreover, there is not only a point here about how to *feel* but how to *act*. We should seek to do what is best for all, but often this is impossible, and then there is no reason why all moral people cannot support what I would call a moral 'principle of *proximity*'. This means that when we only can assist some people, the closeness involved in being of the same family or church or village or even nation, is a *relevant* consideration, both in respect to how we should feel and how we should act in times of stress.[18]

The last example of caricature I shall give here is found in a number of writers who are suspicious of religions because they can appear to downgrade altruism, and make the search for heaven or nirvana or some other blessed state, the *motive* for all good action. As in so many cases, this distortion is partly the fault of religious people. Many Christian sermons have portrayed the penalties of hell in lurid colours and begged the listener to consider their own true interests in gaining heaven. One of the worst sermons I ever heard likened the human condition to someone who was asked to choose between a box of stones and a box of chocolates, the implication being that the rational and moral choice involved in being a Christian was like the sensible choice of the chocolates! In the seventeenth and eighteenth centuries, this danger was accentuated by a particular view of rationality which was related to a new stress on individuality, and which saw the truly good person as the one who prudently maximized well-considered options, in the marketplace or elsewhere. I came across this startling example in Locke, significantly within his book called The **Reasonableness** of Christianity (my emphasis), published in 1695.

> How has this one truth [the existence of eternal life] changed the nature of things in the world, and given the advantage to piety ... virtue now is visibly the most enriching purchase, and by much the best bargain ... Upon this foundation, and upon this alone, morality stands firm, and may defy all superstition.[19]

In contrast, we can take the words of St Francis de Sales' hymn 'My God I love Thee, not because I hope for heaven thereby', ending with the assertion that I will love God in response to what he has done, and just because 'Thou art my God, and my eternal King'.

Behind this caricature lies a misunderstanding of the context in which Jesus and the great prophets warned about the dangers of evil and the rewards of the blessed. There are at least three levels at which a selfish person might be reached, and the level at which it is appropriate to start depends on the context. Let us suppose I am visiting a petty criminal in prison and making the argument that crime simply doesn't pay. I might take this approach because I thought it likely to be the only one that would 'get through' to the person in their present state of moral development. This would be level one, in which one simply relies on the short-term foolishness of doing wrong. However, I now meet a more sophisticated person who ought to be in prison, but isn't, who argues that if you go in for crime in a big way, especially white-collar crime, it may well pay, and discovery is a risk worth taking. This is where we find the level two argument, which essentially claims that this kind of selfish life does something to the person that makes the higher forms of happiness impossible. For example, the good life involves real friendships, and (for many) happy marriages, and these *cannot* be achieved by systematic 'faking' – that is, acting *as if* one really cared for another person. It is like the truth expressed by Aristotle and Mill, mentioned in Chapter 2, whereby happiness is seen to be a by-product of virtuous action rather than an object of search in itself. A sustained example of this argument can be found in Plato's *Republic* where Socrates seeks to show that the unjust person *cannot* participate in the Good because injustice inevitably injures the soul, making it incapable of real blessedness. Jesus' remarks about the stupidity of gaining the whole world only to lose one's own soul are of the same kind.[20] I think that a wise materialist is able to use an equivalent argument, although without any reference to an after-life. I can see nothing wrong in the use of these second-level arguments, in sermons or elsewhere, provided this is not the last word. If it is the last word, then any sensitivity to the spirit of the great religions will sense that there is something unsatisfactory or, more strictly, that something is lacking, even if it is felt that these may be the only kinds of argument that have a chance of getting through to people like my sophisticated criminal. Thus there is a reaching towards a third level, and this is found in all the great religions, and also in secular form, in the acknowledgement that with love, in its fullest sense, the very idea of motive simply disappears. In Plato we find this in the *Symposium*, where one is simply caught up in the divine beauty, and in the *Republic* at the highest level of knowledge indicated in the allegory of the cave. Christian versions include the poem of St Francis de Sales already quoted, but have their real source in a recurrent theme in St John's gospel, where those who are of the light are simply attracted to the light, for its own sake.[21] Judaism, Islam, and all the great religions, have their own way of expressing this important truth. It is not an exclusive reserve of any religion or philosophy, but a common insight whenever people have a real understanding of love.

The Role of a Religious Community

In the following sections I shall follow the quest for rational answers in the context of Christianity. However, some of the discussion, with suitable adaptations, applies to those who have opted for another form of theism, or even for some non-theistic ways of life. For example, much of what I say about the need for *community* applies to people as human beings, and not just as members of a particular religion.

Most Christians distinguish between the 'invisible' church, which is the company of true believers, united in heaven and earth, and the 'visible' church, manifested in particular denominations and congregations. The latter has been the subject of polemic from the earliest days because it is all too easy to see how far below the ideals the average physical community falls. However, one must not go overboard here. My own experience of a large number of actual congregations has been generally positive. At the core of each one (representing a number of denominations) has been a group of men and women who were sincerely trying to live a Christian life, even though they were anything but perfect. When I meet people who report extremely negative experiences of these communities, I am often lost for comment. I don't know if they have really been unlucky, or whether I have been lucky, or whether they have come into a church with unrealistic expectations. If someone is really seeking a community in which to worship, and has had truly negative experiences, perhaps they should go on seeking until they find a community in which they feel welcome, and which they feel is genuinely trying to follow the way of Christ. This could be more important than seeking a denomination which perfectly represented one's beliefs. In general, there is a tendency for theologians to stress the importance of correct doctrine at the expense of the living spirituality of a particular church. However, if our priorities are really spiritual, joining a community in which one can find strength, and to which one can contribute, should have a high priority. However, there must be two reservations about this openness with respect to denomination. The first is that one should avoid permanently joining any congregation which involves having to affirm belief in something one really does not believe. The second is that one should seek, if possible, to find a community that expresses a view of faith, and a manner of worship, that one is at home with. For example, I would find it very hard to be permanently at home in a church which did not have a traditional liturgy in which there was a kind of *rhythm* that ran through the church's year and the church's principal services. This is not to say that others ought to find the same place, but that we all need, most of the time, to express worship in ways that reflect how we feel and think.

The foregoing has assumed that a community, along with corporate worship, is something that all Christians ought to find, and this has been disputed, so that we must consider the option of being a Christian *as* a member of a worshipping community, over and against being a Christian with no such affiliation or commitment.

The argument for finding a Christian community in which to worship is based on two claims. The first relates to human nature in general, and has nothing specifically Christian about it. Although I have argued for the kind of individualism that is founded in the classic exposition of Jeremiah, I have also indicated that a sense of 'solidarity' is not to be rejected, only those aspects of it which imply collective guilt or which deny individual responsibility. While there is a place for solitary reflection, many aspects of human fulfilment and flourishing can only take place within a community and, ideally, a loving, caring community, which for Christians represents the *body* of Christ. Music can have its solitary side, but it is typically a cooperative enterprise, between players, and between players and listeners. Family life, conversation, the enjoyment of good food and wine, political action, education, to name just a few of the manifold activities in which people can find fulfilment, are either exclusively, or partially communal enterprises. We are social beings.

The second claim relates to Christian experience, especially that of the Eucharist, which both symbolizes and fortifies the sense of being 'in Christ' and in the 'communion of saints'. Of course, those who say that they want to worship at the top of a mountain, or in some other private way, need not be quarrelled with. There are countless, legitimate, personal ways for religious people to express their worship. The point is simply that the Christian tradition, for good reasons, has stressed both how much we need the strength and support of corporate worship, and also our duty to support this worship, even if, some of the time, it runs counter to our immediate inclinations.

Is There 'One, True Church'?

In this section I shall argue against the view that *any* denomination, or sect, represents the 'one, true church'. (There is 'one, true church', but it is the invisible one I have referred to.) The claim to be this true church is made by innumerable Protestant sects, and also, although nowadays expressed in a softer way, by the official Roman Catholic church. I shall not detail the claims of the sects since they all depend on particular interpretations of the Scriptures which it is hard for a rational person to see to be the *only* justifiable interpretation. Frequently, there are also rejections of evolution, and claims to special revelations which defy rational analysis. In a recent discussion with a missionary from the Church of Jesus Christ and the Latter Day Saints (the Mormons), the missionary responded to my doubts with the claim that he *knew* his position was the true one, and that the revelation to Joseph Smith, the founder, was true. But, of course, this is exactly parallel to the claim of special knowledge made by Jehovah's Witnesses when their faith is challenged, and of countless other sects which make equivalent claims, even though (in so far as they are rivals) they are manifestly proclaiming different teachings. Instead of responding to such assertions I shall concentrate on the official Roman Catholic claims, since they have the merit of being based in an argument that does not depend on a special revelation to a few chosen people. First, however, we must be clear about the different ways in which the word 'catholic' is used.

In its initial, and most original sense, 'catholic' simply reflects the Greek word that lies behind it, meaning 'universal'. In this sense, all Christians are likely to claim that they are 'catholic' in being part of the universal church of God.

In a second sense, the word refers to a set of emphases that tend to separate off more 'catholic' churches or individuals from others. I shall list what I consider to be the six most important emphases, and it will be clear that in many cases they are interrelated. These comprise: i) the attempt to represent many kinds of people within a community, rather than a 'gathered' or eclectic group of true believers; ii) a stress on the need for a liturgy which represents a certain *rhythm* that runs through both individual services of worship and the church's whole year; iii) a sense of tradition, along with a respect for ancient authorities, according to which changes from ancient ways of doing things (which have acquired a certain rhythm) need special justification; iv) a sacramental view of the universe, which is felt to mirror God in many positive ways, so that there is less emphasis than in radicalism on Christians being 'different' in their manner of life through a denial of 'worldly' pleasures; v) a view that the central moments of Christian worship are sacramental, centred in particular on the celebration of the Eucharist, or 'Last Supper'; vi) a belief that although humans are fallen, this has not so vitiated our minds that some truths, both religious and moral, cannot be apprehended by human reason.

As with many other words (such as 'rationality'), since we are dealing with a number of criteria rather than a single criterion, marking off people in terms of whether or not they are 'catholic' (in sense two) involves using a very blunt instrument. However, this usage does explain why, for example, many Anglicans, and also a number of Methodists and other Protestants, consider themselves to be 'catholic', in this important sense of the term. This list of desiderata, which a 'catholic' such as myself would like to uphold, also helps to explain the hesitation of catholic Christians fully to identify with bodies such as the Quakers (or more accurately, the 'Society of Friends'). It will be apparent from many passages in this book that I am much impressed with the Quaker tradition, both in terms of its attempt to illuminate the heart of Christian doctrines and in terms of its witness. Apart from the work of some isolated individuals, Quakers were the first actively to oppose slavery, the first Christians who were interested in serious dialogue with aboriginal peoples in which one listened to what they had to say, among the first to promote social legislation for the betterment of the poor, the first to open a hospital for the humane treatment of the mentally ill, and have been ahead of their time in many other ways. However, as a complete statement of what Christianity stands for, the 'catholic' (in sense two), will clearly think that some things are lacking. In the first place, I have argued that the church is right to make a doctrine of the Trinity a part of its traditional teaching. Further, although every person should listen to the inner light that is the Spirit within them, the awareness of this inner light, for the average Christian, is within a context of church teaching and worship that makes it much less likely to become the special claim to personal revelations that typifies the warring sects. Ideally, as I see it, the Quaker movement could be seen as a movement *within* the church, a movement that encourages us to listen to the inner light in a way that many catholic Christians neglect. Seen in this way, I would have no difficulty in seeing myself as both Anglican and Quaker. This suggestion would also solve another problem (but not a criticism) that faces the Quaker tradition. It is one thing for a group of like-minded people to share a spiritual experience in which silence is specially valued, and in which those who feel moved to speak do so; it is another thing for this form of worship to work when it becomes the principal form of worship for Christians of many different kinds, when one or two people who, quite frankly, have too much to say, can render the form of worship unworkable. It is worthy of notice that in the present Society of Friends this is only rarely a problem – which is yet another tribute to the tradition.

In a third sense, 'catholic' is simply another term for 'Roman Catholic'. There are, as is not always appreciated, a number of local differences between Roman Catholic churches in different countries. Some of these churches have been granted special dispensations, as in the 'Uniate' church in Greece, but all owe allegiance to Rome, and are held to be bound by the Magisterium – that is, the teaching authority of the church as expressed through papal bulls, encyclicals or other clear determinations of teaching. It is well known that many people who are catholics in the third sense have grave doubts about some of these teachings, and in what follows I shall be concerned with the 'official' Roman Catholic view, recognizing the fact that some, and possibly all, the criticisms that follow would be accepted by many individual Roman Catholics. My target is the official Vatican position, which is that the Roman church represents the one true church, and alone guards faithfully the keys given to St Peter. All other churches, it is held, even the ancient and venerable Orthodox churches, have in some degree strayed from the right path.

Behind this claim there are two principal kinds of argument. The first is historical. Quoting the famous passage in Matthew where Jesus says that Peter is the 'rock' on which the church will be built, and that to him will be given the keys of the kingdom, a special case is argued for the primacy of Peter among the apostles.[22] The argument then goes as follows: Peter, charged with this unique responsibility centred his later ministry in Rome, where he became the first bishop. Prior to his death he ordained Linus to be the second bishop, and handed over his unique primacy to him. This historical argument is often combined with a second, *a priori* kind of argument that goes like this: there are certain beliefs that it is *essential* for the church to hold if it is to be the guardian of the faith, and if it is to offer a guaranteed way of salvation for Christians. God cannot have left such a vital matter to chance, but in accordance with his promises to give us a way of salvation in Jesus, there has to be a discernible body that represents this way for us. In view of the historical argument just outlined, this can only be the Roman Catholic church. (This is an *a priori* argument in that it does not in its early stages refer to any observable feature of the church, but to the kind of church, which it is alleged, there *must* be.) There are also a number of ancillary arguments that are often used, for example, about the alleged failures or inadequacies of other churches, and about the heroic examples of Catholic saints. Before concentrating on the two crucial arguments just given I shall just make this comment on the ancillary arguments. Although all the churches may indeed be proud of their saints, one of the things that makes many honest seekers suspicious of the whole church is the negative parts of its history, especially (mostly relating to Western Christianity) the horror of the Crusades and of the anti-Semitic pogroms, the toleration of slavery, the use of torture, and so on. Protestant churches, once established, may have an equal share of the blame here – but the point has to be made that such terrible imperfections are particularly hard to reconcile with the claims of any church to be the only true church.

The foregoing point can be put in another way. One can be a committed member of a Christian church and still admit that *all* churches, including one's own, are 'defective' in certain ways. The Vatican, in its recent declaration (*Dominus Jesus*, September 2000) asserts that all *other* churches are 'defective'. However it also makes a distinction between moral fault (which elsewhere is admitted) and 'defect' in matters of church order and doctrine. But whether a sharp distinction along these lines can be maintained is questionable. Some moral faults appear to be interconnected with authoritarian and patriarchal structures within the church which encourage a lack of sensitivity to certain issues, or with doctrines of salvation which encourage intolerance towards those thought to be heading for damnation. More generally, in the normal sense of 'defective', it seems to me that all the churches, in terms of their human components, are 'defective'.

Let us turn to *a priori* argument, since it tends to provide a context for the historical argument. Is it the case that there are some *essential* articles of belief, if one is to be guaranteed salvation? This question, it should be noted, is not the same as the question 'Are there some central Christian teachings?' or the question 'Are there some "truths" that Christianity has succeeded in expressing that are not found elsewhere?'. It will be apparent from Chapter 7 that I would defend an affirmative answer to the two latter questions, since I think that a traditional doctrine of the Trinity is a legitimate part of Christian teaching, and that this doctrine succeeds in articulating a truth that is not, at least in any clear way, expressed elsewhere. However, it will also be clear that I do not see the holding of any particular *belief* as, in the strict sense, something *essential* for salvation. If God is good, in the way already described, and if he is the source of our rationality, then it is reasonable to assert that 'salvation' depends upon a sincere following of the Good in the ways that it is manifested to us. This, however, is quite different from the ancient claim that unless you believe x and y, and any other belief that is *de fide* (as part of some essential core of beliefs), you will be condemned by God, a claim that cannot be justified if God is indeed 'good'. This ancient claim was just as typical of early Protestantism as of Roman Catholicism, and relatively few Christian writers dissented explicitly from it before the eighteenth century – among the exceptions being the Anglican, William Chillingworth and the Quaker apologist, Robert Barclay.

However, a more moderate version of the claim may emerge, and it is important to consider this if we are to be fair to the official Roman Catholic position. While no belief may be *essential*, in the strict sense, to any single person's salvation, there may still be a central core of beliefs which it is essential for the church to hold and to teach if it is to carry out its historic mission. The mainstream churches share a number of such central teachings, notably those of the Trinity, incarnation and redemption. Are there others, including all those that have developed in accordance with a doctrine of what is 'latent' within the Catholic tradition, such as the doctrines of the Immaculate Conception and of the Assumption of the Blessed Virgin Mary? Here, there is wide disagreement among Christians, for even if one takes these later doctrines as representing actual truth, it is hard to see how they can be *central* for Christianity in the way that, for example, the doctrine of redemption is. On this matter Chillingworth made a powerful case for the view that we must distinguish genuine 'fundamentall' points of belief from the 'non-fundamentall'.[23] In sum, while the *a priori* argument might bolster the claim that there must be churches that witness to certain central Christian claims or insights, the added claim that there must be one unique repository of a series of other 'essential' truths, guaranteed by God, is highly controversial.[24]

With respect to the claim that a central core of beliefs must be guaranteed by an ancient tradition, there is this to be said in favour of the Roman Catholic and Eastern Orthodox positions. When Christians have broken away from churches which have had a long tradition, there has been a tendency for the part that broke away to fragment into many smaller parts. One of the reasons for this is a crisis in the question of 'authority' once the ancient body has been abandoned. Hence, today, one can sympathize with those who wish to remain loyal to one of the ancient bodies, claiming that within these bodies we know where we stand and what we believe, while the break-away groups tend to squabble among themselves, and often seem to be unsure of what to teach in a variety of areas. The negative side of this conservatism is that many things are demanded in the name of ancient tradition, either as matters of belief or practice, which reflective people have major difficulties with, as we shall see when we come to consider the Magisterium. One example in the area of belief is the doctrine of original guilt, enshrined in many ancient formulations, which are now a source of embarrassment to many, even in the traditional churches. An example in the area of practice is the support for the institution of slavery which typified the established churches for nearly eighteen hundred years. It was not by chance that opposition to slavery, in the first decades of the movement, came almost entirely from Protestant churches. Overall, this is one of many areas where some kind of balance seems to be needed, in which tradition is not lightly set aside, and yet is not accepted in an unquestioning manner.

Let us turn to the historical claim. Here we can distinguish a series of steps, the first three of which comprise the claims (i) that Jesus did in fact say what Matthew's gospel records him as saying, (ii) that Jesus' statement did refer primarily to the *person* of Peter, and not just to his act of faith (which was the contention of many of the early Fathers[25]), and (iii) that Jesus' words did imply some kind of primacy to the apostleship of Peter. Personally I would be prepared to grant all three of these claims, given the evidence that exists,[26] but it is important to notice how already we are not dealing with proof, but with personal interpretation of probabilities. There are many scholars who would deny one or more of these three steps, and this is relevant when it comes to considering what *weight* the whole argument can bear. The remaining steps are much more problematic. They comprise the claims (iv) that Peter was the first *bishop* of Rome, (v) that he handed on his special authority to his successors, and (vi) that his special kind of primacy was not only pastoral, but related to the guardianship of true belief. In each case my position is not that these claims are certainly false, but that they can legitimately be doubted, and cannot bear the weight that is necessary if they are to support claims about the unique authority of the Roman See.

With regard to claim (iv), there is much dispute among scholars regarding the relationship of the apostles to the orders of bishop (*episcopos*) and priest (*presbuteros*) in the early church, terms which are probably better rendered as 'overseer' and 'elder' if we are to respect the Greek sense of the terms. A common, scholarly view is that none of the apostles became 'bishops' because they had a wider, itinerant role, which included setting up bishops in local areas. It is possible that Peter was an exception to this, but we simply don't know. We do know that by 200 CE the *claim* was made that Peter was the first bishop of Rome, for Iranaeus, at about this time, provides a list of those who were believed to be the early bishops, starting with Peter.[27] Commenting on this, a leading Roman Catholic historian writes : 'The list [of Iranaeus] is certainly a good deal tidier than the actual transition to rule by a single bishop can have been.'[28] I have no doubt that by 200 CE it was sincerely believed that Peter held the position of bishop, but this can easily be explained as analogous to countless examples of the growth of claims that support some kind of power. My point here is not original, but based on a long period of scholarly reflection on the sources. For example, John Hales, writing in the first half of the seventeenth century wrote 'that he [Peter] was bishop at all (as now the name of bishop is taken) may be very questionable … .'[29] In sum, the Roman Catholic statement, much repeated, that Peter was bishop of Rome is an historical *claim*, not an historical *fact*.[30] The evaluation of claim (v) is clearly dependent on this matter, as is the evaluation of claim (vi). This final claim is again subject to much dispute, and my view is, once again, that we are not in a position to be sure. In the early church, some kind of special leadership seems to have been granted to at least three people: James, the brother of Jesus, who presided at the Council of Jerusalem,[31] Peter and Paul.[32] Not only is there uncertainty about the relationship between these key figures in terms of pastoral leadership, there is still more uncertainty about the authority of any of these figures in matters of doctrine. The Council of Jerusalem, as a body, is the closest thing we find in the New Testament to a source of final authority, apart from the words of Jesus himself.

Doubts about the strength of the two central arguments for the special teaching authority of the Roman Catholic church are multiplied when we look at some of the issues surrounding the doctrine of papal infallibility and of the Magisterium. On the question of infallibility I shall say little, since it relates to a small range of teachings (arguably only three, in explicit terms),[33] and does not have the daily effect on the lives of Roman Catholics that many pronouncements of the Magisterium do. I shall indicate just one of the rational ground for disquiet. The defining document relating to the doctrine of the Immaculate Conception of Mary, proclaimed in 1854 (the bull, *Ineffabilis Deus*), and subsequently treated as an infallible, *ex cathedra* truth, centres on the claim that by a special act of grace Mary was not born as we are, subject to 'original sin'. I have already indicated that, as with the nature of Jesus, any suggestion that here was a special 'advantage' when it came to facing life's problems tends to make Mary less relevant as a role model. With regards to infallibility, a particular difficulty arises over an essential accompaniment to the doctrine of the Immaculate Conception, namely that all other human beings (Jesus excepted) are born under original sin. The text includes approval of what is claimed to be the teaching of Scripture, the Fathers and approved Councils that 'all men are born infected with original guilt' (*omnes homines nasci originali culpa infectos*).[34] In other words, it is not simply original *sin* (*peccatum*) that we are all said to be born with, but original *guilt* (*culpa*). We have already seen that such a claim raises major problems for any rational reflection on the human condition. A possible way out is to redescribe the meaning of the Latin *culpa* in ways that separate it from the ordinary connotations of the English 'guilt', and were I briefed to defend the papal teaching this is the line I would take.[35] However, an historical awareness of how most Christians at the time really did believe in collective human guilt, and often did rely on Jerome's mistranslation of Romans, make this a shaky undertaking. This is one rational ground for a serious questioning of the doctrine of papal infallibility. The assertion of Mary's immaculate conception appears to carry as a corollary a doctrine that many have problems with on both logical and moral grounds.[36]

Let us turn to the more relevant issue of the Magisterium. According to the important encyclical *Veritatis Splendor* (1993), good Catholics cannot pick and choose between the teachings of the Magisterium; in effect, they are all to be treated *as if* they were infallible (even though they are not, of course, actually claimed to be infallible decrees).[37] However, consider how often papal teaching has been wrong, and now universally acknowledged to be wrong, both over questions of ethics and of fact. Here are some examples:

- *Laudabiliter* – the bull of 1155 or 1156, in which Adrian IV granted Henry II of England political dominion over Ireland.[38]
- *Ad extirpanda* – the bull of 1252 in which Innocent IV approved torture for heretics (perhaps the most scandalous of all papal decrees).
- *Inter Caetera*– the two bulls of 1493 in which Alexander VI divided parts of South America between Spain and Portugal, provided that the governments assumed responsibility for the conversion of the natives. Here the white invaders were given political dominion over the native peoples.
- *Regnans in Excelsis* – the bull of 1570 in which St Pius V not only excommunicated Elizabeth (which was certainly defensible in the circumstances), but withdrew her subjects' allegiance, effectively putting England under Spanish rule. (The vast majority of Roman Catholics living in Elizabethan England wanted to remain loyal to Elizabeth, but this position was strenuously opposed by Cardinal Allen and a minority of priests.[39])
- The papal indexing of Copernicus' *De Revolutionibus* in 1616 along with the subsequent condemnation of Galileo's views.[40]
- *Miriam Vos* – the encyclical of 1832 in which Gregory XVI attacked the separation of church and state, and demanded support for monarchical regimes.

In the light of such egregious errors (as now admitted by almost all Roman Catholics), it is hard to see why the Magisterium should *now* be treated *as if* infallible, especially since more recent teachings have included a large number of matters that are subject to much controversy among Catholic Christians. I am not denying that the church has a teaching function, or 'Magisterium' of a general sort, which should command respect and attention; my critical comments concern the demand for a complete intellectual acceptance of and obedience to this Magisterium. Here is an indication of some of the more recent teachings that raise legitimate questions:

- The encyclical *Providentissimus Deus* of 1893 in which Leo XIII demanded a belief in the verbal inspiration of the Bible. This is of a piece with a number of later documents, some of which emanated from the Pontifical Biblical

Commission, established in 1902, and which by a decree of 1907, all Catholics are bound in conscience to accept.[41] A number of determinations were made which very few scholars would now accept, such as the Mosaic authorship of the Pentateuch,[42] the traditional authorship of all four gospels,[43] and the unity of the Book of Isaiah.[44] (The situation has been remedied in some degree by the more liberal encyclical *Divino Afflante Spiritu* in 1943 and by the Commission's own acceptance of a more liberal view of the Pentateuch in 1948.[45]) Also relevant here are the antimodernist encyclicals of 1907 which, among other matters, repeated the insistence on verbal inerrancy regarding all the Scriptures.[46]

- The encyclical *Sacra Virginitas* of 1954 in which virginity (undertaken for the right reasons) is a *higher* state than that of matrimony.

- The encyclical *Humani Generis* of 1950 in which it is declared that Adam was an individual historical person, and original sin is a quality in us 'only because it has been handed down in descent from him'.

- The encyclical *Casti Connubi* of 1930 which insists on the primacy of the husband, and 'the ready subjection of the wife and her willing obedience' (except when the husband's command is not in harmony with 'right reason' – because it suggests something manifestly evil).

- The encyclical *Humanae Vitae* of 1968, in which (among other matters) all artificial methods of birth control, even within the context of conjugal love, are outlawed. (Contrary to what is often asserted, this encyclical does not deny the right to limit one's family, but the methods must be either those of abstinence or of 'rhythm' – which, even if it makes use of thermometers, is deemed to be in accordance with nature.)

Notoriously it is the last mentioned encyclical that has drawn most attention, and the reason for this is not only its rejection by many Roman Catholics, but the manner in which the encyclical came about. The papal commission, originally set up by John XXIII, contained fifty-five Catholic experts, clerical and lay, who debated the issue for many months and eventually produced a 'Theological Report' that had the backing of fifty-one of the members. In this report a reasoned case was presented, argued in the language of natural law, for lifting the ban on the use of contraception within marriage. The other four members produced what is sometimes called the 'minority report' (actually a working paper) which argued for maintaining the ban. Amidst a sea of controversy, a new, extremely conservative body was set up to review the findings, and under the influence of this new body the pope (Paul VI) issued the encyclical.[47]

In reviewing this second list of rulings from the Vatican, it should be stressed that we are not dealing with the same scale of problem as in the earlier list, for there are individual, intelligent people who agree with many and, in a few cases, all of the foregoing. Also, although I have singled out questionable teachings, the encyclicals also contain many things which liberal Christians fully endorse. *Veritatis Splendor*, for example, begins with an interesting exegesis of Jesus' discussion with the rich young man that has much of value to say about social justice. The negative point is that, in view of the perfectly rational objections that are felt by many people to many or all of the teachings in this second list, to insist that the whole Magisterium must be treated as if it were infallible is highly unsatisfactory. This point can be put much more strongly when we turn to the first list. When Roman Catholics admit that there has been error in the past, both on matters of morals (as in the approval of torture for heretics), and on matters of fact (such as the authorship of the gospels and the rejection of the Copernican theory), it is hard to see why the Magisterium should now be treated *as if* it were infallible.[48] In other words, when we recall the dreadful errors indicated by the first list, the claim that all good Catholics should treat the Magisterium as if it represented infallible truth becomes an extraordinary claim. Recent apologies by the Vatican for some of the errors of the past may be welcomed, but they do not provide new grounds for accepting the Magisterium in an uncritical way. As I have indicated, it is one thing to be a Roman Catholic, and certainly this can be a rational option, but it is another thing to accept the official Vatican position on the foregoing issues, which to many people amounts to the acceptance, not only of the non-rational, but of the irrational.

Verbal Inspiration and Infallibility

Claims to be the 'one true church', and similar claims to represent the 'one true religion', are frequently linked with belief in the verbal inspiration of a sacred text. Consider the following debate between a Muslim and a sceptical critic which mirrors fairly accurately one that I have heard:

Muslim: For us the Qur'an is the inspired word of God, and no one has shown that it contains any errors, which is remarkable for a book written some 1400 years ago.

Doubter: With respect to errors, my principal problem is not with any alleged contradictions, but with the moral standing of some of the teaching. Similarly, I reject the verbal inspiration of the Old Testament not primarily because of the contradictions I find there, but because of the morality, for example, of the book of Joshua, where one appears to find divine approval of wholesale slaughter, even of children.

Muslim: But what are your moral objections to the Qur'an?

Doubter: They are not on the same scale as my objections to the book of Joshua, but they are still important. One example is the inequality of men and women. Men may have several wives, but women may not have several husbands, and the evidence of a female witness is given half the weight of that of a man.[49] Also, the accounts of heaven are described in terms of the future happiness of men, and women seem to be there to serve them.

Muslim: But you misunderstand the matter. Islam teaches the *equal* value of men and women in the eyes of God. They are equal in spiritual matters, but have natures that are different in certain respects, and this leads to them having complementary, but different roles.[50] The Vatican, in its teaching of the incapacity of women for the priesthood has an equivalent doctrine.

Doubter: But when you say that men and women are equal but different this sounds like a genuine equality until one asks where complementarity involves differences. Then it turns out that *leadership* roles are essentially a male reserve, and this leads to a doctrine that is very convenient to men, for they alone are to occupy the major leadership roles in religion, and according to more conservative Muslims, in society as well. But what is the justification for such 'patriarchy'? The biology of the past was full of false claims that defended a hierarchical system, alleging the innate superiority of men in a range of areas,[51] but although there may be some differences in terms of the gifts that are more typical of one gender rather than the other, I know of no reputable scientist, speaking as a scientist, who would defend any general superiority, or anything that indicates a greater leadership capacity in men. Further, even if it were the case that men are generally more suited to leadership roles (which I deny), it is obvious that many individual women are more suited to leadership than many individual men. I agree that the Vatican has an equivalent official teaching on the leadership role of men within the priesthood, and also, come to mention it, so do many conservative Protestants, but I object equally to all these claims. Equality is asserted, but it is an 'unequal equality' that puts men in command over a whole series of crucial questions that apply to women as much as to men.

Muslim: But I insist, we do believe in the equality of women in the things that really and ultimately matter. In fact, Muhammad, on whom be the peace, was a liberator of women, for example, against the practices of slavery and female infanticide. You should also know that the veil is not, in the Qur'an, obligatory for all time.[52] However when the teaching of the Qur'an is clear we must submit to it as the word of God. In Islam, women are equal, but their roles are different.

At this point, the debate is likely to grind to a halt, both in this exchange and in parallel debates when the doubter is faced with a conservative Protestant for whom the literal text of the Bible is an unquestioned authority, or a conservative Roman Catholic, for whom the Magisterium's interpretation of the Bible is not to be questioned. The debate can get some way because important misunderstandings can be cleared up. For example, many Christians are not aware of the ways in which the lot of women was improved in the early days of Islam. However, in the later stages, the argument begins to go round in circles because when a *reason* is asked for a doctrine, that is (for the doubter at least) morally questionable, the 'answer' is in terms of an *authority*, be it that of Bible or Magisterium or Qur'an. Here, even if there were only one alleged authority rather than three or more rivals, the doubter is unlikely to be satisfied, and when confronted with a plurality of authorities the doubts multiply. The response that has developed within the liberal tradition is to claim that we have to learn to live without such ultimate authorities or 'infallibilities'. Psychologically the demand for them is understandable, but not only has past reliance on such authorities sometimes proved disastrous, there are major problems with any rational defence of them. They either depend on questionable historical or *a priori* arguments (like those described earlier in this chapter), or they tend to become circular. The proposed reason is that we should submit to this authority because God has authorized it. Then, if we ask how we know that God has authorized it, one of the common responses is to point to its intrinsic quality.[53] Up to a point I am sympathetic to this reply, since the Biblical and Qur'anic texts do have great intrinsic quality, but when this intrinsic quality is questioned with respect to a particular point, as in the foregoing debate, then we are told to submit to the higher wisdom of God. Now the circle is complete.

Nevertheless, this suspicion of infallible authorities does not have to lead to extreme forms of scepticism. Within the boundaries of what can be called 'moderate scepticism', I have tried to show that a reasoned defence of a religious philosophy of life can be given, which can still make use of 'inspired' texts. The process that leads to what I have called an 'indirect' form of inspiration, in which a sacred text is seen to consist, at least for the most part, of *human* words, but based on a genuine vision of the divine, is likely to involve several steps. In the early stages, the more difficult or morally dubious passages are handled by an acknowledgement that there are different 'levels' of understanding the text, and then the *interpretation* can move away from the literal reading to the moral or spiritual teachings that can be found there. This was typical, especially, of the Alexandrine school in early Christianity, but can be found in all religions once time has allowed for reflection on the sacred texts. A good example of this process is the allegorization of Israel's conquest of Canaan, in which the Canaanites were held to represent vices which needed to be stamped out.[54] At first, this would simply redirect the emphasis from fighting against people to fighting against vice, but it would open the door, in due course, to a new reading of the sacred texts in which there is no need to believe that God actually sanctioned ethnic cleansing. Another step can be taken when the authority of certain parts of the text is held to be greater than others. For example, in the New Testament, St Paul sometimes distinguishes teachings that come 'from the Lord' and those that are his.[55] Thus, in regard to some passages, it may be said that although the text accurately describes what St Paul wrote, his view does not necessarily reflect the will of God in this matter, especially in changed circumstances. Here a liberal view, for example, of the status of women in the church, becomes possible, without having to say that the Bible is 'mistaken' or 'inaccurate' – as these terms would normally be understood. An interesting variation on this approach can be found in Calvin. Here we find strong support for the general subordination of women that typified the Reformers but, somewhat unexpectedly, Calvin insists that when St Paul refers to women being veiled and silent in church,[56] the passages relate to the category of things that are in themselves 'indifferent'. In the context of human freedom 'both should be received as respected advice but not as eternal law that binds the conscience. Both should be adapted to changing circumstances for the edification of the church.'[57]

It is fortunate that what I have called the more liberal approach to matters such as exclusivity and the status of women can emerge gradually, through interpretative devices such as these, for otherwise liberal doctrines would always be associated with an account of inspiration that is just too radical for many to accept. The same point applies to the interpretation of the Qur'an. Although the conservative view, reflected in the foregoing dialogue, is that 'women and men are created differently and are suitable for different roles in their social and private lives',[58] some recent interpretations of the Qur'an within Islam, or in those sympathetic to Islam, take an alternative position. It is argued that the Qur'anic allowance of polygamy was part of Muhammad's general protection and liberation of women, for it was to protect widows and orphans during a time of war, and has wrongly been taken to be an endorsement of a general practice.[59] (This is in line with the scholastic treatment of polygamy in the Old Testament, which is seen as a secondary rather than a primary, precept of natural law, and therefore to be allowed in special circumstances.) Another interpretation of the Qur'an, from within Islam, is to distinguish that part which deals with universal spiritual and moral issues – which comprises 'the eternal message of Islam' – and another part which concerns social and practical questions, which should be understood in relation to particular socio-political situations, and is therefore subject to change.[60] With interpretations such as these, all the likely moral objections that are voiced to the teaching of the Qur'an might well be taken care of, including the troublesome Qur'anic teaching about the witness of women. However in the long term, I cannot see any benefit, or adequate rational defence, of a doctrine of verbal inspiration for any of the sacred texts, and until it is abandoned there will always be a tendency to run into the kinds of problem that the foregoing dialogue illustrated.

It is instructive to observe an equivalent process in the movement away from the claim that God *directly* controls every event in history. In Judaic, Christian and Muslim thought there has been a tendency to interpret belief in the omnipotence of God as involving the consequence that every event is directly willed by God. Gradually, as we have seen, this has given way to a realization that (as Aquinas put it), God works chiefly through 'secondary' causes, and (as Austin Farrer put it), God has made a world that makes itself. This allows for a contingency in the daily events of life that is required both for a predictable science and for a domain of human freedom. However, this more subtle understanding is hard for many traditionalists to accept because they believe that the power of God is being challenged. (Whereas, in fact, Aquinas and Farrer are making *sense* of what it means to claim that God has power.) Hence, once again, we find that a more liberal view can emerge through intermediate steps. For example, following the tragic earthquake in Turkey, of August 1999, the papers recorded a number of Muslims as saying 'This was not the work of God, but the work of evil people who made money out of poor and illegal buildings'. They meant that, whereas the earthquake was the work of God (like every natural event 'it was God's will'), the shoddy buildings were not. Of course, on a more traditional view, *everything*, including the evil and shoddy workmanship would have to be put down to God's inscrutable will; while on the view of omnipotence that I have suggested, *neither* earthquake nor human evil are direct expressions of God's will. However, these newspaper reports indicate a welcome compromise which enables human responsibility to be taken more seriously.

An Anglican Option

The position I shall defend here is *not* that the Anglican church is the one true church, but (i) that it represents *one* branch of the universal catholic church; (ii) that in the special case of the Church of England, there is a certain historical primacy, in that it is a continuation of an original Christian community; (iii) that it represents an attractive *via media* in which, at its best, Catholic and Protestant elements are blended.

Let us begin with one of the common caricatures. The Anglican church is often said to have been founded by Henry VIII. However, this is the position of its critics, not its own teaching. As a context for a better characterization it should be stressed that *Anglicana ecclesia* was the medieval name for the church in England, so named, for example, in the *Magna Carta* of 1215, and the early defenders of the reformed Anglican church had no hesitation in using this ancient Latin name for the

Church of England that they supported.[61] At the Reformation and the separation from Rome, not only did most of the *people* remain in the reformed body, virtually the same congregations continued to believe the same basic doctrines of redemption, incarnation and Trinity, recite the same creeds, worship in the same buildings and use essentially the same types of service, of which the Eucharist (or Holy Communion or Mass) was the most important. Many of the people, especially in the days of Henry, Edward and the early years of Elizabeth's reign, still considered themselves Catholic, and internal loyalty to many of the reforms only came gradually. Later this loyalty was enormously stimulated by the Spanish Armada, after which loyalty to Rome seemed more and more like disloyalty to England. In sum, the Church of England was essentially *the same church*, but reformed in matters such as more use of the vernacular, the marriage of priests and the communion in two kinds.[62] It could only be said to be a totally *new* church, with a new beginning, if one claims that the link with Rome was more important than the continuity of *people*, basic beliefs and acts of worship. Moreover, the claim that the link with Rome is central to this degree runs into difficulties when it is recalled that prior to the Synod of Whitby in 664 CE the sway of Rome in parts of England, especially the North, was very unclear.[63] The ancient Celtic church gradually evolved into the indigenous churches of England, Wales, Scotland and Ireland, all of them branches of Western Christendom. Thus the true beginnings of the Church of England are to be found with the first Christians to reach England, possibly before the end of the first century. It would not be correct to say that reformed Anglicanism was simply a return to the Celtic tradition, among other reasons because there was no return to the use of the Celtic rite, but nor is it correct to say that a degree of independence from Rome was totally outside the ancient tradition in England. In sum, although the word 'Anglicanism' is most naturally used today to refer to the reformed body, and this is what I normally mean to connote by the term, in its strict sense it applies equally to catholicism in England before the Reformation. For this reason it is appropriate for Anglicans to celebrate some of the great names within the Church in England prior to the Reformation, such as Cuthbert, Aelred and Julian of Norwich.

This continuity with the medieval church was something that many of the Reformers were most anxious to stress. Thus in 1567 Jewel, the most famous of the first generation of Anglican apologists writes: 'we have forsaken the church as it is now, not as it was in old times past.'[64] (He adds that, in terms of falling away from the original, the Roman church has fallen away from the Greek church 'from whom they first received their faith'.[65])

Later, we find William Chillingworth making the same claim. We did not leave the church, he says, only its errors.[66] Earlier, Archbishop Parker had been among those who claimed a continuity with the ancient Celtic church – which he believed (almost certainly mistakenly) went back to Joseph of Arimathea.[67] Henry was a cause of the change, but not the founder of a new church. Moreover, the reformed Anglican church, as we know it now, has its origins in the time of Elizabeth rather than of Henry, following a return to the Roman allegiance at the time of Mary. Most leaders of reformed Anglicanism saw the continuance of the 'apostolic succession' of bishops from the time of the Apostles as one sign (although not the most important sign[68]) of continuity with the ancient church.[69] Another, though less important sign, has been the continuation of the use of pre-Reformation Canon Law within the Church of England, 'except when that Canon Law has been affected by statute or custom in England'.[70] Hence it was quite appropriate for an Elizabethan Canonist to refer to Pope Alexander III (one of the great medieval Canonists) as a 'predecessor'.[71] Even the royal power in the appointment of clergy was not primarily the result of the Reformation, it was rather a hardening of practice following the Statutes of Provision and Praemunire (1351–65): 'A common history of appointments [of English medieval bishops] was that the king nominated and the Pope provided the same person, the chapter duly electing him.'[72] In the early days of the Reformation, the symbolic importance of the removal of papal jurisdiction in appointments was more important than the practical consequences.

With hindsight, there is much to be said for the view that the faults lay equally on both sides. Many Christians were appalled at the papal support for the Inquisition and at the character of many Reformation popes. In these and many other ways the church urgently needed reforming. However, many of the needed reforms came with the Council of Trent. More immediately, Henry's chief motive for the initial break, namely his desire for a legitimate son, and thence for a divorce, while understandable in the context of the times, does not – at least in my view – justify his actions. At the same time, the reason *why* he was not granted a divorce may well be connected with the fact that the pope was under the influence of Spain (which, naturally enough, supported Catherine of Aragon) as much as with the intrinsic merits of the case.[73] On both sides the issues were political as well as religious. However one evaluates the rights and wrongs of what happened, what emerged was a reformed Anglicanism that has both gained and lost from the separation. It gained the speedy introduction of many reforms, and there was also a new sense of liberty. Both Hales and Chillingworth, for example, stressed the need to ask *why* with respect to any belief, rather than the blind acceptance of tradition.[74] On the negative side, the Anglican church was established by means of the same kind of intolerance that it criticized in others. As a result, it lost many courageous Christians and a communion with a larger body of Christians that was only partly compensated for by relationships with Continental Protestants, and, from early on, by increased links with the Greek Orthodox church.

On the issue of the 'head' of the church, there is a similar misunderstanding. According to the reformed Church of England, in the strict sense of the term, the head of the church is Jesus Christ.[75] The head, or governor, 'on earth' or 'in earth' was declared to be the 'sovereign', which indicates the king or queen 'in Parliament'.[76] Like many other Anglicans I do not think that this is a satisfactory arrangement, especially in present circumstances where the relationship of Parliament and church is quite different from that of Elizabethan times, and when there have been instances of inappropriate interferences with the appointment of some bishops by recent prime ministers. In the past, although this was not a perfect arrangement, it was defensible in terms of the relationship between church and state that characterized many national churches. As Jewel pointed out, the Roman church had a very close relationship with the emperors who both called and presided over some of the great Councils.[77] What is clearly needed now is a new relationship of that (relatively small) part of the Anglican church known as the Church of England with the state. This does not need to involve total disestablishment, but a much less formal link between church and state, perhaps akin to that between the Church of Scotland and the state. In view of the historical links with the first Christians in England that I have described, it is perfectly appropriate for the Church of England to claim a certain historical primacy in England, just as it is proper for Roman Catholic churches to make an equivalent claim in places like Ireland, France, Spain and Italy, Lutheran churches in Scandinavian countries, the Orthodox churches in Greece and Russia, and so on. (There are also some more doubtful cases of alleged continuity, where there can be legitimate differences of opinion, but I shall not discuss any of these here.) In all of the named cases, there is a substantial *continuity* of a Christian body from ancient times. Meanwhile, in some parts of the world it is not clear that *any* church has a parallel claim, given the way in which Christianity was introduced by many churches and, in some cases, as much by force as by conversion.

Like all churches, the Anglican church has its weaknesses and, as throughout this book, a rational exploration of options must include an admission of these. However, my overall argument is to the effect that these failings are acceptable within the context of a church that does not claim to be the only true church, and an awareness that *all* the other churches also have weaknesses. I shall comment briefly on two of these.

First, there is the question of authority. Clearly, there is a measure of authority exercised by convocations and synods, and by the regular Lambeth conferences of bishops. However, these all work by consensus or majority vote, and the way in which the decisions are binding on all dioceses is often left unclear. This may be acceptable if one is nervous about centres of authority, but it can make for an ambiguity about exactly what the church teaches on certain matters that is unacceptable to those who desire a more definite, authoritative voice. The same ambiguity applies to exactly what is the Anglican 'tradition', which although loosely defined, for example in the 'Chicago-Lambeth Quadrilateral' adopted in 1886,[78] is better found by sampling Anglicanism than by reading one or two authoritative texts.

Second, in recent decades there has been the introduction of a huge variety of liturgy and language, and this has produced great problems with respect to forms of service. Although my personal preference is for a traditional liturgy, along with the beauty and uniformity of the ancient rites, I am not arguing that this should be standard fare for all Christians or all Anglicans. In fact, at a recent Anglican service in which some members of the congregation danced in the aisles, I was much impressed by the sense of engagement and liveliness, and I am quite sure that for some Christians this can properly represent their normal mode of worship. But there are problems, for example, in the deadness, which quite frankly characterizes many services (be they traditional or radical) and the uncertainty concerning what one is going to find on entering an unfamilar church. The fact that this is equally true of most other churches does not help matters, but rather explains the present attraction of the Orthodox churches for those who seek a really traditional liturgy, and who are not disturbed (as I am) by the conservative stand on issues such as the ordination of women.

Moving on to the strengths of the Anglican tradition, I shall mention three. First, there is the rational tradition, in the positive sense of one that seeks to apply reason to the fullest possible extent, while not in any way denying the importance of religious experience and of those aspects of Revelation that are felt to be integral to primitive Christianity. Closely linked to this rational tradition is the attempt to stress a relatively small number of *essential* doctrines, especially those related to the Apostles' creed. This emphasis was not invented by Anglicanism, but was taken over from earlier liberals within Catholicism, notably Erasmus.

Second, there is the *relative* tolerance of traditional Anglicanism after the early days of the Elizabethan settlement. It is important to stress the word 'relative' with respect to toleration here, for it is not difficult to find many examples of intolerance within the reformed Anglican church or, more often, within the Anglican 'estab-lishment'.[79] Real toleration was something that Anglicans, along with all other branches of the Christian church *that have had political power*, have been slow to learn. Among critics of Anglicanism, much is made of the persecution of both Roman Catholics and 'dissenters' in England, especially in Elizabethan and Stuart times but, serious as these were, they were less severe than the systematic torture and death of Protestants in Roman Catholic Spain and France.[80] An equivalent reign of terror was run by the Calvinists of Geneva. Prior to the Emancipation Act of 1829,[81] ordinary Roman Catholics and many kinds of dissenter suffered signifi-cant disabilities, and their treatment cannot be defended by the norms of today, but most of the time they were allowed to maintain their faith, although in the case of Roman Catholics there was a major problem in its *practice* while the saying of mass was illegal. Meanwhile, in some parts of Continental Europe, merely main-taining a different faith was subject to severe penalties, or even death. Another indication of the *relative* toleration of reformed Anglicanism can be seen in the approach to witchcraft. Prior to the Commonwealth period, and the temporary triumph of puritanism over Anglicanism, witch trials in England were relatively uncommon, partly because of a general scepticism among the higher ranks of the clergy concerning most of the accusations. This changed dramatically during the Commonwealth years, when Anglican compromises tended to be set aside, and, in addition to an escalation of the persecution of Catholics in Ireland, there was a huge increase in the trials and cruel treatment of those alleged to be witches.

An apparent inconsistency concerns the terrible treatment of Roman Catholic missionary priests in Tudor and early Stuart England. This, it must be stressed, was largely the result of the political programme already alluded to, especially after the papal decision to remove Elizabeth's title to the throne of England. As a result, these priests were seen as men who would have England subjected to Spanish rule, along with its Inquisition. The result was particularly tragic in cases like that of Edmund Campion, who was cruelly killed in 1581 even though he clearly accepted Elizabeth's right to the throne. The decision of the authorities cannot be defended in such cases by the standards of today (and, in my view, by the standards that should have been evident at the time),[82] but the authorities were genuine in their belief that political stability was at stake. As is so often the case, it is a combination of political and religious pressures that produces the worst excesses. (Following the events of St Bartholomew's Day 1572, when between ten and twenty thousand Huguenots were killed in Paris and other French cities in a coordinated massacre, Pope Gregory XIII attended a special service of thanksgiving and ordered an annual *Te Deum* to be observed. However, in fairness it must be observed that it was believed, wrongly, that this massacre prevented a political plot against the French monarchy. This was another case of mixing politics with religion.) My general point is that, despite the evils that affected *all* churches that gained political influence, Anglicanism, especially after the Toleration Act of 1689, gradually developed a tolerant spirit that was rooted in the writings of some of its early apologists. Seventeenth-century Anglicans like Chillingworth,[83] Edward Stillingfleet and Jeremy Taylor argued strenuously for the toleration of other Christians, including Roman Catholics. Taylor's *Liberty of Prophesying* (1647) has a title page which indicates how the book shows 'the iniquity of persecuting differing opinions',[84] and is possibly second only to the earlier work of Sebastion Castellio in the advancement of real toleration. Moreover, even in the sixteenth century, the contrast between the treatment of Protestant leaders under Mary (some three hundred of whom were burned alive) contrasts remarkably with the treatment of Catholic leaders in the Elizabethan settlement.[85]

Third, there is the way in which Anglicanism, at its best, is a kind of 'bridge' between traditional Catholicism and Protestantism. This very fact makes it unacceptable to those who identify strongly with the pure form of one or other of these traditions, but makes it attractive to those who search for a *via media*, even if this involves some compromises that inevitably seem untidy. However, it is very easy to underestimate the way in which a tradition *does* work within Anglicanism. This is a tradition that does not have as a primary aim the production of a distinctive Anglican theology, but rather the desire to express a basic theology that can be common to almost all Christians, based, in particular, on respect for the first five hundred years of Christian experience as portrayed in the New Testament and the Fathers of the early church. The tradition has included a special place for the writings of Hooker and other seminal writers. In recent Anglican scholarship, this 'tradition' is sometimes referred to as a 'distinctive standpoint' (Stephen Sykes[86]) or as a 'Spirit' (Henry McAdoo[87]). Here there is an analogy with the common law tradition of England, which works as much by precedent and custom as by statute, in contrast with the civil law tradition of Continental Europe, which depends much more on the letter of a legal code. In a recent, generally friendly exchange of ideas between Anglican and Roman Catholic theologians, the Anglicans were asked for definitive documents expounding their position. Here, I suggest, there was a misunderstanding that parallels misunderstandings of the English common law tradition by those not familiar with it from the inside.

Conclusion

The views expressed in this book are not original. Most, perhaps all of them, will be found in recent books that are concerned with 'rational theology' or 'liberal Christianity' or similar topics. For example, there have been a number of recent books which portray a dialogue between the great religions in a sympathetic and creative manner, which contrast sharply with earlier polemics.[88] What I have tried to do is to present liberal views in a systematic way so that instead of being a series of scattered beliefs or insights they comprise a coherent system.[89] In this way they can more easily be both understood, in their relation to each other, and rationally defended.

A recurring theme of the rational tradition this book attempts to expound can be summarized as follows: although the Christian faith asks for a commitment that goes *beyond* reason, it does not ask for any commitment to a belief that is *against* reason. Closely related to the theme of expounding the nature of the liberal tradition in Christianity is that of the *urgency* of it being understood. We live in an age of great spiritual hunger and, at the same time, in an age when countless people are persuaded that all the great spiritual traditions are not worth consideration because of irrational elements within them. In other words, not only Christianity, but all the great religious traditions are often rejected, not on account of what – at their best – they stand for, but because intelligent people are frequently presented with caricatures. If anyone with a spiritual hunger is persuaded to look again at what any of these great traditions might have to offer, then this book will have achieved much.

If there is any originality in this book, it is primarily in the way I have tried to interrelate the ideas. The logic of the presentation, I have tried to show, must begin by defending the meaningfulness of the fundamental questions; it must go on to establish some universal criteria of rationality; it must then include a systematic review of materialism, monism and theism. It must also take some account of agnosticism, in the popular sense of the term. Within this context, a coherent 'liberal Christian' philosophy emerges that includes support for some fundamental Christian doctrines. This philosophy emerges not only as one of the possible ways of viewing the world in a consistent way, but as a challenging and attractive way that falls within the broader Christian tradition. Finally, in a very tentative way, I have suggested how an individual might be drawn to some more particular tradition within the Christian fold.

In order to attempt a systematic presentation of liberal theology, it may seem that I have painted on a very broad canvas. However, if we are thinking of an overall Christian philosophy, there are many issues that have only been addressed in a very peripheral way, and others that have not been addressed at all. These include a series of ethical issues which are of great importance, but peripheral to the principal concerns of this book. (In my view, the kind of liberal theology described in this book has significant implications for areas of life such as politics, education and medical ethics, and this is one reason for its importance.[90]) Also omitted is any consideration of the doctrine of the 'second coming' (apart from the use of the lightning analogy in Chapter 7), although this has been a significant topic in the history of Christian thought. A more complete statement of liberal theology could explore at least four approaches to this issue.[91] Another of the serious omissions is any adequate account of a Continental, Christian rejection of the kind of liberalism I have defended, although when I have discussed the role of reason and the need to go beyond a *via negativa* I have sometimes felt as if Karl Barth were looking over my shoulder, disapprovingly. While Barth and his followers would approve my claims that religious experience must be taken very seriously and that we should centre Christian doctrine in 'the logos made flesh', they would be unhappy with any notion of building theological truth upon a basis of natural, or reasoned theology. God's word challenges us amidst the corruption that infests this world, and calls us to an existential response, simply because it is recognized as

God's word. 'Christian humanism', says Karl Barth, 'is a contradiction in terms.' The gospel, he goes on, 'is neither principle, system, world view, nor morality; it is spirit and life ...'.[92]

An evaluation of this movement must include an appreciation of the context in which this 'dialectical' theology developed. This includes Barth's expulsion from his professorship by the Nazis, and the two great wars, in which the evil and corruption of human society were all too manifest. Also to be noted is the way in which the total rejection of natural theology has tended to be softened, for example, in a famous exchange between Karl Barth and Emil Brunner in the 1930s. My general comment on the movement is this: if we were faced with a radical choice between the evil represented by Adolf Hitler and the word of the gospel, with no way of making any rational evaluation, my heart would certainly lead me to say 'yes' to the gospel. However, this is not the way in which the fundamental existential choice comes to most people. We hear all kinds of voices calling us to be followers, and within the area of what is felt to be 'good' there are still many voices. A *leap* towards one of them seems more like the dangerous commitment associated with a hundred different cults, or the blind acceptance of some Sartrean idea of freedom. The psychological certainty which many members of the cults have is not the same as a 'justified' certainty, and may easily lead to fanatical behaviour. Further, it is a distortion of what the Biblical tradition describes as 'faith'. Moreover, although much of the world that we experience is evil, it is not totally evil. Outside terrible contexts, such as that of the Holocaust, we find many things that are 'true, honest, just, pure, lovely, of good report',[93] and these things include the serious and often courageous attempt to follow reason, while, in the very name of reason, seeing what the limitations of reason must be. Thus if I must classify my own position on this matter, it is unashamedly closer to a Neothomism[94] that seeks to build a revealed theology upon a natural theology, and to see in revelation, not a rejection of everything 'worldly', but a *fulfilment* of the higher aspirations of all people. Grace does not destroy nature, but fulfils it. These 'higher aspirations' must include the search for an objective truth (and consequentially for the logos of God), recalling Coleridge's aphorism: 'He who begins by loving Christianity better than Truth, will proceed by loving his own Sect or Church better than Christianity, and end in loving himself better than all.'[95]

I shall refer here to only one of the other omissions. I strongly suspect that more evangelical readers of this book will accuse the proposed liberal theology of being irredeemably 'Pelagian', because there is insufficient stress on our absolute need of the grace of God. Here, in addition to a series of problems concerning the exact meaning of 'Pelagian',[96] several issues need to be disentangled. First, any recognizably theistic doctrine of creation must stress the absolute need of God's grace if we are to exist at all, and have the physical, mental and spiritual capacities that we are born with. Second, with regard to our basic response to the Word of God, as it comes to us in what appears as good or true or beautiful, there must be a genuine human ability that is part of our freedom, and which cannot be entirely evaporated in terms of special acts of divine grace assisting us to be good. It may well be true that we always find God, as it were, 'going before us', helping us and encouraging us, but the final choice of the good cannot simply be the result of an extra helping of grace. (One is reminded of Augustine's claim that the good angels did not fall because they were given additional grace – a view which I reject on similar grounds.) If this involves being a 'semi-Pelagian', so be it, for I cannot see how the logic of moral discourse can be preserved without some assertion of real human freedom, along with the frightening responsibilities that this entails.[97] Third, if we speculate that there may be rare individuals who are wholly good, without any special act of divine grace, even in such cases the promise of God, namely to be children with an eternally blessed and loving communion with him, goes beyond any possible merit. This has to be a matter of grace and mercy, not of pure justice. More generally, the practical experience of all the good people I know is that our need of forgiveness and reconciliation is manifest and, in the context of any Christian theology, this involves looking at the special act of grace given through the life, death and resurrection of Jesus.

A final comment concerns the relevance of poetry to the whole discussion. In opposition to many writers in the field of religion, I have denied that God is *totally* ineffable. If God is real, then he is indeed transcendent, but not *totally* transcendent *to us*, because our minds – according to the Thomistic doctrine of analogy and the related doctrine of the image of God – are also transcendent, although in a lower degree. They are transcendent because, at their best, they already *participate* in the divine Mind. This is the way they have been created. For this reason, statements such as 'God is love', expressed with understanding by our minds, can be held to be *true*, and are not only emotive utterances. At the same time, the doctrine of analogy, which allows us to say this coherently, demands that our language about God is seen to be severely limited – for any other view does indeed begin to bring God down to our level. It is in this context that the power of poetry can be better understood, for it may well be the case that what is evoked by powerful imagery and metaphor may be better than straight narrative for describing what we apprehend 'through a glass, darkly':[98]

> I dimly guess what Time in mists confounds;
> Yet ever and anon a trumpet sounds
> From the hid battlements of Eternity;
> Those shaken mists a space unsettle, then
> Round the half-glimpsed turrets, slowly wash again.[99]

Recalling the first paragraph of this book, we may seem to have made a complete circle. But we have returned to a very different castle. Instead of looking out *from* secure battlements we are looking *towards* the 'battlements of eternity'. We seek a truth that we believe is there, although we only glimpse it through the shaken mists. Also, the eternal castle is not designed to keep other people out – it is there to welcome everyone in. The drawbridge is permanently down. Paradoxically, the eternal castle does not represent the stronghold of eternal invulnerability (even though it suggests eternal joy); rather it represents the strength of a love that involves accepting our vulnerability.

Notes and References

1   The Qur'an, Sura 2, 256.

2   The *Ne'ematullahi Sultanalishahi*.

3   Tabendeh, S. (1966), trans. F.G. Goulding (1970), *A Muslim Commentary on the Universal Declaration of Human Rights*, London: Goulding and Co., pp. 71–3.

4   John XXIII, *Pacem in terris*, trans. with comments, H. Waterhouse (1980), London: Catholic Truth Society, sect. 14, p. 8.

5   Aquinas, *ST* 2a 2ae. Qs. 11 and 12.

6   *ST* 2a 2ae. Q. 11, 4.

7   Pius IX, *Syllabus of Errors*, 8 Dec. 1864; 77 and 78.

8   D'Arcy, E. (1967), 'Freedom of Religion' in *The New Catholic Encyclopedia*, New York: McGraw-Hill, vol. 6, p. 112a. Cf. Garrigou-Lagrange, R. (1925), *De Revelatione*, 3rd edn, Rome, pp. 632–3.

9   The modern world has moved towards toleration of belief, but not of actions that are held to be pernicious. There is something initially paradoxical here, since it can be argued that spiritual ends should take precedence over political ends. Indeed, this is the understandable starting-point for arguments such as that of Garrigou-Lagrange. However, not only has history shown the dire consequences of justifying persecution of belief on this ground, Sebastion Castellio, in 1554, put his finger on the essential fallacy. The principal argument for his position (in the *De Haereticis*) is precisely the inability to have *rational certainty* in the spiritual matters under dispute.

10 This forged *Gospel of Barnabas* must not be confused with the second-century *Epistle of Barnabas*, in the pseudopygrypha of the New Testament, or with an early, but lost, *Gospel of Barnabas* that might once have existed. See James, M.R. (corrected edn 1953), *The Apocryphal New Testament*, Oxford: Clarendon Press, p. xxvi; and Ragg, L. and Ragg, L. eds and trans. (1907), *The Gospel of Barnabas*, Oxford: Clarendon Press. The introduction to this edition includes the only known fragment of an early gospel, sometimes associated with Barnabas (p. xlvi). According to the forged gospel Jesus was taken by the angels into heaven while Judas, miraculously changed to look like Jesus, took his place on the cross. His body was then stolen by other disciples. See also Sox, D. (1984), *The Gospel of Barnabas*, London: Allen and Unwin.

11 *Ofudesaki*, 7–21–647. See also The Headquarters of Tenrikyo Church (1958), *The Doctrine of Tenrikyo*, 2nd edn, Tenri Jihosha, p. 90. Tenrikyo teachings raise a number of questions, for example, about claims that all misfortunes arise from past sins and from the will of God, *Ofudesaki*, 6–22–514; cf. *The Doctrine of Tenrikyo*, p. 75. However the suggestion that the sacred texts contain allegory (*tatoe*) is also made (*Ofudesaki*, 1–46–46), so that, once again, the essential texts can be interpreted in more liberal ways.

12 Abdu'l-Baha (1922), *The Promulgation of Universal Peace*, Wilmette, Illinois: Bahai Publishing Trust, p. 455.

13 An interesting indication of this is provided by the seventeenth-century Quaker marriage rite which adapted the form of civil marriage given in the Commonwealth Law of 1653. The Quakers deliberately omitted the wife's vow of obedience, thus making the promises of husband and wife identical. It might be argued that Christianity in general is committed to equality of the sexes in accordance with the spirit of the gospels, and the specific claim that in Christ there is neither male nor female (Gal. 3: 28). However, all the mainstream churches, at least until recently, have clearly approved many forms of inequality in their *practice*. Sikhism might be considered as another example of a religion that espouses complete gender equality and that antedates the Bahai faith. Here it is certainly the case that God is said to transcend the categories of male and

female. (See Cole W.O. and Sambhi, P.S. (1995), *The Sikhs*, 2nd edn, Brighton: Sussex Academic Press, p. 69.) Once again, however, there can be different views as to what counts as actually *practising* complete equality, and here we may note that all ten great gurus were men, and that the eldest *son* has a certain priority (see ibid., p. 150).

14 In its early days the Bahai faith allowed bigamy, but monogamy was subsequently demanded in the teaching of Abdu'l-Baha. See Elder, E.E. and Miller, W. McE. eds and trans.(1961), *The Most Holy Book*, (the *Katib al-aqdas*), London: The Royal Asiatic Society, p. 40 (section 22). Also to be noted is that, according to *The Most Holy Book*, fathers and brothers are to get a greater share of estates than mothers or sisters. Ibid. p. 29 (sections 8–9).

15 Luke 19: 41; John 11: 35; cf. Luke 6: 21.

16 Rorty, R. (1989), *Contingency, Irony, and Solidarity*, Cambridge: Cambridge University Press, p. 191.

17 See especially his *De Spirituali Amicitia*, probably written around 1160.

18 On occasions actual *physical* proximity could be relevant because one is likely to act more quickly and effectively if one is near to someone in need. However, in general I refer to psychological and spiritual proximities.

19 Locke, J., *The Reasonableness of Christianity*, in *Works*, (1823 corrected edn), London: Tegg, vol. VII, pp. 150–51. Note the use of economic, capitalistic language.

20 For example, Mark 8: 36.

21 For example, John 3: 19–20; 8: 12.

22 Matt. 16: 18–19. There is a play on the meaning of Peter's name (*cephas*) which means 'rock'.

23 Chillingworth, W. (1638), *The Religion of Protestants*. See, for example, the heading to his 'The answer to the third chapter [of his opponent]'.

24 One counter-argument asserts that church teachings form a sort of 'seamless web', so that no one of them should be rejected. However, if this has the effect of putting a controversial teaching, such as that of the bodily assumption of Mary, on the same footing as the doctrine of redemption through the cross, this seems a very strange position for a Christian to defend.

25 See, for example, Jewel, J. (*c.* 1562), 'Epistola ad D. Scipionem' in *Works* (1845), Cambridge: University Press, Cambridge, vol. 4, p. 1119.

26 For example, in the letter known as the *First Epistle of Clement to the Corinthians*, probably written about 96 CE. This (along with other early documents) gives good evidence for the claims (a) that Peter died in Rome, and (b) that by this date the bishop of Rome was recognized as having a pastoral influence beyond his own see. However, it does not provide evidence for the claims numbered iv to vi.

27 Iranaeus, *Adv. Haer.* 3.3, probably written between 190 and 200 CE.

28 Duffy, E. (1997), *Saints and Sinners*, New Haven, CT: Yale University Press, p. 11.

29 John Hales (of Eaton) (1765), *Works*, Glasgow, vol. 1, p. 109.

30 One can argue about the precise meaning of 'bishop', and claim that in a broad sense all the apostles were 'overseers', but in the narrower sense that the term had acquired by the year 200 CE it is not at all certain that Peter was a 'bishop'. The quotation from John Hales shows sensitivity to this point.

31 Acts 15; cf. ch. 21.

32 For an interesting discussion of the relationship between James, Peter and Paul, see Chadwick, H. (1959), *The Circle and the Ellipse*, Oxford: Clarendon Press.

33 That is to say, the doctrine of the Immaculate Conception, 1854, the doctrine of Papal Infallibility itself, 1870 (for statements made *ex cathedra*, after an appropriate process), and the doctrine of the Assumption, 1950.

34 *Ineffabilis Deus* (1854) trans. and ed. U.J. Bourke (1868), Dublin, p. 36.

35 For a valiant attempt to do this, by a Presbyterian who wished to uphold the language of the *Westminster Confession*, see Tulloch, J. (1878), *The Christian Doctrine of Sin*, Edinburgh: Blackwood, pp. 192–3.

36 The logical grounds concern how 'guilt' can be inherited; the moral grounds concern the way in which doctrines of 'collective guilt' have been used to justify cruelty.

37 John Paul II (1993), 'Veritas Splendor', London: Catholic Truth Society, see especially pp. 8–9, 49, 104, 123, 165, 174.

38 Since there is no original copy of this bull, there has been some dispute about it. However, it is mentioned by John of Salisbury (in his *Metalogicon*), and according to the *New Catholic Encyclopedia*, Adrian's successor, Alexander III, gave recognition to the rights granted to Henry.

39 On this matter see Bossy, J. (1975), *The English Catholic Community – 1570–1850*, London: Dartman, Longman and Todd, pp. 35–7.

40 Strictly, *De Revolutionibus* was indexed until the hypothetical nature of the claims was made more explicit, and after four years a modified version of the book became permissible.

41 The papal decree *Praestantia Scripturae*, of 1907, bound all Catholics to accept in conscience the decrees of this Commission, past and future.

42 *De Mosaica Authentia Pentateuchi*, *Acta Santae Sedis* 1906, pp. 377–8. The teaching allows for some flexibility in terms of glosses on the original text.

43 *Acta Sanctae Sedis*, 1907, pp. 383–4 which deals with the authorship of St John's gospel and the first Epistle of John (also said to be by the apostle). For the authorship of Matthew see *Acta Apostolicae Sedis* (which replaces *Acta Sancae Sedis* in 1909), 1911, pp. 294–6. According to most Biblical scholars, in the case of Luke the attribution is probable, of Mark possible (on these see ibid., 1912, pp. 463–5), but of Matthew and John, exceedingly unlikely. For the Davidic authorship of the Psalms see ibid., 1910, pp. 354–5.

44 *Acta Sanctae Sedis*, 1908, pp. 613–4. In addition to the insistence that the whole of Isaiah is the work of one prophet, this document also insists that the prophet was divinely inspired to see the distant future.

45 In a letter from the Commission to Cardinal Suhard of Paris, responding to questions he had raised.

46 *Pascendi Dominici Gregis* and (the decree) *Lamentabili Sane*. Note especially the condemnation of error 11 in the latter.

47 For the process involved see Harris P. et al. (1968), *On Human Life*, London: Burns and Oates, written by a number of Roman Catholics who were upset by the process.

48 It is interesting to note the shift in official thinking between the 1911 *The Catholic Encyclopedia*, New York: Appleton and the 1967 *New Catholic Encyclopedia*, New York: McGraw-Hill. In the articles on St Matthew's gospel the former clearly upholds the traditional authorship and puts the balance of Catholic thinking on the date as 40–45 CE, while the latter thinks Matthew's authorship unlikely (except for an early document which the present gospel made use of) and puts the probable date at around 80 CE.

49 The Qur'an, Sura II, 282 (where the context is giving evidence relating to a matter of debt). See also Yamani, M. (1996), 'Introduction' to *Feminism and Islam*, ed. M. Yamani, Reading: Ithaca Press, pp. 6–7.

50 See Raga' El-Nimr (1996), 'Women in Islamic Law' in ibid., p. 91.

51 Within the many writings on this subject see Daston, L. (1992), 'The Naturalized Female Intellect' in *Science in Context*, Cambridge: Cambridge University Press, **5** (2), pp. 209 ff.; and Schiebinger, L. (1989), *The Mind Has No Sex? Women in the Origins of Modern Science*, Cambridge, Mass: Harvard University Press. Note too this aston-

ishing (to us) statement by an eminent nineteenth-century historian: 'Intellectually, a certain inferiority of the female sex can hardly be denied ....' See Lecky, W.E.H. (1869, 3rd edn 1877), *History of European Morals*, London: Longmans, Green, and Co., vol. 2, p. 358. (Lecky goes on to defend the *moral* superiority of women.)

52   See Yamani, M. (1996), 'Introduction' to *Feminism and Islam*, p. 19.

53   Another common response has been to justify a particular text by reference to alleged miracles, either reported in it or performed by those who have been faithful to it. Here one runs into the problem of *rival*, miraculous claims.

54   See Bainton, R.H. (1969), *Erasmus of Christendom*, Tring: Lion Press, p. 178.

55   For example, 1 Cor. 7: 10–12, 25.

56   1 Cor. 11: 4–13; 14: 34 and 1 Ti. 2: 11–12.

57   Douglass, Jane D. (1985), *Women, Freedom, and Calvin*, Philadelphia: The Westminster Press, p. 62; cf. Calvin, J., *Institutes* (1569 edn), IV, 10, 30–31 and *Commentary on I Corinthians*, verses 33–4.

58   A. Najmabadi (describing the conservative views she is opposing), in 'Hazards of Modernity and Morality: Women, State and Ideology', in D. Kandiyoti, ed. (1991), *Women, Islam and the State*, Basingstoke: Macmillan, p. 50.

59   See Goodwin, J. (1994), *Price of Honour*, London: Little, Brown and Co., p. 33. For some other writers on liberal interpretations of Islam, see M. Afkhami, ed. (1995), *Faith and Freedom*, London: Taurus.

60   See Ghada Karmi (1996), 'Women, Islam and Patriarchalism' in *Feminism and Islam*, ed. M. Yamani, pp. 80–1.

61   Hence the title of John Jewel's *Apologia ecclesiae anglicanae* (1562).

62   On the marriage of priests, see Jewel, J., *A Defence of the Apologie*. The 1845 edition (Parker Society), Cambridge: University Press, 4 vols, includes the additions made in 1570 among which is an approving reference to the marriage of priests in the Greek Orthodox church – vol. 3, p. 157. On the communion in two kinds see the 1567 version (London, 1567), p. 579, again with a positive reference to the Greek Orthodox church.

63   St Augustine of Canterbury, who reached England in 597, did much to strengthen the ties of the English church with Rome, but he met considerable resistance in the North.

64   Jewel, J., *An Apologie or Answere, in defence of the Church of England*, in *The Apology of the Church of England*, trans. Anne Lady Bacon, London: SPCK, p. 111 (a 1900 copy of the 1564 translation of the original Latin text of 1562).

65   Ibid., p. 110–11.

66   Chillingworth, *The Religion of Protestants*, iii, 11; cf. v, 31–2 and 73.

67   See Avis, P. (1989), *Anglicanism and the Christian Church*, Edinburgh: T and T Clark, p. 24.

68   The most important sign was the continuity of a community that gave witness to Christ by its life and teaching; cf. Article 19 of the 39 Articles of Religion.

69   At least three questions complicate the issue of the apostolic succession. First, there is the question of whether or not bishops (*episcopoi*) and priests (*presbuteroi*) were actually distinct orders within the early church. On this matter see the dissertation by Lightfoot, J.B., *The Christian Ministry*, appended to *St Paul's Epistle to the Philippians*, 3rd edn 1873, London: Macmillan. Second, there is the question of whether the succession was strictly necessary for the continuity of the church (as maintained, for example, by the High Church Anglican theologian William Palmer, 1803–85), or whether it was rather an ancient and venerable form that was consistent with Scripture, and should be maintained, although not, in all circumstances, absolutely necessary for the continuance of the church. The latter was the view of both Jewel and Hooker. (It is also my own view.) Third, there is the question of whether or not the episcopal succession was actually broken during the Elizabethan era. A claim to this effect lies

behind the Vatican's rejection of Anglican orders. The central problem here does not concern the episcopal status of those who ordained Archbishop Parker in 1559 (at least three of whom, and probably all four of whom, were in episcopal orders), but the form and intent of the Ordinal of 1552 that was used. On this, see the *Answer of the Archbishops of England to the Apostolic Letter of Pope Leo XIII* (1897) in *Anglican Orders* (1932), London: SPCK. As I see it, pp. 48–9 (of the English version) deal effectively with the issue of intent, and expose a gap in the reasoning of the papal encyclical of 1896.

70   Halsbury's *Laws of England*, 4th edn 1975, London: Butterworth, vol. 14, pp. 142–3. See also, The Report of the Archbishops' Commission on Canon Law (1947), *The Canon Law of the Church of England*, London: SPCK, ch. 4.

71   (1583) *An Abstract, of Certain Acts of Parliament*, London (?), p. 8. (The attached commentary on the abstract was strongly criticized in *An Answer* to this abstract, London 1584.) The 1947 proposals for Canon Law revisions include annotations that are studded with medieval as well as later authorities.

72   See J.R. Tanner et al., eds (1932), *The Cambridge Medieval History*, Cambridge: Cambridge University Press, vol. 7, p. 451; cf. p. 277 and the Archbishops' Commission, *The Canon Law*, p. 51.

73   The situation was complicated by the fact that Henry's first marriage was only possible because of a papal dispensation allowing marriage to the widow of Henry's elder brother, and this meant that the pope was now being asked to reject the decision of a predecessor. However, Wolsey had been in negotiations which might well have allowed some kind of compromise had the politics not changed.

74   Chillingworth, *The Religion of Protestants*, Preface to the author of *Charity Maintained*, 2. However, Chillingworth adds that if we have grounds to say that God says something is true, this is a reason for us to hold it to be so. John Hales writes 'Without the knowledge of *why*, of the true ground or reasons of things, there is no possibility of not being deceived': *Works*, 1765 edn, Glasgow, vol. 3, p. 152, original emphasis.

75   See John Overall's *Convocation Book*, 1606, Book II, Canon V. The canons were never authorized (because James I objected to the implied rejection of the Divine Right of Kings in some of them), but they did express theological thinking within the Church of England. See also Hales, John, *Works*, vol. 1, p. 106. The theological headship of Christ is clear in the repeated claim that the sovereign is supreme governor 'under God' and 'on earth', also in Article 36 of the 1553 Articles of Religion (the basis for Article 37 in the later 39 Articles), where the king is described as supreme head on earth 'next to Christ'; cf. Eph. 5: 23.

76   See Avis, P., *Anglicanism and the Christian Church*, p. 39. According to the Supremacy Act of 1534 the king is 'the only supreme head in earth of the Church of England called Anglicana Ecclesia ...', while according to the Supremacy Act of 1559, the queen is the 'supreme governor' in matters civil and ecclesiastical. These and other acts made it clear that this did not allow the sovereign to define doctrine.

77   Jewel, *An Apologie*, pp. 130–4.

78   That is, the acceptance of the Scriptures as the word of God, the principal creeds, the dominical sacraments of baptism and Eucharist, and the 'historic episcopate'.

79   For example, many Quakers died in prison as a result of the Conventicle Acts of 1664 and 1670, and the Unitarian, John Biddle, died from the effects of imprisonment in 1662.

80   While the Edict of Nantes was in effect (from 1598 to 1685), French Protestants had a measure of legal protection, and in some areas they flourished.

81   Some disabilities had to wait for further legislation, and even today certain disabilities remain, for example, concerning the faith of the sovereign.

82 I have in mind the reasoned defence of toleration that had already been made by writers such as Castellio.
83 Chillingworth, *The Religion of Protestants*. See especially i, 14–17 and v, 96.
84 Taylor, J., *Works*, 1828 edn, London, vol. 7, facing p. 390.
85 On this matter, see Starkey, D. (2000), *Elizabeth*, London: Chatto and Windus, pp. 300 ff.
86 See Sykes, S.W. (1978), *The Integrity of Anglicanism*, Oxford: Mowbray, p. 73; and idem (1995), *Unashamed Anglicanism*, London: Darton, Longman, Todd.
87 See McAdoo, H.R. (1965), *The Spirit of Anglicanism*, London: Adam and Charles Black (an important study in seventeenth-century theological method).
88 For example, in the writings of Ninian Smart. See, for example, Smart, N. (1995), *Choosing a Faith*, London: Boyars.
89 The extent to which any philosophy, Christian or other, can or should be presented as a complete system is itself highly controversial. I have set about the much more modest task of trying to see how our different insights that concern the fundamental questions are related to each other.
90 A possible sequel, perhaps subtitled *A Reason for Passion*, is envisaged.
91 In one (under the name of 'realized eschatology'), many of the gospel sayings that appear to relate to a second coming are taken to be references by Jesus to the crucial events associated with the cross and resurrection, sayings that many Christians mistook as references to a later time. In a second, Jesus' references to his coming are held to refer, at least primarily, to the way in which he said he would come to all his disciples in the persons of the poor and the needy – for inasmuch as we help the stranger, feed the hungry, visit the prisoner, and so on, 'you do it unto me' (Matt. 25). In a third, the second coming refers to our confrontation with the word of God at our death; in a fourth, there is postulated some kind of world event in the future in which Christ will be manifested in a new way. Some or all of these approaches can be combined in various ways.
92 From a 1950 lecture, see Erler, R.J. and Marquard, R. eds, (1986), *A Karl Barth Reader*, trans. G.W. Bromiley, Edinburgh: T and T Clark, p. 54.
93 Phil. 4: 8. Even within the context of the holocaust we find heroic good, namely in some of the resistance to it.
94 The approach taken in this book is also Neothomist in a still more fundamental sense, in that God is held to be the ultimate reality, or (in Scholastic language) 'Being'. Interestingly, on this point, although many recent forms of theology, like that of Don Cupitt, would disagree, Karl Barth would have much in common. See Webster, J. (1995), *Barth's Ethics of Reconciliation*, Cambridge: Cambridge University Press, pp. 2–3. At the same time, it must be admitted that many contemporary Neothomists would part company with me on the approach I take to the issues raised by panentheism and ecclesiastical authority. A related matter concerns the nature of the contemporary dialogue between thinkers of all persuasions, the importance of which I have stressed in my account of 'liberalism'. In principle, Neothomists can be fully committed to such a dialogue, but in practice there is a tendency to rely on traditional and authoritarian positions that make significant debate, for example, with process theologians, quite rare.
95 Coleridge, S.T. in *Aids to Reflection, Collected Works*, vol. 9, ed. J. Beer (1993), Princeton: Princeton University Press, p. 107.
96 Our knowledge of Pelagius' views are almost entirely dependent on writers who oppose him, which has led some critics to suggest that Pelagius himself was probably not a 'Pelagian'!
97 In some humans, this essential freedom may be diminished or rendered absent by

severe disabilities, such as extreme chemical imbalances in the brain. In such cases, moral responsibility, and all notions of guilt, begin to disappear. Our inability always to assess this situation is *one* of the reasons why we ought not (in moral terms) to judge one another.

98   1 Cor. 13: 12. Here we might recall Aristotle's view that poetry is more philosophical and of deeper import than history, because it deals with universal truths. See *Poetics* 1451b 5 ff. (in ch. 9).

99   From Francis Thompson's *The Hound of Heaven*.

Appendix 1

Miracles Revisited

In Chapter 1 it was admitted that there were several places where the issues had been oversimplified in order to write a book that was more accessible to the general reader. Among these places were the references to miracle, and here I shall attempt to go some way to correct the oversimplification. In this appendix I shall expand on what has already been suggested.

It is a mistake to look within the Bible for a definition of 'miracle' as that term is now used. The principal reason for this is not the difficulty of translating Hebrew or Greek words, but the fact that the modern distinction between ordinary events and events that, it is alleged, cannot have a 'naturalistic' or 'scientific' explanation, is foreign to earlier ways of thinking. For the Biblical writers, the events that we call 'miracles' were *signs* of the power of God, and in all cases were astonishing,[1] but this did not mean that they were in conflict with 'laws of nature'. Although, for these writers, nature was what we might call 'law-like', the idea that one could discover a series of 'laws' by which one could explain what had happened and then, to an increasing degree, predict what was going to happen, was not developed. However, although Aquinas wrote before what is often called the dawn of modern science (around the sixteenth century), the kind of distinction that we now make between ordinary events and the miraculous was already implicit, because of his emphasis (which was discussed in relation to Providence in Chapter 5) on 'secondary' or 'proximate' causation.[2] As a result, Aquinas' definition of miracle succeeds in capturing what most people now mean by the term. According to Aquinas, although we often use the word 'miracle' in a broad sense to mean anything beyond human capability and vision, in the *strict* sense of the term (*miraculum proprie dicitur*), it is an event 'in nature' that cannot be explained by natural means, because it is 'something that happens outside the whole realm of created nature',[3] and is done by God. In a sense all things are done by God, because he is 'first cause' of all things, but in ordinary events the standard explanation is in terms of 'secondary' causes, which is why (what *we* might call) a naturalistic explanation is possible, whereas in the case of miracles, God is the direct cause.

In modern speech, when the word 'miracle' is used loosely, simply to mean something astonishing or (in a religious context) to refer to an event that is claimed to be revelatory, then no significant problem arises concerning the use of the word, and there is little problem in alleging that in these senses miracles sometimes occur. Most atheists will admit that some surprising events have occurred and that some of these have been given profound religious significance. However, in the narrower sense of the term (that accords with Aquinas' definition), many issues arise. One concerns Hume's suggestion that miracles are (alleged) 'violations' of the law of nature.[4] However, Hume's position is essentially circular, since he defines laws of nature simply in terms of our observations of constant conjunction, which leads, among other problems, to *defining* miracles out of existence. If a miracle, in Hume's sense, were to occur, then there would no longer be *constant* conjunction, and therefore no miracle after all. On the other hand, if, more in line with contemporary science, we think of laws of nature as statistical generalizations, then miracles, if they ever occur, do not have to be seen as 'violating' laws of nature, although some people would say that these laws were 'overridden'.

There are two other points that have been stressed in the body of the book. First, when we adopt Aquinas' usage, creation, redemption, and (I have argued) other events such as the incarnation, are not miracles in the strict sense, because they are not events 'within nature'.[5] Second, I have suggested that theological liberalism is reluctant to stress the role of the miraculous, in the strict sense of the term, not primarily because of problems of evidence, but because the occurrence of miracles seems to be in tension with God's typical, providential activity within the world, and because they seem also to be in tension with the autonomy of nature that is required for freedom and responsibility. If such miracles do occur, they must have, from the human perspective, a certain ambiguity, as a result of which they cannot properly be used as 'proofs' for the non-believer.

A more extensive investigation of the issues involved must explore further the suggestion I have made that when relationships are as they can be and should be, then many things become possible that were not so before. For example, when we are 'in tune' with nature, or 'at peace' within ourselves, then the body is able to find new ways of healing, not through the intervention of totally new forces, but by the harnessing of forces that are already present within us. Both religious and non-religious people often stress this insight. If we now add to this the belief that God's Spirit is always at work within us, working in and through nature, then, when our relationships with God are also as they should be, it is hard to put limits on what God's Spirit may achieve, even within the workings of nature. When I have described the lives of the saints as being part of the saga of the spirit, I suggested that except for relatively few events taking them seriously did not require belief in a series of 'interventions' in nature.

It must be admitted that this suggestion introduces new difficulties, for if nature, in terms of what it can be when relationships are perfect, is infinitely flexible, then I, like Hume, may have defined miracles out of existence – although for a different reason. (A rigid distinction between events that could have a 'naturalistic' explanation, and those that could not, would now be hard to sustain.) A parallel problem arises with the suggestion that 'science' is evolving, so that what counts as a 'naturalistic' interpretation is not cast in stone. If this evolution of science allows for too much flexibility, then the idea of a scientific explanation may become so vague that it may be impossible to distinguish the miraculous from other events.

My response is that although nature (and along with it, the science of the future) is far more open, in terms of possibilities, than most of us imagine, there are *limits* written into what is possible, outside some 'direct' intervention by God, as the author of the created order. The natural order has within it much greater possibilities that we realize, but it is an 'order' in which there are still many things that are 'naturally' *impossible*. The notion of 'natural impossibility' must not be confused with 'logical impossibility'. The latter involves breaking the law of non-contradiction, and applies to any possible order of nature. The former relates to the order of nature as it is, and according to theists, to the particular way in which God has chosen to make it, in which, as Aquinas puts it, there are certain 'natural powers' (*virtutes naturales*).[6] Commenting on Kant, I suggested that the principle of the conservation of energy *may* reflect a natural necessity of this kind. What is possible or impossible, in this 'natural' sense, is not discoverable by pure logic, but is gradually discovered by observation and experience. If this suggestion is accepted, then it is rational to believe that many things are possible, within nature, that we do not now realize to be possible, but it is not the case that *all* things that are logically possible are also naturally possible. Therefore, 'miracles' in Aquinas' strict sense, are not defined out of existence, and whether or not they occur can be a matter of genuine disagreement.

Given the foregoing usages, it has been claimed not only that a Christian should deny that the incarnation was a miracle in the strict sense (because it was not, in its essence, an event 'within nature'), but that miracles, in this sense, are not essential for the viability of Christianity – or of any other form of monotheism. I repeat that the chief ground for this claim is not a matter of the evidence, but a tension with the view of Providence described earlier. However, I am not committing myself to the view that miracles, in this strict sense, could not happen, or that they have *never* occurred. For example, I left open the possibility that the event known as the resurrection might have had, as an *ancillary* event, an empty tomb that demanded a miracle in this strict sense. My point is that belief in such miracles is not *demanded* by monotheism. Whether or not such miracles occur is one of the many issues where there can be legitimate differences in points of view, several of which are rationally viable. However, when alleged miracles are used in an attempt to prove something to the unbeliever, then I am very doubtful of the rationality of the process.[7] For the unbeliever, alternative accounts of what really happened, or alternative explanations of what is agreed to have happened, will always be possible. It might be rational for the believer to accept some miracles, in the strict sense of the term, *given* belief in the God of theism, but I doubt their value as evidence for a belief not already possessed. Jesus, we should recall, consistently played down the *public* demonstration of his works of healing, and seems to have made his primary appeal in terms of the spiritual quality of his message and the way in which it fulfilled the expectations of the Old Testament prophets. For the public, 'there shall be no sign ... but the sign of Jonah.'[8] The sign (in what I take to be a parable, although possibly one with some historical basis), so far as the people of Nineveah were able to observe, was simply the preaching and message of Jonah, for the deliverance from the great fish was not observed by them. Congruently, the resurrection appearances are only reported as being to the faithful, with the single exception of Paul, who was most certainly an ardent believer in God. At the same time I admit that the appearance of an 'extraordinary' event (in whatever sense it turns out to be miraculous), while not providing a proof of theism, might quite properly cause a sceptic to be shaken into a reassessment of their position, a reassessment that might lead to faith.

A reasonable objection to the foregoing might come from the Muslim camp. In traditional Islam, it is often held that there is only one miracle that is essential, and that is the Qur'an itself – being, it is claimed, the unique example of a revelation made directly by God. This would seem to place the Qur'an in the same category as miracles in the strict sense, as defined by Aquinas. It will be apparent from the discussion of the Qur'an in Chapter 8 that I can see no reason why a liberal version of Islam may not emerge in which, while the miraculous nature of the Qur'an is still affirmed, the claim is interpreted in new a way that does not require 'verbal inspiration'. If this is so, Islam, like Christianity, is not dependent on miracles in the strict sense.

Another part of my suggestion is that it is not enough to distinguish three senses of 'miracle' in ordinary language, that is a surprising event, a revelatory event, and an event that requires God's 'direct' intervention. At least two more senses are needed. In a fourth sense, I would put events like creation, redemption and incarnation that, although not 'within nature', are certainly, *in ordinary language*, often referred to as miracles (although I think that Aquinas was right to make his distinction – when we are thinking with more precision). Also, a fifth sense is needed to indicate events that are not only revelatory but depend upon such an extraordinary manifestation of the Spirit, working at the limits of what is possible in the relationships of nature, persons and God, that we want to single them out as being revelatory in a particularly powerful sense. A characteristic of miracles, in this fifth sense, is that an adequate naturalistic explanation cannot be given *now*, but – unlike the case of miracles in the third sense – it is not denied that an explanation might be forthcoming when nature is better understood.

Consider, for example, the miracles associated with the Roman Catholic system of canonizing new saints (other than martyrs). Although I doubt whether this is the best way of delineating those people whom we ought to hold in special reverence and honour in our calendars, I am not as negative on the existence of these miracles as the general tone of this book might suggest, especially since in recent years the Vatican has been very careful in its investigation of alleged miracles. In terms of our ordinary experience, it should indeed be stressed to our secular world that 'There are more things in heaven and earth, Horatio, Than are dreamt of in your philosophy',[9] and the lives of the truly holy are surrounded by events that clash with the expectations that typify the secular world. But there do seem to be limits. I know of no cases where, for example, someone who lost a leg in an explosion is given, suddenly or gradually, a new leg. (Perhaps this would require a miracle in the third sense, at least if it were to happen suddenly, and not as a result of some genetic modification.) On the other hand, I do know of cases where an apparently incurable cancer has suddenly gone into remission, or disappeared between one scan and the next. I think there is a good case for using 'miracle' in the fifth sense, to refer to such events, especially when they occur in the context of faith. However, the sophisticated monotheist ought to be aware of the distinctions I have made.

In the light of these suggestions, I shall conclude with a reflection on one of the most important miracles in the Judaeo-Christian tradition, namely the crossing of the red sea. The delivery of Israel from Egypt, along with the covenant at Sinai that followed, form the central act of the Old Testament, corresponding to the life, death and resurrection of Jesus in the New Testament. Both were seen as events that led to 'covenantal' relationships that give the two testaments their names.

It is well known that the Bible gives two accounts of this crossing of the red sea. In one, 'Moses stretched out his hand over the sea; and the Lord caused the sea to go back by a strong east wind all that night, and made the sea dry land'.[10] When this account of the event is stressed, then we have a miracle in senses one and two (a surprising and revelatory experience), and possibly sense five – if we stress the way in which the *timing* of the event indicated a special relationship of Moses to the divine mind. However, there is no need to introduce sense three, and this suggestion can be strengthened by pointing out that the Hebrew translated as 'red sea' (*yam suph*) is more naturally translated as 'sea of reeds' or 'sea of weeds', suggesting a shallow estuary rather than a deep body of water. Whether or not there was a miracle in sense three is a matter about which theists can legitimately disagree. In a second, and perhaps later account, the waters are said to stand up as a 'heap', or wall (*ned*),[11] and this view, which does seem to demand a miracle in sense three, has been popularized in Hollywood films.

Whichever view one takes of the crossing of the red sea, there is an important way in which for Jews, Christians, Muslims and Bahais a miracle in sense four (an event that is not 'within nature') is involved. Just as the key to any understanding of the resurrection is to be found in a claim about the living presence of Christ, leading to a new kind of relationship with God, so the key to understanding the whole Sinai experience is the claim that through the deliverance from Egypt and the new covenant made through Moses, a new relationship with God became possible, and became the actual experience of the pious Jew. This new relationship cannot be identified with any particular happening, and so it is not an event 'within nature'. It is the outcome of a new covenantal relationship that the accompanying events symbolized and explained. A 'redemption' is involved that transcends any particular historical event.

Notes and References

1 Cf. Aquinas in *ST*, 1a, Q. 105, 7 *miraculi nomen ab admiratione sumitur*. The passage is prior to the 'reply', but the claim appears to be accepted in the main body of the article.
2 For example, *ST* 1a, Q. 22, 3; Q. 195, 5.
3 *ST*, 1a, Q. 114, 4.
4 *An Enquiry Concerning Human Understanding*, X, part 1
5 *ST*, 1a, Q. 105, 7.
6 *ST*, 1a, Q. 114, 4. Aquinas uses this notion to defend the possibility that some of the 'magical' events described in the Bible – for example, the wonders produced by Pharaoh's magicians – did actually happen, even though they were not, properly speaking, 'miracles'. We may be unhappy about Aquinas' acceptance that some of these events actually happened, while accepting the general principle, that we do not know the limits of 'natural powers'.
7 It is interesting to note that Hume is concerned to argue that 'no human testimony can have such force as to prove a miracle, and make it a just foundation for any such system of religion': Ibid., X, part II. I agree with this assertion.
8 Matt. 16: 4
9 Shakespeare, *Hamlet*, I, iv.
10 Ex. 14: 21.
11 Ex. 15: 8; cf. Ps. 33: 7; 78: 13.

Appendix 2

Three Suggested Creeds

The creeds that follow are not put forward with the serious suggestion that any church should adopt them now. The adoption of new creeds, or of revised creeds, could only properly be made after a careful process of reflection and consultation, a process that ought to involve as many churches as possible. These creeds are put forward as discussion papers which may be helpful in promoting such a process.

Preamble to Creeds 1 and 2

At baptism, all those who are of sufficient age to receive instruction shall be expected first, to make an act of repentance for their sins; second, to ask for baptism; and third, to proclaim a basic creed, expressed in either of two forms. Creed 2 shall be used unless the person to be baptized specifically asks for Creed 1. In those churches that accept infant baptism for those who are to be brought up in Christian families, the parents, and sponsors or godparents shall proclaim one of the first two creeds, and the corresponding formula for the actual baptism shall be used. Those baptized as infants shall be encouraged to proclaim one of the creeds for themselves when they reach a suitable age, either at a service of confirmation, or at a service in which baptismal vows are renewed.

Creed 1 runs: 'I acknowledge Jesus Christ to be Lord. I seek to find in him a model for how I should live and how I should pray.' The corresponding formula for use by the baptizing minister runs: 'M or N, I baptize you in the name of the Lord Jesus.'

Creed 2 runs: 'I believe in God the Father, creator of all things; I believe in Jesus Christ, the express image of God who shows us in time what God is like in eternity; I believe in the Holy Spirit whereby God himself is active within the world and within the human heart.' The corresponding formula for baptism runs: 'M or N, I baptize you in the name of the Father, and of the Son, and of the Holy Spirit. Amen.'

Preamble to Creed 3

With respect to the doctrine of the Trinity, there can be seen to be four steps that lead up to the traditional position of the church. In the first step, Jesus is acknowledged as Lord, in accordance with the simple creed implicit in the Acts of the Apostles, and used in the first formula for baptism. Here Jesus is accepted as the Messiah who is to be taken as a model for how to live and how to pray. This is the step that is required of all persons wishing to be baptized as adults, and expresses the essential belief for church membership. In the second step, it is acknowledged that we have experienced God in three principal ways, as creative power – referred to as Father; as the concrete expression of God's love shown to us in the life and death of Jesus – referred to as the Son; and as active energy in the world and within people – referred to as the Holy Spirit. In step three it is acknowledged that these three ways of experiencing God can be related to the three 'persons' of the Christian doctrine of the Trinity, and that, potentially, God has shown himself to all persons in these ways. In step four it is acknowledged that the three persons of the Trinity relate not only to human experiences of the divine, but to profound relationships within the very nature of God himself. God is one, but this 'one' is a special and unique kind of unity in which Father, Son and Spirit have always shared. The Father is the creative and ultimate source of all things, and especially of love. The Son is the eternal object of this love, in union with whom all of us can fully experience this love. The Spirit represents the love itself that is the bond that unites Father and Son. Step three represents the minimum requirement for the holding of any teaching office within the church. Step four expresses the traditional teaching of the church which, on appropriate occasions, members of the church should expect to find expounded.

Those who are to be admitted into a teaching office within the church, whether it be as a lay reader, deacon, priest or bishop, shall be expected to assent to the basic teaching of the church as expressed in the creed that follows. This creed assumes that at least the third of the foregoing steps has been taken, and it encourages, but does not specifically demand, the language of the fourth step.

Creed 3

I believe in God the Father, who created all things, either through acts of instantaneous power, or through a gradual, creative process at work at every moment of history, as in the formation of each individual person's body.

I believe in God the Son, the express image of God, incarnate in the historical person of Jesus. Here God's eternal word was made flesh and we see, in time, the character of God in eternity. Here God identified with humankind as far as it is possible for the eternal creator so to do. Jesus was born of Mary, suffered under Pontius Pilate, was crucified, died, and was buried. On the third day, the day of Resurrection, he was found to be alive, and continued to be known by his disciples as an individual person until his Ascension. In union with him, 'in Christ', we experience both forgiveness and a new life that is already a foretaste of eternal life.

I believe in God the Holy Spirit, the active power of God, at work in creation, manifested at Pentecost, and continually at work within the hearts and minds of people.

I believe in the Bible as the supreme written witness to God's work in history. In the Old Testament we see the emergence of the understanding of one God, a God both of justice and of love, who at Sinai entered into a special relationship with Israel after the deliverance from captivity. We also see the expectation of a Messiah who would fully reveal God's loving nature. In the New Testament we see the fulfilment of God's promise in the life and teaching of Jesus, in his death upon the cross, where he fully accepted and identified with the vulnerability of the human condition, and in the experience of his living presence at Easter.

I believe in the Holy Catholic Church, the community of believers both on earth and in heaven in which all the churches on earth that teach the faith of Christ participate.

I believe in the forgiveness of sins, made available to us by the work of Christ, both in his life of obedience to the Father, and by his death on the cross.

I believe in the sacraments of Baptism by which we are made members of Christ's church, and Holy Communion, or Eucharist, in which we truly experience the presence of Christ in the community of saints.

I believe in God's gift of resurrection to eternal life for all who truly respond to his word.

Appendix 3

A Meditation

I sit in the garden and close my eyes. I am aware, not by means of my physical senses but by an act of conscious reflection, that I am sitting on a particular point on the surface of this planet. Gradually, I extend this awareness to the realization that this planet on which I am placed is a tiny part of a solar system, and with my mind's eye I can see myself reaching out from this garden to the whole physical context; this village, this county, this country, this planet, this solar system, this galaxy, the whole physical universe. I am filled with an immense sense of awe. My mind, in so far as it has a location, is centred in one spot, and yet it has this transcending power to envisage the context in which this garden is placed. The fact that I am 'here', rather than 'there', from the perspective of this understanding, seems irrelevant. It is almost as if I were not really in any particular place at all, and yet, paradoxically, everywhere. My concentration can either be centred on one place in this vast universe, which can as well be on a distant star as on a blade of grass in this garden, or it can, as it were, step back, and view the whole.

But then I wonder, is the *size* of the context in which this garden is placed what really matters? After all, questions of size are all relative, and quite independent of a searching mind. Instead of going outwards from this garden I can start to go within. My body, including my brain, is made up of a myriad tiny cells. But each cell is made up of tinier atoms which are made up of still smaller subatomic particles. Where does this all end? Are there some ultimate 'building-blocks' if we go small enough and, if there are, should they be described as 'strings' or in some other way, and do they consist of 'substance', or of energy, or of something different again? Whatever the correct answer to these questions, in the great order of things, *size* is something that is only relative to my body, which as it happens, seems to be a sort of median between the ultimate building-blocks, if such there be, and the system of galaxies. Size by itself is not the chief source of wonder. Wonder and awe at the presence of my single mind is just as appropriate, for in a way it transcends all questions of size.

However, I also need to question how all our physical descriptions are reflections of the way whatever is 'out there', or 'in there' is actually constituted. Perhaps the whole physical description is a construct of my mind. I cannot bring myself to believe this, but while I cling to the notion that there is 'something' out there – a universe of some kind – and 'something' in there – building-blocks of some kind – at best my pictures reveal only inadequate models, mediated through the particular five senses I have been given.

Next, I realize that this meditation is taking place in a particular time. I am aware that I have a past, and that the universe has a past – possibly an infinite one. I am aware that there is to be a future, possibly an infinite one. I am aware too that I am asking questions that are timeless. What is real? Why is there a reality? Who or what am I? Are these three questions genuine questions? At least this *fourth* question is a genuine one, for any transcending intelligence can see that this must be so, and therefore the significance of at least this question is guaranteed.

Then there is another question that can be asked. Even while thinking about the physical universe, I found that size is not what really 'matters', and as soon as this word is introduced and its significance realized, questions of value emerge, for to say that something matters or does not matter is to imply what *ought* to be seen as primary. But if value arises even in the very notion of understanding, then questions of value are inescapable, and I can go on to ask whether in all our experiences there are things that really *matter*, that matter not just in the sense that I am concerned with them, but in the sense that any conscious intelligence that can frame them ought to be concerned with them? To put this another way, are there values that we discern or discover?'

At once I realize the fallacy of so many arguments that reject the possibility of seriously asking this question. I am told – 'Look how *tiny* and *insignificant* I am, or all human consiousnesses are, compared to the *vastness* of the cosmos, or, in its own way, the *vastness* of the world of subatomic entities.' But my meditation has already shown how this observation is totally irrelevant to my questions. My awareness ranges over and within the whole macrocosm and microcosm. The fact that my mind is centred (and, carried away with the power of thought, I had almost forgotten this) in a spot in this garden, is quite irrelevant. My four levels of reflection – those on the grand scale, the tiny scale, the time scale and now the value scale – are all questions that are asked by any probing mind; or could it better be said, by probing Mind? 'How can there be a divine mind that transcends place and time?' asks the sceptic, but I already find that my own mind does just this, at least to a degree. Even my mind is not so much here as everywhere, and even my mind is not simply tied to this 'moment', but ranges over past events and future possibilities and questions of what really matters. I can imagine a greater mind that not only thought about all space and all time, but which had the added powers of actually knowing what is there and of interacting with it. If there is a divine mind, and if conscious beings are truly given the responsibility to share in the divine order, then within my own mind I begin to glimpse a reflection of the divine mind. It does not follow that the divine mind is the human mind 'writ large', since there must be whole dimensions of the divine mind that are totally beyond our reach; but in conscious reflection, there is one aspect of the divine mind 'writ small'.

I realize that I do not *know* the answer to my questions about whether anything is 'really' important, or whether there are values to be discovered. But I realize that the answers – if there be answers – are not to be found by simply observing individual bits of the physical universe, although there might be a clue when the system as a whole is appreciated. Thought, and value, and most especially love, could not be subject to sight, in the physical sense. But what follows from this? Only that such things are not physical objects in space and time. The materialist has consistently looked for answers in the wrong place – and this is truly paradoxical when the questioning mind of the materialist who asks these questions is itself an example of transcending the physical order. The belief, if this is the right word, that my mind that meditates is related to other minds and to a universal Mind does not directly answer my fundamental questions, but it begins to make sense of my own ability to ask them. In me the universe is conscious of itself. Perhaps in God, Consciousness is conscious of all of consciousness.

Index